Analysis of Machine Elements
Using SolidWorks® Simulation 2013

SolidWorks® Simulation Premium 2013

John R. Steffen, Ph.D., P.E.
Valparaiso University

ISBN 978-1-58503-782-7

Publications

Schroff Development Corporation

www.SDCpublications.com

Schroff Development Corporation
P.O. Box 1334
Mission, KS 66222
(913) 262-2664
www.SDCpublications.com
Publisher: Stephen Schroff

Trademarks and Disclaimer

SolidWorks, SolidWorks Simulation, and its family of products are registered trademarks of Dassault Systemes, SolidWorks® Corporation. Microsoft Windows®, Word®, Excel®, and its family of products are registered trademarks of the Microsoft Corporation.

Every effort has been made to provide an accurate, error free text. The author and manufacturers shall not be held liable for any parts developed or designed based on this book or for errors appearing in this text.

Copyright © 2013 by John R. Steffen

Examination Copies

Examination copies (whether marked or not) are for review purposes only and may not be made available for student use. Resale of examination copies is prohibited.

Electronic Files

Any electronic files associated with this book are licensed to the original user only. These files may not be transferred to any other party.

About the Cover

An artistic interpretation of a mechanical device is chosen for the cover because, although finite element analysis is a highly sophisticated, mathematically based software program, its application requires a certain amount of art to be used properly.

Dedication

For family and friends who have provided guidance, inspiration, encouragement, and much delight. Also Kraig Olejniczak, Ph.D., Dean of Engineering, Valparaiso University, Valparaiso, IN is thanked for his encouragement and support.

About the Author

Dr. John Steffen obtained his B.S.M.E. from Valparaiso University, M.S.M.E. from The University of Notre Dame, and Ph.D. from Rutgers, The State University of New Jersey. His areas of interest include Machine Design, Mechanisms and Mechanism Synthesis, Finite Element Analysis, and Experimental Stress Analysis. Dr. Steffen is Professor Emeritus of Mechanical Engineering and the Alfred W. Sieving Chair, Emeritus, in Engineering at Valparaiso University, Valparaiso IN. He is a life member of the American Society of Mechanical Engineers (ASME) and longtime member and supporter of the American Society for Engineering Education (ASEE).

Acknowledgements

The author would like to acknowledge the following individuals and corporations for their support, encouragement, and invaluable assistance in preparation of this book.

- The SolidWorks Corporation and the SolidWorks Solution Partner team for their support and assistance, especially Ms. Heather Haas.

- Mr. Stephen Schroff and Ms. Mary Schmidt of Schroff Development Corporation, for their guidance and assistance preparing the manuscript for publication.

- Mr. Michael A. Steffen, and Mr. Carl Jurss for their assistance with preparation of many SolidWorks models and drawings.

- Ms. Cami Gudino, Administrative Assistant in the College of Engineering, for knowing the answers to numerous logistical questions.

- Prof. Scott Duncan, Ph.D for assistance with SolidWorks Simulation and for suggesting revisions.

- Valparaiso University and the College of Engineering who provided an environment that encouraged and supported this effort.

This publication marks the 8th edition of this learner centered, step-by-step guide to using SolidWorks Simulation. Every attempt has been made to make this book error free so that it best serves first-time SolidWorks Simulation users. In many instances, the software provides alternative approaches to perform the same tasks. Some alternative methods are presented, however, it is not possible to include every option while keeping the text of manageable length. In an effort to improve future editions of this text, the author welcomes error corrections and suggestions to enhance the presentation at john.steffen@valpo.edu.

NOTES:

Table of Contents

Chapter 2
Curved Beam Analysis

Chapter 3
Stress Concentration Analysis

Chapter 4
Thin and Thick Wall Pressure Vessels

Chapter 5
Interference Fit Analysis

Chapter 6
Contact Analysis

Chapter 7
Bolted Joint Analysis

Chapter 8
Design Optimization

APPENDIX A

APPENDIX B

INDEX

PREFACE

Intended Audience for This Text

This text is written primarily for first-time users of SolidWorks Simulation® who wish to understand finite element software capabilities applicable to stress analysis of virtually any mechanical component or assembly. As such, the focus of this text is upon mastering software use. Mastery is accomplished by exploring problems that students should be familiar with from undergraduate engineering courses in Mechanics of Materials, Design of Machine Elements, or similarly named courses. Because students and practicing engineers already are familiar with topics from these courses, they are able to focus primarily on learning the software capabilities introduced herein. Other novice users of SolidWorks Simulation, possessing background in the above named courses, will also benefit by using the self-study format employed throughout this text.

Many chapter example problems are accompanied by solutions based on the use of classical equations for stress determination. This approach amplifies two fundamental tenets of this text. The first is that a better understanding of course topics related to stress determination is realized when classical methods *and* finite element solutions are considered together. The second tenet is that finite element solutions should always be verified by checking, whether by classical stress equations or by experimentation.

Although it is assumed that readers have working knowledge of SolidWorks, practicality dictates that many users will be new to SolidWorks and/or the SolidWorks Simulation work environment or are transitioning to it from other solids modeling or finite element programs. For these reasons, this text is organized so that individuals with no prior SolidWorks or SolidWorks Simulation experience will be successful. To assist overcoming any lack of SolidWorks familiarity, models of parts or assemblies for all examples and end of chapter problems can be downloaded and unzipped from the publisher's web site at: http://www.SDCpublications.com. Before proceeding, download and unzip chapter examples and end-of-chapter problems from the publisher's web site at:

> **http://www.SDCpublications.com** From the **Browse Books** menu, select **FEA/CAE** followed by **SolidWorks Simulation**. Next, scroll to find the current edition of this text, select it, then open the **Downloads** tab and select **Book Files**.

Using this SolidWorks Simulation User Guide

Each chapter of this text begins with a list of *Learning Objectives* related to specific features of SolidWorks Simulation introduced in that chapter. Most software capabilities are repeated in subsequent examples so that users become familiar with their purpose and are able to apply them to future problems. However, successive use of repeated steps is typically accompanied by briefer explanations. This approach is used to minimize document length, to permit users to work at their own pace, and to devote more emphasis to new concepts being introduced.

Unlike many step-by-step user guides that only list a succession of steps, which if followed correctly lead to successful solution of a problem, this text attempts to provide insight into *why* each step is performed in a "just-in-time" manner. A consequence of this approach is somewhat lengthier explanations of new topics. However, these explanations ensure a deeper understanding and ultimately enhance knowledge about the software and the finite element method.

Numerous traditional design of machine elements textbooks[1,2,3,4,5,6] were reviewed prior to embarking on the writing of this SolidWorks Simulation user guide. The goal was to identify common organizational schemes such that this text would be compatible with the bulk of commonly used undergraduate machine design texts. However, considerable organizational differences exist between textbooks, compounded by the fact that course outlines often vary by instructor, made it unlikely that a common format would accommodate all organizational needs. Perhaps the only common theme found is that chapters in the first-half of the referenced texts focus on topics related to special states of stress found in mechanical components.

For these reasons, this text begins with problems that can be solved with a basic understanding of mechanics of materials. Problem types quickly migrate to include states of stress found in more specialized situations common to a design of mechanical elements course. Paralleling this progression of problem types, each chapter introduces new software concepts and capabilities. Therefore, it is recommended that chapters be followed in the sequence presented. However, despite this recommendation, each chapter is self-contained, thus examples can be worked in any order.

Each example is divided into several major sections that are designated by a descriptive title or sub-title. This division of topics is done to focus attention upon a specific set of software tasks within each section. For example, individual sections are devoted to: material selection, application of fixtures and external loads, meshing the model, etc. Each section is subdivided into a series of numbered steps intended to lead the user through a logical sequence of actions necessary to accomplish the overall goal of that section. However, numbered steps do not necessarily imply a rigid order to an analysis. Rather, the numbers are to serve as "location finders" when working back-and-forth between this user guide and a computer screen. Each menu selection is printed in **bold font** to facilitate locating the corresponding word or phrase on the computer monitor.

---

[1] Collins, J.A., Busby, H.R., Staab, G.H., Mechanical Design of Machine Elements and Machines, 2nd ed, John Wiley & Sons, Inc, 2010.
[2] Hamrock, B., Schmid, S.R., Jacobson, B., Fundamental of Machine Elements, 2nd ed., McGraw-Hill, 2007.
[3] Mott, R.L., Machine Elements in Mechanical Design, 4th ed., Pearson-Prentice Hall, 2004.
[4] Budynas, R.G., Nisbett, J.K., Shigley's Mechanical Engineering Design, 9th ed., McGraw-Hill, 2011.
[5] Spotts, M., Shoup, T.E., Hornberger, L. Design of Machine Elements, 8th ed., Pearson-Prentice Hall, 2004.
[6] Ugural, A.C., Mechanical Design an Integrated Approach, McGraw-Hill, 2004.

Because SolidWorks Simulation is a Windows® based program, the left mouse button serves the usual purposes of clicking to select an item or clicking-and-dragging to draw a line and/or to create or select a geometric shape. References to left mouse button selections are simply denoted by the words "click," "select," or "choose." Clicking the right mouse button provides access to numerous pull-down menus and options within the software. A "right-click" is always specifically indicated where applicable. Subsequent selections from within pull-down menus are always made with the left mouse button. It is frequently necessary to reorient SolidWorks models or assemblies by zooming, rotating, or otherwise manipulating the model to facilitate application of loads or restraints to specific geometric entities such as faces, edges, or vertices. To facilitate these operations without the need for menu or icon selections, the following "short-cut" key and mouse combinations are summarized in Table 1.

Table1 - Short-cut key and mouse button selections

Key and Mouse Button Combinations	Resulting Model Motion
Roll the Middle Mouse Button (MMB) 'up' or 'down.'	Zoom 'out' or 'in,' respectively, to the *current* cursor location on the model.
[Shift] + MMB and move mouse 'away from' or 'toward' the user.	Zoom 'in' or 'out' on the model respectively, by *smooth* motion.
Press [Z] key	Zoom 'out' on current view of the model in incremental steps.
Press [Shift] + [Z]	Zoom 'in' on current view of the model in incremental steps.
Press MMB and move the mouse.	Rotates the model in 3-dimensions.
Arrow keys [↑], [↓], [←], [→]	Rotates the model about the X and Y axes, respectively, in incremental steps.
[Alt] + Arrow keys [←], [→]	Rotates the current model view clockwise or counterclockwise in incremental steps.
[Ctrl] + MMB and move the mouse.	Moves the model 'left' or 'right' and/or 'up' or 'down' on the graphics screen.
[Ctrl] + Arrow keys [↑], [↓], [←], [→]	Pans the model: i.e., moves the model 'up,' 'down,' 'left,' or 'right' respectively.

Instructors Preface

This text is intended for use by students with background in an introductory Mechanics of Materials course. However, the focus of most examples and end of chapter problems is on more advanced topics commonly found in a Design of Machine Elements or similarly named course. A quick review of chapter titles in the Table of Contents highlights these topics. Hence this text is better suited to students enrolled in such a course and, may in fact, simultaneously enhance their understanding of course topics and use of SolidWorks Simulation.

While it is fairly common knowledge that virtually anyone with a technical background can become proficient at using a finite element program, what is frequently lacking is the ability to discern and interpret meaningful results from the copious output produced by such programs. To address this perceived weakness, chapter example problems and most end-of-chapter problems request students to compare finite element results with results found using classical stress equations. Instructors can elect to emphasize or de-emphasize this aspect by assigning selected parts of end-of-chapter problems.

To accommodate organizational differences between design of machine elements textbooks and between individual course outlines, chapters of this text can be worked in any order. However, it is strongly recommended that Chapters 1 and 2 serve as a common starting point. Chapter 4 introduces the topic of symmetry boundary conditions (fixtures), which is expanded upon in Chapter 5 and applied again in Chapter 6. Depending upon course goals, either Chapter 4 or 5 should be included at a minimum. While other chapters may refer to techniques mastered in earlier (skipped) chapters, all necessary analysis steps are included so that users are able to complete each example. Also, because default graphical software output includes von Mises stress plots, von Mises stress is introduced briefly in Chapter 2. Instructors should be aware of this fact and attempt to fill in any gaps in understanding until von Mises stress is addressed in your course.

Finally, evaluation "check sheets" are provided to facilitate grading end-of-chapter problems. These check sheets are created in MS Word® and, thus, can be edited to emphasize (add or delete) particular aspects of a problem and/or to change point values to emphasize instructor desired importance of specific portions of an analysis. Check sheets can be downloaded at the publisher's web site http://www.SDCpublications.com. This is the same web site where model files for all textbook problems are found. It can be instructional to provide these sheets to students when problems are assigned so that instructor expectations and grading criteria are clearly understood.

INTRODUCTION

Finite Element Analysis

Finite element theory was introduced over sixty five years ago. However, implementation of this theory only became practical after the advent of high-speed computers. This section introduces one method of understanding the numerous sets of simultaneous equations that must be solved as part of the finite element method, and therefore, why this technique requires computer solution. Other more refined mathematical formulations exist; however, they are not the subject of this text. Suffice it to say that finite element theory applied to the solution of any realistic problem results in a computationally intensive exercise. Additional insight into the number of equations that must be solved in a finite element analysis (FEA) is related to the number of nodes and elements in a model as described in the next section.

The following discussion provides a simplified overview of the mathematical basis of a finite element solution based on the *stiffness* approach. Begin by considering a simple member of original length **L** subject to an external axial load **F** as shown in Fig. 1. Due to force **F**, the member undergoes an axial deformation shown as Δ**L**. For this simple case, the well-known equation relating force and deformation is given by equation [1].

$$\Delta L = \frac{FL}{AE} \qquad\qquad [1]$$

Notice that the material property (**E** = modulus of elasticity) along with the applied force **F**, length **L**, and cross-sectional area **A**, must be known to solve for Δ**L**.

Figure 1 – A simple member subject axial force **F** illustrates the relationship that exists between the applied force and the resulting deformation Δ**L**.

The next step in a stiffness formulation is to compute strain based on the deformation determined using equation [1] above. To do so, the simple definition of strain is used where change of length, Δ**L**, was found above. Strain can be expressed verbally as:

strain = (change of length) / (original length)

or mathematically as:

$$\varepsilon = \frac{\Delta L}{L} \qquad [2]$$

Finally, since the goal of analysis is to determine stress in a member, stress can be determined by substituting strain (ε) into the following classic stress-strain relationship.

$$\sigma = E\varepsilon \qquad [3]$$

Of course, equation [3] is valid only in the elastic region where stress is proportional to strain. This fact is fundamental to *linear* finite element analysis described in this text.

In summary, the finite element method begins with a mathematical description of deformation, it then proceeds to calculate strain and finally solves for member stress.

Nodes, Elements, Degrees of Freedom, and Equations

To permit mathematical analysis by the finite element method requires simplification of modeled parts. If the cylindrical member, shown in Fig. 1, were divided into an arbitrary number of *nodes* and *elements*, its model might appear as shown in Fig. 2.

F   1   2   3   4   5   6   7   8   F

Figure 2 – Simplified model of the cylindrical member sub-divided into a series of nodes and elements.

In Fig. 2, *elements* are represented by short line segments between successive numbered points. The small numbered circles, which represent points of connection between adjacent elements, are called *nodes*. For tracking purposes, elements are also numbered within the finite element software. However, for simplicity, they are not numbered in Fig. 2.

Many different types of elements are found in commercial finite element software. SolidWorks Simulation beam elements *could* be used to model the part shown in Figs. 1, 2 and 3. However, only simple one degree of freedom elements are included here to introduce the concepts of *degrees of freedom* and the *number of equations* that result during a finite element solution. To assist with this understanding, we isolate an arbitrary element and its two nodes (n and n+1) from the model in Fig. 2 to obtain an enlarged view of a single element and its two nodes shown in Fig. 3.

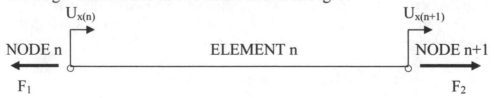

Figure 3 – A simple one-dimensional model represented using two nodes and one element.

First, we assume that displacements at nodes n and n+1 are restricted to lie in the X-direction. This restriction ensures that the problem is one-dimensional (i.e., displacements are limited to a single direction, the X-direction). $U_{x(n)}$ and $U_{x(n+1)}$ represent displacements in the X-direction at *each* node. These displacements correspond to one *degree of freedom* at each node. Thus, since displacement at *each* node results in one set of equations, like equations [1, 2, and 3] above, it is logical to conclude that two sets of equations result for the element shown in Fig. 3 (one set of equations for each node). If one were to extrapolate the above observation to all seven elements, each with two nodes, for the model shown in Fig. 2, it is evident that:

(7 elements)*(2 nodes/element)*(1 degree of freedom/node) = 14 degrees of freedom [4]

A mathematical solution for the fourteen displacements requires simultaneous solution of fourteen equations to solve this very simple problem. The following section examines primary element types currently available within SolidWorks Simulation.

SolidWorks Simulation Elements

Having established a fundamental understanding of nodes, elements, and degrees of freedom, we next introduce the various types of elements available within SolidWorks Simulation. Basic element types include a *Solid* element, a *Shell* element, and *Beam* or *Truss* elements. *Solid* and *shell* elements are available as either first-order or second-order element types while *Beam* elements have unique characteristics as described in a later section. Descriptions of each element type follow.

Solid Elements

The majority of components analyzed by finite element methods are 3-dimensional models based on solid geometry used to define boundaries of a part or assembly. In this context *solid* refers to parts or assemblies that have significant volume or thickness relative to other component dimensions. The SolidWorks Simulation *solid* elements used to model this type of geometry are named tetrahedral elements. A first-order tetrahedral element, shown in Fig. 4, is comprised of six straight sides, four flat faces, and four nodes that join the edges at each of its four corners. All edges and faces of first-order elements remain straight and flat after deformation. First-order elements are also called "draft quality" elements.

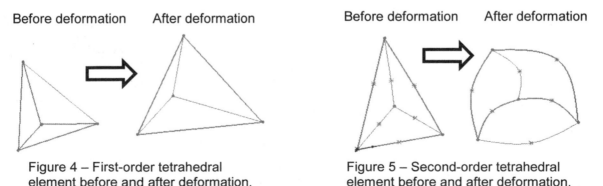

Before deformation   After deformation

Before deformation   After deformation

Figure 4 – First-order tetrahedral element before and after deformation.

Figure 5 – Second-order tetrahedral element before and after deformation.

A second-order tetrahedral element, illustrated in Fig. 5, is characterized by the addition of another node on each edge of the element for a total of ten nodes per element. These additional nodes, typically called "mid-side nodes," permit element edges and surfaces to conform and deform in a second-order (curved) manner. The obvious advantage of second-order elements is their ability to provide better mapping of curved surfaces. And, a better fit of elements ensures improved modeling of deformations, strains, and hence stresses computed within modeled parts. Whether a first-order (draft quality mesh) or second-order (high quality mesh) is used, the overall mesh density (i.e., total number of elements) is essentially the same for identical model geometry. However, second-order elements yield better results at the expense of greater computational resources.

Solid Element Degrees of Freedom

Both first-order and second-order tetrahedral elements within SolidWorks Simulation allow three degrees of freedom at each node. These degrees of freedom permit *displacements* in the X, Y, and Z directions. The number of degrees of freedom for each element type is summarized below.

First-order (draft quality) element –
A typical first-order element is shown in Fig. 6 (a) along with its three degrees of freedom (permissible displacements in the X, Y, and Z directions) at each node. For this element, the total number of degrees of freedom is given by:

   (3 degrees of freedom/node) * (4 nodes/element) = 12 degrees of freedom/element   [5]

Figure 6 (a) – Draft quality element with three degrees of freedom at each of four nodes.

Figure 6 (b) – High quality element with three degrees of freedom at each of ten nodes. (Labels omitted at mid-side nodes)

Second-order (high quality) element –
Figure 6 (b) shows three degrees of freedom at each of ten nodes on a high quality element. The total number of degrees of freedom for this element is given by:

   (3 degrees of freedom/node) * (10 nodes/element) = 30 degrees of freedom/element   [6]

Recalling the relationship between degrees of freedom and the corresponding number of simultaneous equations requiring solution for each degree of freedom, it is easily seen that computational intensity increases dramatically as model size and order of the element type increase. Although more computationally intensive, second-order elements yield more accurate results and are almost always recommended for finite element solutions.

Shell Elements

The second type of element available within SolidWorks Simulation is the *shell* element. As implied by its name, *shell* elements are primarily used to analyze thin-walled components such as sheet metal parts or other thin surfaces regardless of material type. Examples of components that might be modeled using shell elements include a propane gas tank, beverage containers, fan blades, a kayak, a cell-phone case, or the oil pan on your car. Although the above examples may appear to present clear-cut differences between uses for *solid* and *shell* elements, in reality there exist numerous situations where a relatively thin member can be modeled equally well using either solid or shell elements. Usually the nature of desired results dictates the choice of element type.

As with solid elements, *shell* elements are also available as first-order "draft quality" or second-order "high quality" mesh types. Figure 7 (a) illustrates a first-order shell element. This element appears two dimensional with straight sides and one flat surface with one node at each of its three corners. Figure 7 (b) illustrates a second-order shell element with its additional mid-side nodes yielding a total of six nodes per element.

Figure 7 (a) – First-order shell element.

Figure 7 (b) – Second-order shell element showing additional mid-side nodes.

Once again, mid-side nodes permit shell elements to conform to curved geometry of the original component and to better model curvature associated with displacements in deformed parts. Although shell elements are considered two dimensional, a thickness must be defined for them to properly model a part. There are two ways to define a shell mesh. One method creates a shell mesh based on the *mid-surface* of a part while the other approach allows the user to select the surface to be meshed. For example, the 'top' or 'bottom' surface may be specified. Since assignment of mesh thickness varies according to how a shell mesh is defined, this topic is investigated further in Chapter 4.

Shell Element Degrees of Freedom

Because shell elements are two dimensional, it might be presumed that they have fewer degrees of freedom (i.e., displacements) allowed at each node point. However, just the opposite is true because, in addition to translational displacements at each node, thin members (a.k.a., shells or membranes) may be subject to bending displacements. These bending displacements are typically referred to as "rotations." Therefore, each node of a shell element has six degrees of freedom. They include three displacements (X, Y, Z) and three rotations, one about each of the global X, Y, Z axes as illustrated in Fig. 8.

Figure 8 – Six degrees of freedom occur at *each* node of a shell element.

Beam and Truss Elements

Beam or truss elements are the logical choice when modeling structural members due to the significantly reduced number of nodes and elements required to create a model. Beam elements are used where length of the member is large when compared to its cross sectional dimensions. For example, beam elements are typically used where the length/height ratio is 20:1 or greater. To gain an appreciation for the simplicity of beam elements, consider Figs. 9 (a, b, and c). If the structural channel shown pictorially in Fig. 9 (a) were created using solid or shell elements, thousands of nodes and elements would be required to model each beam as shown in Fig. 9 (b). However, use of beam elements reduces model size to a series of "cylinders" (the *elements*) joined end-to-end (by *nodes*) with one *joint* at each end shown in Fig. 9 (c). A smaller model size results in a reduction of computational resources used during a beam analysis while still yielding accurate results.

| Figure 9 (a) - Schematic of a structural channel. | Figure 9 (b) - Channel modeled using solid tetrahedral elements consists of over 19,000 nodes. | Figure 9 (c) – Simplified beam element model consists of 59 nodes 57 elements and two joints. |

Extensive tables of common beam cross-sections are available within SolidWorks. Also, definition of beam cross-section dimensions is needed so that the program can compute its moment of inertia and neutral axis location. No matter what the actual shape of the original structural member is, when it is represented as a beam or truss element, it appears like the simple cylinder illustrated in Fig. 9 (c). However, SolidWorks Simulation permits stress results to be displayed on either a cylindrical representation of the beam or on the actual beam geometry.

Based upon their application, structural members can be defined as either *truss* or *beam* elements. The difference between these definitions lies in the connections defined between the members. For example, a *truss* consists of structural members connected by pin joints at both ends. As such, truss members are classified as two force members that carry only axial loads (tension or compression). A *beam*, on the other hand, assumes rigid connections, such as welded or bolted joints, exist between members. These rigid connections are capable of transmitting not only axial loads, but also bending moments, and even torsion between connected members.

Because beam and truss elements are not investigated in this text, this brief introduction should suffice to alert the interested reader to their existence and general use.[1]

Meshing a Model

The process of subdividing machine elements into an organized set of nodes and elements is called *meshing,* or creating a *mesh,* on a model of the component to be analyzed. As implied above, mathematical solution of a finite element analysis depends upon sets of simultaneous equations that describe small displacements at the element level. Therefore, subdividing a model into a continuous set of nodes and elements, i.e., meshing a model, is a necessary prerequisite in the solution process. Fortunately, within SolidWorks Simulation meshing occurs automatically. However, users have the ability to control mesh size and distribution as is investigated in Chapter 3.

To understand this process it is helpful to outline the progression from an actual part to a meshed finite element model. This process is illustrated in Figs. 10, 11, and 12. Typically

Figure 10 – Solid model of an actual machine shaft to be meshed prior to FEA.

Figure 11 – Solid model of shaft modified to simplify its geometry prior to meshing. (two end chamfers are deleted)

---

[1] For more on analysis of beam and truss elements, see: Shih, Randy H., Introduction to Finite Element Analysis Using SolidWorks Simulation, Schroff Development Corporation, 2013.

part geometry is simplified to reduce or eliminate geometric features that have little or no impact on the ensuing analysis. This step is known as "defeaturing" the model. In this example, 45° chamfers are removed from both ends of the shaft shown in Fig. 10, which leads to the simplified model illustrated in Fig. 11. This change is minor, but an accumulation of similar small changes made to a complex part or assembly can significantly reduce model complexity and hence solution time. Of course, the user must use good engineering judgment when weighing whether or not simplifying changes alter important aspects of stress within a model.

Figure 12 shows the simplified shaft model after meshing it using first-order (draft quality) solid tetrahedral elements. The model below consists of approximately 1543 elements and 7192 nodes. Automatic meshing of this part is accomplished in less than three seconds using SolidWorks Simulation 2013 and a late model PC.

Figure 12 – Meshed model of the shaft using first-order (draft quality) tetrahedral elements.

Figure 13 – Close-up of the fillet reveals the approximate nature of first-order tetrahedral elements.

Figure 13 shows a close-up view of the fillet at the transition between small and large shaft diameters. This image reveals the approximate nature of first-order tetrahedral elements with straight edges when used to model a curved surface. The modeling errors that are visible when first-order elements are used contribute to larger approximations (more error) in computed results of a finite element analysis. For this reason, second-order (high quality) elements are recommended to achieve more accurate results.

The following section provides insight into differences observed when comparing solutions based on nodal and element averaging of stress results.

Stress Calculations for Nodes and Elements

Now that nodes, elements, and mesh have been introduced it is important to understand how stress values are determined based on these three items. In brief, stress results are reported in two basic ways. One is referred to as *nodal stress* and the other is called *element stress*. The following sections describe the basis for interpreting results given by these two different methods.

Nodal Stress Values

Begin by considering the L-Shaped cantilever beam shown in Fig. 14 (a). The model is fixed at its left end and includes an external load applied to its top right edge. A high quality tetrahedral mesh is applied to the model. Following a finite element analysis, *nodal* stresses are shown on a front view of the model by a series of colored bands called "fringes" shown in Fig. 14 (b). At this point it is not necessary to understand the steps required to build the model and accomplish this solution. Rather, the goal is to understand the difference between *nodal stress* and *element stress* and how they are calculated. To do this, focus your attention on the elements in the region circled on Fig. 14 (b).

(a)   (b)

Figure 14 – (a) Finite element model showing, fixtures, loads, and mesh. (b) Model showing stresses as colored fringes following a finite element analysis.

Figure 15 shows an enlarged image of selected nodes and elements in the circled region of Fig. 14 (b). In Fig. 15, black circles ● at the corner of each element represent nodes while hollow circles **0** and **0'** within each element represent Gauss points. Gauss points are defined as locations within each element at which stress results are calculated.

In Fig. 15, notice that the central node is shared by several elements. Stress at the central node is calculated by extrapolating stress values from Gauss points labeled **0'** to the one central node and then averaging the results from those Gauss points to determine the *nodal stress* value at the central node. This averaging of Gauss point values occurs at every shared node location throughout the entire model. Nodal stress magnitudes are typically used in analysis. However, for the sake of completeness, the following section describes the usefulness of element stress values.

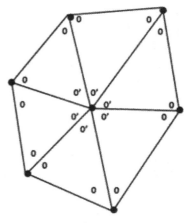

Figure 15 – Stress values at Gauss points labeled **o'** are used to compute the average *nodal stress* at the central node point.

Element Stress Values

Once again refer to Fig. 15, except this time focus attention on any *one* element. *Element stress* is calculated by averaging stress values from all Gauss points *within a single element*. Because *element stress* is calculated on a 'per element' basis, an *element* plot of the stress distribution illustrated in Fig. 14 (b) is shown in Fig. 16. Notice that element stress plots typically appear like a "patch work" pattern of colors, where each element is all the same color. This occurs because each element shows its own *individual* stress value, which is *not* averaged with surrounding elements. When large differences of stress level occur between adjacent elements, as evidenced by different colored elements, it is a good indication that a smaller mesh size should be used to obtain a better estimate of true stress magnitudes in that area. This phenomenon typically occurs in regions of high stress gradient (i.e., regions where large stress differences occur).

Figure 16 – Element stress plot showing stress magnitudes calculated on a per element basis.

The number of Gauss points varies according to the type of element. Table 1 summarizes the number of Gauss points found in various element types.

Table 1 – Number of Gauss Points Found in Typical Solid and Shell Elements

Element Type	Number of Gauss Points
First order Tetrahedral element (draft quality)	1
Second order Tetrahedral element (high quality)	4
First order Shell element (draft quality)	1
Second order Shell element (high quality)	3

Assumptions Applied To Linear Static Finite Element Analysis

Three limiting assumptions apply to all finite element solutions studied in this text. They are: (a) loads are applied statically; (b) materials behave in a linear manner; and (c) deformations are small. Each of these limiting assumptions is reviewed below.

Static Loading

Assumption #1
   Loads are applied quasi-statically (i.e., very slowly). Dynamic loads, damping, and inertial effects are not allowed.

Although analyses described in this text are limited to static loading situations, SolidWorks Simulation Premium does provide the capability to solve problems involving dynamic loads, drop test (impact) problems, and to determine the natural frequencies and mode shapes of vibrating systems.

Linear Material Behavior

Assumption #2

> Linear assumptions apply to all calculations. This means that system response is proportional to load.

For example,

- if a 1000 N load causes 0.01 mm displacement,

- then a 2000 N Load will cause a 0.02 mm displacement

The linear assumption also implies that parts and assemblies undergo *no* permanent deformation. Or, stated another way, a body returns to its original *un-deformed* shape when loads are removed.

Taken together, the above statements are equivalent to stating that the material of which a body is made does not exceed its yield strength (a.k.a., yield point, or elastic limit). In other words, *all* analyses are presumed to occur on the *linear elastic* portion of the stress strain curve shown in Fig. 17. Recall that the modulus of elasticity "**E**" (a.k.a., Young's modulus) is determined from the linear portion of the stress versus strain curve.

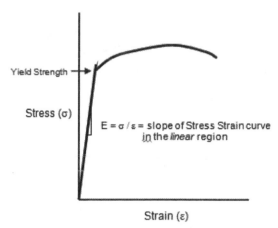

Figure 17 – Stress versus strain curve for a typical ductile material.

The observation stated above for the stress versus strain curve is consistent with the mathematical relationship between stress and strain given by equation [4], which states that stress is proportional to strain.

$$\sigma = E * \varepsilon \qquad [4]$$

In equation [4], modulus of elasticity, **E,** is the constant of proportionality determined from the linear portion of a stress versus strain graph shown in Fig. 17.

Note, however, that SolidWorks Simulation Premium software also offers the capability of solving non-linear problems (referred to as "post yield" problems).

Small Deformations

Classification of deformations as "small" is a relative concept. For example, a 7 mm (approx. ¼ in) deformation at the mid-span of a 30 m (approx. 98.5 ft) roof support beam might be considered small for a beam that supports its own weight plus the weight of roofing materials and a significant snow load on the roof exterior. Conversely, a 1 mm (0.04 in) deformation of a small, hand-size, "C"-clamp subject to clamping forces might be considered a relatively large deformation. The Simulation software features a large displacement solver that automatically warns users when large deformations are encountered in a solution. A large displacement solution option can be invoked in such cases.

Closing Comments

Remaining steps of a finite element analysis are analogous to steps involved when solving stress related problems by long-hand methods. In particular, loads and restraints are applied to the model (like creating a free-body diagram), and material properties are selected so that stress levels can be compared to material strength at the conclusion of an analysis. Because these aspects of problem solution are familiar to individuals who have completed a fundamental Mechanics of Materials course, discussion of the equivalent finite element steps is deferred to example problems in subsequent chapters. For these reasons, the remainder of this chapter shifts emphasis to acquaint users with various aspects of the SolidWorks Simulation user interface.

Introduction to the SolidWorks Simulation User Interface

Perhaps the most awkward part of getting started using SolidWorks, SolidWorks Simulation, or any other complex software program, is finding your way around in a new software work environment. Because some users might be new to both SolidWorks Simulation *and* SolidWorks, this introduction begins by providing orientation to the SolidWorks work environment, also known as a Graphical User Interface or GUI.

Proficient SolidWorks users can skip the SolidWorks orientation section below. However, the toolbars and reading associated with Figs. 18 and 20 should be examined. These toolbars are important because many SolidWorks icons are also useful when working in SolidWorks Simulation. Click the SolidWorks [icon] icon on your screen to open SolidWorks. Select **[Accept]** when the SolidWorks license agreement appears.

Orientation and Set-up of the SolidWorks Work Environment

First time users of the combined SolidWorks / SolidWorks Simulation software must become acquainted with both the vocabulary and the location of items in the work environment. Thus, we begin by investigating how to add or delete menus to the default SolidWorks graphical user interface. The default 'start-up' SolidWorks screen is shown in Fig. 18. Most menu items are inactive (grayed out) at this time. Click in the gray screen area to close the **SolidWorks Resources** menu.

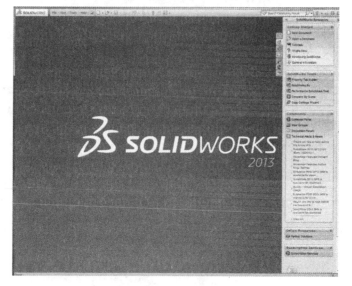

Figure 18 – SolidWorks start-up screen showing default menus and toolbars.

Depending upon your work environment, particularly at public access computers, the default SolidWorks work environment may or may not appear as shown in Fig. 18 due to alterations made by other users or individuals who installed the software. Therefore, this section outlines how to return all settings to the factory default settings followed by steps to customize the work environment. Begin by permanently opening and displaying the SolidWorks main menu on the screen as outlined below.

1. If the **Main Menu**, labeled on Fig. 19, appears at the top left of the screen, skip to step 3. Otherwise, move the cursor over the [DS SOLIDWORKS] button at top left of the screen. This action opens the main menu illustrated in Fig. 19.

Main Menu

Figure 19 – The SolidWorks button provides access to the **File**, **View**, **Tools**, and **Help** items in the main menu.

2. Because these menu items are used frequently, click to select the "push-pin" icon, circled in Fig. 19. This action permanently displays the main menu.

The next step is to reset to the system default settings. Begin by opening a *new part* file in SolidWorks as follows.

3. In the SolidWorks main menu, click **File**, and from the pull-down menu select **New…**

NOTE: Steps 4 and 5 may or *may not* occur during your first session. Skip to step 6 if step 4 does not appear.

4. The SolidWorks **Units and Dimension Standard** window opens. Within this window, beneath **Units:**, click ▼ to open the pull-down menu and select **IPS (inch, pound, second)** if not already selected.

5. Next, beneath **Dimension Standard:**, click ▼ to open the pull-down menu and select **ANSI** as the dimension standard, if not already selected, and click **[OK]** to close the **Units and Dimension Standard** window.

6. The **New SolidWorks Document** window opens. Within this window, click the **Part** icon.

7. Click **[OK]** to close the **New SolidWorks Document** window. A *new* part file is opened in the graphics area. The default SolidWorks screen appears similar to that in Fig. 20.

Various areas of the *default* SolidWorks start-up screen are labeled in Fig. 20. The **Features** tab, circled in Fig. 20, is *usually* selected by default on the start-up screen. If not, click its tab to select it. Next, explore other *tabs* beneath the **Main Menu** by clicking on the tab name and then examining the contents contained within each tab.

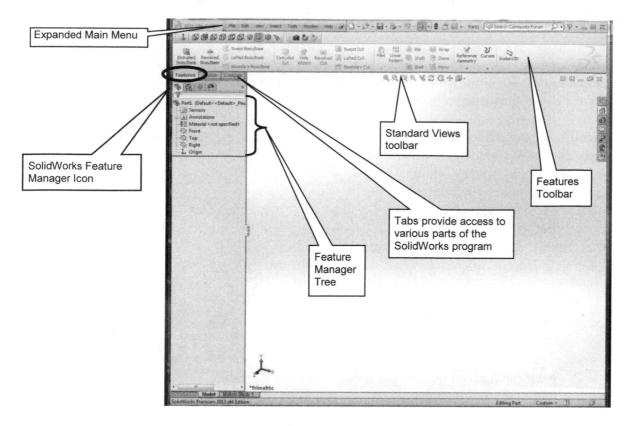

Figure 20 – Definitions identifying basic portions of the SolidWorks screen. Several default toolbars are shown.

If your screen looks like Fig. 20, skip to the section titled **Customizing the SolidWorks Screen** on the next page. If not, proceed to step 8 where the default screen settings are reset.

8. In the main menu, click **Tools** and near the bottom of the pull-down menu, select **Options…** The **System Options - General** window opens (not shown here).

9. At the lower left corner of this window, click the **[Reset…]** button. Immediately a **SolidWorks** window opens as shown in Fig. 21.

10. Select the **[Reset all options]** option to return all settings to the SolidWorks factory default settings.

Figure 21 – SolidWorks confirmation window.

11. Click **[OK]** to close the **System Options – General** window. Your screen should now appear like that shown in Fig. 20.

Customizing the SolidWorks Screen

If the large graphics area of the screen appears grey, blue, or some other shaded color as shown in Fig. 20, continue to the next paragraph. However, if the background color is *white*, skip to the sentence following step 7.

Because a shaded background can mask details of a screen image and because printing images on this background wastes considerable ink/toner . . . "think green" . . ., most users prefer to work on a white background. Change the background color as follows.

1. In the main menu, at top left of screen, click **Tools** to open a pull-down menu.

2. Near the bottom of this menu, click **Options...** The **System Options - General** window opens.

Figure 22 – Selections used to change the **Viewport Background** color.

3. Beneath the **Systems Options** tab, select **Colors** and immediately the right half of the window appears similar to that shown in the background of Fig. 22.

4. Within the **Color scheme settings** box, the top entry should read, **Viewport Background**. Click to select **Viewport Background** (if not already selected).

5. To the right of the previous selection, click the **[Edit...]** button. The **Color** window opens as also shown in the foreground of Fig. 22.

6. Within the **Basic colors:** section, select the *white* color box circled in Fig. 22; then click **[OK]** to close the **Color** window.

7. Finally, click **[OK]** to close the **System Options - Colors** window. The main graphics area should now appear white. *(See step 8 if the above procedure failed).*

8. See **Appendix B** for an alternate way to alter the screen background color.

The next task leads you through the addition of various toolbars to the screen and the modification of some existing toolbars.

9. In the main menu, select **View**. Then from the pull-down menu select **Toolbars ►**. This action opens the Command Manager pull-down menu shown at the right of the partial screen image in Fig. 23. *CAUTION: Two **Toolbars** options exist! Choose the one indicated by an arrow.*

10. Click the **Standard Views** icon, circled in Fig 23. Immediately the **Standard Views** toolbar appears (shown boxed) in the menus above the graphics window. *NOTE: It may be necessary to scroll down the list to locate the **Standard Views** icon.*

Figure 23 – The Command Manager menu from which toolbars are selected for display.

Although the following steps detail how to add toolbars to the menu, be aware that most necessary toolbars already appear on the screen due to default settings within SolidWorks. Thus, to gain practice with this procedure, follow steps below to *turn off* the toolbars and subsequently to *turn them back on*.

11. Once again select the **Standard Views** icon (circled in Fig. 23) by selecting **Views / Toolbars ►**, and finally select **Standard Views**. The menu closes and the **Standard Views** toolbar is deleted from menus at the top of the screen.

12. Open the Command Manager pull-down menu again, but this time use the following shortcut. Right-click anywhere on the top menu bar. This shortcut directly opens the Command Manager menu.

13. Again, locate and select the **Standard Views** icon. The Command Manager closes and the **Standard Views** toolbar is again added to the top of the screen.

14. To gain familiarity with this process, repeat steps 11 and 12 but, this time select the **Sketch** icon. The **Sketch** toolbar typically appears along the right edge of the graphics window. If not, its location can be adjusted by clicking-and-dragging a 'drag handle' located at the top or left end of the toolbar.

Finally, observe the system default icons appearing at the top-middle of the graphics screen as shown in Fig. 24. Because not all of these icons are useful for the purposes of this text, those shown *boxed* will be removed from this toolbar and others will be added.

Figure 24 – Default icons appearing at top-middle of the start-up screen

Proceed as follows.

15. In the main menu, select **Tools** and from the pull-down menu select **Customize...** The **Customize** window opens and is *similar* to Fig. 25.

16. Within this window, select the **Commands** tab. Then, near the bottom, left-side of the **Categories:** scroll list, select **View**. Your screen should appear like Fig. 25.

Figure 25 – Menu used to add and delete icons from the **Heads-Up View** toolbar.

17. To remove an unwanted *(boxed)* icon from the toolbar, click-and-drag it to deposit it into the **Customize** window shown in Fig. 25. Repeat for each icon to be removed.

18. Next, examine images of the desired icons shown in Fig. 26. To add the missing icons, simply click-and-drag the appropriate icon from the right-half of Fig. 25 to its desired location at the top of your screen.

19. After updating the icons displayed, close the **Customize** window by selecting **[OK]**.

The icons shown in Fig. 26 are most useful throughout this text. Selecting any of these icons allows the user to perform various graphic manipulations on part models.

Figure 26 – Adjusted listing of icons used most frequently to manipulate models.

A brief description of each icon is provided below.

Zoom to Fit – Resizes the model and places it at the center of the screen.

Zoom to Area – Zooms to an area of the model enclosed in a user defined box.

Zoom In/Out – Move mouse up or down to zoom 'out' or 'in' on the model.

Zoom to Selection – Zooms to a selected location on a part or sub-assembly.

Previous View – Returns image to its previous view.

Rotate View – Rotates view about 3-dimensional axes.

Roll View – Rotates view about a specific X, Y, or Z axis.

Pan – Moves model left/right, up/down, or diagonally without rotation.

View Orientation – The ▼ arrow provides access to multiple standard views and window display configurations. These views are also accessible using **Standard Views** icons previously added to the upper menu.

20. Additional toolbars can be added to or removed from the screen by right-clicking anywhere on the **Main Menu** and either selecting or deselecting items that appear in the pull-down menu.

21. If the pull-down menu remains open, close it by clicking anywhere outside the menu.

Although short-cut methods for manipulating the model were introduced in the **Preface**, (see **Table 1**, page ix), new users may find the visual display of icon capability helpful.

Seasoned SolidWorks users might choose to place additional toolbars on the screen, or to customize those now appearing by adding or removing specific icons. The procedure to do this is much the same as adding or removing icons in any Windows® program. For this reason it is not uncommon for slight differences of screen images to occur. The next section outlines steps to add SolidWorks Simulation icons to the graphics screen.

Orientation to the SolidWorks Simulation Work Environment

Following procedures like those outlined above, essential SolidWorks Simulation toolbars are next added to the screen. However, it is first necessary to deal with the probability that *Simulation*, the finite element component of SolidWorks, has not yet been added to the work environment. Thus, proceed as follows to activate SolidWorks *Simulation*.

1. In the main menu, click **Tools** and from the pull-down menu select **Add-Ins...** The **Add-Ins** window opens as shown in Fig. 27.

2. Within the **Add-Ins** window, click to place a check mark to the *left* of ☑ **SolidWorks Simulation** and also in the **Start Up** column located to the *right* of **SolidWorks Simulation** ☑. This latter selection ensures that Simulation is active every time SolidWorks is started.

3. Click **[OK]** to close the **Add-Ins** window.

NOTE: It is necessary for first time users to **[Accept]** the **Simulation License Agreement** at this time.

Figure 27 – Activating SolidWorks Simulation software.

The above steps add the name "**Simulation**" to the **Main Menu** located at the top of the screen and a **Simulation** *tab* is located just above the graphics area as shown in Fig. 28.

Figure 28 – Work environment modified by the addition of SolidWorks Simulation capability.

4. In the **Main Menu**, click **Simulation** to open a pull-down menu of capabilities within the finite element portion of the program. Briefly examine this list.

5. Click anywhere outside the menu to close it.

Note that a new *tab*, labeled **Simulation**, appears just above the graphics area as shown in Fig. 28. If this tab does not appear, proceed as follows. Otherwise skip to step 8.

6. Right-click on any of the *tabs* (labeled: **Features, Sketch, Evaluate, DimXpert,** or **Office Products,** etc.) located at the top left of the graphics area. A pull-down menu opens as shown in Fig. 29.

This menu shows a check mark ☑ adjacent to the name of each tab that is currently displayed at the top left of the graphics area. It also contains a list of other tabs that can be added to or deleted from those currently displayed.

Figure 29 – List of menu tabs that can be added to or removed from the top left of the screen.

7. In the pull-down menu, click to place a check mark adjacent to ☑ **Simulation** (if not already checked). This action opens the **Simulation** tab at the top of the screen. This tab contains icons used during a finite element analysis.

8. Click the **Simulation** tab *name* to display icons used during a finite element analysis.

Next, proceed as follows to remove un-needed tabs.

9. Right-click on any tab *name*. In the pull-down menu clear the check mark "✓" adjacent to ☐ **DimXpert** (if it appears). The menu closes automatically and **DimXpert** is removed from the list of tabs.

10. Repeat step 9 to remove the **Office Products** tab (if it appears at top left of the graphics area).

11. Right-click anywhere in the top menu bar to open the **Command Manager** pull-down menu.

12. Near the top of this menu, select ☑ **Use Large Buttons with Text** (if not already selected). This action adds descriptive labels beneath each icon.

The upper portion of the SolidWorks Simulation window should now appear similar to that shown in Fig. 28. The number of icons appearing on a toolbar may vary. Also, because a finite element analysis is not currently active, most icons appear grayed out.

Property Managers and Dialogue Boxes

Property managers and dialogue boxes are, perhaps, the most frequently used items when developing a finite element analysis in SolidWorks Simulation. The importance of these two interfaces cannot be overstated because the specific meaning of each aspect of the finite element modeling process is defined within them. However, these interfaces are only encountered when an actual analysis is being performed. For this reason, this section only attempts to define their location on the screen and provide basic insight to their general role in an analysis. No user interaction is required for the remainder of this chapter.

When opened, a *property manager* is typically located at the left side of the graphics area, shown boxed in Fig. 30. Numerous property managers exist and each is somewhat unique. However, the general observations described below apply to each. The property manager, shown boxed in Fig. 30, is enlarged in Fig. 31.

Figure 30 – Image showing the location of a property manager in the SolidWorks Simulation graphical user interface.

Figure 31 shows an example of the **Force/Torque** property manager with its name prominently displayed at the top. This property manager is used when defining different types of loads applied to a finite element model.

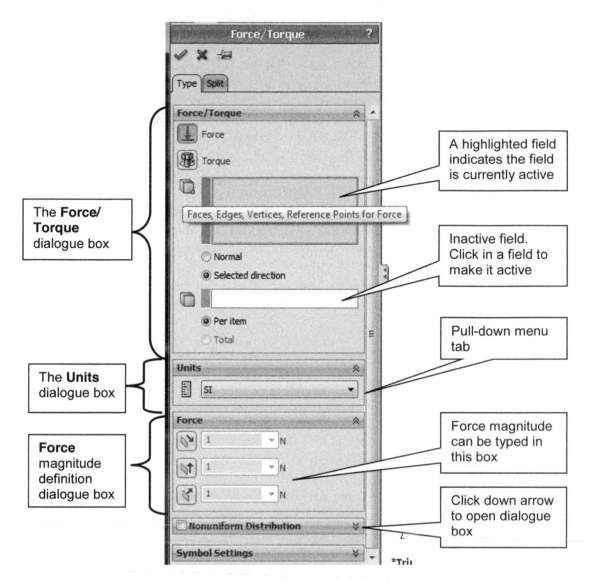

Figure 31 – Overview of features common to property managers and dialogue boxes.

Each *property manager* contains several *dialogue boxes*. Five different dialogue boxes appear in the **Force/Torque** property manager shown above, they are: **Force/Torque**, **Units**, **Force**, **Nonuniform Distribution**, and **Symbol Settings**. Dialogue boxes group related items in a single location and their names help the user quickly locate items to be defined.

For example, the **Force/Torque** dialogue box lists various types of forces or torques that can be selected by clicking within the ⊙ symbol to the left of a specific load type. Also within the **Force/Torque** dialogue box are two *fields*. Moving the cursor over a field, or the icon adjacent to a field, causes specific field information to appear much like prompts that occur for other Windows® icons. In Fig. 31, the prompt for the upper field is displayed as "**Faces, Edges, Vertices, Reference Points for Force**". This field is also highlighted a light blue color (here shown in grey), which indicates it is currently "active" and awaiting user input.

Many dialogue boxes contain pull-down menus that can be accessed by clicking the symbol ▼ adjacent to a field. For example, the **Units** dialogue box in Fig. 31 permits the user to switch between **English (IPS)**, **SI**, or **Metric (G)** units. Some boxes, such as the **Force** dialogue box, permit the user to type a force value into a data box. And finally, as is often the case, insufficient space is available to display the contents of all dialogue boxes simultaneously. Therefore, only the titles of some dialogue boxes appear. In these instances the user must click the ![symbol] symbol to display contents of a dialogue box. Such is the case for the ☐**Nonuniform Distribution** and the **Symbol Settings** dialogue boxes located at the bottom of Fig. 31.

This completes the introduction to underlying fundamentals of finite element analysis and the SolidWorks and SolidWorks Simulation graphical user interfaces. Familiarize yourself with this work environment so that you are able to work comfortably within it.

Step-by-step examples focusing on the application of SolidWorks Simulation to solve finite element modeling problems begin in the next chapter.

Cautions and Other Facts You Should Know

1. Always download example problems and end of chapter problems to the local hard drive of the computer being used. If problem files reside on a remote file server or a USB drive plugged into the computer, execution times that should take a matter of seconds could increase to forty minutes or more.

2. If a pop-up SolidWorks Warning window, such as that shown in Fig. 32, appears when a model file is opened, simply click **[OK]** to dismiss the window. The fact that some models were created using the student version of SolidWorks makes no difference; the files are still valid.

   Figure 32 – SolidWorks Warning window can be ignored.

3. Beginning in 2011 a **Curvature Based Mesh**, seen in Fig. 33 (a), became the new system default mesh recommended for finite element analysis when using SolidWorks Simulation. However, the majority of examples and problems encountered in the first several chapters of this text use a **Standard Mesh**. The reason for using a **Standard Mesh** is that it results in a more *orderly* mesh as illustrated in Fig. 33 (b). A more orderly mesh is useful when selecting nodes to better approximate data along a straight line across a model.

Figure 33 - (a) **Curvature Based Mesh**   (b) **Standard Mesh**

4. Problem and exercise statements throughout this text indicate items such as a **Force** applied in the **X**, or **Y**, or **Z** direction. Always refer to the SolidWorks coordinate system triad, Fig. 34, when uncertain about model orientation in the global X, Y, Z coordinate system.

Figure 34 – Cartesian Coordinate system Triad.

NOTES:

CHAPTER #1

STRESS ANALYSIS USING SOLIDWORKS SIMULATION

This chapter is intended to familiarize first-time users of SolidWorks Simulation with basic software capabilities. Particular aspects of the software to be mastered are listed below. This example problem also serves as a model for subsequent Finite Element Analysis (FEA) problems because, once mastered, the sequence of solution steps is fairly consistent. These steps closely parallel the six learning objectives outlined below.

Learning Objectives
Upon completion of this unit, users should be able to:
- Create and execute a linear, static Finite Element Analysis (FEA). SolidWorks Simulation names this process is named a *"Study."*

- Assign *Material Properties* using the material editor.

- Apply *Fixtures* and *External Loads* to a model.

- Use a *Standard Mesh* definition to subdivide a part into nodes and elements.

- Execute a standard *Solution* to a Finite Element Analysis problem.

- Selectively view appropriate stress *Results* of a Finite Element Analysis.

- Use the *Probe* feature to create graphs of stress variation within a part.

- Develop insight into practical decisions that influence how a *Study* is defined to obtain desired results.

Problem Statement
The goal of this example is to determine stresses in the reciprocating cam follower illustrated in Fig. 1. In particular, stresses to be determined are those in the circled region near the upper end of the cam follower where it passes through its support in the frame.

Positions of the cam and follower shown in Fig. 1 and Fig. 2 are assumed to correspond to the locations of maximum cam pressure angle and maximum dynamic load on the cam follower. Although not shown here, a dynamic analysis should be performed using SolidWorks Motion and the resulting dynamic loads applied to the model.

Figure 1 – Concept sketch showing the region of interest on the cam follower.

Figure 2 shows specific dimensions and loads applied to the cam follower. Force components F_x = -368 lb and F_y = 1010 lb exerted by the cam on the follower in the X and Y directions are applied on the roller-pin at the bottom of the follower. Because a static stress analysis is to be performed, the upper-end of the cam follower is considered "fixed", analogous to the fixed end of a cantilever beam, and corresponding reaction forces R_x, R_y, and a resisting moment M_z are shown at the upper support. We will soon discover one of these end conditions is not possible if solid tetrahedral elements are used to model the cam follower. Do you recall from the element description why this is true?

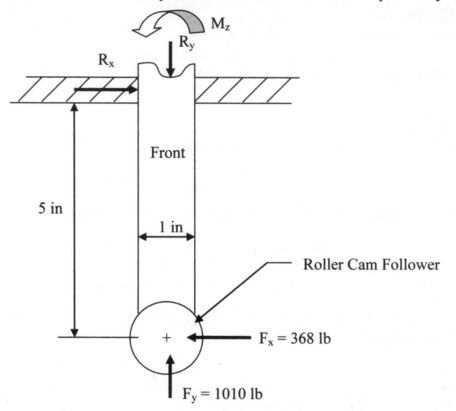

Figure 2 – Two-dimensional model of the reciprocating cam follower. The *Front* surface is labeled for later reference. The follower stem is ½ in thick into the page.

Design Insight
Although finite element programs are powerful computational tools, you should be aware that engineering assumptions are often necessary to advance the design process. In this example, at least three significant engineering assumptions are applied. They are:

- The list of possible materials must be narrowed to a group that provides a strong yet heat-treatable class of steels. Heat treatment is important to produce a hard, long wearing surface for contact between the cam follower and frame in which it slides.

- Because the focus of this analysis is on stress at the *upper* end of the cam follower, modeling of the roller and its pin connection to the follower can be neglected thereby resulting in a considerable saving of modeling effort.

- Assuming that the upper-end of the cam follower is "fixed" results in significant simplification for this initial example (i.e. a static rather than a dynamic analysis results).

Creating a Static Stress Analysis (Study)

Before proceeding, download and unzip chapter examples and end-of-chapter problems from the publisher's web site at: **http://www.SDCpublications.com** see pg. vii for complete details.

1. Open SolidWorks by making the following selections. These steps are similar to opening any Windows program. (*NOTE:* The ">" symbol is used to separate successive menu selections.)

Start>All Programs>SolidWorks 2013>SolidWorks 2013 x64 [or x32] Edition (or) Click the **SolidWorks** icon on your screen.

2. After SolidWorks opens, in the main menu, select **File > Open...** and browse to the location where you saved the downloaded problem files. Click the file named **Cam Follower (Part)** and select **[Open]**, see Fig. 3.

Figure 3 – Solid model of the cam follower.

If a pop-up SolidWorks window appears and states: **Warning: The File C:\Users\Jack\Documents\ ... etc. ... xxx.SLDPRT is from educational version. This file is for instructional use only.** Click **[OK]** to close the window.

NOTE: If SolidWorks **Simulation** is not listed in the main menu of the SolidWorks screen, then in the main menu click **Tools** > **Add-Ins...** Next, in the **Add-Ins** window place check marks "✓" in the left *and* right columns adjacent to ☑ **SolidWorks Simulation** ☑ then click **[OK]** to close the **Add-Ins** window. The **SolidWorks Simulation** License Agreement appears *(for first-time users only)*. Click **[Accept]**.

At this point **Simulation** is added to the main menu displayed at the top of the screen. If the main menu is not displayed, go to the bottom of page I-13 of the Introduction and perform steps 1 and 2. In fact, if the graphical user interface is not set up as outlined on pages I-14 through I-21 of the Introduction, it is *strongly recommended* to do so at this time because instructions below are based on the work environment defined there.

3. In the main menu, select **Simulation**. Then from the pull-down menu select ⚲**Study...** Alternatively, in the **Simulation** *tab*, near top-left of the graphics area, click the down arrow ▼ beneath the **Study Advisor** icon and from the pull-down menu select ⚲**New Study**. A partial view of the **Study** property manager opens as shown in Fig. 4

4. In the **Name** dialogue box, replace "**Study 1**" by typing a descriptive name. For this example type, "**Cam Follower #1**" as the Study name.

5. Next, in the **Type** dialogue box, verify that the system default **Static** analysis icon appears shaded to indicate it is selected. If not, click to select it.

6. Click **[OK]** ✓ (the green check mark) to close the **Study** property manager.

Figure 4 – Initial selections shown in the **Study** property manager.

After completing the above steps, an outline of the current SolidWorks Simulation Study is created in the boxed area of Fig. 5. The SolidWorks feature manager, containing steps used to construct the solid model, appears above the box.

The Study name, **Cam Follower #1 (-Default-)**, appears at the top of the box. Beneath this name is the **Cam Follower (Part)** folder.

Also shown are:
   a. the **Connections** folder, where interactions between parts are defined. Connections are not applicable here because only one part exists.

   b. next is the **Fixtures** folder where restraints are applied to the model,

   c. next is the **External Loads** folder where forces, torques, pressures, etc. are applied to a model,

   d. the **Mesh** folder appears next,

   e. and finally, the **Result Options** folder appears at the bottom of the list. It is not used in this example.

Figure 5 – The **SolidWorks Simulation** manager showing various components used to define a Study.

The finite element analysis steps listed in Fig. 5 proceed in a logical order from beginning to end of a Study. Thus, this sequence of steps is followed in all subsequent examples. It is, however, worth noting that steps shown in the outline can be executed in any order.

Assigning Material to the Model

Begin by defining the material of which the cam follower is made. To do this, proceed as follows. *NOTE: For simplicity in the remainder of this text, the SolidWorks Simulation manager will be referred to as the "Simulation manager."*

1. In the Simulation manager *right*-click the **Cam Follower (Part)** folder; see Fig. 6, and from the pull-down menu, select **Apply/Edit Material...** The **Material** window opens as shown in Fig. 7.

2. In the left-hand column of the **Material** window, do the following:

    a. Click the "+" adjacent to **SolidWorks Materials** (if not already selected).

Figure 6 – Selecting the part to which material properties are assigned.

Figure 7 – Material properties of a part are specified in the **Material** window.

    b. Click the "+" adjacent to **Steel** (if not already selected) and scroll down the list to select **AISI 1045 Steel, cold drawn**. Immediately, properties of 1045 steel appear in the right half of the table.

    c. If material properties are listed in SI units, click ▼ to open the **Units:** pull-down menu. From the list, select the **English (IPS)** system of units, where IPS indicates units of inches, pounds, and seconds.

Familiarize yourself with information in this table by reading **Property** names listed in the left-hand column and their corresponding magnitudes in the **Value** column. For example, **Yield Strength = 76870 psi** for AISI 1045 cold drawn steel. Occasionally values like yield strength appear at greater precision than is truly known for this property. This is because S.I. units are default within SolidWorks Simulation and extra digits frequently occur when values are converted to English units. Examine other values listed in the table to become familiar with data available in the material library.

3. Click **[Apply]** followed by **[Close]** to close the **Material** window. In the Simulation manager tree, notice that a check mark "✓" now appears on the **Cam Follower (Part)** icon and **(-AISI 1045 Steel, cold drawn-)** is listed next to the part name. The check mark indicates that material properties have been defined.

Applying Fixtures

Restraints must be applied to stabilize and support the model as it is supported in its actual application. In this example, the top surface of the model, i.e., the location where the cam follower enters the frame, is assumed to be "fixed." This restraint is consistent with a cam follower whose upper end is located in a near-zero clearance slot in the frame and for which a static analysis is assumed. Define fixtures for the model as follows.

1. In the Simulation manager, right-click **Fixtures**, then from the pull-down menu select **Fixed Geometry...** The **Fixture** property manager appears as shown in Fig. 8. Also, the **Example** dialogue box contains an animation depicting the effect of this type of restraint.

2. Within the **Type** tab, locate the **Standard (Fixed Geometry)** dialogue box and select the **Fixed Geometry** icon (if not already selected). This option sets all translations in X, Y, and Z directions to zero. From the Introduction, recall that tetrahedral elements used to model solid parts allow only three degrees of freedom (three translations) at each node.

Figure 8 – Selections made in the **Fixture** property manager.

As with other Windows® operations, placing the cursor over an icon causes a brief description of the icon to be displayed. Placing the cursor on the icon located to the left of the light-blue colored field in the **Standard (Fixed Geometry)** dialogue box reveals that **Faces, Edges, Vertices for Fixture** can be selected as entities to which restraints can be applied. In this example the top surface of the cam follower is selected as described next.

The light-blue color indicates that the **Faces, Edges, Vertices for Fixture** field is *active* and waiting for the user to specify what part of the model is to be designated as **Fixed**. If, in the following step, selecting the top surface of the model is difficult due its orientation or size, use the graphics controls to rotate, and/or zoom-in on the top surface. If rotate or zoom icons are used, press **[Esc]** to return to the standard cursor (pointer).

3. Move the cursor over the model and when the top *surface* is indicated by a small green square next to the cursor *and* when **Fixture** symbols appear on the top surface, click to select the surface.

Fixture symbols appear as arrows in the X, Y, and Z directions as shown in Fig. 9 and an information "flag" labels the surface as **Fixed Geometry:**. Also, the notation **Face<1>** now appears in the **Fixture** property manager as shown in Fig. 8.

Figure 9 – **Fixed** restraint applied to top surface of the cam follower model.

NOTE: If the *bottom* surface (surface with a line on it) or an edge, vertex, or other surface of the model is selected incorrectly, right-click the incorrect item in the dialogue box (light blue field) and from the pop-up menu, select **Delete**. Then repeat step #3.

4. To change color or size of the restraint symbols, click the down-arrow ⌄ to open the **Symbol Settings** dialogue box located at the bottom of the **Fixture** property manager. Next click the **[Edit Color...]** button to open a color palette. Select the desired color and click **[OK]**. In this example you are encouraged to leave the fixture color as pre-defined because additional symbols, applied to the model later in this analysis, use different default colors to differentiate fixtures from applied loads. To change symbol size, click the up or down arrows adjacent to the **Symbol Size** spin box. Fixture symbols in Fig. 9 were increased in size to 120 and their color changed for emphasis.

5. Click **[OK]** ✓ (green check-mark) at top of the **Fixture** property manager to accept this restraint and close the window. The above steps render the top face of the cam follower **Immovable** and create an icon named ⚓ **Fixed-1** beneath the **Fixtures** folder in the Simulation manager.

Aside:

It is important to note that, although the **Fixture** property manager allows the user to specify **Fixed** restraints at desired locations on a model, the effect of this restraint type produces different restraints when applied to different element types. However, the software recognizes the type of element to which the restraints are applied (solid model, shell elements, truss elements, or beam elements), and applies the proper fixture to each type.

In the case of a solid model, such as the cam follower, application of **Fixed** restraints prevents translations of the top surface in the X, Y, and Z directions. This type of restraint is referred to as being "immovable" because it prevents only three degrees of freedom at each node selected on the model. Note that the moment acting on top of the cam follower in Fig. 2 is *not* restrained by immovable restraints.

Future examples will reveal that **Fixed** restraints, when applied to shell or beam elements, not only prohibit node translations in the X, Y, and Z directions, but also restrict (i.e., prevent) rotational displacements (i.e., moments) about the X, Y, and Z axes at each restrained node. A shell mesh is investigated in Chapter 4.

Applying External Loads

Following the sequence of steps listed in the Simulation manager, we next apply external forces to the model. Proceed by defining the X and Y force components one at a time that act at the bottom center of the cam follower. Begin by applying the vertical component of force $F_y = 1010$ lb that acts upward on the bottom of the cam follower. Proceed as follows.

1. In the Simulation manager, right-click the **External Loads** folder and from the pull-down menu, select **Force...** The **Force/Torque** property manager appears in Fig. 10.

2. Under the **Type** tab, click the **Force** icon (if not already selected).

3. Beneath the light blue colored field, click to choose ⊙ **Selected direction**. This choice is made to define the direction of the Y-force component in step 5 below.

Figure 10 - Definition of force F_y acting on a *Split Line*.

4. In the **Force/Torque** dialogue box, place the cursor in the upper field. If the field does not appear light-blue, click within the box to change its color. Placing the cursor over this box reveals the message, **Faces, Edges, Vertices, Reference Points for Force**. This text prompts the user to select the entity to which the Y-component of force is to be applied. In the graphics area, rotate the model and zoom-in on the bottom face. Notice that a line is located at the center of the bottom surface. As you move the cursor onto this line, the message *(Split Line1)* should appear. Click to select this line since it is desired to place both X and Y force components at the center of the bottom face. After selecting *(Split Line1)*, **Edge<1>** appears in the top field of the **Force/Torque** dialogue box, shown in Fig. 10.

5. Next, click inside the bottom field in the **Force/Torque** dialogue box. This action changes the field color from white to light blue. Placing the cursor on this field prompts the user to select a **Face, Edge, Plane for Direction**. In other words, to indicate the direction of the Y-force component it is necessary to select a face, edge, or axis in the desired direction. Click to select *any vertical* **Edge** of the model shown in Fig. 11. **Edge<2>** should appear in the active field and force vectors should appear on *Split Line 1*. Ignore incorrect Y-directions at this time. If force vectors do not appear, proceed to the next step; otherwise skip to step 7.

Choose *any* vertical **edge** to specify direction

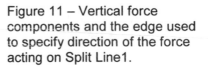

Figure 11 – Vertical force components and the edge used to specify direction of the force acting on Split Line1.

6. Click ⩔ to open the **Symbol Settings** dialogue box located at the very bottom of the **Force/Torque** property manager. Toggle the ☑ **Show preview** check mark "off" and "on" again to display the force vectors.

7. Next, within the **Units** dialogue box use the pull-down menu to set **Units** ⧉ to **English (IPS)** (if not already selected).

8. In the **Force** dialogue box, type **1010**, which indicates magnitude of the Y-force component. Examine the direction of vectors appearing in the graphic image and if they are not directed toward the top of the model, check ☑ **Reverse direction.**

9. Click **[OK]** ✓ (green check-mark) to accept this force definition and close the **Force/Torque** property manager. SolidWorks Simulation applies the 1010 lb force to the model and creates an icon named ⟟ **Force-1 (:Per item: 1010 lbf:)** beneath the **External Loads** folder in the Simulation manager tree.

Next, apply the X-force component (F_x = -368 lb) to *Split Line 1* on the bottom of the cam follower. Try this on your own using a procedure similar to the preceding steps. Alternately, a listing of commands is provided below for those desiring guidance.

10. In the Simulation manager tree, right-click the **External Loads** folder and select **Force...** The **Force/Torque** property manager opens.

11. In the **Force/Torque** dialogue box, choose ⊙ **Selected direction**.

12. Click to activate (light blue) the upper field where **Faces, Edges, Vertices, Reference Points for Force** prompts the user to indicate where the force is to be applied. Again select *Split Line1*. The line is highlighted and **Edge <1>** appears in the active field.

13. Click to activate (light blue) the **Face, Edge, Plane for Direction** field and proceed to select *any* edge of the model parallel to the X-direction (i.e.- parallel to the 1-inch dimension of the cam follower). After selecting an edge, **Edge<2>** appears in the direction field and force vectors in the X-direction appear on *Split Line1*. Ignore incorrect direction at this time.

14. In the **Units** dialogue box set the **Units** 🔲 field to **English (IPS)**.

15. In the **Force** dialogue box , type **368** to define magnitude of the X-force component. If necessary, check ☑ **Reverse direction** to orient force components in the negative X-direction.

16. When the X force component appears as shown Fig. 12, click **[OK]** ✓ to accept this force and close the **Force/Torque** property manager.

17. A new icon named ⊥ *Force-2 (:Per item: -368 lbf:)* appears beneath the **External Loads** folder.

Figure 12 – Front view of cam follower showing force components F_x and F_y applied to the *Split Line 1*.

The model is now complete as far as material property, restraint, and force definitions are concerned. The next step is to Mesh the model as described in the following section.

Aside #1:
Split lines are frequently encountered in the study of SolidWorks, therefore, this example does not review how they are applied. However, they are also extremely useful in Finite Element Analysis, and for that reason, their application is reviewed in future chapters.

Aside #2:
As noted in the **Design Insight** section at the beginning of this example, stresses at the *upper end* of the cam follower are to be investigated. For this reason, the simplified assumption of force loading at the center of the lower end of the model, where the roller is attached to the follower, might be deemed acceptable. After all, why devote considerable time and effort to model contact stress between the roller-pin and cam follower *if* the focus of analysis is to determine stresses elsewhere in the model? On the other hand, if the focus of this analysis were on stresses in the vicinity of the pin that joins the roller to the cam follower, then details of that geometry must be included in the model. Contact stress between a pin and a hole is investigated in Chapter 6.

Meshing the Model

The final task in preparing the model for analysis is to generate a finite element mesh in the solid model. This section explores the meshing process.

1. In the Simulation manager, right-click the **Mesh** icon and from the pull-down menu, select **Create Mesh...** The **Mesh** property manager opens. A partial view of this property manager is shown in Fig. 13.

The **Mesh Density** dialogue box shows a pointer on a sliding scale between **Coarse** and **Fine** mesh sizes. The default setting performs an initial analysis with mesh size set midway between these two extremes.

To learn more about the units, mesh size, and tolerance of the current mesh click to place a check mark "✓" to open the ☑ **Mesh Parameters** dialogue box also shown in Fig. 13. At the top of this dialogue box, select ⊙ **Standard mesh** because this model contains no curved surfaces.

Next, inches (**in**) should appear in the **Unit** ▤ field. If not, change units by accessing the **Unit** pull-down menu.

Also within the **Mesh Parameters** dialogue box observe the **Global Size** of the mesh indicated in the middle field as **0.13576659in**. This value represents the diameter of an *unseen* sphere that circumscribes (surrounds) a typical tetrahedral element in the model. Element size is automatically determined based on geometric features of the model. Values may vary slightly.

Figure 13 – Mesh parameters, can be altered in the **Mesh** property manager.

The third field from the top indicates the mesh **Tolerance**, which is 5% of the global mesh size. In cases where the automatic mesher fails to mesh a model, increasing the tolerance may help. **Tolerance** allows lengths of element sides to deviate from the exact **Global Size** so that the mesh is able to conform to curvature and other irregularities present in a geometrically complex model. Default values usually provide sufficient definition of element size to yield acceptable results for an initial finite element analysis.

Although the **Mesh** property manager is essentially unchanged in this example, its use in modifying mesh size is investigated in Chapter 3.

2. Click **[OK]** ✓ to accept the default values and close the **Mesh** property manager.

Meshing starts automatically and the **Mesh Progress** window appears briefly (< 2 sec). After meshing is complete, SolidWorks Simulation displays the meshed model as shown in Fig. 14. Also, a check mark "✓" appears on the **Mesh** icon in the Simulation manager tree to indicate meshing is complete.

3. To display mesh information, right-click the **Mesh** folder and select **Details…** The **Mesh Details** window opens and is also shown in Fig. 14.

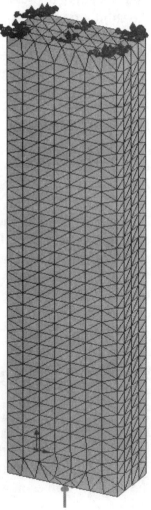

The **Mesh Details** window displays information about the current model such as its **Study name**, **Mesh type (Solid Mesh)**, **Mesher Used (Standard mesh)**, …, **Element size**, **Tolerance** values and other data is repeated. Scroll down in this window and notice that approximately 10539 **Total nodes** and 6546 **Total elements** are created for this model. Because the automatic meshing software attempts to create an optimal mesh for each model, the number of nodes and elements may vary slightly between alternate meshing of complex models.

4. Click ⊠ to close the **Mesh Details** window.

Mesh Details	
Study name	Cam Follower #1 (-Default-)
Include Mesh Auto Loops	Off
Jacobian points	4 points
Element size	0.135767 in
Tolerance	0.00678833 in
Mesh quality	High
Total nodes	10539
Total elements	6546
Maximum Aspect Ratio	3.1862
Percentage of elements with Aspect Ratio < 3	100

Figure 14 – Cam follower with mesh and boundary conditions illustrated. Also shown is the **Mesh Details** window where mesh information can be reviewed.

5. To hide the mesh, right-click **Mesh** and from the pull-down menu select **Hide Mesh**. Conversely, selecting **Show Mesh** in the pull-down menu returns the mesh display to the model. Try this option, but Hide the mesh before continuing.

Aside:
As noted earlier, it is permissible to define material properties, fixtures, external loads, and create the mesh in *any order*. However, all these *necessary* steps must be completed prior to running the Solution portion of a Study.

Running the Solution

After the model has been completely defined, we are ready to proceed to the *Solution* process. This is the second major portion of a finite element program. It is where the numerous equations that define a Study are solved. For all of its complexity, this portion of a Finite Element Analysis is, perhaps, most deceiving in terms of its seeming simplicity from the user's perspective. Time required for an analysis can vary from several seconds to several hours depending upon overall model complexity and the computer hardware used. Most examples in this text should solve in a matter of seconds to five minutes at most. To solve the current example, proceed as follows.

1. To run an analysis, right-click **Cam Follower #1 (-Default-)** located at the top of the Simulation manager tree. Refer to highlighted text in Fig. 15.

2. From the pull-down menu, select **Run** and the solution process begins automatically. A window that tracks progress of the Solution appears, but due to the small size and simplicity of this example, it is displayed only briefly.

After successful solution of this static analysis, SolidWorks Simulation creates a new folder, named "**Results**," at the bottom of the Simulation manager tree. This folder should contain the three sub-folders shown boxed in Fig. 15. These sub-folders contain default plots resulting from a finite element analysis of the current model. If these folders do *not* appear, follow steps (a) through (f) outlined on the next page. Otherwise skip to the section titled "**Examination of Results**."

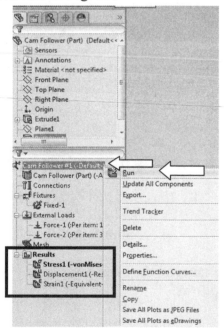

Figure 15 – **Results** folders created as part of the Solution process. Each folder contains solution information indicated by its name.

a) Right-click the **Results** folder and from the pull-down menu, select **Define Stress Plot...** The **Stress Plot** property manager opens.

b) In the **Display** dialogue box, select **VON: von Mises Stress** from the pull-down menu (if not already selected).

c) Also in the **Display** dialogue box, verify that ▦ **Units** are set to **psi**. If not, from the **Units** pull-down menu, select **psi** as the units used to display results.

d) Click **[OK]** ✓ to close the **Stress Plot** property manager and immediately a plot of von Mises stress is displayed in the graphics area.

e) Repeat steps (a) through (d), but in step (a) select **Define Displacement Plot...**; in step (b) accept the default display named **URES: Resultant Displacement**; in step (c) change the **Units** pull-down menu to inches (**in**); and in step (d) click **[OK]**✓.

f) Repeat steps (a) through (d) a third time, but in step (a) select **Define Strain Plot...**; in step (b) accept the default display item named **ESTRN: Equivalent Strain**; in step (c) take no action because strain is unitless; and in step (d) click **[OK]**✓. The three sub-folders should now appear beneath the **Results** folder.

Examination of Results

The outcome of this analysis, in the form of graphs, plots, and data, can be viewed by accessing computed output stored in the various **Results** folders. These results are the ultimate goal of a finite element analysis. It is where validity of finite element calculations should be investigated by cross-checking them against manual calculations or other verifiable experimental or reference results. *Checking computed results is a necessary step in good engineering practice!*

Understanding Default Graphical Results

1. If a color plot of **Stress1 (-vonMises-)** is *not* displayed on the graphics screen, then right-click the **Stress1 (-vonMises-)** folder and from the pull-down menu select **Show**. Alternatively, double-click **Stress1 (-vonMises-)**.

If units on the color-coded stress scale on this plot are *not* in **psi**, then change units as follows.

2. In the Simulation manager, right-click **Stress1 (-vonMises-)** and from the pull-down menu, select **Edit Definition...** The **Stress Plot** property manager opens.

3. In the **Display** dialogue box, verify that ▦ **Units** are set to **psi**. If not, from the **Units** pull-down menu, select **psi** as shown in Fig. 16.

If the model does *not* appear deformed (curved), as shown in Fig. 17, then proceed to step 4. Otherwise, skip to step 5.

4. In the **Stress Plot** property manager, check "✓" to open the ☑ **Deformed Shape** dialogue box. Then click to activate ⊙ **Automatic** as shown in Fig. 16.

5. Click **[OK]** ✓ to close the **Stress Plot** property manager.

Either system default settings or the above actions cause a deformed view of the cam follower along with a color plot of the von Mises stress distribution to be displayed on the model as shown in Fig. 17 and on your screen.

Default information provided near the upper-left corner of the graphics screen, circled in Fig. 17, includes:

Figure 16 – Changing **Units** and **Deformed Shape** of the model in the **Stress Plot** property manager.

- **Model name:** ← Contains the name of the SolidWorks model opened from the parts file at the beginning of this example; it is named **"Cam Follower (Part)."**

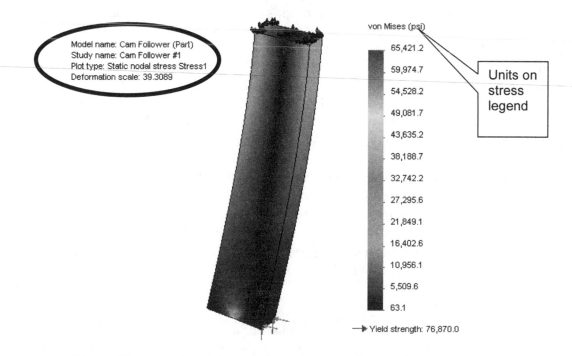

Figure 17 – Default plot of von Mises stress distribution throughout the cam follower model. Stress is shown in English units.

- **Study name:** ← Lists the name selected and typed into the **Study** property manager at the start of this example. If previous instructions were followed precisely, this name should appear as "**Cam Follower #1**".

- **Plot type:** ← Should indicate "**Static nodal stress Stress1**"

- **Deformation Scale:** ← To illustrate a deformed shape, SolidWorks Simulation scales the maximum deformation of the model to 10% of the diagonal of a bounding box around the model (this box is not visible). A number representing the magnitude of the deformation scale for this model appears on the bottom line. This value indicates that the part image is deformed 39.3089 (or similar value) *times larger* than its actual deformation. The intent of the deformed model is to aid visualization of part deflection and does *not* represent the actual deformation magnitude.

- Also appearing on the plot is a color-coded stress scale. Stress magnitudes at various locations throughout the model can be determined by matching colors to those of the color-coded stress scale. Red traditionally corresponds to high stress while dark blue corresponds to algebraically lower stress magnitudes.

Results Predicted by Classical Stress Equations

It is assumed that some users may not yet be familiar with von Mises stress.[1] Therefore, discussion below digresses to examine *other*, more fundamental, stresses that occur within the cam follower model. To accomplish this, a brief, but thorough solution to the current problem is included based on classical equations of stress analysis.

Begin by recalling the original free-body diagram of the cam follower shown in Fig. 2. That figure revealed the part is subject to force components in both the X and Y directions on its lower end. The upward acting force component $F_y = 1010$ lb causes an axial compressive stress given by $\sigma_y = F_y/A$ in the Y-direction. Although this stress is shown near the lower end of the cam follower in Fig. 18, classic stress equations assume it is *uniformly distributed* throughout the model from top to bottom. Similarly, the X-component of force, $F_x = -368$ lb that acts perpendicular to the length of the cam follower, causes bending stress given by $\sigma_y = Mc/I$ shown at the top of the model in Fig. 18. Bending stress is maximum at the top of the model due to maximum length (5 in) of the moment arm acted upon by the X-component of force F_x which is applied at the bottom of the cam follower. Briefly review stress calculations included on Fig. 18 before proceeding. Recall the cam follower is 1.00-in wide by 0.50-in thick.

---

[1] It is presumed that use of this SolidWorks Simulation user guide will be introduced near the beginning of a Design of Machine Elements or Mechanics of Materials course. However, most traditional textbooks on these subjects delay introduction of vonMises stress until later chapters. For this reason, early examples in this user guide involve stresses that are more familiar to individuals who have completed a fundamental mechanics of materials course.

Because all stresses depicted on Fig. 18 act in the Y-direction, they can be combined simply by adding magnitudes of axial and bending stresses provided proper ± signs are included. Combining these stresses yields the following results:

Bending Stress:
$\sigma_y = Mc/I = (368*5)(0.5)/[(.5)(1)^3/12] = \pm 22080$ psi
(Force component F_x causes bending which produces compressive stress at **A** and tensile stress at **C**)

Axial Stress:
$\sigma_y = F_y/A = 1010/(0.5*1.0) = -2020$ psi
(Axial force component F_y causes uniform compressive stress throughout the length of the model)

(Compression) B C A

Length = 5.0 in

$F_x = 368$ lb

$F_y = 1010$ lb

Figure 18 – Schematic of loading and distribution of bending stress (compression on left-side and tension on right-side) and axial stress (compression) in the Y-direction on the cam follower determined using classic stress equations.

Stresses at points **A**, **B**, and **C** *combine* as described below.

Stress at point **A** is in compression due to both axial and bending stresses, thus:

Stress at point **A**: $(\sigma_y)_A = \sigma_{Axial} + \sigma_{Bending} = (-2020) + (-22080) = -24{,}100$ psi

Stress at point **B** is in compression due to axial stress, but bending stress is zero on the neutral axis, thus:

Stress at point **B**: $(\sigma_y)_B = \sigma_{Axial} + \sigma_{Bending} = (-2020) + (0) = -2{,}020$ psi

Stress at point **C** is compressive due to axial stress, but acts in tension due to bending stress. Because the tensile "+" bending stress is greater than the compressive "-" axial stress, the resultant stress at point **C** is:

Stress at point **C**: $(\sigma_y)_C = \sigma_{Axial} + \sigma_{Bending} = (-2020) + (+22080) = +20{,}060$ psi

SolidWorks Simulation Results for Stress in Y-Direction

The above results are next compared with those determined using the finite element analysis performed in this chapter. To do so, it is meaningful to produce a plot of normal stress in the Y-direction (i.e., σ_y). Proceed as follows.

1. In the Simulation manager tree right-click the **Results** folder and from the pull-down menu select **Define Stress Plot...** The **Stress Plot** property manager opens as shown in Fig. 19.

2. In the **Display** dialogue box, click ▼ to open the pull-down menu adjacent to the **Component** field. Initially this field shows that **VON: von Mises Stress** is currently selected. From the list of stresses available in the pull-down menu, locate and select **SY: Y Normal Stress**. This selection identifies normal stress in the Y-direction, commonly represented by σ_y, as the stress to be displayed in a new plot. This is the *same* stress determined using classical equations above.

For future reference it is informative to observe all the other stresses available for analysis within the **Component** field. Briefly return to the pull-down menu and note the list of thirteen stresses included there. Although names, rather than Greek symbols are listed, observe what stresses it is possible to select when defining a new plot. Following is a *partial* list of stresses available.

σ_x, σ_y, σ_z = Normal stresses in X, Y and Z directions listed as **SX**, **SY**, **SZ**.

τ_{xy}, τ_{xz}, τ_{yz} = Shear stresses on X, Y, and Z planes, listed as **TXY**, **TXZ**, **TYZ**.

σ_1, σ_2, σ_3 = 1st, 2nd, and 3rd Principal stresses listed as **P1**, **P2**, **P3**.

And, other stresses not listed here.

3. In the **Advanced Options** dialogue box, change **Units** to **psi** (if needed).

4. Also in the **Advanced Options** dialogue box verify that ⊙ **Node Values** is selected.

Figure 19 – Selections to specify plotting of a different stress component on the model.

5. Because it is often convenient to turn off the deformed shape when viewing stresses within a model, check "✓" to open the ☑ **Deformed Shape** dialogue (if not already open) and select ⊙**True Scale** to display deformation of the model at its true magnitude. Suppressing display of the deformed shape also proves helpful when using the **Probe** feature later in this example.

6. Open the **Property** dialogue box by clicking ⩗. Within this dialogue box, click to place a check mark next to ☑ **Include title text** and type a descriptive title such as: **Sigma-Y,** *Your name*. A descriptive title serves both to identify *what* quantity is plotted and *who* created this new plot in the current study.

7. Click **[OK]** ✓ to accept these changes and close the **Stress Plot** property manager. A plot of normal stress in the Y-direction (σ_y) now appears on the graphics screen and a new plot, named **Stress2 (-Y normal-)**, is listed beneath the **Results** folder. The icon labeled **Stress1 (-vonMises-)** still contains the original plot of von Mises stresses while **Stress2 (Y-normal-)** contains a new plot of normal stress in the Y-direction (σ_y).

Also note that the title and your name entered in step 6 now appears at the top-left of the graphics window. This data helps identify printed output at a public (campus) printer. Next, proceed as follows to modify visual characteristics of the graphics display.

8. Right-click **Stress2 (-Y normal-)** and from the pull-down menu, select **Settings...**. The **Settings** property manager opens as seen in Fig. 20.

9. Within the **Fringe Options** dialogue box, select **Discrete** from the pull-down menu. This action displays stress contours as discrete color bands rather than the rainbow effect created by the **Continuous** display. While on this menu, experiment with other **Fringe Options**, then reset to **Discrete** to correspond with images illustrated on the following pages.

10. In the **Boundary Options** dialogue box, select **Model**. This option outlines the model with a black line thereby making its edges easier to view.

Figure 20 – Altering stress contour display options in the **Settings** property manager.

11. Click **[OK]** ✓ to close the **Settings** property manager. A *partial* image of the **Discrete** fringe plot of normal stress in the Y-direction near the top of the model appears in Fig. 21 (a).

Using the Probe Tool

Although stress contour plots provide a general sense of stress *magnitudes throughout the model*, it is often desirable to determine stress magnitudes *at specific locations*. To do this, use of the **Probe** tool is demonstrated next. To aid in selecting specific points on the model its image is modified by superimposing a **Mesh** on the model.

To alter model appearance, return to the **Settings** property manager and proceed as follows.

1. Right-click **Stress2 (-Y normal-)** and from the pull-down menu select **Settings…** This action returns us to the **Settings** property manager.

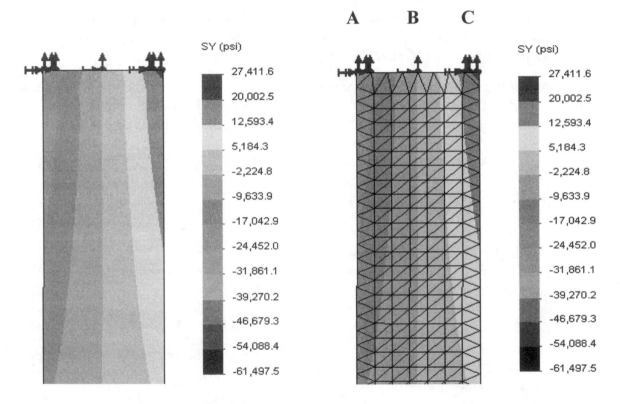

Figure 21 (a) – Upper portion of model showing stress σ_y as **Discrete** fringes.

Figure 21 (b) – Upper portion of the model showing the normal stress σ_y and a **Mesh** superimposed on the model. This action facilitates using the **Probe** feature.

2. Within the **Settings** property manager, open the pull-down menu in the **Boundary Options** dialogue box and select **Mesh**. A mesh is displayed on the model.

3. Click **[OK]** ✓ to close the **Settings** property manager. The upper portion of the model should now appear with the mesh shown as illustrated in Fig. 21 (b).

We are now ready to compare manually calculated stresses with stress values determined using the finite element analysis. To facilitate comparisons, manually calculated stress magnitudes at points **A**, **B**, and **C** on top of the cam follower in Fig. 21 (b) are repeated below.

Stress at point A: $(\sigma_y)_A = \sigma_{Axial} + \sigma_{Bending} = (-2020) + (-22080) = -24,100$ psi

Stress at point B: $(\sigma_y)_B = \sigma_{Axial} + \sigma_{Bending} = (-2020) + (0) = -2,020$ psi

Stress at point C: $(\sigma_y)_C = \sigma_{Axial} + \sigma_{Bending} = (-2020) + (+22080) = +20,060$ psi

The **Probe** tool is used to determine stresses at points **A**, **B**, and **C** on the model and at all points in-between. Occasionally it *may* be necessary to approximate the stress at point **B**. The reason for this is that the automatically generated mesh size depends on model geometry. Therefore, nodes, which typically are used as measurement points, may not lie *exactly* at the location of point **B** on the cam follower centroidal axis. This will be determined as the analysis proceeds.

Begin by zooming-in on the top of the model. An image similar to that shown in Fig. 21 (b) should appear on your screen. Two different methods for using the Probe tool are demonstrated below. Proceed as follows to use the **Probe** tool by the first method.

4. Because stress in the Y direction (σ_y) is to be examined, in the SolidWorks Simulation manager tree right-click **Stress2 (-Y normal-)** and from the pull-down menu, select **Probe**. A partial view of the **Probe Result** property manager opens, but does not initially look like Fig. 22.

5. In the **Options** dialogue box, click to choose ⊙ **On selected entities**. The **Results** dialogue box expands to include a highlighted (light blue) field. This field is active and is awaiting the selection of **Faces, Edges, or Vertices** on the model.

Figure 22 – Partial View of the **Probe Result** property manager.

6. In the graphics screen, slowly move the cursor over faces, edges, and verticies (corners) of the model. The symbol adjacent to the cursor changes to a square, a line, or a small circle to represent selection of a **Face**, an **Edge**, or a **Vertex** respectively. Click to choose the line on the top, front **Edge** of the cam follower. **Edge<1>** appears in the highlighted field and the **[Update]** button becomes active.

7. Click the **[Update]** button. This action fills the **Results** table with the data seen in Fig. 23 and described below.

*NOTE: To view complete results, it may be necessary to enlarge the table <u>and</u> width of individual columns within the table by clicking-and-dragging the right boundary of the **Probe Result** property manager and the individual column boundaries respectively.*

Information contained in each column of the **Results** table includes (from left to right):

- **Node**: This column contains the number of each *sequential* node located across the top front edge of the model. Node numbers are assigned automatically by the software during mesh generation. Seventeen nodes exist across the top edge because high quality tetrahedral elements have nodes at both corner and mid-side locations on each element. Count element sides in Fig. 21 (b) or on your screen.

Figure 23 – **Probe Result** table contains stress values at node locations across the top **Edge** of the model.

- **Value (psi)**: This column contains the magnitude of the *selected* stress (σ_y) at each node location along the top front edge. For the current example, the **Value (psi)** column contains magnitude of stress in the Y-direction.

- **X (in)**: This column contains X-coordinates of each node location across the top of the model. The initial value appears as 1 inch and subsequent values decrease in 1/16 inch increments across the model. (Refer to values shown in Fig. 23)

- **Y (in)**: This column contains Y-coordinates of each node location. Because the original cam follower model was created by locating its bottom left-hand corner at the origin of a global X, Y, Z coordinate system, all points along the top edge lie at a distance of Y = 5.000 inches above that origin.

- **Z (in)**: This column contains Z-coordinates of each node location. Because the original model was extruded ½ inch in the positive Z direction, all Z-coordinates on the top front edge are located at Z = + 0.500 inches.

8. In the **Report Options** dialogue box, located near the bottom of the **Probe Result** property manager, click the **Plot** icon; see Plot flag in Fig. 23. Immediately a graph of stress variation (σ_y) across the top edge of the model is displayed.

Aside:

In this user guide, images of stress within the model are referred to as "stress contour plots" or simply "plots." On the other hand, when an image shows the relationship between two variables X and Y, in the form of a line, the image is referred to as a "graph."

Notice, however, that the graph on your screen displays tensile (positive) stress on its left-hand side and compressive (negative) stress on its right-side. This is just the reverse of the actual stress distribution across the top of the cam follower shown in Fig. 24. The reason for this error is that the top edge of the model is a line with two different ends, but, no means is provided to select data from one end or the other. This logical misrepresentation of data is easily remedied by the following action.

9. First, close the current graph by clicking the ⊠ at its upper-right corner.

10. Next, near the top of the **Results** dialogue box, place a check "✓" adjacent to ☑ **Flip edge plot**. See white arrow in Fig. 23.

11. Again, click the **Plot** icon and a corrected graph, showing variation of σ_y across the top edge of the model, from left to right, appears in Fig. 24. *Do not close the plot window.*

Figure 24 – Graph of stress distribution σ_y from the left side (0.0 in.) to right side (at 1 in.) along top front edge of the cam follower.

The graph in Fig. 24 indicates compressive stress along the left side of the model as expected. This stress gradually decreases to zero near the center of the model and then becomes positive, indicating tensile stress, on the right side of the cam follower. These results are consistent with our understanding of stress distribution on the top edge of the model. However, we next observe that these results do not agree well with results obtained using classical stress equations.

OBSERVATIONS:
Table 1 below compares results of manually calculated stresses with finite element results obtained using the **Probe** tool at locations **A, B,** and **C** at the top-end of the cam follower. Verify results in the Probe Tool Results column of Table 1 below by scrolling through results in the **Values (psi)** column of the **Probe** table on your screen.

Table 1 – Comparison of stress σ_y computed by classical and finite element methods.

Location	Manual Calculation (psi)	Probe Tool Results (psi)	Percent Difference (%)
Point A	-24100	-33129	27.2 %
Point B	-2020	-2123	4.8 %
Point C	+20060	+25750	22.1 %

Results in Table 1 indicate significant differences between results calculated using classical stress equations and those determined using finite element analysis methods. How can this be?

The above question can be answered by recalling St. Venant's principle, which states that stress predicted by classic equations exists only in regions *reasonably well removed* from: (a) points of load application, (b) support locations, and (c) locations of geometric discontinuity. Any of these conditions typically introduces significant *localized* effects. Thus, in these regions, shortcomings of classical stress equations are at odds with more accurate results predicted by finite element methods. For this reason, the **Probe** tool is used again, but this time it is used to select nodes at locations somewhat removed from the upper support. Proceed as follows.

12. Begin by closing the **Edge Plot** graph. Click ☒ to close the graph window.

13. Within the **Options** dialogue box, click to select ⊙ **At location.** This action clears all data from the **Results** table and changes the mode of operation to one that enables display of results at user selected node locations.

Figure 25 – Close-up view of top end of the model showing the first node selected along an *approximate* straight-line across the model.

14. Move the Probe tool into the graphics area and count down to the 4th node below the top-left corner. See the node selected in Fig. 25. This node is somewhat arbitrarily assumed to be "sufficiently removed" from the *immovable* **Fixture** condition applied on top of the cam follower. This location is chosen to reduce the effects predicted by St. Venant's principle.

As you perform the next step, a small information "flag" will appear adjacent to each selected node, like the "flag" shown in Fig. 25. Information listed in this flag includes the *Node Number* in its top row, node coordinates *(X, Y, Z)* on the second line, and stress magnitude is listed in the bottom line; units are included with all values. These values are also listed in the **Results** table of the **Probe Result** property manager. Unfortunately these "flags" tend to overwrite one another for closely spaced node selections. Flags can be moved by clicking them and dragging to arrange them as desired; see Fig. 26. Alternatively, in the **Annotations** dialogue box at the bottom of the **Probe Result** property manager, turn OFF *parts* of these flags by clearing the check "✓" mark from ☐ **Show Node/Element Number** and from ☐ **Show X,Y,Z Location**. However, it is suggested that ☑ **Show Value** remain checked.

15. Proceed across the model *from left-to-right* and click to select *only* nodes at element corners as illustrated by small circles in Fig. 26. If an error is made when selecting nodes, simply click the ⊙ **At Location** button again. This action clears the **Results** table and the selection process can be repeated.

Aside:
Due to the arbitrary mesh generation scheme it may not be possible to select a row of nodes in a *straight line* across the model. Despite this inconvenience, it is still possible to compute stresses at each node location and compare classical results with finite element values listed in the **Results** table. Why? Because its Y coordinate is known.

Figure 26 – **Results** table containing σ_y values and node locations for node selection across the model at a distance "sufficiently removed" from support conditions.

16. Within the **Report Options** dialogue box, once again select the Plot 🗠 icon. The resulting **Probe Result** graph is shown in Fig. 27.

The graph in Fig. 27 reveals the expected variation of stress caused by adding the uniform axial compressive stress to the near linear variation of bending stress. Bending stress varies from compression on left side of the model to tension on the right side.

Figure 27 – Plot of combined axial and bending stress variation (σ_y) across the model.

17. Move the cursor onto the graph and note that cross-hairs (two intersecting dashed lines) appear and move with the cursor. On the default graph, stress **SY (psi)** is plotted on the ordinate and node numbers are plotted on the abscissa. As the cross-hairs move, values of the X and Y coordinates at their intersection update automatically beneath the graph.

18. Move the cursor to the intersection of the curve and the centroidal axis of the model. This location should occur midway between node numbers 531 and 532. Since the cam follower is seven (7) elements wide, its center should lie 3.5 elements from either side of the cam follower.

With the cross-hairs on the curve *at* the centroidal axis, the coordinates displayed beneath the bottom-center of the graph should read either (X = 3.5 nodes, Y = -1902.65 psi) or X = 3.5 nodes, Y = -2123.89 psi. Units are *not* shown with values beneath the graph. The reason for uncertainty of the Y-coordinate is lack of accuracy locating the exact cross-hair intersection with the curve. Thus, the average of these two values

$$(\sigma_y)_{AVG} = [-1903 + (-2124)]/2 = -2013 \text{ psi} \quad \text{(rounded values)}$$

is used for comparison in Table 2.

Table 2 shows a comparison between stresses calculated using classical equations and those computed using the finite element analysis. Results of both methods are compared at *approximately* 0.6 inches below the top of the model. Refer to the Y-coordinate, labeled "**Y (in)**," in the **Results** table of Fig. 26 for the exact distance (4.459-in at nodes on left and right sides of the cam follower). Bending stress components at points A and C in Table 2 are computed at this location, while stress at point B is calculated above.

Table 2 – Comparison of stress σ_y computed by classical and finite element methods at an arbitrary distance below the top of the cam follower.

Location	Manual Calculation (psi)	Probe Tool Results (psi)	Percent Difference (%)
Point A	-21710	-21499	0.98 %
Point B	-2020	-2013	0.35 %
Point C	17670	17635	0.19 %

Note the significant improvement in the comparison of manual calculations and finite element results in Table 2. Differences are less than 1 % at all points **A**, **B**, and **C**. Based on these comparisons, several additional observations are included in the Summary section at the end of this chapter.

19. Do *not* close the **Probe Result** graph. Instead, proceed directly to the next section.

Customizing Graphs

Because default information displayed on SolidWorks Simulation graphs is rather terse, as evidenced by graphs of the previous section, this section briefly examines those graphs and explores means to enhance them. Begin by examining differences between graphs shown in Figs. 24 and 27 (repeated below).

Figure 24 – Repeated   Figure 27 – Repeated

Observations:
- Both graphs bear the same title. Therefore, there is no obvious clue that these graphs represent stress data at different locations on the cam follower.

- The Y-axis label indicates that normal stress in the Y-direction is plotted ($SY = \sigma_y$), but there is no indication that **SY** is a combination of axial and bending stress.

- The X-axis in Fig. 24 plots the **Parametric Distance**, which in this case begins at 0.0 inches at the left side of the model and increases to 1.0 inch at its right side. Recall, the 1 inch wide top *edge* of the model was selected to create Fig. 24.

- The X-axis in Fig. 27 lists the numbers of each **Node** selected as the **Probe** tool moved across the model from left to right.

- A legend, at bottom middle of the graph, indicates the symbols, line color, and units used to plot **SY**. If other lines were plotted on the same graph, additional symbols and colors would appear. Also, because the model *edge* was selected for the graph of Fig. 24, stress at both mid-side *and* corner nodes were plotted for each element. However, only element corner nodes were selected for the plot in Fig. 27, therefore, fewer data points are displayed.

Because properly labeling various parts of a graph is very informative *and* because ability to accomplish this task can be used throughout the remainder of this text, graph labeling is investigated below. However, be aware that graph labeling capability within SolidWorks Simulation is rather limited and somewhat arduous to use. Therefore, steps below outline *only* the most useful tools for customizing graphs. Because the graph shown in Fig. 27 should still be open, proceed as follows.

1. In the menu at the top of the **Probe Result** graph, select **Options**. Then from the pull-down menu select **Properties**. The **2D Chart Control Properties** window opens as shown in Fig. 28.

Begin by replacing the graph title with more descriptive wording.

2. Select the **Titles** tab. Then, within the **Titles** tab, select the **Label** tab.

3. Within the **Text:** box type a descriptive title. Choose wording that fully describes the information displayed on this graph. Press the **[Enter]** key between lines of text. *Hint: Type the _second_ line of text first.* Compare your title to that shown in Fig. 28. Was all the pertinent information included? Click **[Apply]** when done.

4. Explore other options within the **Titles** tab as time and interest permit.

Figure 28 – Creating descriptive graph titles and axis labels within the **2D Chart Control Properties** window.

Next, alter the axis labels. Once again the goal is to provide more descriptive labels. The following step assumes the **2D Chart Control Properties** window remains open. If not, open it again by repeating step 1.

5. Select the **Axes** tab followed by selection of the **Title** tab. Notice that **X** is highlighted (blue) at the top left corner of the current window to indicate X-axis.

6. In the **Text:** box, replace the current axis label, "**Node,**" using wording such as, "**Node Numbers Across the Cam Follower: Left to Right (Node Nos.)**", then click **[Apply]**.

Note that node numbers are the default display when the **Probe** tool is used. The task of altering these values to again represent distance across the width of the cam follower appears to be impossible. Proceed as follows to enhance the Y-axis label.

7. While still on the **Axes** tab, click to highlight **Y** in the **Axes** box located at top left of the **2D Chart Control Properties** window. The **Text:** box changes to show the current Y-axis label, **SY (psi)**.

8. Type a new, more descriptive label of your own choosing for the Y-axis into the **Text:** box. Then click **[OK]** to close the **2D Chart Control Properties** window.

Figure 29 – Graph showing edited title and axis labels to clarify what is displayed on the graph.

An edited version of the graph with a more meaningful title and descriptive axis labels is shown in Fig. 29. **CAUTION: Once the graph is closed, all edits are lost.** Therefore if a graph is to be printed, proceed to step 9 prior to closing the graph.

9. In the **Probe Result** *graph* window, select **File**. Then from the pull-down menu, select either **Save As...** a filename you designate or **Print** the graph immediately.

10. To close the **Probe Result** graph, click ☒. Users should form the habit of always applying *descriptive titles, axis labels,* and *their name* to every graph.

11. Click **[OK]** ✓ to close the **Probe Result** property manager.

Summary

- The effect of *localized* conditions, also known as "end-conditions" or "boundary conditions," which occur at support locations, locations of applied loads, and areas of geometric discontinuity (locales of stress concentration), upon finite element results can be significant. These effects typically are not predicted by classical equations used in manual stress calculations. For this reason care must be exercised when checking finite element results in these regions.

- Excellent agreement typically exists between finite element analysis and manually computed results at locations *sufficiently removed* from localized conditions (examples of St. Venant's principle).

- The importance of selecting the *appropriate stress* within a finite element analysis when comparing results cannot be overstated. For example, the SolidWorks Simulation default plot of von Mises stress does not, and should not, agree when compared with manually calculated values of stress in the Y-direction (σ_y) for the cam follower of this example. Simply stated, *like* stresses must be compared when checking validity of finite element results.

The current example concludes at this point. Most of the software capabilities introduced in this example are fundamental to a successful finite element analysis and will be encountered repeatedly in subsequent examples and end-of-chapter problems. This file either can be saved or deleted. See below for further saving guidance.

To SAVE or Not to SAVE Files, that is the Question?

Whether or not to save your SolidWorks Simulation files depends upon a number of factors. Some general guidelines regarding file retention follow.

- It is highly recommended that all chapter example problems be deleted upon completion. Why? (a) You have already benefitted from the learning experience; (b) these files are not referred to later in the text, and (c) if a chapter problem must be re-worked, you will discover how much more rapidly a solution can be achieved because of your increased software proficiency.

- Do not delete end-of-chapter problem files until all plots, graphs, and tabular data required for an assignment have been printed.

- In the event your work must be interrupted, it is possible to SAVE a file part way through a solution and to continue the solution at a later time (see Option 1 or 2 below).

A brief description of options for closing a file with or without saving it follows. Because a variety of file structures are found in different computer work environments, the guidelines below are quite general. It is suggested that local system guidelines be followed regarding *where* files are saved (i.e., to a personal USB drive, to the hard-drive, or to personal file space allocated on a system network).

To exit SolidWorks Simulation and *save a file and all changes made to that file*, proceed as follows.

OPTION 1 – Close a File and SAVE its Contents Using the Original File Name *(Not recommended for this example)*.

1. From the main menu, choose **File**. Then from the pull-down menu, select **Close.** This action opens the **SolidWorks** window shown in Fig. 30.

2. In this window, select the **Save all** option indicated at the arrow in Fig. 30. This action saves the original SolidWorks file plus all changes made within the Simulation portion of the software.

Figure 30 – Saving a file using a previously assigned file name.

3. The above action saves an up-to-date version of the model under its original file name, which in this example is "**Cam Follower (Part)**."

4. See OPTION 4 for instructions to be used when re-opening this file.

OPTION 2 – Close a File and SAVE it Contents Under a Different File Name *(Not recommended for this example)*.

1. From the main menu, choose **File** and from the pull-down menu, select **Save As...** The **Save As** window opens and the current file name, "**Cam Follower (Part)**," appears in the **File name:** field. Simply replace the existing name and click the **[Save]** button at lower right of the **Save As** window.

2. See OPTION 4 for instructions to be used when re-opening this file.

OPTION 3 - Close a File Without Saving Results *(Recommended)*

It is almost universally recommended that files *not* be saved for the simple expedients of: (a) not having to rummage through the copious files created during a finite element soultion to find a single desired file, and (b) although computer memory is now rather inexpensive, why waste it saving files that will not be accessed again. To close a file without saving results, proceed as follows.

1. From the main menu, choose **File**. Then from the pull-down menu, select **Close.** This action opens the **SolidWorks** window shown in Fig. 30 (repeated).

2. In this window, select the **Don't Save** option indicated at the arrow in Fig. 30 (repeated). This action discards all finite element results, but saves the original SolidWorks model file.

Figure 30 (repeated) – Saving a file using a previously assigned file name.

The only times a file should not be discarded are when: (a) a solution must be interrupted and returned to at a later time; or (b) in an academic environment it is suggested that a solution file be retained until one is certain that all assigned problem parts have satisfactorily been submitted; or (c) in one or two rare instances an end-of-chapter problem may be revisited in a later chapter. In these rare instances, users will be instructed to Save the original solution file . . . just in case an extension is reassigned.

OPTION 4 – Re-opening SolidWorks Simulation Files Saved Using OPTION 1 or OPTION 2

Confusion sometimes results when Simulation files are re-opened within SolidWorks because the Simulation results are not immediatley displayed. Follow steps below to overcome this unexpected file re-opening procedure.

1. In the main menu select **File** followed by **Open...** The **Open** window appears. Alternatively, it might be necessary to browse to a USB, or other file storage device in your system network, to locate and click on the file name to be opened.

2. Select the desired file name and click the **[Open]** button. In the case of the **Cam Follower (Part)**, a reduced size image of the SolidWorks screen is shown in Fig. 31. Note, however, that only the SolidWorks model is displayed; Simulation results are not displayed either on the model or in the Simulation manager tree.

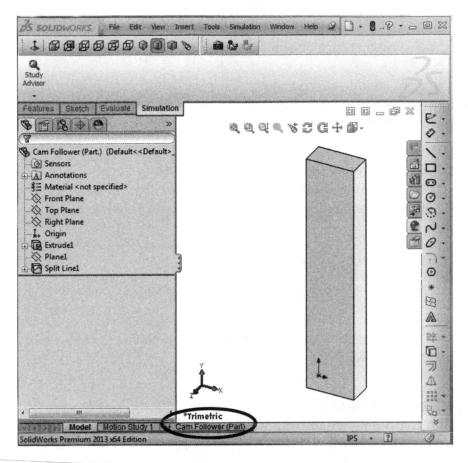

Figure 31 – Screen image after a SolidWorks Simulation model is re-opend.

3. To open the SolidWorks Simulation results, simply click the *tab* labeled **Cam Follower (Part)** located near the lower left corner of the screen; circled in Fig. 31. It contains the Simulation solution up to the point when it was **Saved**.

EXERCISES

End of chapter exercises are intended to provide additional practice using principles introduced in the current chapter. Future chapters also build upon capabilities mastered in preceding chapters. SolidWorks part files for all example and end-of-chapter problems can be downloaded from: **http://www.SDCpublications.com**. To save time, download all files at one time. Use a USB drive or create a file on your PC or network.

Most exercises include multiple parts. In an academic setting, it is likely that parts of problems will be assigned or modified to suit specific course goals.
╫ *Designates problems that introduce new concepts. Solution guidance is provided for these problems.*

Default Expectations (unless specified otherwise)

- Include a *descriptive* Study name and *your name* when naming each Study. This approach uniquely labels each plot with your name.

- Use *discrete* stress contours (colored fringes) and display all plots on an *un-deformed* view of the model.

RECALL: "Plot" – refers to a stress contour plot (i.e., colored fringes depicting stress magnitudes, displacements, etc. within a model).

"Graph" – refers to an X-Y line graph that depicts a relationship between two variables.

EXERCISE 1 – Shear Due to Bending in a Cantilever Beam

The cantilever beam pictured in Fig. E1-1 is rigidly supported (**Fixed**) at its left-end and is subject to forces F_x and F_y applied to its right-end. Either create a beam model using SolidWorks on your own or open problem file **Cantilever 1-1**, which is available at the publisher's web site (see above). Then, perform a finite element analysis of this beam subject to the following guidelines.

- Material: **AISI 1045 Steel cold drawn**

- Mesh: In the **Mesh** property manager, select **Standard mesh**.

- External Load: Assign an axial **Force** F_x = 830 lb that acts **Normal** to the right-end of the beam in the direction shown. Also apply a downward **Force** F_y = 760 lb that acts on the top-right **Edge** of the beam. *Split Lines* are not used.

Figure E1-1 – Basic dimensions (in inches) of a cantilever beam subject to loads F_x and F_y.

- Assign a **Fixed** restraint (not shown in Fig. E1-1) to the left-end of the beam

Determine the following:

a. Create a stress contour plot of shear stress τ_{xy} showing the stress distribution on the front face, which corresponds to the 1.00 x 4.00 inch side of the beam.

b. Use the **Probe** feature to create a graph of τ_{xy} across the left-front edge of the beam. Create this graph by zooming in on the left end of the model and selecting its left edge; use **Flip edge plot** if necessary. Customize the graph title and include your name. Also provide descriptive labels for both the X and Y axes on this graph.

c. Use the **Probe** feature to create a graph of τ_{xy} across the front face of the beam by selecting successive nodes (from top to bottom) at a location approximately 1-in. to the right of the fixed-end of the model. Refer to the **Results** table to ensure the X-value corresponds to approximately 1 in. from the left-end of the model. *Record the actual X- value.* If nodes are not aligned in a straight line across the model, then choose nodes along the best approximation of a straight line at this location. On this plot, manually label the maximum value of τ_{xy} and the X location used to determine shear due to bending. Customize the graph title and include your name. Also provide descriptive labels for both the X and Y axes.

d. Calculate the maximum shear stress due to bending using classical stress equations at the fixed end and at the same distance to the right of the fixed end determined in the **Results** table of step (c). Then, use equation [1] below to compute the percent difference between classical and finite element solutions for maximum shear stress determined half way between top and bottom surfaces of the beam in parts (b) and (c) above.

$$\% \text{ difference} = \frac{(\text{FEA result - classical result})}{\text{FEA result}} * 100 = \underline{\hspace{2cm}} \quad [1]$$

e. Briefly state reason(s) why shear stress determined in parts (b) and (c) differ.

f. Use the **Probe** feature to create a graph of σ_x across the front face of the beam (from top to bottom) at approximately X = 1 in. to the right of the fixed-end. *Record the actual X value.* Select *both* corner and mid-side nodes to yield a more uniform graph. In the **Results** table, observe and record the exact X-coordinate of nodes located on the top and bottom edges of the beam. Assign a descriptive title and axis labels to this graph; include your name in the title.

g. Use classical stress equations to calculate the *appropriate* normal stress on *both* the top and bottom surfaces of the beam at a location approximately 1-in. to the right of the fixed-end. Use the "correct distance" to calculate stress at this location. Hint: the X-coordinate of node location(s), determined in step (f) above, should help to determine the "correct distance."

h. Use equation [1] to compare finite element results for σ_x with manual calculations of the *appropriate* normal stress on both top and bottom surfaces of the beam. Clearly label calculations corresponding to "top" and "bottom" surfaces.

i. If results for the comparison of σ_x at 1 in from the left end differ by more than 3% locate and correct the error(s) in either the finite element model and/or in manual stress calculations.

EXERCISE 2 – Combined Stress in an "L" Shaped Cantilever Beam

The "L"- shaped cantilever bracket, pictured in Fig. E1-2, is rigidly supported (**Fixed**) at its left end. It is made from **2014-T4** Aluminum and is subject to a concentrated tensile load of F = 6.5 kN applied to a *Split Line* located adjacent to the hole on the right end of the beam. Open the file **Cantilever Bracket**. Use the model provided at the publisher's web site **http:\\ www.SDCpublications.com**. Create a finite element model of this beam based on the following information.

- Material: **2014-T4** Aluminum (Use S.I. units)

- Mesh: In the **Mesh** property manager, select **Standard mesh**. Tetrahedral elements are the (system default) high quality elements.

- External Load: Assign a **Force** F = 6.5 kN, directed to the right and applied on the *Split Line* labeled in Fig. E1-2.

- Fixture: Apply a **Fixed** restraint at the left-end of the model.

Figure E1-2 – An "L"-shaped cantilever beam "fixed" at its left-end and subject to a horizontal force F = 6.5 kN applied at its right end. (All lengths in mm).

Determine the following:

   a. Create a stress contour plot of the *most appropriate* normal stress distribution on the front face of the beam. Consider the lower image in Fig. E1-2 to be the "front" view. Include your name and a descriptive title on this plot; see Fig. 19.

   b. On the plot of part (a), state whether or not the material yield strength is exceeded. If it is exceeded, circle the region or regions where this occurs and state the reason for your conclusion.

   c. Use the **Probe** feature to create a graph of the *most appropriate* normal stress across the front face of the beam by selecting successive nodes (from top to bottom) at location A-A. Refer to the **Results** table to ensure the X-value corresponds to approximately 50 mm from the left-end of the model. If nodes are not aligned in a straight line across the model at location A-A, then choose nodes along the best approximation of a straight line. *Record the exact distance value on the graph.* On this graph, manually label the value and location of stress on the top, centroidal, and bottom surfaces of the beam. Customize the graph title and X and Y axis labels, and include your name on this graph. The *most appropriate* normal stresses should correspond to those computed in part (d).

   d. Use classical equations to calculate the combined axial and bending stresses on the top, centroidal (middle), and bottom surfaces of the beam at location A-A. In the event that location A-A does not lie exactly 50 mm from the left end, then use the *exact distance* determined in part (c) above. Clearly label calculations corresponding to each of these surfaces.

   e. Use equation [1], below, to compute the percent difference between classical and finite element solutions for stresses determined on the top, centroidal, and bottom beam surfaces determined in parts (c) and (d) above.

$$\% \text{ difference} = \frac{(\text{FEA result - classical result})}{\text{FEA result}} * 100 = \qquad \qquad [1]$$

   f. If results of part (e) differ by more than 3%, determine the source of the error and, in a brief paragraph, describe the source of the error and how it was eliminated.

⌗ EXERCISE 3 – Stress Distribution in the Yoshida Buckling Model (Special Topic: Soft Spring Restraint)

The part shown in Fig. E1-3 is referred to as the "Yoshida Buckling" model by individuals familiar with experimental stress analysis techniques. It is often used as an experimental model in an academic setting due to the interesting stress distribution that exists within the part. In an experimental course, strain gages and/or photoelastic techniques are used to determine strains, and from them stresses in the part are calculated. This exercise investigates the model using finite element analysis.

Open the file: **Yoshida Buckling Model**. Use the model provided at the publisher's web site **http:** **www.SDCpublications.com**.

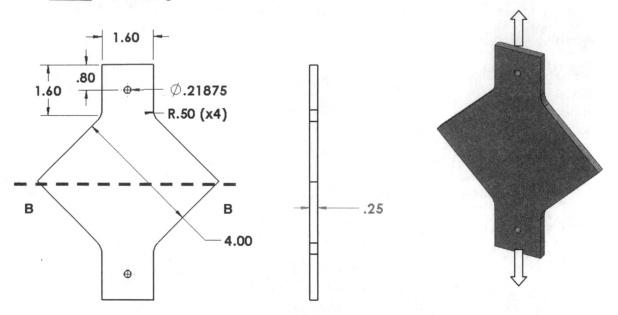

Figure E1-3 – A typical Yoshida Buckling Model. Model dimensions may vary provided proper proportions are retained. Model thickness may also be different than shown. (Units: inches).

Create a finite element model of the above part subject to the following conditions.

- Material: **1060-H18** Aluminum (Use English customary units)

- Mesh: In the **Mesh** property manager, select **Standard mesh**. Tetrahedral elements are the (system default) high quality elements.

- External Load: Assign the applied tensile **Force** of **F = 740** lb directed normal to *Split Lines* provided on top and bottom surfaces of the model.

    HINT #1: When applying **External Loads** within the **Force/Torque** property manager, click ⊙ **Selected direction**. Otherwise it is not possible to apply forces to the *Split Lines*.

    HINT #2: **External Loads** must be applied individually. Why? Try applying both forces within the same property manager and see what happens.

In actuality loads are applied by pins passing through holes at both ends of the model. However, that approach requires a more sophisticated approach than has been introduced thus far. Alternate methods of load application are investigated in future chapters.

- Support the model using **Soft Springs**. The reason for applying soft springs to the model is that finite element models must be restrained against the possibility of "rigid body motion." It is logical to ask . . . "Why might there be any rigid body motion for the current model? The answer to this question is discussed in the following Analysis Insight section.

Analysis Insight

The Yoshida Buckling model is the *only* part file in Chapter #1 that does *not* have a **Fixed** restraint applied somewhere on the part. Recall that **Fixed** restraints, when applied to tetrahedral elements, restrict translations in the X, Y, and Z directions at each node to which they are applied. Thus, equilibrium for externally applied forces in all of those directions is guaranteed due to the **Fixed** restraints. But, that is not the case for the current model where only external forces are applied, but *no* **Fixtures** are used.

It also might logically be argued that the model is in static equilibrium under the action of equal but opposite forces acting on opposing ends of the model. However, the traditional understanding of equilibrium of forces, such as are applied to a free-body diagram, is subject to subtle differences in a finite element analysis. Those differences include possible asymmetry of the mesh, small inaccuracies in the model, and/or mathematical round-off in calculations. These factors can produce extremely slight differences in what we ordinarily assume to be a body in equilibrium. Thus, in a finite element analysis, even the smallest difference from a "zero" force balance results in an unbalanced force acting on the body. And, according to Newton's second law of motion, any unbalanced force acting on a body results in an acceleration in the direction of that unbalanced force. Such motion is not tolerated in a *static* finite element analysis. Therefore, one way to deal with unbalanced forces is to apply *soft springs* to support the model. These springs also stabilize the model against any unbalanced forces. Instructions in the application of soft springs are provided in the Solution Guidance Section.

Solution Guidance

Soft Spring Restraints
Discussion below provides guidance in the assignment of soft springs to the current model. This section also assumes the model is already open and a Study is started. Soft springs can be assigned any time before the Solution is **Run**.

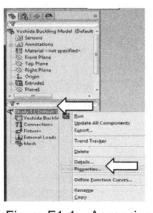

- Right-click the Study name you entered at the top of the Simulation manager (not to be confused with the name at top of the SolidWorks feature manager tree). A pull-down menu appears as shown in Fig. E1-4. From the pull-down menu, select **Properties…** The **Static** window opens as shown in Fig. E1-5.

Figure E1-4 – Accessing the Study pull-down menu.

Solution Guidance (continued)

- Within the **Options** tab, select ☑ **Use soft spring to stabilize model**, circled in Fig. E1-5.

- Also select ⊙ **Direct Sparse** as the equation solver method. This solver must be used in conjunction with the soft spring option. Discussion of solver types available within SolidWorks Simulation is included in a later chapter.

- Click **[OK]** to close the **Static** window.

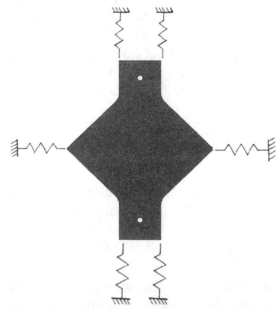

Figure E1-5 - Selecting **Soft Springs** to stabilize the model.

Springs shown in Fig. E1-6 are schematic representations only. Springs *do not appear* on a screen image of the model. However, they are mathematically present between *every* surface node and the ground. Thus, these springs effectively restrain the model in the X, Y, and Z directions.

Figure E1-6 – Schematic representation of **Soft Springs** applied to stabilize a model with insufficient **Fixtures**. In actual fact, soft springs are attached to *all* surface nodes.

Determine the following:

a. Create a plot of von Mises stress throughout the model. On the screen image, zoom in on high stress regions to get an accurate assessment of stress magnitude in the affected region(s). Use the **Probe** tool to estimate the maximum stress at top and bottom ends of the model. Either manually record the maximum stress magnitude on the plot adjacent to where it occurs or position the data "flags" so they are readable on the plot. Also, on an image of the entire model, circle the region(s), if any, where the material yield strength is exceeded.

b. Create a plot of stress in the **Y**-direction on the model. Display the mesh on this model.

c. Use the **Probe** tool to create a graph of stress in the **Y**-direction across the middle of the model. Proceed *from right to left* across the model along imaginary line **B-B** shown in Fig. E1-3. Select only corner nodes in as straight a line as possible across the face of the model. Provide a descriptive graph title (include your name) and descriptive labels for both the X and Y axes.

d. Like part (b), except plot stress in the X- direction. Include the mesh on this image.

e. Use the plot of part (d), but select nodes along a vertical center-line extending between edges of the two holes that are closest to the center of the model.

f. For the plot of part (a), were the maximum stresses at both ends of the model equal? If not, at what end of the model (top or bottom) is stress the greatest? Knowing that, (**Stress**) * (**Area**) = **Force**, and based on your observation regarding differences, if any, between stresses at opposite ends of the model, discuss whether or not the finite element model is in static equilibrium. Does your finding support or refute the idea that soft springs might be needed to stabilize the model?

g. Beneath images of the two graphs created for part (c) and for part (e), discuss general observations regarding the magnitude of σ_y and σ_x within the part. Consider questions such as whether or not the distribution of stress magnitude makes sense and explain "why" or "why not?" Why is this part referred to as a buckling model?

Textbook Problems
It is highly recommended that the above exercises be supplemented by problems from a design of machine elements textbook. A great way to discover errors made in formulating a finite element analysis is to work problems for which the solution is known by independent calculation or experiment. Typical textbook problems, if well defined in advance, make an excellent source of solutions for comparison.

NOTES:

CHAPTER #2
CURVED BEAM ANALYSIS

This example, unlike that of the first chapter, will lead you quickly through those aspects of creating a finite element Study with which you already have experience. However, where new information or procedures are introduced, additional discussion is included. For consistency throughout this text, a common approach is used for the solution of all problems.

Learning Objectives

In addition to software capabilities studied in the previous chapter, upon completion of this example, users should be able to:

- Use SolidWorks Simulation *icons* in addition to menu selections.

- Apply a *split line* to divide a selected face into one or more separate faces.

- Simulate *pin loading* inside a hole (or other loading on a curved surface).

- Use **Design Checks** to determine the *Factor of Safety* or lack thereof.

- Determine *reaction* forces acting on a finite element model.

Problem Statement

A dimensioned model of a curved beam is shown in Fig. 1; English units are used. Assume the beam is subject to a downward vertical force, $F_y = 3800$ lb applied through a cylindrical pin (not shown) in a hole near its upper end. Beam material is 2014 Aluminum alloy. The bottom of the curved beam is considered "fixed." In this context, the *actual* fixed end-condition is analogous to that at the end of a cantilever beam where translations in the X, Y, Z directions and rotations about the X, Y, Z axes are considered to be zero. However, recall from Chapter 1 that **Fixture** types within SolidWorks Simulation also depend on the type of element to which they are applied. Therefore, because solid tetrahedral elements are used to model the curved beam, **Immovable** restraints are used.

Figure 1 – Three dimensional model of a curved beam. (Dimensions in "inches")

Design Insight
Numerous mechanical elements occur in the shape of initially curved beams. Examples include: C-clamps, punch-press frames, crane hooks, and bicycle caliper brakes, to name a few. This example examines the stress at section A-A shown in Fig. 2. The center of section A-A is chosen because its centroidal axis is the furthest distance from the applied force **F** thereby creating reaction force **R** = **F** and the maximum bending moment **M** = **F*L** at that location. Accordingly, classical equations for stress in a curved beam can be used to predict stress at section A-A. In this example, the validity of this assumption is investigated while exploring additional capabilities of SolidWorks Simulation software listed in the Learning Objectives.

Figure 2 – Traditional free-body diagram of the upper portion of a curved beam model showing applied force **F** acting at a hole, and reactions **R** = **F**, and moment **M** acting on cut section **A-A**.

Creating a Static Analysis (Study)

1. Open SolidWorks by making the following selections. (*NOTE:* The symbol ">" is used below to separate successive menu selections).

Start>All Programs>SolidWorks 2013 (or) Click the **SolidWorks 2013** icon on your screen.

2. In the SolidWorks main menu, select **File > Open...** Then browse to the location where SolidWorks Simulation files are stored and select the file named "**Curved Beam**;" then click **[Open]**.

> **Reminder:**
> If you do not see **Simulation** listed in the main menu of the SolidWorks screen, click **Tools** > **Add-Ins...**, then in the **Add-Ins** window check ☑ **SolidWorks Simulation** in both the **Active Add-Ins** and the **Start Up** columns, then click **[OK]**. This action permanently adds **Simulation** to the main menu every time a file is opened.

Because one goal of this chapter is to introduce and to use Simulation icons during the solution process, set-up of the Simulation toolbar is described below. If you previously set up the Simulation toolbar as outlined in the Introduction to this text, large Simulation icons with captions should appear (grayed out) near the top of your screen. In that case, click on the **Simulation** *tab* and skip to step 5.

Setting up the Simulation Toolbar

If the **Simulation** *tab*, shown in Fig. 3, does not appear at the top left of your screen, add it to the other tabs as follows. Otherwise, skip to step 2.

Figure 3 – Useful *tabs* located beneath the main menu.

1. Right-click on any of the *tab names* (**Features**, **Sketch**, **Evaluate**, etc.) and from the pull-down menu, click to place a check "✓" adjacent to ☑ **Simulation**. This action adds the **Simulation** tab beneath the main menu.

2. Click the **Simulation** tab to display its contents.

Initially the **Simulation** tab and its associated toolbar contain only the **Study** 🔍 icon with remaining icons grayed out as shown boxed in Fig. 4.

Figure 4 –Common icons associated with a **Simulation** finite element analysis.

Presuming the **Simulation** icons to be unfamiliar to new users, the display mode illustrated in Fig. 5, which includes descriptive captions, is used throughout the remainder of this chapter. To display icons with captions, proceed as follows.

3. Right-click anywhere on any toolbar at the top of the screen to open the **Command Manager** menu shown in a *partial* view in Fig. 5.

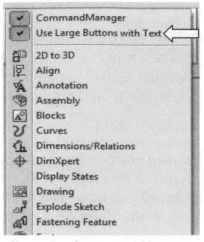

Figure 5 – **Command Manager** pull-down menu.

4. Just below **Command Manager** at top of this menu, click to select ☑ **Use Large Buttons with Text**. This action adds a brief description beneath each icon as illustrated in Fig. 6. NOTE: Fig. 6 will not appear with *active* icons until a new study is initiated in step 8 below.

Figure 6 – View of the **Simulation** toolbar with descriptive captions applied beneath each icon.

5. In the **Simulation** tab begin a new study by selecting the ▼ symbol located on the **Study Advisor** icon. From the pull-down menu select 🔍 **New Study**. The **Study** property manager opens (not shown).

6. In the **Name** dialogue box, replace **Study 1** by typing **Curved Beam Analysis - YOUR NAME**. Including your name along with the Study name ensures that it is displayed on each plot. This helps to identify plotted results sent to public access printers.

7. In the **Type** dialogue box verify that 🔬 **Static** is selected as the analysis type.

8. Click **[OK]** ✓ (green check mark) to close the **Study** property manager.

Notice that an outline of the new Study is now listed beneath the Simulation manager tree.

Now that an icon-based work environment is established, our Study of stress in the curved beam continues below. As in the previous example, the sequence of steps outlined in the Simulation manager, at the left of your screen, is followed from top to bottom as the current Study is developed.

Assign Material Properties to the Model

Part *material* is defined as outlined below.

1. On the **Simulation** *tab*, click to select the **Apply Material** icon. The **Material** window opens as shown in Fig. 7.

2. In the left column, select **SolidWorks Materials** (if not already selected). Because the left column typically defaults to **Alloy Steel** or displays the last material selected, click the minus "-" sign to close the **Steel** folder if necessary.

Figure 7 – Material properties are selected and/or defined in the **Material** window.

3. Click the plus sign next to the **+ Aluminum Alloys** and scroll down to select **2014 Alloy**. The properties of 2014 Aluminum alloy are displayed in the right half of the window.

4. In the right-half of this window, select the **Properties** tab (if not already selected), and change **Units:** to **English (IPS)** if needed.

In the table, note the material **Yield Strength** is a relatively low 13997.56 psi (essentially 14000 psi). Material with a low yield strength is intentionally chosen to facilitate discussion of *Factor of Safety* later in this example. Examine other values in the table to become familiar with data listed for each material.

Within the table, also notice that some material properties are indicated by red text, others by blue, and some by black. Red text indicates material properties that *must* be specified because a stress analysis is being performed. Conversely, material properties highlighted in blue text are optional, and those in black text primarily refer to thermal or vibration damping properties and, as such, are not needed for this stress analysis.

5. Click **[Apply]** followed by **[Close]** to close the **Material** window. A check mark "✓" appears on the **Curved Beam** folder to indicate a material has been selected. Also, the material type **(-2014 Alloy-)** is listed adjacent to the model name.

Aside:

If at any point you wish to *change the material specification* of a part, such as during a redesign, simply right-click the name of the particular part whose material properties are to be changed and from the pull-down menu select **Apply/Edit Material…** The **Material** window opens and an alternative material can be selected.

However, be aware that when a different material is specified *after* running a solution, it is necessary to run the solution again using the revised material properties.

Applying Fixtures

For a static analysis, adequate restraints must be applied to stabilize the model. In this example, the bottom surface of the model is considered "fixed."

1. In the **Simulation** tab, click ▼ beneath the **Fixtures Advisor** icon, boxed in Fig. 8 at right, and from the pull-down menu select **Fixed Geometry**. The **Fixture** manager opens as shown in Fig. 9.

2. Within the **Standard (Fixed Geometry)** dialogue box, select **Fixed Geometry** (if not already selected). 4

Figure 8 – Selecting the **Fixture** icon.

3. The **Faces, Edges, Vertices for Fixture** field is highlighted (light blue) to indicate it is active and waiting for the user to select part of the model to be restrained. Rotate, and/or zoom to view the bottom of the model. Next, move the cursor over the model and when the bottom surface is indicated, click to select it. The surface is highlighted and fixture symbols appear as shown in Fig. 10. Also, **Face<1>** appears in the **Faces, Edges, Vertices for Fixture** field.

If an incorrect entity (such as a vertex, edge, or the wrong surface) is selected, right-click the incorrect item in the highlighted field and from the pop-up menu select **Delete**; then repeat step 3.

4. If restraint symbols do not appear, or if it is desired to alter their size or color, click the down arrow ⬇ to open the **Symbol Settings** dialogue box, at bottom of the **Fixture** property manager, and check the ☑ **Show preview** box.

5. Both color and size of the restraint symbols (vectors in the X, Y, Z directions) can be changed by altering values in the **Symbol Settings** dialogue box of Fig. 9. Experiment by clicking the up ▲ or down ▼ arrows to change size of restraint symbols. A box of this type, where values can be changed either by typing a new value or by clicking the ▲ ▼ arrows, is called a "spin box." Restraint symbols shown in Fig. 10 were arbitrarily increased in size to 200%.

Figure 9 – **Fixture** property manager.

6. Click **[OK]** ✓ (green check mark) at top of the **Fixture** property manager to accept this restraint. An icon named 🔧 Fixed-1 appears beneath the **Fixtures** folder in the Simulation manager tree.

Figure 10 – **Fixtures** applied to bottom of the curved beam model.

Aside:
Restraint symbols shown in Fig. 10 appear as simple arrows with a small disk added to its tail. These symbols indicate **Fixed** restraints when applied to shell or beam elements. **Fixed** restraints set both *translational* and *rotational* degrees of freedom to zero (i.e., both X, Y, Z displacements and rotations (moments) about the X, Y, Z axes are zero). However, when applied to either solid models or truss elements, only *displacements* in the X, Y, and Z directions are restrained (i.e., prevented). This latter type of restraint is referred to as **Immovable**. The software applies appropriate fixtures based on element type. Watch for this subtle difference in future examples.

Applying External Load(s)

Next apply the downward force, $F_y = 3800$ lb, at the hole located near the top left-hand side of the model shown in Figs. 1 and 2. This force is assumed to be applied by a pin (not shown) that acts through the hole.

Analysis Insight:
Because the goal of this analysis is to focus on curved beam stresses at Section A-A, and because Section A-A is well removed from the point of load application, modeling of the applied force can be handled in a number of different ways. For example, the downward force could be applied to the vertical *surface* located on the upper left side of the model, Fig. (a). Alternatively, the force could be applied to the upper or lower *edge* of the model at the extreme left side, Fig. (b). These loading situations would require a slight reduction of the magnitude of force **F** to account for its additional distance from the left-side of the model to section A-A (i.e., the moment about section A-A must remain the same).

Figure (a) – Force applied to left surface.   Figure (b) – Force applied to lower edge.

The above loads are simple to apply. However, the assumption of pin loading allows us to investigate use of a *Split Line* to isolate a *portion* of the bottom surface of the hole where contact with a pin is assumed to occur. This surface is where a pin force would be transferred to the curved beam model. The actual contact area depends on a number of factors, which include: (a) geometries of the contacting parts (i.e., relative diameters of the pin and hole), (b) material properties (i.e., hard versus soft contact surfaces of either the pin or the beam), and (c) magnitude of the force that presses the two surfaces together. This example arbitrarily assumes a reasonable contact area so that use of a *Split Line* can be demonstrated. If, on the other hand, contact stresses in the vicinity of the hole were of paramount importance, then determination of the true contact area requires inclusion of the actual pin and use of *Contact/Gap* analysis. This type of analysis is investigated in Chapter #6.

Inserting Split Lines

The first task to simulate downward pin loading on the hole bottom is to isolate a small area at the bottom of the hole. This can be accomplished by using a *Split Line*. The method described below outlines the use of a reference plane to insert a *Split Line*.

1. In the drawing toolbar, at top center of the graphics area, reorient the model by clicking the **Trimetric** or **Isometric** view icon.

2. From the main menu, select **Insert**. Then, from succeeding pull-down menus make the following selections: **Reference Geometry** ▶ followed by **Plane...** In Fig. 11 the **Plane** property manager opens to the left of the graphics area. However, a SolidWorks "flyout" menu appears at the top left of the graphics area to provide access to SolidWorks options; see Fig. 11.

Figure 11 – The **Plane** property manager and SolidWorks flyout menu.

3. Within the **Plane** property manager, under **First Reference**, the field is highlighted (light blue) to indicate it is active and awaiting selection of a plane from which a *new* plane can be referenced.

Figure 12 (a) - The **Plane** property manager and selections to create a reference plane passing through the bottom of the hole.

Fig. 12 (b) – Flyout menu (enlarged view).

4. Begin by clicking the "+" sign to open the SolidWorks flyout menu circled in Figs. 12(a) and (b). Within the flyout menu select the **Top Plane**, see arrows. The **Plane** property manager changes appearance as shown in Fig. 12(a) and **Top Plane** appears in the **First Reference** dialogue box. For those using the **Curved Beam** part file from the textbook web site, the top plane passes through the part origin, which is located on the bottom of the model[1] in Fig. 12 (a).

5. Return to the **First Reference** dialogue box and in the **Offset Distance** spin-box and type **14.75**. This is the distance *from* the **Top Plane** to a **Reference Plane** located so that it intersects the bottom portion of the hole in Fig. 12 (a).

Aside:

The 14.75-in. dimension is determined from the following calculation. Refer to Fig. 1 to determine the source of values used in the equation below.

> 10 in (height of straight vertical sides) + 3 in (radius of concave surface) + 1.75 in (distance from the horizontal edge beneath the hole and extending an arbitrary distance into the bottom portion of the hole) = 14.75in.

It is emphasized that the area intersected on the bottom of the hole is chosen *arbitrarily* in this example!

---

[1] Users who created a curved beam model from scratch can also follow these instructions. The *only* difference would be specification of the proper *distance* from the **Top Plane** (used as a reference in *your* model) to the bottom of the hole.

6. Click **[OK]** ✓ to close the **Plane** property manager.

The reference plane labeled **Plane1**, depending on model size, created in the preceding steps appears highlighted on your screen. In the following steps this plane is used to create *Split Lines* near the bottom of the hole. These *Split Lines* enable us to define a small "patch" of area on the bottom of the hole where the downward load will be applied.

7. From the **Main Menu**, select **Insert**. Then, from the pull-down menus choose: **Curve ▶** followed by **Split Line...** The **Split Line** property manager opens as shown in Fig. 13.

8. Beneath **Type of Split**, select ⊙ **Intersection**. This choice designates the means by which *Split Lines* are defined for this example (i.e., *Split Lines* will be located where the reference plane *intersects* the hole).

9. In the **Selections** dialogue box, **Plane1** should already appear in the **Splitting Bodies/Faces/ Planes** field. If **Plane1** does not appear in this field, click to activate the field (light blue), then move the cursor onto the graphics screen and select the upper plane when it is highlighted. **Plane1** now appears in the top field.

Figure 13 – **Split Line** property manager showing selections.

10. Next, click inside the **Faces/Bodies to Split** field. This field may already be active (light blue). Then move the cursor over the model and select anywhere on the *inside surface* of the hole. It may be necessary to zoom in on the model to select this surface. Once selected, **Face<1>** appears in the active field. Figure 14 shows a partial image of the model with *Split Lines* appearing where **Plane1** intersects the bottom portion of the hole.

Figure 14 – Close-up view of hole showing *Split Lines* where **Plane1** intersects near the bottom of hole.

Remain zoomed-in on the model to facilitate applying a force to the inside of the hole.

11. In the **Surface Split Options** dialogue box, select ⊙ **Natural**. A **Natural** split follows the contour of the selected surface.

12. Click **[OK]** ✓ to close the **Split Line** property manager.

13. *If* an information "flag" appears adjacent to the *Split Lines*, click ⊠ to close it.

Applying Force to an Area Bounded by Split Lines

Now that a restricted area on the bottom of the hole has been identified, the next step is to apply a downward force, $F_y = 3800$ lb, on this area. Proceed as follows.

1. On the Simulation tab, click ▼ beneath the **External Loads...** 🔲 icon and from the pop-up menu select the 🔲 **Force** icon. A partial view of the **Force/Torque** property manager appears in Fig. 15.

2. Within the **Force/Torque** dialogue box, click the 🔲 **Force** icon (if not already selected). Also, click ⊙ **Selected direction**. Then click to activate (light blue) the upper field titled **Faces, Edges, Vertices, Reference Points for Force**.

3. Move the cursor over the model and when the *bottom inside surface* of the hole is outlined, click to select it. **Face<1>** appears in the active field of the **Force/Torque** dialogue box.

4. Next, click to activate the second field from the top of the **Force/Torque** dialogue box. Passing the cursor over this field identifies it as the **Face, Edge, Plane for Direction** field. This field is used to specify the direction of the force applied to the bottom of the hole.

Because a downward, vertical force is to be applied, select a *vertical* edge . . . *any vertical edge* . . . on the model aligned with the Y-direction. After selecting a vertical edge, **Edge<1>** appears in the active field and force vectors appear on the model as seen in Fig. 16.

5. In the **Units** dialogue box, set **Units** 🔲 to **English (IPS)** (if not already selected).

Figure 15 – Specifying a force and its direction on the hole bottom.

6. In the **Force** dialogue box, type **3800**. As noted in an earlier example, it may be necessary to check ☑ **Reverse Direction** if the force is not directed downward.

7. Click **[OK]** ✓ to accept this force definition and close the **Force/Torque** property manager. An icon named **Force-1 (:Per item: 3800 lbf:)** appears beneath the **External Loads** folder in the Simulation manager.

Figure 16 – Downward force applied between *Split Lines* on bottom of hole. A wireframe view of the model is shown.

The model is now complete as far as material, fixtures, and external load definitions are concerned. The next step is to Mesh the model as described below.

Meshing the Model

1. Within the Simulation tab, select ▼ beneath the **Run** ⌄ icon. From the pull-down menu, select the 🔲 **Create Mesh** icon. The **Mesh** property manager opens as shown in Figs 17 (a) and (b).

2. Check ✓ to open the ☑ **Mesh Parameters** dialogue box and verify that a ⊙ **Standard mesh** is selected. Also set the **Unit** field to **in** (if not already selected). Accept the remaining default settings (i.e., mesh **Global Size** and **Tolerance**) shown in this dialogue box.

3. Click the down arrow ⌄ to open the **Advanced** dialogue box, Fig. 17 (b). Verify that **Jacobian points** is set at **4 points** (this setting indicates high quality tetrahedral elements are used). These default settings produce a good quality mesh. However, verify that the settings are as listed and only change them if they differ.

Figure 17 (a) – **Mesh** property manager showing system default **Mesh** settings applied to the current model.

2-13

4. Finally, click **[OK]** ✓ to accept the default mesh settings and close the **Mesh** property manager.

Meshing starts automatically and a **Mesh Progress** window appears briefly. After meshing is complete, SolidWorks Simulation displays the meshed model shown in Fig. 18. Also, a check mark "✓" appears on the **Mesh** icon to indicate meshing is complete.

Figure 17 (b) – Views of the **Advanced** and **Options** portions of the **Mesh** property manager.

5. Since it is no longer needed, hide the reference plane by right-clicking it and, from the pop-up menu, select the 👋 **Hide** icon.

OPTIONAL:

6. Display mesh information by right-clicking the **Mesh** folder (not the Create Mesh icon) and select **Details...**

The **Mesh Details** window displays a variety of mesh information. Scroll down the list of information and note the number of nodes and elements for this model is 12578 nodes and 7229 elements (numbers may vary slightly due to the automated mesh generation procedure).

Rotate the model as illustrated in Fig. 18 (a Trimetric view) and notice that the mesh is two elements *thick*. Two elements across the model's thinnest dimension are considered the minimum number for which *Solid Elements* should be used. Thus, two elements are considered an unofficial dividing line between when *Shell* or *Solid Elements* should be used. Therefore, either element type could be used for this model. But, keep in mind that shell elements are typically reserved for thin parts.

6. Click ⊠ to close the **Mesh Details** window.

Figure 18 – Curved beam with mesh and boundary conditions illustrated.

> **Reminder**
>
> Recall that it is permissible to define material properties, fixtures, external loads, and create the mesh in any order. However, all these necessary steps must be completed before running a solution.

Solution

After the model has been completely defined, the solution process is initiated. During a solution the numerous equations defining a Study are solved and results of the analysis are automatically saved for review.

1. On the **Simulation** tab, click the **Run** icon to initiate the solution process.

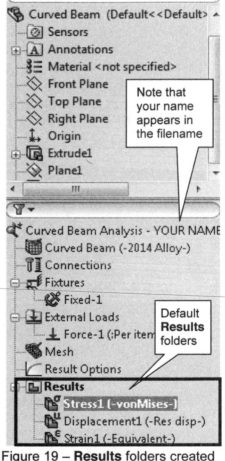

After a successful solution, a **Results** folder appears below the Simulation manager. This folder should include three default plots saved at the conclusion of each Study. These folders are named as illustrated in Fig. 19. If these folders do *not* appear, follow steps (a) through (f) outlined on page 1-14 of Chapter #1.

If **Units** for the **Stress1** and **Displacement** plots are not **psi** and **in** respectively, then change them as outlined in steps 2 through 5. Otherwise, skip to the next section.

2. If the von Mises stress plot is not shown, double-click **Stress1 (-von Mises-)** to display the plot.

3. Next, right-click **Stress1 (-vonMises-)** and from the pull-down menu select **Edit Definition...** In the **Display** dialogue box, verify **Units** are set to **psi**. If not, use the pull-down menu to change **Units** from **N/m^2** to **psi**.

Figure 19 – **Results** folders created during the Solution process.

4. Click **[OK]** ✓ to close the **Stress Plot** property manager.

5. Repeat steps (2) through (4), however, in step (2), double-click **Displacement1 (-Res disp-)** and in step (3) in the **Display** dialogue box alter the Units field from **mm** to **in**. NOTE: **Res disp** is short for "resultant displacement."

Examination of Results

Analysis of von Mises Stresses Within the Model

Outcomes of the current analysis can be viewed by accessing plots stored in the **Results** folders listed in the previous section. This step is where validity of results is verified by cross-checking Finite Element Analysis (FEA) results against results obtained using classical stress equations or by experiment. *Checking results is a necessary step in good engineering practice!*

1. In the Simulation manager tree, double-click the **Stress1 (-vonMises-)** folder (or) right-click it and from the pull-down menu, select **Show**. A plot of the vonMises stress distribution throughout the model is displayed.

Figure 20 reveals an image *similar* to what currently appears on the screen. The following steps convert your current screen image to that shown in Fig. 20.

Figure 20 – Front view of the curved beam model showing von Mises stress *after* making changes outlined below. Note arrows indicating Yield Strength on the stress scale at right.

NOTE: *Stress contour plots are printed in black, white, and grey tones. Therefore, light and dark color areas on your screen may appear different from images shown throughout this text.*

2. Right-click **Stress1 (-vonMises-)** and from the pull-down menu select **Chart Options...** A portion of the **Chart Options** property manager is shown in Fig. 21.

3. Within the **Display Options** dialogue box, click to place check marks to activate ☑ **Show min annotation** and ☑ **Show max annotation**.

4. Click **[OK]** ✓ to close the **Chart Options** property manager. The minimum and maximum vonMises stress locations and magnitudes are now labeled on the model.

Figure 21 – Upper portion of **Chart Options** property manager showing current selections.

5. Right-click **Stress1 (-vonMises-)** and from the pull-down menu select **Settings...**. A partial view of the **Settings** property manager opens as illustrated in Fig. 22.

6. From the **Fringe options** menu, select **Discrete** as the fringe type to be displayed.

7. Next, in the **Boundary options** pull-down menu, select **Model** to superimpose an outline of the model on the image.

8. Click **[OK]** ✓ to close the **Settings** property manager.

Figure 22 – Selections in the **Settings** property manager.

9. In the **Simulation** tab, repeatedly click the **Deformed Result** icon to toggle between a deformed image of the model (default state) and an un-deformed image. See images in Fig. 23. When done, leave the model in the un-deformed state and rotate it to the front view.

Figure 23 – Deformed and un-deformed model images.

The following observations can be made about the figure currently on your screen.

OBSERVATIONS:

- Areas of low stress (dark blue) occur at the top-left side of the model. Also observe the dark blue region through the vertical center of the model. This region overlaps the neutral axis. The minimum von Mises stress is approximately 18.1 psi. Regions of high stress are indicated in red. The maximum stress indicated is 24867.6 psi, which occurs along the concave surface. (numbers may vary slightly)

- Material *Yield* Strength =13997.6 ≈ 14000 psi is also listed beneath the color-coded **von Mises** stress legend. A red arrow adjacent to the color chart indicates where the Yield Strength lies relative to all stresses within the model. In this instance, it is clear that some stresses in the model *exceed* the material yield strength. *Yield Strength* and *Safety Factor* are investigated later in this chapter.

Modern software makes conducting a finite element analysis and obtaining results deceptively easy. As noted earlier, however, it is the validity of results and understanding how to interpret and evaluate them properly that is of primary importance. For these reasons, we pause to consider two questions that should be intriguing or, perhaps, even bothering you, the reader.

First, why are all stress values positive in Fig. 20? ("+" stress values typically indicate tension). However, compressive stresses are known to exist along the concave surface for the given loading. Second, why does the solution show stresses above the material yield strength when stresses that exceed the yield strength indicate yielding or failure? These, and many others, are the types of questions that should be raised continually by users of finite element software. Attempts to address these questions are included below.

To answer these questions, we briefly digress to investigate the definition of von Mises stress as a means to determine a *Safety Factor* predicted by the software.

Von Mises Stress -
The example of Chapter 1 avoided the issue about what the von Mises stress is or what it represents. That example further assumed that some readers might not be familiar with von Mises stress. For the sake of completeness and because von Mises stress typically is not introduced until later in a design of machine elements course, its basic definition is included below. Although this SolidWorks Simulation user guide is not intended to develop the complete theory related to von Mises stress, the usefulness of this stress might be summed up by the following statement-

> The equation for von Mises stress "allows the most complicated stress situation to be represented by a single quantity."[2] In other words, for the most complex state of stress that one can imagine (e.g., a three-dimensional stress element subject to a

---

[2] Budynas, R.G., Nisbett, J. K., <u>Shigley's Mechanical Engineering Design</u>, 9th Ed., McGraw-Hill, 2010, p.224.

combination of shear and normal stresses acting on every face (as illustrated below), these stresses can be reduced to a single number. That number is named the von Mises stress. This number represents a stress magnitude, "which can be compared against the yield strength of the material"[3] to determine whether or not failure by yielding is predicted. As such, the von Mises stress is associated with one of the theories of failure for *ductile* materials; theories of failure are briefly discussed below. The von Mises stress is always a *positive, scalar* number.

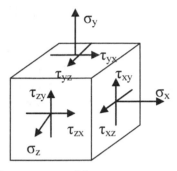

The above statement answers the question about the positive nature of von Mises stress shown in Fig. 20 and on your screen. It also should provide some insight into why von Mises stress, which is *a single number*, can be used to determine whether or not a part is likely to fail by comparing it to the part yield strength *(yield strength is also listed as a single value)*. The method of comparison used is the *Safety Factor,* which is explored later in this chapter.

Although the above definition indicates that von Mises stress is always a positive number, that superficial answer might continue to bother readers who intuitively recognize that compressive stresses result along the concave surface of the curved beam.

More fundamentally the issue in question gets to the heart of any analysis. That question is, "*What stress should be examined* when comparing finite element results with stress calculations based on the use of classical equations?" The answer, of course, is that one must examine the *appropriate stresses* that correspond to the goals of an analysis. For example, in Chapter 1 it was decided that normal stress in the Y-direction (σ_y) was the primary stress component that would provide favorable comparisons with stress calculated using classic equations. The **Verification of Results** section below reveals the *appropriate stress* for the current example. Before continuing, answer the question: "What is the appropriate stress?" Then, check your answer below.

Verification of Results

In keeping with the philosophy that it is *always* necessary to verify the validity of Finite Element Analysis (FEA) results, a quick comparison of FEA results with those calculated using classical stress equations for a curved beam is included below.

Results Predicted by Classical Stress Equations

Although not all users may be familiar with the equations for stress in a curved beam, the analysis below should provide sufficient detail to enable reasonable understanding of this state of stress. The first observation is a somewhat unique characteristic of curved beams, namely, for a symmetrical cross-section its neutral axis lies closer to the center of curvature than does its centroidal axis. These axes can be observed in Fig. 24. By definition the centroidal axis, identified as r_c, is located half-way between the inside and outside radii of curvature. However, the neutral axis, identified by r_n, lies closer to the

---

[3] Ibid

inside (concave) surface. Based on this observation, a free body diagram of the upper portion of the curved beam is shown in Fig. 24. Included on this figure are important dimensions used in the following calculations. Dimensions shown are defined below.

w = width of beam cross-section = 4.00 in (see Fig. 1)
d = depth (thickness) of beam cross-section = 0.75 in (see Fig. 1)
A = cross-sectional area of beam = w*d = (0.75 in)(4.00 in) = 3.00 in^2
r_i = radius to inside (concave surface) = 3.00 in
r_o = radius to outside (convex surface) = r_i + w = 3.00 + 4.00 in = 7.00 in
r_c = radius to centroid of beam = r_i + w/2 = 3.00 + 2.00 = 5.00 in
r_n = radius to the neutral axis = w/ln(r_o/r_i) = 4.00/ln(7.00/3.00) = 4.72 in. [determined
       by equation for a curved beam having a rectangular cross-section]
c_i = distance from the neutral axis to the inside surface = $r_n - r_i$ = 4.72 – 3.00 = 1.72 in
c_o = distance from the neutral axis to the outside surface = $r_o - r_n$ = 7.00 – 4.72 = 2.28 in
e = distance between the centroidal axis and neutral axis = $r_c - r_n$ = 5.00- 4.72 = 0.28 in

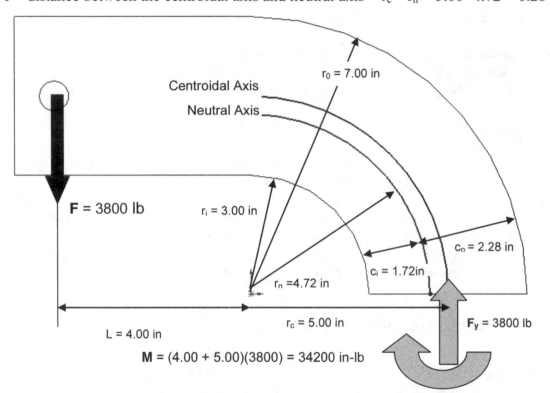

Figure 24 – Geometry associated with calculation of stress in a curved beam.

The reaction force F_y and moment **M** acting on the cut section are necessary to maintain equilibrium of the upper portion of the curved beam. Equations used to compute the combined bending and axial stresses that result from these reactions are included below. Each equation is of the general form,

Curved beam stress = ± bending stress ± axial stress

Where the "±" sign for bending stress depends on what side of the model is being investigated. Bending stress, caused by moment **M**, is compressive on the concave surface of the curved beam. Hence a minus "-" sign is assigned to the bending stress term in equation [1]. However, on the convex side of the beam bending stress causes tension on the beam surface thereby accounting for a "+" sign associated with the first term in equation [2]. Reaction force $\mathbf{F_y}$ acts to produce a compressive stress on the cut section. Therefore, a minus "-" sign is used with the axial stress component in both equations [1] and [2] below. In what direction do both of these stresses act?

Stress at the inside (concave) surface:

$$\sigma_i = \frac{Mc_i}{Aer_i} - \frac{F_y}{A} = \frac{-(34200 \text{ in-lb})(1.72 \text{ in})}{(3.00 \text{ in}^2)(0.28 \text{ in})(3.00 \text{ in})} - \frac{3800 \text{ lb}}{3.00 \text{ in}^2} = -24610 \text{ psi} \qquad [1]$$

Stress at the outside (convex) surface:

$$\sigma_0 = \frac{Mc_o}{Aer_o} - \frac{F_y}{A} = \frac{(34200 \text{ in-lb})(2.28 \text{ in})}{(3.00 \text{ in}^2)(0.28 \text{ in})(7.00 \text{ in})} - \frac{3800 \text{ lb}}{3.00 \text{ in}^2} = 11990 \text{ psi} \qquad [2]$$

Comparison with Finite Element Results

In addition to serving as a quick check of results, this section reviews use of the **Probe** tool. Both bending and axial stresses act normal to the cut surface in Fig. 24. Therefore, it is logical that the finite element analysis stress acting in the Y-direction (σ_y) should be compared with values computed using equations [1] and [2] above. You are encouraged to produce a plot of stress σ_y on your own. However, abbreviated steps are outlined below if guidance is desired.

1. In the **Simulation** tab, click ▼ on the **Results Advisor** icon and from the pull-down menu, select **New Plot**. Then from the next pull-down menu select the ![Stress icon] **Stress** icon. The **Stress Plot** property manager opens.

2. In the **Display** dialogue box, select **SY: Y Normal Stress** from the pull-down menu. Also in the **Display** dialogue box, set the **Units** field to display **psi**.

3. Click to un-check ☐ **Deformed Shape**.

4. Click **[OK]** ✓ to close the **Stress Plot** property manager. A new plot named **Stress2 (-Y normal-)** now appears beneath the **Results** folder and a plot of stress σ_y is displayed as shown in Fig. 25. If the plot does not appear, right-click **Stress2 (-Y normal-)** and select **Show** from the pull-down menu.

5. Right-click **Stress2 (-Y normal-)** and from the pull-down menu select **Settings...** The **Settings** property manager opens.

6. Within the **Settings** property manager, set the **Fringe Options** to **Discrete**.

A plot of normal stress σ_y in the Y-direction should now appear as shown in Fig. 25. The following observations can be made about Fig. 25.

SY (psi)

19,072.6
15,464.9
11,857.2
8,249.5
4,641.8
1,034.1
-2,573.6
-6,181.3
-9,789.0
-13,396.7
-17,004.4
-20,612.1
-24,219.8

Sign change from "+" to "-"

Region of high compressive stress

Region of high tensile stress

Figure 25 – Plot of **SY: Y Normal Stress** (σ_y) on the curved beam model.

OBSERVATIONS:

- Tensile (i.e., positive "+") stress is shown in lime green, yellow, orange, and red. This stress occurs primarily along the right vertical side and convex region of the model. Because this region is subject to tensile stress, positive "+" stress magnitudes are expected.

- Compressive (i.e., negative "-") stress is shown by some green, light blue, and dark blue regions are located along the left vertical and concave regions of the model. Once again compressive stress should correspond with the user's intuitive sense of stress in that region.

- **Max** and **Min** stress can be labeled on the plot in the **Chart Options** property manager.; add these labels on your own.

- Low stress regions, corresponding to the neutral axis, or neutral plane, which runs near the vertical center of the model. Notice the sign change from "+" to "-" in the light green color coded region of the stress chart adjacent to the model.

- Note that **Yield Strength** is *only* labeled on the vonMises stress plot. It does not appear on the current plot.

The model is next prepared to examine stresses at section A_i-A_o shown in Fig. 26.

7. Within the **Settings** property manager, set the **Boundary Options** to **Mesh**. A mesh is displayed on the model.

8. Click **[OK]** ✓ to close the **Settings** property manager.

9. Zoom in on the model to where the curved beam section is tangent to the straight, vertical section, shown as A_i and A_o in Fig. 26, where subscripts "**i**" and "**o**" refer to the inside and outside surfaces of the model respectively.

Figure 26 – Use the **Probe** tool to determine stress magnitudes at locations on the concave and convex sides of the curved beam model.

10. On the **Simulation** tab click the [Plot Tools ▾] icon and from the pull-down menu, select the [Probe] **Probe** tool icon. The **Probe Result** property manager opens as shown on the left side of Fig. 26.

11. In the **Options** dialogue box, select ⊙ **At location** (if not already selected).

12. Move the cursor over the straight vertical edges on the left and right sides of the model. Each edge is highlighted as the cursor passes over it. Click to select two nodes, indicated by a small circle, (one on the left and one on the right) located at the *top* end of each line. These nodes are located at the *intersection* between the straight vertical section and the beginning of the curved beam section. Selected nodes correspond to A_i and A_o in Fig. 26. If an incorrect node is selected, simply click ⊙ **At location** in the **Options** dialogue box to clear the current selection and repeat the procedure. *Do not close the **Probe Result** property manager at this time.*

The above action records the following data in the **Results** dialogue box: **Node** number, **Value (psi)** of the plotted stress (σ_y), and the **X, Y, Z** coordinates of the selected node. Also, a small information "flag" appears adjacent to each node on the model and repeats data listed in the **Results** table. *It may be necessary to click-and-drag column headings to view values in the **Results** table.*

2-23

Table I contains a comparison of results found by using classical equations and the finite element analysis results at these locations. Rounded values are used.

Table I – Comparison of stress (σ_y) from classical and finite element methods at Section A-A.

Location	Manual Calculation (psi)	Probe Tool Results (psi)	Percent Difference (%)
Point A_i	-24610	-21619	13.8%
Point A_o	11990	14180	15.4%

Examine all values and the **Percent Difference (%)** column. Although, differences of this magnitude occasionally do occur, as an engineer you should be disappointed and, in fact, quite concerned at the significant difference between these results given the validity of the curved beam equations. However, when results differ by this magnitude it is always appropriate to *investigate further* to determine the cause for the disparity and not simply "write off" the differences as due to the fact that two alternative approaches are used. Can you provide a valid reason *why* such large differences exist?

Further thought should reveal that St. Venant's principle is once again affecting the results. In this instance, a traditional engineering approach would dictate using classical equations for a straight beam in the straight vertical segment of the model below Section A-A, see Fig. 1 (repeated), and curved beam equations in the portion of the model above Section A-A. Therefore, common sense suggests that there is a *transition region* between the straight and curved segments where neither set of classical equations is entirely adequate. In fact, due to the finite size of elements in this region, it is logical to presume that the finite element analysis provides a more accurate solution than do classical equations in the transition region.

Figure 1 (Repeated) – Basic geometry of the curved beam model.

Given the above observations, we next proceed to sample stress magnitudes at Section B_i-B_o in Fig. 26. This new section is located slightly above the transition region. Proceed as follows.

13. Move the cursor over the curved edges of the model. Then, on the concave side click to select the *first* node *above* the previously selected node.

14. Next, on the convex side of the model, select the *second* node *above* the previously selected node. This procedure selects nodes B_i and B_o in Fig. 26.

Observe the two new stress magnitudes listed in the **Results** dialogue box and compare them to values listed in Table II. Nodes **B$_i$** and **B$_o$**, thus selected, lie on a radial line that forms an approximate angle of 7.5° above the horizontal. Stress values calculated using the classical equations are modified to account for a slight shift of the centroidal axis due to beam curvature and for the change in angle of the axial force. Using these values, a comparison of classical and FEA results in Table II reveals that values differ by at most 4.1%, which is a significant improvement over previous calculations.

Table II – Comparison of stress (σ_y) for classical and finite element methods at Section B$_i$-B$_o$. (Rounded values are used)

Location	Manual Calculation (psi)	Probe Tool Results (psi)	Percent Difference (%)
Point **B$_i$**	-24515	-23781	3.1%
Point **B$_o$**	11940	12453	4.1%

15. Click **[OK]** ✓ to close the **Probe Result** property manager.

This concludes the verification of Finite Element results, but note that even better results are expected at locations further from the transition region.

Assessing Safety Factor

SolidWorks Simulation provides a convenient means to determine and view plots of Safety Factor distribution in the model. To use this capability, proceed as follows.

1. In the **Simulation** tab, click ▼ on the **Results Advisor** icon and from the pull-down menu, select **New Plot**. Then, from a second pull-down menu, select **Factor Of Safety**. The **Factor of Safety** property manager opens as shown in Fig. 27 and displays the first step of a three step procedure.

2. Read text in the yellow **Message** dialogue box *and* at bottom of the **Step 1 of 3** dialogue box. These messages indicate Safety Factor is based on the failure criterion noted in the **Materials** window. That criterion was specified as **Max von Mises Stress.**

3. In the upper pull-down menu of the **Step 1 of 3** dialogue box, select either **All** or **Selected Bodies**. Because there is only one part to be analyzed the result is the same in either case.

4. Next, in the **Criterion** field, click the pull-down menu to reveal names of the four failure criteria available for determination of the safety factor.

Figure 27 – **Factor of Safety**, Step #1 of safety factor check.

A brief overview of the four failure criteria is provided below.

- **Max von Mises Stress** – This failure criterion is used for ductile materials (aluminum, steel, brass, bronze, etc.). It is considered the best predictor of actual failure in ductile materials and, as such, provides a good indication of the true safety factor. This criterion is also referred to as the "Distortion Energy Theory."

- **Max Shear Stress (Tresca)** – This criterion also applies to ductile materials. However, it is a more conservative theory thereby resulting in lower predicted safety factors. As a consequence of its conservative nature, parts designed using this criterion may be somewhat oversized.

- **Mohr-Coulomb Stress** – This failure criterion is applied to the design and analysis of parts made of brittle material (cast iron, etc.) where the ultimate compressive strength exceeds the ultimate tensile strength ($S_{uc} > S_{ut}$).

- **Max Normal Stress** – Also applicable for brittle materials, this failure criterion does not account for differences between tensile and compressive strengths. This theory is also regarded as the least accurate of the methods available.

- Other failure criteria apply for *shell* elements made of composite materials. These criteria are not described here.

5. Because the curved beam is made of aluminum and because a good estimate of safety factor is desired, choose **Max von Mises Stress** from the pull-down menu.

Upon making the above selection, the **Factor of Safety** property manager changes to that illustrated in Fig. 28. Immediately below the **Criterion** field notice that the factor of safety check is currently defined as

$$\frac{\sigma_{vonMises}}{\sigma_{Limit}} < 1$$

Figure 28 – The failure criterion is selected in **Step 1 of 3** of the **Factor of Safety** dialogue box.

In other words, the above equation is currently set to identify locations in the model where the ratio of von Mises stress to the "limiting" value of stress (i.e., the Yield Strength) is < 1.

Thus, the above criterion identifies locations where yielding of the model is *not* predicted because model Yield Strength, the denominator, is greater than the von Mises stress, the numerator. As initially defined, the above ratio is the *inverse* of the traditional safety factor definition, where:

Safety Factor = n = strength/stress

To plot only critical regions of the part, i.e., regions where the Yield Strength is exceeded and the safety factor is < 1, proceed as follows –

6. Advance to the second step by clicking the right facing arrow button ➡ at the top of the **Factor of Safety** property manager. The **Step 2 of 3** dialogue box appears as shown in Fig. 29. It may be necessary to click and drag its bottom edge to expand the **Factor of Safety** dialogue box.

7. In the top pull-down menu, select **psi** as the set of **Units** to be used (if not already selected).

8. Under **Set stress limit to**, click to select ⊙ **Yield strength** (if not already selected).

9. Do *not* change the **Multiplication factor**.

Notice that the material, **2014 Alloy** aluminum, and its Yield and Ultimate strengths for the model appear near the bottom of this dialogue box.

Figure 29 – **Step 2 of 3** in the **Factor of Safety** process.

Design Insight – Focus attention near the top of the **Step 2 of 3** dialogue box.

In the event that a *brittle* material is being analyzed using the Mohr-Coulomb or the Max Normal Stress failure criteria, it is appropriate to select the ⊙ **Ultimate strength** as the failure criterion since brittle materials do not exhibit a yield point.

The ◯ **User defined** option is provided for cases where a user specified material is not found in the **Material Property** table.

---

10. Click the right facing arrow button ➡ at top of this property manager to proceed to **Step 3 of 3** in the **Factor of Safety** property manager shown in Fig. 30.

Two options are available for displaying the factor of safety. Brief descriptions of each are provided below.

- **Factor of safety distribution** – Produces a plot of safety factor variation throughout the entire part.

- **Areas below factor of safety** – A desired value for safety factor is entered in the field beneath this option. The resulting display shows all areas of the model below the specified safety factor in the color red and areas with a safety factor greater than the specified value in blue. This approach easily identifies areas that need to be improved during the design process.

Figure 30 – Redefinition of **Factor of Safety** and values to be displayed on the new plot.

11. Beneath **Step 3 of 3**, select ⊙**Areas below factor of safety** and type "**1**" in the **Factor of safety:** field (if not already "1").

At the bottom of this dialog box the **Safety result** field informs the user that the *minimum* factor of safety is **0.562883** which indicates that the design is *not* safe in some regions of the model. Recall that this value is based on a comparison between Yield Strength and the maximum von Mises stress. *(Values may vary slightly from those shown).*

Also note that the above value of safety factor closely matches that computed by the reciprocal of the equation appearing in the first **Factor of Safety** window. That is:

$$\frac{\sigma_{Limit}}{\sigma_{vonMises}} = \frac{\text{Yield Strength}}{\text{Max. von Mises Stress}} = \frac{13997}{|-24866|} = 0.56289$$

12. Click **[OK]** ✓ to close the **Factor of Safety** property manager. A new plot folder, named, **Factor of Safety1 (- Max von Mises Stress-)**, is listed beneath the **Results** folder. Also, a plot showing regions of the model where the Safety Factor < 1.0 (red) and where the Safety Factor > 1.0 (blue) is displayed.

13. Right-click **Factor of Safety1 (-Max von Mises Stress-)**, and from the pull-down menu, select **Chart Options...** The **Chart Options** property manager opens.

14. In the **Display Options** dialogue box, check ☑ **Show min annotation** and click **[OK]** ✓ to close the **Chart Options** property manager.

The preceding step labels the location of minimum Safety Factor on the curved beam as shown in Fig. 31. As expected, this location corresponds to the location of maximum compressive stress previously illustrated in Fig. 20.

The figure now on your screen should correspond to Fig. 31. This figure shows regions where the factor of safety is less than 1 (unsafe regions) in red. Regions with a factor of safety greater than 1 (safe regions) are shown in blue. Localized regions, along the right and left vertical edges and extending into the concave region, have a safety factor less than one.

The line of text, circled near the top-left in Fig. 31, provides a "key" to interpret safe and unsafe regions on the model.

Figure 31 – Curved beam model showing areas where FOS > 1 (safety predicted) and where FOS < 1 (yield predicted).

15. Double-click **Factor of Safety (-Max von Mises Stress-)** and repeat steps 1 through 12 above, but this time set the **Areas below factor of safety** to **2** instead of **1**, in step 11. How does the plot change?

A designer can repeat the above procedure for any desired level of safety factor check.

In summary, an important aspect of the von Mises stress is that it can be used to predict whether or not a part might fail based on a comparison of its stress *magnitude* to the value of yield strength. This topic is aligned with the study of theories of failure found in most mechanics of materials and design of machine elements texts.

Analysis Insight #1:

Faced with the fact that the above part is predicted to fail by yielding, a designer would be challenged to redesign the part in any of several ways, depending upon design constraints. For example, it might be possible to change part dimensions to reduce stress magnitudes in the part. Alternatively, if part geometry cannot be changed due to size limitations, a stronger material might be selected, or some combination of these or other possible remedies might be applied. Because part redesign might be considered an open-ended problem, it is not pursued here.

Analysis Insight #2:
Return briefly to the vonMises stress plot by double-clicking **Stress1 (-vonMises-)** beneath the **Results** folder.

Refer to Fig. 32 or your screen and notice that the material yield strength (13997.6 psi) is displayed beneath the color coded stress scale. Also, an arrow appears adjacent to the stress scale at a magnitude corresponding to this yield strength. Thus, all stresses above the arrow *exceed* the material yield strength. Given this observation it is logical to ask, "What is the meaning of stress values above the material yield strength?"

Figure 32 – von Mises stress plot for the curved beam model.

The answer to this question is quite straight forward. Stress values greater than the yield strength are *meaningless!* Why is this true?

Recall that the stiffness approach, described in the Introduction, indicated a finite element solution starts by determining deflection ΔL of a part subject to applied loads. Then, based on deflection, strain is calculated as $\varepsilon = \Delta L/L$. And finally, from strain, stress is calculated from the relation $\sigma = E\varepsilon$. In words, the last equation states that "stress is proportional to strain," where the constant of proportionality E (i.e., the modulus of elasticity) is determined from the *linear* portion of the stress strain curve illustrated in Fig. 33.

Because this solution is based on a *linear* analysis, stress values *above* the yield strength in Fig. 32 are *assumed* to lie along a *linear* extension of the stress-strain curve shown dashed in Fig. 33. However, above the yield strength, the actual stress-strain curve follows the *solid* curved line where stress is no longer proportional to strain. Thus, stress values reported above the yield strength are meaningless.

Figure 33 – Stress vs strain curve for a typical elastic material shown by the solid curve.

Problems where stress exceeds the yield strength can be solved in the Professional version of SolidWorks Simulation where *non-linear* analysis capabilities are available to conduct post-yield analysis.

Alternate Stress Display Option

Because some users might prefer more immediate feedback to identify areas where material yield strength is exceeded, this section outlines steps to quickly identify those regions in a part. This option is only valid for von Mises stress plots. Another restriction is that this display option only applies to individual parts. It does not apply to assemblies because individual parts within an assembly might be made of different materials each with its own yield strength. Change the display as follows.

1. Beneath the **Results** folder, right-click **Stress1 (-vonMises-)** and from the pull-down menu, select **Chart Options**. The **Chart Options** property manager opens. The bottom *portion* of this property manager is shown in Fig. 34.

2. At the bottom of this property manager, click ≽ to open the **Color Options** dialogue box.

3. Place a ✓ mark to select ☑ **Specify color for values above yield limit** and accept the default gray color specified.

Figure 34 – Customizing displays where stress exceeds yield strength on von Mises plots.

4. Immediately shades of gray are displayed on regions of the model where the Safety Factor < 1 as shown in Fig. 35. The shades of gray are unimportant.

Figure 35 – Altered plot displays stresses greater than the yield strength in shades of grey.

5. Because it is not desired to keep this display, click ✖ to close the **Chart Options** property manager.

The plot produced using this technique appears in Fig. 35 where all stress magnitudes greater than the material yield strength are displayed in gray tones. Although this plot does not provide insight into magnitude of the Safety Factor, or lack thereof, it does reinforce the concept that stress magnitudes above the yield strength are meaningless by assigning them a non-descriptive color.

Determining Reaction Forces

It is always good engineering practice to verify that results obtained correlate well with the given information. One simple way to confirm that results correlate with given information is to check whether or not reaction forces are consistent with external loads applied to the model. This section examines how to determine reaction forces at the base of the curved beam model. To accomplish this, proceed as follows.

1. On the **Simulation** tab, click ▼ on the **Results Advisor** icon and from the pull-down menu, select **List Result Force**. The **Result Force** property manager opens as shown in Fig. 36.

2. In the **Options** dialogue box, verify that ⊙**Reaction Force** is selected.

3. In the **Selection** dialogue box, set **Units** to **English (IPS)** (if not already selected).

4. The **Faces, Edges, or Vertices** field is active (highlighted light blue) and awaiting selection of the entity on which the reaction force is to be determined. Rotate the model so that its bottom (restrained) *surface* is visible and click to select it. **Face<1>** appears in the active field. This is the only face where reactions occur.

5. Click the **[Update]** button and the **Reaction force (lbf)** table at the bottom of the property manager is populated with data. Also, X, Y, and Z reaction force components appear at the base of the model and force magnitudes are contained within an information "flag".

Figure 36 – Data appearing in the **Result Force** property manager.

2-32

The **Component** column in this table lists names for the sum of reaction forces in the X, Y, and Z directions and the **Resultant:** reaction. Reaction force magnitudes listed in the **Selection** column are identical to those in the **Entire Model** column. This result is expected because the entire model is restrained at only this one location.

Results interpretation is as follows: (values may vary)
    SumX: -0.22832 (essentially zero) no force is applied to model in the X-direction
    SumY: 3800 (essentially 3800 lb) equal and opposite to the applied force
    SumZ: 0.19026 (essentially zero) no force is applied to model in the Z-direction
    Resultant: 3800 (essentially 3800 lb = the applied force)

It should be noted that a *moment* reaction at the base of the curved beam is missing from the **Reaction Force** table. Also, opening the **Reaction Moment (lbf-in)** dialogue box, near the bottom of the property manager, reveals no data entries. This outcome does not agree with the usual conventions for reactions associated with a free-body diagram, but it is consistent with our understanding of **Immovable** restraints applied to three-dimensional tetrahedral elements. The **Immovable** restraint only restricts translations in the X, Y, Z directions at each restrained node. This observation accounts for the fact that there are only three force reactions and no moments in the **Reaction Force** table of Fig. 36. Note, however, that calculated reaction forces do not *exactly* match the applied force. This difference confirms the observation that slight mathematical errors exist.

    6. Click **[OK]** ✓ to close the **Result Force** property manager.

The reaction force results above are valid for the **Entire Model**. However, in many instances a model is supported (i.e., restrained) at more than one location. In those instances it is necessary to determine reaction forces at other locations on a model. Performing a reaction check is quite simple and can be viewed as an additional means for users to verify the validity of boundary conditions applied to a model.

Although a surface was selected to examine reaction forces in the above example, it should be evident that other geometric features, such as edges or vertices can also be selected at other restrained locations on a model.

Logging Out of the Current Analysis

This concludes an introduction to analysis of the curved beam model. It is suggested that this file *not* be saved. Proceed as follows.

    1. On the **Main Menu**, click **File** followed by choosing **Close**.

    2. The **SolidWorks** window opens in Fig. 37, and provides the options of either saving the current document or not. Select **[Don't Save]**.

Figure 37 – **SolidWorks** window prompts users to either save changes or not.

EXERCISES

End of chapter exercises are intended to provide additional practice using principles introduced in the current chapter plus capabilities mastered in preceding chapters. Most exercises include multiple parts. In an academic setting, it is likely that parts of problems may be assigned or modified to suit specific course goals.

╬ *Designates problems that introduce new concepts. Solution guidance is provided for these problems.*

EXERCISE 1 – Curved Beam Stresses in a "C"- Clamp

C-clamps, like that illustrated below, must pass minimum strength requirements before they can be qualified for general purpose use. Clamps are tested by applying equal and opposite loads acting on the two gripping faces. Part of the federal test criteria requires that the movable (lower) jaw be extended a certain percentage of the distance of the fully-open state to ensure that column failure of the screw is an integral part of the test. Presuming that the movable jaw of the clamp satisfies the prescribed test criterion, perform a finite element analysis of the C-clamp subject to the following guidelines.

Open file: **C-Clamp 2-1**

- Material: **Cast Carbon Steel** (use S.I. units)

- Mesh: In the **Mesh** property manager, select **Standard mesh**.

- Fixture: **Fixed** applied to the upper gripping surface of the C-clamp.

- External Load: **950 N** applied normal to the lower gripping surface.

SECTION A-A

Figure E2-1 – "C"-clamp frame and cross-section dimensions.
Stress to be determined at Section A-A. (All dimensions in mm.)

Determine the following:

a. Use classical equations to compute stress at the inside and outside surfaces of the C-clamp frame at section A-A. Section A-A is located where the straight and curved sections are tangent. Include a free body diagram of the lower portion of the clamp and use curved beam equations.

b. Create a stress contour plot of von Mises stress in the frame of the C-Clamp. Include automatic labeling of maximum and minimum von Mises stress on this plot.

c. Use the **Probe** feature to produce a graph of the *most appropriate stress* acting on section A-A. In other words, because values from this plot are to be compared with manual calculations of part (a), it is necessary to choose the corresponding stress from those available within the finite element software. Include a descriptive title, axis labels, and your name on this graph. When using the **Probe** feature, begin at the concave (left inside) surface and select nodes across the model continuing to the outside of the "T" cross-section. Use equation [1] to compare percent differences between classical and FEA determination of stresses at the inside and outside surfaces.

$$\% \text{ difference} = \frac{(\text{FEA result - classical result})}{\text{FEA result}} * 100 = \qquad [1]$$

d. Assuming the C-clamp is made of a ductile material, produce a plot showing regions where the safety factor < 2.0. Also, if the safety factor is < 1.0 at any location within the C-clamp, produce a second plot to highlight any un-safe regions.

EXERCISE 2 – Curved Beam Stresses in Hacksaw Frame

A common, metal-cutting "hacksaw" is shown in Fig. E2-2. A solid model of the hacksaw is available as file: **Hacksaw 2-2**. The model is simplified to include two 0.125 inch diameter holes that pass through the lower left and lower right ends of the hacksaw "backbone" labeled in Fig. E2-2. For analysis purposes, the inside surface of the left-hand hole is to be considered **Fixed** (i.e. immovable). Use split lines to create a small "patch" of area on the inside surface of the hole located at the right end of the backbone. On this surface apply a 50 lb force induced by a tensile load in the saw blade, which is ordinarily held in place between these two holes. Assume the following.

- Material: **AISI 1020 Steel** (use English units)

- Mesh: In the **Mesh** property manager, select ⊙ **Standard mesh**; use the default mesh size.

- Units: **English (IPS)**

- Fixture: **Fixed** applied to inside of left hole.

- External Load: **50 lb** applied parallel to the X-direction on the inner surface of the right-hand hole (split lines needed; placement of these lines is user defined).

Figure E2-2 – Basic geometry of a hacksaw frame. Stress is to be determined at Section Q-Q.

Determine the following:

a. Use classical curved beam equations to compute stress at the inside (concave) and outside (convex) surfaces of the hacksaw frame at section Q-Q. Section Q-Q is located where the straight and curved sections are tangent. Include a labeled free body diagram of the right-portion of the model.

b. Include a zoomed-in image of the right-hand hole so that the 50 lb applied load can clearly be seen to act between user specified *Split Lines*.

c. Create a stress contour plot of von Mises stress in the saw backbone. Include automatic labeling of maximum and minimum von Mises stress on this plot.

d. Use the **Probe** feature to produce a graph of the *most appropriate stress* across section Q-Q, beginning at the inside (concave) surface and continuing to the outside (convex) surface of the backbone cross-section. Use the **Stress Plot** property manager to select the *appropriate stress* for this plot to enable comparison with manual calculations of part (a). Include a descriptive title, axis labels, and your name on this graph. Also, below the graph, cut-and-paste a copy of the **Probe Results** table showing values used in this comparison [see Appendix A for procedures to copy SolidWorks images into a Word® document]. Then use equation [1], repeated below, to compute the percent difference between classical and finite element solutions at the inside and outside surfaces of the saw backbone.

$$\% \text{ difference} = \frac{(\text{FEA result - classical result})}{\text{FEA result}} * 100 = \qquad [1]$$

e. Based on von Mises stress, create a plot showing all regions of the model where Safety Factor < 2.2 and circle these regions on the plot. Include a software applied label indicating the maximum and minimum values for Factor of Safety.

f. Question: If stresses at section Q-Q, calculated using both classical equations and the finite element solution, differ by more than 4%, state the reason for this difference and describe at least one method to reduce the percent difference calculation at this location.

EXERCISE 3 – Stresses in a Curved Anchor Bracket

The curved beam shown in Fig. E2-3 is subject to a horizontal load applied by means of a pin (not shown) that passes through a hole in its upper end. A solid model of this part is available as file: **Anchor Bracket 2-3**. The lower-left end of the part is attached to a rigid portion of a machine frame (also not shown). Because three-dimensional tetrahedral elements are to be used to model this part, the restraint at this location should be considered **Immovable**. Use split lines to create a small "patch" of area on the inside surface of the 16 mm diameter hole. Locate these split lines 24 mm from the right edge of the model. On this inner surface of the hole apply a horizontal force of 8600 N acting in the positive X-direction (to the right). Assume the following.

- Material: **AISI 1010 Steel, hot rolled bar** (use SI units)

- Mesh: In the **Mesh** property manager, select ⊙ **Standard mesh**; use the default mesh size.

- Fixture: Apply a **Fixed** (immovable) restraint on the inclined surface.

- External Load: **8600 N** in the X-direction applied on the right, inside surface of the 16 mm diameter hole between user defined split lines.

Determine the following:

a. Use classical equations to compute stress at the inside (concave) surface and the outside (convex) surface of the anchor bracket at section B-B. Section B-B passes through the center of curvature of the curved beam and is considered to be a vertical line. Include a labeled free body diagram of the portion of the anchor bracket to the right of section B-B.

b. Include a zoomed-in image of the hole so that the force $F_x = 8600$ N can clearly be seen to act between user specified *Split Lines*.

c. Create a stress contour plot of von Mises stress in the anchor bracket. Include automatic labeling of maximum and minimum von Mises stress on this plot.

Figure E2-3 Dimensioned view of the Anchor Bracket. Stress is to be determined at Section B-B.

d. Using von Mises stress, create a plot showing all regions of the model where Safety Factor < 1.5 (if any). Indicate these regions, if any, by circling their location(s) on the figure and labeling them as "FOS < 1.5". Include a software applied label indicating locations of maximum and minimum values of Safety Factor.

e. Use the **Probe** feature to produce a graph of the *most appropriate stress* across the bracket at section B-B. Begin at the inside (concave) surface and continue to the outside (convex) surface. (See the *"HINT"* on next page for guidance when making this graph). Use the **Stress Plot** property manager to select the *appropriate stress* for this plot to enable comparison with manual calculations of part (a) above. Add a descriptive title and axis labels to this graph.

Below the graph or on a separate page either: (a) cut-and-paste a copy of the **Probe Results** table that includes values used for this comparison [See Appendix A for procedures to copy images from SolidWorks Simulation into a Word® document], or (b) click the **Save** icon located in the **Report Options** dialogue box, to create an Excel spreadsheet containing all values in the **Probe Results** table. [See Appendix A- pg. 12]

After determining both classical and FEA results at section B-B, use equation [1] to compute the percent difference between classical and finite element solutions at the inside and outside surfaces of the bracket.

$$\% \text{ difference} = \frac{(\text{FEA result - classical result})}{\text{FEA result}} * 100 = \qquad [1]$$

2-38

f. If results of part (e) differ by 4% or more, determine the source of error in either the classical solution or finite element solution and correct it. If no error is found, state why results differ by this significant percent difference.

HINT: Because the **Standard mesh** generation scheme within SolidWorks Simulation creates an optimized mesh, it is probable that (a) a straight line of nodes may *not* exist across the model at section B-B (thus, choose the best straight line available), and (b) it is also *unlikely* that node points *occur exactly on a vertical line through the center of curvature.* For these reasons, and to obtain the best estimate of stress on a vertical line through section B-B, proceed as follows.

- Zoom in on a *front* view of the model at section B-B.

- On the **Simulation** tab, select the **Plot Tools** icon and from the pull-down menu, click the **Probe** tool icon. This action opens the **Probe Results** property manager.

- In the SolidWorks Feature manager, move the cursor over the **Right Plane** label. This action highlights an edge view of the **Right Plane** at the desired location, which will assist in locating nodes closest to a vertical line at Section B-B. Unfortunately, the line disappears when the cursor is moved, but it is very useful none the less.

- Complete the graph using the **Probe** tool.

⌗ EXERCISE 4 – Stresses in a Curved Photoelastic Model
(Special Topics Include: Custom material definition, and using a "Hinge" joint for Fixture)

A curved beam model, made from a photoelastic material and subject to axial load **F**, is shown in Fig. E2-4. Beams such as this might be used in an experimental stress analysis laboratory where photoelastic techniques are studied. Photoelastic material has a unique optical property known as birefringence. Thus, when a photoelastic model is subject to applied loads in a field of polarized light, the light passing through the model undergoes changes of wavelength that produce visible "fringes" within the model as shown.

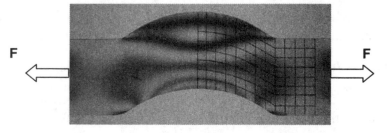

Figure E2-4 – "Fringes" appearing in a photoelastic model subject to a tensile load applied through pin joints (not shown). A grid is superimposed on the model to facilitate locating specific stress magnitudes and directions.

These "fringes" are analogous to, but not equal to, stress contour plots produced upon completion of a finite element analysis. In this exercise, stresses produced within the curved beam model are examined. Dimensioned views of a typical photoelastic beam are shown in Fig. E2-5.

Figure E2-5 – Top view (above) and front (edge) view of a curved beam model. (Dimensions: inches)

Create a finite element model of this part that includes custom material specification, fixtures, external loads, mesh, solution, and results analysis.

Open the file: **Curved Bracket**

- Material: Material properties not found in SolidWorks material library (use custom properties below)
  - $E = 360e3$ psi Modulus of Elasticity (use English units)
  - $v = 0.38$ Poisson's ratio
  - $S_y = 2200$ psi Yield Strength

- Mesh: In the **Mesh** property manager, select a ⊙ **Standard mesh**; use the default mesh size. (Although this model is very thin, use a solid mesh.)

- Fixture: **Hinge Joint** applied at hole on left end of the model.

- External Load: **72** lb in the X-direction applied between user defined split lines on the inner surface of the hole located at the right end of the model.

Two aspects of this exercise are unique. First, properties of the photoelastic material are not available in the SolidWorks material library. And second, the fixture at the left hole of the curved bracket is considered to be a **Fixed Hinge** joint. Guidance in the application of these two items is provided below.

Solution Guidance

It is assumed that the user has opened the model file and started a Study in SolidWorks Simulation. The following instructions are to serve as a "guide;" they are less detailed than the step-by-step procedure found in example problems.

<u>Custom Material Specification</u>

The recommended way to create a custom material definition is to begin with a *similar* existing material and then edit material properties as outlined below.

- Open the **Material** window by right-clicking the **Curved Bracket** folder and selecting **Apply/Edit Material…**

- Close all open pull-down menu(s) beneath **SolidWorks Materials**.

- Because photoelastic material is a special, clear "plastic like" material, open the **Custom Materials** folder at the bottom of the **SolidWorks Materials** list.

- Next click "+" to open the **Plastic** folder and beneath it select **Custom Plastic**. The right side of the window is populated with property values for the current material.

- On the **Properties** tab, select **Units:** as **English (IPS)**.

- Adjacent the **Name:** field, change the name "Custom Plastic" to "**Photoelastic Material**." The **Description** and **Source:** fields can be left blank.

- Within the **Property** column of the lower table notice that red, blue, and black colors are used to indicate different **Property** names. Red lettering indicates information *required* for a stress solution. Blue lettering indicates *desirable, but not necessary* information. And, property names appearing in black *are not required* for the current solution. For each red item, enter the values listed beneath "Material" in the problem statement, but do not change the existing value in the **Mass density** field. Do not alter other values listed in the table.

- Click **[Apply]** followed by **[Close]** to exit the **Material** window. A check "✓" appears on the **Curved Bracket** part folder and the **Name:** assigned above appears on the part folder. You have successfully defined a custom material.

<u>Fixed Hinge Specification</u> A **Fixed Hinge** joint acts like a door hinge. This joint type allows rotation about a fixed axis on the model, but prevents translation along that axis. A **Fixed Hinge** is used at the left end of the **Curved Bracket** to prevent translations in the X, Y, Z directions, but allows the model to rotate thereby maintaining alignment with the external load as the part deforms. Proceed as follows.

Solution Guidance (continued)

- Right-click the **Fixtures** folder and from the pull-down menu select **Fixed Hinge...** The **Fixture** property manager opens as shown in Fig. E2-6.

- In the **Standard (Fixed Hinge)** dialogue box, the **Cylindrical Faces for Fixture** field is highlighted (light blue).

- Zoom in on the left hole of the model and select its *inner surface*. **Face<1>** appears in the highlighted field, shown in Fig. E2-6. This cylindrical surface has an axis perpendicular to the model face.

Figure E2-6 – Specifying a **Fixed Hinge** restraint.

- Click **[OK]** ✓ to close the **Fixture** property manager.

A **Fixed Hinge** restraint allows the model to undergo rotations about the selected hole, but no translations perpendicular to the hole. The remainder of this solution uses previously mastered procedures.

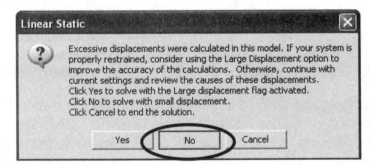

Special Solution Note:
Due to specification of a **Fixed Hinge** on this model, it is highly likely that the above warning message will appear during the **Solution** portion of this analysis.

Click the **[No]** button if the above **Linear Static** window appears and continue with the "small displacement" Solution.

Determine the following:

    a. Use classical equations to compute stress at the inside (concave) surface and the outside (convex) surface of the curved bracket model at section C-C. Section C-C passes through the center of curvature and is considered to be a horizontal line in the top view of Fig. E2-5. Include a labeled free body diagram of the portion of the model to the right of section C-C.

b. Turn *off* the deformed image. Then, include a zoomed-in image of the right hole so that the external load, $F_x = 72$ lb, can clearly be seen to act between user specified *Split Lines* on the inner surface of the hole.

c. Create a stress contour plot showing the *most appropriate stress* that should be analyzed acting across section C-C. The *most appropriate stress* should correspond to the stress calculated in part (a). Do stress fringes on the FEA model loosely approximate those shown in the photograph in Fig. E2-4?

d. Use the **Probe** feature to produce a graph of the *most appropriate stress* across section C-C, beginning at the inside (concave) surface and continuing to the outside (convex) surface of the beam. (See the *"HINT"* near the end of this problem for guidance when making this graph). Use the **Stress Plot** property manager to select the *appropriate stress* for this plot to enable comparison with manual calculations of part (a) above. Include a descriptive title, axis labels, and your name on this graph.

Below the graph, or on a separate page, either: (a) cut-and-paste a copy of the **Probe Results** table that includes values used for this comparison [see Appendix A for procedures to copy SolidWorks Simulation images into a Word® document], or (b) click the **Save** 🖫 icon, located in the **Report Options** dialogue box, to create an Excel spreadsheet containing all values in the **Probe Results** table. [See Appendix A, pg. A-12]. This spreadsheet can be inserted onto the page beneath the current graph. In either table, circle the magnitudes of stress on the concave and convex surfaces.

After determining both classical and FEA results at section C-C, use equation [1] (repeated below) to compute the percent difference between these results at the concave and convex surfaces of the model.

$$\% \text{ difference} = \frac{(\text{FEA result - classical result})}{\text{FEA result}} * 100 = \qquad [1]$$

e. On the **Probe** graph created in part (d), label the distance of the neutral axis (neutral plane) from the concave edge of the model at section C-C. Write a brief statement indicating how this value was determined. Compare this value with the location of the neutral axis determined using classical equations?

f. Return to the plot produced in part (c). This time, use the **Probe** tool to sample stress magnitudes along the concave edge of the model beginning at point **A** and proceeding from node-to-node until reaching point **B**. Include a graph of these results with your analysis. Add a descriptive title, axis labels, and your name to this graph.

g. QUESTIONS: Answer the following questions on a separate page.

- Is the variation of stress through the middle of the model shown in the graph of part (d) expected? Why?

- Is the variation of stress shown on the graph of part (f) expected? Why?

- Is the location of the neutral axis determined in part (e) located where it is expected to occur on the curved bracket model? Does the neutral axis of a curved member subject to axial load *always* occur at a location *like* that shown in the plot of part (e)? Explain why or why not.

HINT: Because the mesh generation scheme within SolidWorks Simulation creates an optimized mesh, it is probable that (a) a straight line of nodes may *not* exist across the model at Section C-C, and (b) it is also *unlikely* that node points *occur exactly on a horizontal centerline through the center of curvature.* For these reasons, and to obtain the best estimate of stress on a straight line through the center of the curved section, proceed as follows.

- Zoom in on a top view of the model at section C-C.

- On the **Simulation** tab, select the **Plot Tools** icon and from the pull-down menu, click the **Probe** tool icon. This action opens the **Probe Results** property manager.

- Open the SolidWorks flyout menu, located at top right of the graphics area, and move the cursor over the **Right Plane** label. This action superimposes an edge view of the **Right Plane** onto the model. This plane will assist in locating nodes closest to a straight line at Section C-C. Unfortunately, the line disappears when the cursor is moved, but this action can be repeated and it is very useful.

⌗ EXERCISE 5 – Curved Beam Stress in a Trailer Hitch (Special Topic Includes: Application of Remote Loads)

The trailer hitch shown in Fig. E2-7 is subject to both vertical and horizontal force components when towing a trailer. The vertical component, or "tongue weight," (**W**) is defined as the downward force due to trailer weight that acts on the hitch. For safety reasons, tongue weight should lie between 9% to 15% of the gross trailer weight (i.e. weight of the trailer plus its cargo). Towing force (**F_T**) is the force required to pull the trailer. Tow force is zero when the trailer is at rest; is reasonably steady when pulling a trailer at constant speed; and is maximum during acceleration or deceleration.

Figure E2-7 – Trailer hitch and ball assembly.

Open file: **Trailer Hitch 2-5**. The trailer hitch, minus the ball, appears in Fig. E2-8. The hitch is bolted to a rigid frame on the towing vehicle (not shown) at the two ½ in holes. Because application of forces to the hitch "ball" may require abilities not yet introduced, and because stress in the ball are not the objective of this analysis, the problem can be simplified by defining applied forces using the **Remote Load/Mass** feature within SolidWorks Simulation. Guidance in the application of a remote load is provided below.

Figure E2-8 – Isolated view of the trailer hitch emphasizes its curved beam shape.

Assume the following.

- Material: **Alloy Steel** (use English units, **IPS**)

- Mesh: In the **Mesh** property manager, select ⊙ **Standard mesh** and use the default mesh size.

- Fixture: To mimic bolt fasteners, apply a **Fixed** (immovable) restraint on the inside surface of the two, 1/2-in bolt holes. Bolted joints are considered in Chapter 7.

- External Load: Apply force components using the **Remote Load/Mass** feature.
  Tongue weight **W = 200 lb** (vertical downward).
  Tow force **F$_T$= 550 lb** (horizontal) in the +X-direction.

Use of the **Remote Load/Mass** feature is described below. This feature permits application of remote forces, moments, displacements, and masses (in the case of static, frequency, linear dynamic, or buckling studies). Application of remote forces is the only new topic introduced in this example. **Remote Load/Mass** is used primarily where modeling simplification can be realized. For example, application of force components to curved surfaces of the hitch ball can be accomplished using several methods. But, using the **Remote Load/Mass** option is one of the more direct approaches. Also, it allows introduction of this useful feature for application in other situations.

Solution Guidance
It is assumed that the user has opened a Simulation file and started a Study. The following instructions are to serve as a "guide;" they are less detailed than step-by-step procedures found in example problems.

Remote Load/Mass
When used, the **Remote Load/Mass** feature, in effect, replaces a more complex portion of a model (or) part of the model that, itself, is not essential to the final analysis. Because the focus of this analysis is upon curved beam stresses, the hitch "ball" can be replaced using a **Remote Load/Mass**. When applying the force components, proceed as follows.

- In the Simulation **Property Manager** right-click the **External Loads** folder and select **Remote Load/Mass…**

- In the **Type** dialogue box, select ⊙ **Load/Mass (Rigid connection)**. This option is used when stiffness of the part to be *replaced* is significant relative to the rest of the model. It is also selected because it can be applied to a **Face**, **Edge**, or **Vertices** of the part. NOTE: The ○ **Load (Direct Transfer)** option could also be used, however it is less convenient in this case because it can only be applied to **Faces** (i.e., entire surfaces) of a model.

- Also in the **Type** dialogue box the **Faces, Edges, Vertices, for Remote Load/Mass** field is active (highlighted light blue). Move the cursor onto the *edge* of the "ball" hole on *top* of the hitch and click to select it.

- In the **Reference Coordinate System** dialogue box, choose ⊙ **Global** as the coordinate system *origin* from which *some* (not all) coordinates of the remote loads are defined.

- If the Global coordinate system triad is not visible at the bottom of the selected hole, in the **Main Menu** click **Insert** and from subsequent pull-down menus, select **Reference Geometry** followed by **Coordinate System…** The *origin* of the **Global** coordinate system now appears on the model. Click ✓ **[OK]** to close the **Coordinate System** property manager and a "ghost" coordinate system triad is displayed.

Design Insight:
The trailer *hitch* was intentionally designed with the **Global** coordinate system *origin* at the base of the ball hole. This location was chosen because it permits easy application of a **Remote Load/Mass** on the model as outlined below. Further, it is desired to apply forces **W** and **F_T** at the center of the ball.

Aided by the SolidWorks **Sketch** in Fig. E2-9, it is seen that the center of the "ball" is located **1.616-in** above the ball shoulder. Also, the ball center is located above the **Global** coordinate system origin at X = 0, Y = 0.625 (hitch thickness) + 1.616-in, and Z = 0. Force components **W** and **F_T** are defined in the following steps.

Figure E2-9 – Determination of height above the hitch surface at which forces are applied to the "ball."

Solution Guidance (continued)
Return your attention to the **Remote Load/Mass** property manager shown in Fig. E2-10.

In the **Location** dialogue box, verify that **Unit** is set to inches **in**.
Then, in the **X-Location** field, accept the zero (**0**) value shown. In the **Y-Location** field, type **1.616**, which is the distance above the hole edge selected on the top surface of the hitch. Finally, in the **Z-Location** field, accept the default zero (**0**) value shown.

If necessary, check ☑ **Force** to open this dialogue box. Verify that **Unit** is set to **lbf**. Then in the **X-Direction** field type **550**. In the **Y-Direction** field, type **200** and, if the Y-force vector is directed upward, check ☑ **Reverse Direction**. Finally, accept the **Z-Direction** default value of zero (**0**) since no force acts in the Z direction on the ball.

Click ✓ [OK] to close the **Remote Loads/Mass** property manager.

Figure E2-10 – Specifying **Location** coordiniates and **Force** magnitudes in the **Remote Loads/Mass** property manager.

Determine the following:

a. Use classical equations to compute stress at the inside (concave) surface and the outside (convex) surface of the trailer hitch model at section A-A. Section A-A passes through the center of curvature and is considered to be a horizontal line in the front view of Fig. E2-8. Include a labeled free body diagram of the portion of the model to the right of section A-A. Use definitions provided for a rectangular cross-section model above Fig. 24, p. 2-20 and equations [1] and [2] on p. 2-21, or use equations from your design of machine elements textbook. Clearly label each calculation.

b. Include an image of the hitch showing fixtures applied to lower two bolt holes and the **Remote Load/Mass** applied above the "ball" hole.

c. Create a stress contour plot showing the *most appropriate stress* that should be analyzed at section A-A. The *most appropriate stress* should correspond to the stress calculated in part (a).

d. Use the **Probe** feature to determine magnitudes of the *most appropriate stress* on both the concave and convex sides of the model at section A-A. (*HINT* – Display a mesh on the model. Also, to avoid edge effects, sample stress magnitudes near the middle of the model. To accurately locate the middle of the model, click the **Front** plane in the SolidWorks feature manager tree or in the SolidWorks flyout menu. Then rotate the model to left and right side views).

Cut-and-paste a copy of the model that includes **Probe** information flags showing stress magnitudes at the locations sampled. See Appendix A for procedures to copy SolidWorks Simulation images into a Word® document.

After determining both classical and FEA results at section A-A, use equation [1] (repeated below) to compute the percent difference between these results at the concave and convex surfaces of the model.

$$\% \text{ difference} = \frac{(\text{FEA result - classical result})}{\text{FEA result}} * 100 = \qquad [1]$$

e. QUESTIONS: Answer the following questions on a separate page.

- Are stress magnitudes near the middle (on front plane) of the concave and convex sides of the trailer hitch in good agreement with stresses calculated using classical curved beam equations? (Include a definition stating what you consider to be "good agreement").

- Use the **Probe** tool to explore stress magnitude on section A-A, but at increasing distances from the model center. Does stress magnitude vary as distance from the model center increases? If stress magnitude varies, does it increase, or decrease? Is the variation of stress expected? Why?

Textbook Problems

In addition to the above exercises, it is highly recommended that additional curved beam problems be worked from a design of machine elements or mechanics of materials textbook. Textbook problems provide a great way to discover errors made in formulating a finite element analysis because they typically are well defined problems for which the solution is known. Typical textbook problems, if well defined in advance, make an excellent source of solutions for comparison.

NOTES:

CHAPTER #3
STRESS CONCENTRATION ANALYSIS

This chapter explores stress in the vicinity of a geometric discontinuity in a part where stress concentration is known to occur. Because geometric discontinuities can assume a variety of shapes, they often are referred to generically as "notches." Stress concentrations and their related stress concentration factors are typically studied in mechanics of materials and/or design of machine elements courses. This example focuses on the validity of Finite Element Analysis (FEA) solutions in the vicinity of these geometric discontinuities and on the effects of mesh size on solution accuracy. General principles studied in this example apply to a wide variety of finite element analysis problems. More specifically, since it is generally accepted that improved finite element solutions result when a smaller mesh size is used, this example examines convergence to a solution through the application of successive mesh refinement.

Because this is the third example problem, fewer figures and briefer step-by-step procedures are included. In fact, where you already are familiar with procedures and where *no new* procedures are introduced, special instructions encourage users to complete specific tasks on their own. The combination of these two approaches should permit users to work more at their own pace while allowing expanded discussion of new topics.

Learning Objectives

In addition to software capabilities mastered in previous chapters, upon completion of this example, users should be able to:

- Recognize when, how, and why to *defeature* and *simplify* a model.

- Apply *mesh refinement* to a model and understand the influence of mesh density on stress and displacement results.

- Create *copies* of related studies quickly and easily within SolidWorks Simulation.

- Check *convergence* to gauge validity of a finite element solution.

- Use multiple *viewports* to compare results of different finite element analyses.

Problem Statement

The rectangular bar illustrated in Fig. 1 is fixed at its left end and is subject to an axial, tensile load **F = 6000** lb applied to the opposite end. A rounded "notch," which causes stress concentration, is located in the center of the member.

Figure 1 – Axially loaded bar with a geometric discontinuity.

Dimensions of the notched bar, shown in Fig. 2, reveal that the member is sufficiently long so that boundary-conditions (i.e., fixtures and external loads) do not significantly affect stress near the notch. The bar is made of **AISI 1020** steel. Analysis of this model begins below.

Figure 2 – Dimensioned drawing and a three-dimensional model of a notched bar. (All dimensions in inches.)

1. Open SolidWorks by making the following selections. (*Note:* ">" is used to separate successive menu selections.)

Start>All Programs>SolidWorks 2013 (or) Click the **SolidWorks** icon on your screen.

2. In the **Main Menu**, select **File > Open...** Then use procedures common to your computer environment to locate and open the file named **"Notched Bar."**

Create a Static Analysis (Study)

The new Study is to be named "**DRAFT Mesh-DEFAULT Size**." Individuals comfortable with setting up a **Static** analysis using a **Solid Mesh** are encouraged to proceed on their own. Abbreviated steps, 1 through 3 below, are provided for those desiring guidance. *NOTE: This and future chapters make use of right-clicking menu items to make selections. Users who prefer to use SolidWorks Simulation icons, as demonstrated in Chapter #2, are encouraged to do so.*

1. In the main menu, select **Simulation** and from the pull-down menu click to select **Study...** Or, click the **Study Advisor** icon and from the pull-down menu, select **New Study**. The **Study** property manager opens (not shown).

2. In the **Name** dialogue box, replace the name "**Study 1**" by typing "**DRAFT Mesh-DEFAULT Size**" where the word "DRAFT" refers to the *type* of mesh (no mid-side nodes) and the word "DEFAULT" refers to the mesh *size*.

3. Verify that a **Static** study is selected, then click **[OK]** ✓. An outline for the study is opened in the Simulation manager tree.

Defeaturing the Model

Before beginning an analysis, it is always a good idea to examine the model to determine whether or not its geometry can be simplified without significantly impacting the results. The reason for this examination is that a simpler model results in a more computationally efficient analysis. Thus, the user must ask, "Is it necessary to include all geometric features on the model in order to obtain a valid solution?" If the answer is "no," then the model can be simplified by *suppressing* (i.e., defeaturing) unimportant features or by making use of model *symmetry*. Typical items that can be suppressed without significantly affecting results are minor geometric features, such as fillets, rounds, and chamfers. *You are cautioned, however, that defeaturing a model can have dire consequences if improper choices are made.* Begin by defeaturing the current model as described by two alternate methods outlined below. It is strongly recommended that both methods be attempted as this will provide flexibility in your approach to new problems.

Method 1:

1. Depress and *hold* the **Shift** key and move the cursor onto the graphics screen. Then click to select each of the eight rounded surfaces on the model. NOTE: Release the **Shift** key when rotating the model. Some of these surfaces are shown shaded in Fig. 3.

2. After selecting all rounds, right-click anywhere in the graphics screen and the pop-up menu shown in Fig. 3 appears. On this menu, select the **Suppress** icon circled in Fig. 3. The suppressed rounds are effectively "removed" from the model as illustrated in Fig. 4.

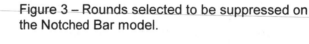

Figure 3 – Rounds selected to be suppressed on the Notched Bar model.

The above procedure works well when only a few geometries are chosen for defeaturing. However, an alternative and somewhat simpler means can be used when the goal is to suppress *all* rounded edges on this model. Next, use the alternative approach, but first the rounded edges must be returned to the model. Proceed as follows.

Figure 4 – Notched Bar after defeaturing.

3. In the SolidWorks manager tree, located *above* the SolidWorks Simulation manager at the left of the graphics screen, locate **Fillet1** and right-click this icon.

In the pop-up menu, select the **Unsuppress** ⬚ icon. Fillets reappear on the model.

Method 2:

4. Once again, locate **Fillet1** in the SolidWorks manager tree and right-click its label. From the box above the pop-up menu, select the **Suppress** ⬚ icon. All fillets are removed from the model.

Analysis Insight:
Clearly **Method 2** is the easier of the two methods. However, its implementation requires planning ahead when the SolidWorks model is created. For example, if rounds of the same size were included elsewhere on a more complex model, but if only one set of rounds were to be suppressed, then the SolidWorks part should be created with two different sets of rounds each of which is easily identified by a different name.

Aside:
SolidWorks Simulation also provides a **Simplify** tool found under the **Tools** menu: **Tools>Find/Modify>Simplify**. See **Help>SolidWorks Simulation>Help Topics** and type **Simplify** in the **Search** box for more information.

Assign Material Properties to the Model

If possible, specify the material for this model on your own. Choose **AISI 1020** steel and select **English (IPS)** units. An abbreviated, step-by-step procedure is provided below if guidance is desired.

1. In the SolidWorks Simulation manager right-click the model name, **Notched Bar**. From the pull-down menu, select **Apply/Edit Material**.

2. In the **Material** window, select **AISI 1020** steel from the list of available steels. *Caution: Avoid selecting AISI 1020 Steel, Cold Rolled.*

3. On the **Properties** tab, adjacent to **Units:**, select **English (IPS)**.

4. Click **[Apply]** followed by **[Close]** to close the **Material** widow. A check "✓" appears on the **Notched Bar** folder and **(-AISI 1020-)** appears next to this folder.

Apply Fixtures and External Loads

Loads and fixtures acting on this model include an **Immovable** restraint applied on its left-end and a **6000** lb axial force applied normal to its right-end. Practice applying these restraints and loads on your own. After applying restraints and loads, a partial view of the Simulation manager should appear as shown in Fig. 5 and the model should appear as shown in Fig. 6. A step-by-step procedure is provided if guidance is desired.

FIXTURES

1. In the SolidWorks Simulation manager, right-click **Fixtures** and from the pull-down menu, select **Fixed Geometry...** The **Fixture** property manager opens.

2. In the **Standard(Fixed Geometry)** dialogue box, the **Fixed Geometry** icon should already be selected. The **Faces, Edges, Vertices for Fixture** field is highlighted (light blue) and is awaiting selection of the surface to be **Fixed**.

3. Rotate the model as necessary and select the surface on the left end of the model. **Immovable** restraints are applied to the left end of the model as seen in Fig. 6.

Figure 5 – SolidWorks Simulation manager with **Fixtures** and **External Loads** defined.

4. Click **[OK]** ✓ to close the **Fixture** property manager. **Fixed-1** appears beneath the **Fixtures** folder as seen in Fig. 5.

EXTERNAL LOADS

1. Right-click the **External Loads** icon and from the pop-up menu, select **Force...** The **Force/Torque** property manager opens.

2. Within the **Force/Torque** dialogue box, select the **Force** icon (if not already selected) and click to select ⊙ **Normal** as the direction of the force.

3. The **Face and Shell Edges for Normal Force** field is highlighted (light blue) to indicate it is active. Rotate the model and select the right end of the part. Force vectors appear on the right-end; *ignore force direction at this time.*

Figure 6 – Notched Bar restrained on its left end and with a **6000** lb force applied normal to its right end.

4. Verify that the **Units** field is set to **English (IPS)**.

5. In the **Force Value** field, type **6000**.

6. Because the default orientation for forces applied normal to a surface is directed *toward* the surface, it is necessary to check ☑ **Reverse direction** to apply a tensile load.

7. Click **[OK]** ✓ to close the **Force/Torque** property manager. **Force-1 (:Per item: -6000 lbf:)** is now listed beneath the **External Loads** folder in Fig. 5. The model should now appear as shown in Fig. 6.

Meshing the Model

Because a primary goal of this example is to examine differences between results obtained when a different mesh *type* or *size* of mesh is used, it is suggested that the following mesh definition steps be followed carefully. The model will be meshed five times, each time using a different size or type of mesh. This example concludes with a comparison of results obtained when using different meshes and corresponding observations about solution accuracy.

Proceed as follows to define the first mesh.

1. In the Simulation manager, right-click the **Mesh** icon and select **Create Mesh…** The **Mesh** property manager opens as shown in Fig. 7.

2. Check "✓" to open the ☑ **Mesh Parameters** dialogue box and verify that a ⊙ **Standard Mesh** is chosen and that ▤ **Unit** is set to **in**. Accept the remaining default settings for mesh size and tolerance. A pointer at the top of this dialogue box is initially located in the center of the scale between **Coarse** and **Fine** mesh sizes. This setting corresponds to the default mesh size; do *not* change it.

3. Near the bottom of the **Mesh** property manager, click ▼ to open the **Advanced** dialogue box, which is also shown in Fig. 7. In this dialogue box, check ☑ **Draft Quality Mesh**.

Figure – 7 Default settings for mesh size in the **Mesh** property manager.

This marks the first time a draft quality mesh is used to perform an analysis. A draft quality mesh is introduced here to reveal some of its shortcomings.

4. Verify that other system default settings appear as shown in Fig. 7 and click **[OK]**
   ✓ to close the **Mesh** property manager and mesh the model.

The meshed model appears in Fig. 8.

Figure 9 shows an enlarged view of the notch and the resulting straight-line approximation of the curved notch that results when a **Draft** quality mesh is used. Although rarely used for a final study, a draft quality mesh can be useful where quick results are needed for a large, complex model. Zoom-in to look at your model, then return the display to an **Isometric** or **Trimetric** view.

Figure 8 – Draft quality mesh shown on the Notched Bar model.

Figure 9 – Close-up view of **Draft** quality mesh reveals straight-line approximation of the curved surface.

Solution

Proceed directly to the solution. You are encouraged to run the **Study** on your own or follow the one-step procedure below.

1. In the SolidWorks Simulation manager tree, right-click the study name **DRAFT Mesh-DEFAULT Size (-Default-)** and from the pull-down menu, select **Run**.

The analysis runs and, upon completion, the now familiar **Results** folders are added at the bottom of the Simulation manager tree. Next, proceed to examine the results of this analysis.

Examination of Results

Stress Plots

Recall that this example will be solved five different times, each time using a different mesh size, mesh type, or mesh control technique. Also, a second goal of this example is to introduce a simple method of creating additional studies that are identical to the first except that different mesh characteristics are used. For this reason, it is necessary to consider carefully exactly *what results* are to be examined and what plot characteristics are defined to *display* those results. If these factors are addressed when the *first* set of results is being defined, then similar results can be produced automatically for all subsequent solutions. Proceed as follows to specify the desired plot characteristics.

1. If the **Stress1 (-von Mises-)** plot appears in the graphics area, skip this step. Otherwise, beneath the **Results** folder, double-click on **Stress1 (-vonMises-)** to display the vonMises stress contour plot and the color-coded stress legend.

The following steps are used to specify certain desired characteristics of the current plot. While some selections are arbitrary, to demonstrate how solution output display can be controlled from one study to the next, other selections represent the author's preferences. In each case a brief justification is given. In practice, however, these selections depend upon user preference and/or standard practices within a specific company or industry. As selections below are made, the current image of the Notched Bar is altered to appear like that shown in Fig. 10.

2. Right-click **Stress1 (-vonMises-)** and from the pull-down menu, select **Edit Definition…** The **Stress Plot** property manager opens. *SHORT CUT:* Double-click the plot title at upper left or center of screen to open the **Stress Plot** property manager.

3. In the **Display** dialogue box, verify ⫼ **Units** are set to **psi**.

4. Check ☑ **Deformed Shape** to open this dialogue box (if not already open) and select ⊙**True Scale**.

5. At bottom of this property manager, click ☒ to open the **Property** dialogue box.

6. Click to check ☑ **Include title text:** and type **YOUR NAME** and any other information pertinent to this plot. *Justification:* It is important to document the author and context of a Study so that other users of this information know who to contact if questions arise. See top left of Fig. 10.

7. Click **[OK]** ✓ to close the **Stress Plot** property manager. The information just entered (your name, etc.) appears at the top-left of the graphics screen along with default information about the plot. Briefly examine information included there.

8. Again right-click **Stress1 (-vonMises-)**. From the pull-down menu, select **Chart Options…** The **Chart Options** property manager opens. *SHORT CUT:* Double-click the color coded stress legend to open the **Chart Options** property manager.

9. Beneath **Display Options** click to check ☑ **Show max annotation**. The location of maximum stress is immediately labeled on the plot as shown near the notch in Fig. 10. *Justification:* This choice is made to determine the location of maximum stress in the part. Rotate the model if the location of maximum stress is unclear.

10. Click **[OK]** ✓ to close the **Chart Options** property manager.

11. Right-click **Stress1 (-vonMises-)** and from the pull-down menu select **Settings…** The **Settings** property manager opens. *Sorry, no short cut.*

YOUR NAME -Stress Concentration Study using Draft Mesh
Model name: Notched Bar
Study name: DRAFT Mesh-DEFAULT Size
Plot type: Static nodal stress Stress1
Deformation scale: 1

von Mises (psi)

15,402.8
14,344.6
13,286.4
12,228.2
11,170.0
10,111.8
9,053.7
7,995.5
6,937.3
5,879.1
4,820.9
3,762.7
2,704.5

Location of YOUR NAME and special plot caption.

Max: 15,402.8

→ Yield strength: 50,991.

Figure 10 – Trimetric view of the Notched Bar with user specified display options.

12. Beneath **Fringe Options**, select **Discrete**. *Justification:* This option is selected because discrete fringes reproduce better when printed in black, white, and gray tones used in this text. Otherwise, fringe display is a user preference.

13. Beneath **Boundary Options**, select **Mesh**. This option displays the current mesh on the model. *Justification:* Since one goal of this example is to investigate effects of mesh modification upon results, viewing the mesh provides visual feedback about mesh size.

14. Click **[OK]** ✓ to close the **Settings** property manager.

A completed view of the model displaying von Mises stress contours appears in Fig. 10. Note the maximum magnitude of von Mises stress (15,402.8 psi - values may differ) determined by this analysis. To more clearly understand results obtained using different meshes, you are *strongly encouraged* to enter results for: maximum von Misses stress, maximum stress in the X-direction (Sigma-X), and maximum X-displacement into **Table 1**, on page 3-30. Place a pencil or scrap of paper at that page to make it easily found and record values for these quantities as each Study is completed. *It only takes a few seconds and the benefit to your understanding is well worth the effort!*

*[**Record:** max. von Mises stress in the first row of Table 1]*

Analysis Insight

Two views of the Notched Bar showing discrete vonMises stress contours are displayed in Figs. 11 and 12. For these plots, the following observations are made.

OBSERVATIONS for Fig. 11:
- The magnitude and distribution of stress at left and right ends of the model are different due to the **Immovable** restraint applied at the left end and a uniform tensile force applied normal to the right-end. This is another example of localized effects explained by St. Venant's principle. However, due to length of the model, these effects are negligible near the middle of the model (the area of primary interest).

To view items described in the second bullet below, alter the model as follows.
- a. Right-click **Stress1 (vonMises)** and select **Edit Definition...**
- b. In the **Stress Plot** property manager, open the ☑ **Deformed Shape** dialogue box and select ⊙**Automatic** to emphasize model deformation.
- c. Click **[OK]** ✓ to close the **Stress Plot** property manager.
- d. Right-click **Stress1 (-vonMises-)** and select **Settings...**
- e. In the **Settings** property manager, change **Boundary Options** to **Model.**
- f. Click **[OK]** ✓ to close the **Settings** property manager.

- A comparison of deformed and *un*-deformed shapes of the model can be made by moving the cursor over the model. This action causes an outline of the *un*-deformed shape to be superimposed on the model. Zoom in on the *front view*, seen in Fig. 11, to observe a slight narrowing of the model in the Y-direction. Notice a small gap between the un-deformed model outline and the colored stress contour plot. This change of lateral dimension is due to Poisson's ratio effect. Also, on the right end of the model, note the increased length which extends to the right from the original line of force application.

Narrow gap between model outline and the stress contour plot is due to Poisson's ratio effect.

Stress due to Immovable restraint.

Max: 15,402.8

Figure 11 – vonMises stress contours and comparison of deformed and un-deformed models of the Notched Bar. The **Mesh** is not shown on this plot so that Poisson's effect is more easily seen. Deformation is exaggerated 346.858 times; see plot caption.

- g. Repeat steps (a) through (f) above except in the **Deformed Shape** dialogue box, select ⊙**True Scale** and in the **Boundary Options** dialogue box return the display to show the **Mesh.**

Analysis Insight (continued)

<u>OBSERVATIONS for Fig. 12</u>:
- Superimposing the current mesh onto the model reveals slight differences between element geometry near the top and bottom notches. Carefully observe these differences on Fig. 12 or on your screen. Zoom in on the notch area.

- Stress *distribution* adjacent to notches located at the top and bottom of the bar is different. This difference is, in part, be due to somewhat different mesh shapes in these two areas of the model and mathematical round-off.

NOTE: Because the meshing process is automated and because it "starts from scratch" and seeks an optimum mesh each time a part is meshed, it is possible that a user obtained mesh might differ from that shown in Fig. 12.

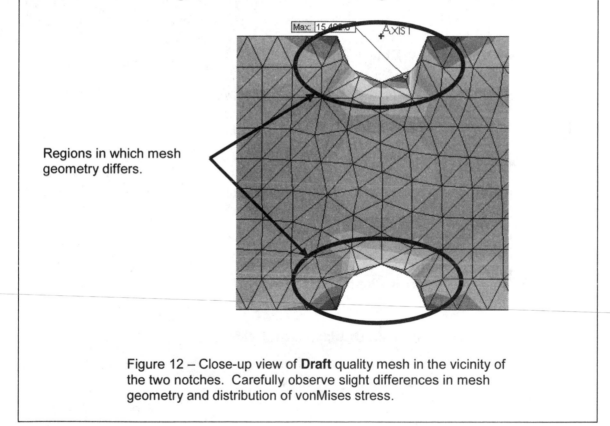

Regions in which mesh geometry differs.

Figure 12 – Close-up view of **Draft** quality mesh in the vicinity of the two notches. Carefully observe slight differences in mesh geometry and distribution of vonMises stress.

Creating a "Copy" of a Plot

Due to the *axial* tensile force of 6000 lb applied to the Notched Bar in the X-direction, it is logical to examine stresses in the X-direction (i.e., σ_x). To do so requires definition of another **Stress Plot** similar to that defined for the von Mises stress plot displayed above. However, repeating all steps required to produce a new plot with the *same* characteristics is somewhat tedious and time consuming. Therefore, use the following shortcut to create a *copy* of the current graph and all its display settings.

1. In the Simulation manager tree *click-and-drag* the **Stress1 (-vonMises-)** folder upward and drop it onto the **Results** folder as illustrated in Fig. 13.

    A new copy of the contents of the **Stress1 (-vonMises-)** folder appears at the bottom of the **Results** list and is labeled **Copy[1] Stress1 (-vonMises-)**, shown at the arrow in Fig. 13. This new folder contains an exact duplicate of all commands used to define the original **von Mises** plot. The following steps outline how to modify this *copied* folder to obtain a plot of σ_x.

2. Click-*pause*-click on the name **Copy[1] Stress1 (-vonMises-)** and type a new descriptive name for the new plot. Since this new folder is to contain σ_x, type: "**Sigma-X**" and press **[Enter]**.

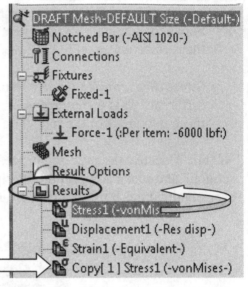

Figure 13 – Making an exact copy of a plot folder.

The *changed name* now appears as **Sigma-X (-vonMises-)**. This name, of course, makes no sense since these names represent two different stresses. The reason for this is that, although the folder *name* was changed, the copied contents (namely vonMises stress) still reside within the folder. However, this is easily corrected by the following steps.

3. Right-click **Sigma-X (-vonMises-)** and the pull-down menu shown in Fig. 14 opens. Select **Edit Definition...** The **Stress Plot** property manager opens.

4. In the dialogue box beneath **Display**, open ▼ the **Component** pull-down menu and from the list of possible stresses select **SX: X Normal Stress**.

5. Click **[OK]** ✓ to close the **Stress Plot** property manager.

Figure 14 – Partial view of pull-down menu.

The *correct* name for the stress now appears in the Simulation manager tree as **Sigma-X (-X normal-)**. This name is a combination of the name you typed to identify the stress plus a system applied label to identify σ_x

6. To display the plot of **Sigma-X (-X normal-)**, right-click its name and from the pop-up menu select **Show**.
   *[**Record:** max. Sigma-X in the first row of Table 1]*

Figure 15 – Graphic display of normal stress in the X-direction (σ_x).

Analysis Insight

OBSERVATIONS for Fig. 15:

- Maximum stress in the X-direction σ_x = 15,761.0 psi is 2.3% larger than the vonMises stress σ' = 15,402.8 psi and it occurs in a different location.

- All display settings established for **Stress1 (-vonMises-)** are copied into the **Sigma-X (-X normal-)** plot folder, (i.e., discrete fringes are shown, your name and a brief description appear at top-left of the graphics screen, the maximum stress magnitude and its location are labeled on the plot, and the mesh is superimposed on the model). NOTE: If the description appearing next to your name in the top line is no longer valid, it can be changed; see steps 2, 6, and 7 of the previous section.

Displacement Plot

Another goal for this example is to determine when an analysis converges to a solution. Although both stress and displacement can be used to make this determination, it turns out that displacement plots typically yield better information about solution convergence than do stress contour plots. Based on your reading of the Introduction to this text, can you explain the reason for this? This question is answered later in this example. Based on this discussion, a **Displacement** plot is created next.

1. Double-click the **Displacement1 (-Res disp-)** folder to display the default displacement plot. Recall that **(-Res disp-)** is an abbreviation for "resultant displacement." If the **Displacement** plot does *not* appear beneath the **Results** folder, perform step (e) found on page 1-14, or try this on your own.

The resultant displacement image, **(-Res disp-)**, is simply a plot of the square root of the sum of the squares of the X, Y, and Z displacement components at any point within the model as given by equation [1].

$$Resultant\ Displacement = \sqrt{X^2 + Y^2 + Z^2}$$ [1]

It is entirely acceptable to use **(-Res disp-)** for this analysis. However, we next select the X-displacement to be displayed for two reasons. First, the X-displacement is in the direction of the applied load and therefore it accounts for the primary displacement component (Y and Z displacements due to Poisson ratio effects are *very* small relative to X). And, second, choosing the X-displacement provides an opportunity to demonstrate selection of a different displacement component as outlined in the following steps.

2. Right-click **Displacement1 (-Res disp-)**, and from the pull-down menu select **Edit Definition…** The **Displacement Plot** property manager opens as shown in Fig. 16. *SHORT CUT:* Double-click the plot title.

3. In the **Display** dialogue box, open the **Component** pull-down menu and select **UX: X Displacement** to display the X-component of displacement.

4. In the **Units** pull-down menu, select inches **in**.

5. In the ☑ **Deformed Shape** dialogue box, select ⊙**Automatic** to exaggerate the actual displacement.

6. Click **[OK]** ✓ to close the **Displacement Plot** property manager.
   [Record: max. Displacement1 in Table 1]

Below, two cosmetic changes are made to this plot.

Figure 16 – Selecting the X-component of displacement.

7. Right-click **Displacement1 (-X disp-)** and from the pull-down menu, select **Settings…** The **Settings** property manager opens as shown in Fig. 17.

8. Beneath **Fringe Options** select **Discrete** for the type of fringe display and beneath **Boundary Options** select **Model** (if not already selected) to turn on a black outline of the model. A mesh display is not needed here.

Figure 17 – Display options in the **Settings** property manager.

9. Click **[OK]** ✓ to close the **Settings** property manager and a plot of **UX: X Displacement** is displayed like that shown in Fig. 18.

Figure 18 – Displacement plot modified to show **UX: X Displacement** using an outlined model and discrete fringes.

Recall that default plots show exaggerated displacements. The exaggeration in this case is 346.858 times larger than actual. See caption at top of the graphics screen. If it is desired to toggle quickly back-and-forth between an exaggerated view and the *true* displacement view, the short-cut of Chapter 2 can be used. Simply click the **Deformed Result** icon located on the **Simulation** tab.

10. Click **[OK]** ✓ to close the **Displacement** property manager.

Because both stress and displacement plots are defined above, it is possible to produce additional nearly identical *copies* of a *Study*. A copy of this *entire* Study can be created in which everything remains the same except for mesh type and mesh size. Proceed as follows to define these new studies. Three different ways of *copying* a Study are illustrated.

Creating New Studies

Basic Parts of the Graphical User Interface

Before outlining different methods of duplicating a Study, the names used to identify various parts of the graphical user interface are reviewed. Also, a previously unused part of the graphical user interface is introduced. Reviewing these parts of the screen image is essential because several names are quite similar. Refer to Fig. 19 while reading the descriptions below.

- SolidWorks Feature Manager Tree – Users familiar with SolidWorks should already be familiar with the Feature manager tree. It is located at the top left side of the graphics screen. See label on Fig. 19. Its name derives from the fact that various features of a model created in SolidWorks, such as sketches, holes, fillets, extrusions, mates, etc. are listed in this portion of the manager tree.

- <u>Simulation Manager Tree (also referred to as the "Simulation manager")</u> – The Simulation manager tree refers to the finite element portion of a Study. It also appears at the left side of the screen and is located just below the SolidWorks Feature manager. Both these entities are referred to as manager trees because they contain a list of items added to the model as an analysis proceeds.

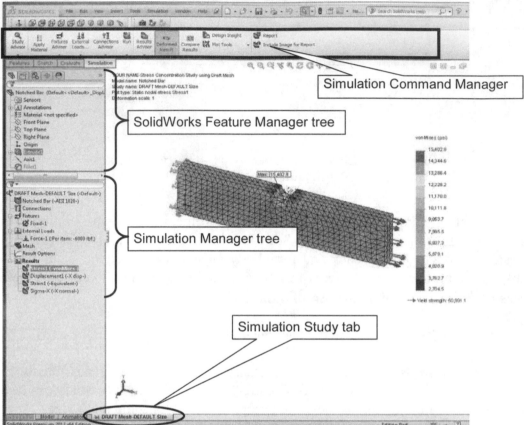

Figure 19 – Identification of various portions of the graphical user interface.

- <u>Simulation Command Manager (also simply referred to as the **Simulation** tab)</u> – This command manager contains icons for commands used to develop the finite element portion of a Study. Command manager icons appear "boxed" across the top of the image shown in Fig. 19. Icons located in the Simulation Command manager were used extensively in Chapter 2.

- <u>Simulation Study Tab</u> – This *new* tab has always been present, but is not emphasized to until now. It is located beneath the graphics screen and is circled in Fig. 19. The tab is identified by the name of the current study, **DRAFT Mesh-DEFAULT Size**, and contains all information used to define the current Study. This information includes items such as **Material** specification, **Fixtures**, **External Loads**, **Mesh,** and all **Results** folders that are currently displayed in the Simulation manager tree.

The following sections outline three different methods for copying the contents from one Simulation Study tab to create a new Study.

Study Using High Quality Elements and COARSE Mesh Size

Method 1 – Item by item Copying

The main reason so much emphasis was placed upon refining plots for the draft quality mesh is that all those settings can be copied as we proceed to examine other mesh types and sizes applied to the model. Begin by copying parts of the current Study as outlined below.

1. At bottom of the screen, right-click to select the Simulation Study *tab* named **DRAFT Mesh-DEFAULT Size**. A pop-up menu opens as shown in Fig. 20.

2. In the pop-up menu, click to select **Create New Simulation Study**. The **Study** property manager opens.

Figure 20 – Pop-up menu revealed by right-clicking on the current Study name.

3. In the **Study** property manager verify that **Static** is selected as the Study **Type**, and click **[OK]** ✓ to close the **Study** property manager.

4. A new Simulation Study *tab* named **Study 1** appears at the bottom left of the screen. Also, an outline for that new Study, named **Study 1 (-Default-)**, appears in the Simulation manager tree.

Observe that all folders (**Notched Bar** (material specification), **Connections**, **Fixtures**, **External Loads**, and **Mesh**) in **Study 1** are currently empty, i.e., undefined. The following steps outline the procedure to copy *individual* items from the original Study into this new Study

5. On the Simulation Study tab, located at the bottom of the screen, return to the **DRAFT Mesh-DEFAULT Size** Study by clicking its tab.

6. Then, within the Simulation manager tree, drag-and-drop the folder named **Notched Bar (-AISI 1020-)** *from* the **DRAFT Mesh-DEFAULT Size** Study onto the **Study 1** tab as illustrated in Fig. 21. Notice a check mark "✓" now appears on the *new* **Notched Bar** folder in **Study 1**.

Figure 21 – Copying **Material** properties from one Study to another using the *click-and-drag* technique.

7. Return to the Study named **DRAFT Mesh-DEFAULT Size** by clicking its name on the Simulation Study *tab*.

8. This time, drag-and-drop the **Fixtures** folder from the **DRAFT Mesh-DEFAULT Size** Study onto the **Study 1** tab as illustrated in Fig. 22. Notice that both the **Fixtures** folder and its contents, namely **Fixed-1**, now appear in **Study 1**.

Figure 22 – Copying the **Fixtures** folder from one Study to another using the *click-and-drag* technique.

9. Again click the **DRAFT Mesh-DEFAULT Size** tab, but this time drag-and-drop the **External Loads** folder onto the **Study 1** tab. Verify that the words **Force-1 (:Per item: -6000 lbf:)** appear beneath the **External Loads** folder on the **Study 1** tab. This move is not illustrated in a figure.

10. If *symbols* representing **Fixed-1** or **Force-1** do not appear *on the model* for **Study 1**, right-click the **Fixtures** folder and from the pull-down menu, select **Show All**. Repeat for the **External Loads** folder.

Do NOT copy the Mesh folder!

11. Finally, repeat the drag-and-drop procedure by copying the **Results** folder from the **DRAFT Mesh-DEFAULT Size** Simulation manager tree to the **Study 1** tab.

Notice that the **Mesh** folder is *not* copied. The reason for this is that each new study in this chapter uses a different mesh. Proceed as follows to re-name the new Study and to define a new mesh type and mesh size.

12. At the bottom of the screen, right-click the **Study-1** tab.

13. From the pop-up menu, select **Rename**.

14. On the Study *tab*, type the name of the new Study as: **COARSE Mesh** and press **[Enter]**. The Study name is updated on the Simulation Study tab and in the Simulation manager tree. Ignore the ⚠ and ⚠ symbols in the manager tree.

Proceed as follows to create the new mesh.

15. In the newly created **COARSE Mesh** Study, right-click the **Mesh** icon and from the pull-down menu select **Create Mesh...** The **Mesh** property manager opens.

16. In the **Mesh** property manager, check ☑ **Mesh Parameters** to open this dialogue box. Select ⊙ **Standard mesh** and note the current mesh size is (0.16846771 in).

17. Next, within the **Mesh Density** dialogue box, click-and-*drag* the **Mesh Factor** slide-control to **Coarse** at the far left-end of the scale. Mesh size is now (0.33693541 in), which is twice as large as the default mesh size indicated when the pointer is at the middle of the scale.

18. At the bottom of the **Mesh** property manager, select ⩔ to open the **Advanced** dialogue box. If necessary, click to *clear* the check mark adjacent to ☐ **Draft Quality Mesh**. This action changes the mesh from **Draft** quality to **High** quality as evidenced by the notation that shows **Jacobian points** are now set to **4 points**. This subtle message is not easily interpreted by new users, but it signifies that a **High** quality mesh is now active. From this point forward, *all meshes* used in this example are **High** quality meshes.

Again observe the **Mesh Parameters** dialogue box and notice that changing the mesh *type* from **Draft** quality to **High** quality does *not* change the mesh *size*. The coarse mesh size is still 0.33693541 in. Using a **High** quality mesh simply adds mid-side nodes to each side of a tetrahedral element, thereby making it better able to model curved surfaces and distortions. This added ability to model curvature makes **High** order elements more *flexible* (i.e. less stiff) than **Draft** quality elements. The effects of this change are examined later in this example.

19. Click **[OK]** ✓ to close the **Mesh** property manager. Re-meshing of the model occurs automatically and the mesh appears relatively large ("coarse").

The Solution is next run as follows.

20. At top of the Simulation manager tree, right-click **COARSE Mesh (-Default-)** and from the pull-down menu, select **Run**. Aside: Note the speed with which this solution is completed (2 seconds or less).

Briefly examine contents of the **Results** folder to observe maximum stress magnitudes shown on **Stress1 (-vonMises-)**, and **Sigma-X (-X normal-)** plots. Also note the maximum displacement shown on **Displacement1 (-X disp-)** plot.
[Record: max. von Mises stress, max. Sigma-X, and max. Displacement1 in Table 1]

Because the **Results** folder was *copied* from the previous study, notice that all plots are displayed using the previously selected format. Thus, no additional work is required to adjust each plot.

A plot of **Sigma-X (-X normal-)** is included in Fig. 23. This figure shows the **COARSE** size **High** quality mesh used for the current study. Compare it to the **DEFAULT** size **Draft** quality mesh shown in Fig. 15. Which has more nodes and elements? Which is more accurate? These questions are answered at the conclusion of this example.

OBSERVATIONS:

- Both the von Mises stress and normal stress in the X-direction (σ_x) are larger for the **High** quality **COARSE** mesh than predicted by the **Draft** quality default size mesh.

- The magnitude of the X-displacement is also larger for the **High** quality coarse mesh than that predicted using a **Draft** quality mesh of default size. Recall an earlier statement that **High** quality elements are not as "stiff" as **Draft** quality elements. This lower mesh stiffness results in larger and more accurate deflections being modeled as is observed again later in this example.

- Increased model stiffness is another reason that a **Draft** quality mesh yields less accurate results.

Figure 23 – A high quality, coarse mesh and stress (σ_x) displayed on the Notched Bar model.

Study Using High Quality Elements and DEFAULT Mesh Size

Method 2 – Copying Multiple Items Simultaneously
In this section the Notched Bar example is solved again, but this time using a high quality **Default** size mesh. A default size mesh is smaller than the coarse mesh of the previous Study. However, to demonstrate additional software capabilities, a different and faster approach to copying the previous Study is outlined below.

1. At bottom of the screen, right-click the Simulation Study *tab* named **COARSE Mesh**. A pop-up menu opens as shown in Fig. 24.

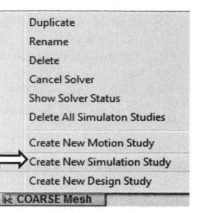

2. In the pop-up menu, select **Create New Simulation Study**. The **Study** property manager opens.

3. In the **Study** property manager verify that **Static** is selected in the **Type** dialogue box, then click **[OK]** ✓ to close the **Study** property manager.

Figure 24 – Pop-up menu revealed by right-clicking on the current Study name.

4. A new Simulation Study *tab,* named **Study 1**, appears at the bottom of the screen and an outline of the new Study, named **Study 1 (-Default-)**, appears in the Simulation manager tree to the left of the graphics area.

Once again note that all of the folders (**Notched Bar**, **Connections**, **Fixtures**, **External Loads**, and **Mesh)** within this *new* Study are empty, (i.e., undefined). The following steps outline a different, more efficient procedure for copying multiple items into this new Study.

5. At bottom of the screen, re-open the Study named **COARSE Mesh** by clicking its tab.

6. Within the Simulation manager tree, click the folder named **Notched Bar (-AISI 1020-)**. Next, *press-and-hold* the **[Shift]** key while clicking the **External Loads** folder. This action highlights all items between the first and last items selected. Finally, click-and-drag all highlighted items to the **Study 1** tab at the bottom of the screen. See Fig. 25.

Figure 25 – Copying all highlighted items from one Study to another using the *click-and-drag* technique.

7. Once again re-open the Study named **COARSE Mesh** by clicking its tab.

8. Repeat the copy procedure by clicking-and-dragging the **Results** folder from the **COARSE Mesh** Simulation manager to the **Study 1** tab.

Do NOT copy the Mesh folder!

9. If symbols representing **Fixed-1** or **Force-1** (**:Per item: -6000 lbf:**) do not appear on the model, right-click their parent folders in the Simulation manager and from the pull-down menu select **Show All**.

10. At the bottom of the screen, right-click the **Study-1** tab and from the pop-up menu, select **Rename**.

11. On the Study *tab*, type the name of the new Study as: **DEFAULT Mesh** and press **[Enter]**. The Study name is updated on the study tab and in the Simulation manager tree. Once again, ignore the ⚠ and ⚠ symbols in the manager tree.

The method of creating a default size mesh for the *new* Study tab parallels that of the previous section. Therefore, try defining it on your own or use the following the steps.

12. Right-click the **Mesh** folder and select **Create Mesh…**

13. In the **Mesh** property manager, check ☑ **Mesh Parameters** to open this dialogue box. The current default mesh size should be 0.16846771 in. If any other value appears, click the **[Reset]** button below the sliding pointer scale to reset the default mesh size to the mid-scale value; slight round-off may occur.

14. Also in the ☑ **Mesh Parameters** dialogue box, select ⊙**Standard mesh**.

15. To discover another feature of the software, in the **Options** dialogue box, check ☑ **Run (solve) the analysis**. Checking this box causes the model to be meshed *and* solved in two consecutive steps.

16. Click **[OK]** ✓ to close the **Mesh** property manager. The model is re-meshed and the Solution is run automatically. Aside: Note the speed with which this solution is completed (about 3 seconds or less).

In the **Results** folder, briefly examine maximum magnitudes on plots of **Stress1 (-vonMises-)**, **Sigma-X (-X normal-)**, and **Displacement1 (-X disp-)**. Because a smaller mesh typically yields more accurate results, all values should *exceed* those of the previous **COARSE Mesh** Study.
[Record: max. von Mises stress, max. Sigma-X, and max. Displacement1 in Table 1]

Study Using High Quality Elements and FINE Mesh Size

Method 3 – Duplicating an Entire Study
Next, the Notched Bar example is solved a fourth time but, this time a fine size high quality mesh is used. However, the solution process differs from that of the preceding sections by introducing a third method for *duplicating* an entire Study.

Any previous studies can be used as the starting point *(except the DRAFT Mesh)* because the **Material, Fixtures, External Loads**, and **Results** folders are identical in each.

1. Beneath the graphics screen, right-click *any* Simulation Study tab. A pop-up menu opens as shown in Fig. 26. *CAUTION:* Do *not* select the **DRAFT Mesh-DEFAULT Size** tab. Why?

2. In the pop-up menu, select **Duplicate**. The **Define Study Name** window opens as shown in Fig. 27.

3. Highlight and delete the existing name in the **Study Name:** field and type **FINE Mesh** as the name of the new Study.

Figure 26 – Selecting the **Duplicate** command to produce an identical Study.

4. Click **[OK]** to close the **Define Study Name** window. A tab with the new Study name "**FINE Mesh**" is added beneath the graphics screen and an *identical copy* of the source Study appears in the Simulation manager tree.

Figure 27 – Defining a new **Study Name:** for a **Duplicate** Study.

The above process creates a new Study that is an *exact duplicate* of whatever study was selected in step 1 above, *including the prior mesh specification*. However, because the new Study is to use a **FINE** mesh, it is necessary to re-mesh the model.

5. Within Simulation manager, right-click **Mesh** and from the pull-down menu, select **Create Mesh...** A **Simulation** warning window opens with the message:

    "**Remeshing will delete the results for study: xxxx Mesh.**"
(Where, "xxxx" corresponds to either the COARSE or DEFAULT mesh selected in step 1).

6. Because it is desired to define a different mesh for the current Study, click **[OK]**. The **Mesh** property manager opens.

7. In the **Mesh Density** dialogue box, click-and-*drag* the **Mesh Factor** slide-control to **Fine** at the far right-end of the scale.

8. Check ✓ to open the ☑ **Mesh Parameters** dialogue box. Notice the mesh size is now (0.08423385 in), which is half as large as the default mesh indicated when the pointer is at the middle of the scale.

9. If the **DRAFT Mesh-DEFAULT Size** tab was erroneously selected in step 1, then open the **Advanced** dialogue box and clear the check "✓" from ☐ **Draft Quality Mesh**. Otherwise skip this step. If you are unsure, perform this step.

10. Click **[OK]** ✓ to close the **Mesh** property manager and the model is re-meshed.

In the Simulation manager, Fig. 28, notice that SolidWorks *warning* symbols and appear adjacent to the **Study Name** and the **Results** folders. If these symbols do not appear, simply move the cursor over these two names. Perhaps you noticed these symbols earlier in this example, but they were ignored at that time.

The meaning of these SolidWorks Simulation symbols is summarized below.

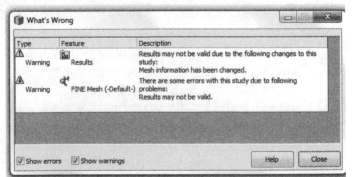

Figure 28 – SolidWorks Simulation manager tree showing one error and one warning.

Icon	Description
⚠	This icon indicates a warning in the Study. It appears adjacent to the Study name because previous calculations do not correspond to the revised mesh.
⊗	This icon indicates an error with a feature in the Simulation study tree. Because no feature errors exist, this symbol does not appear in Fig. 28.
⚠	A warning icon appears next to the **Results** or **Mesh** folders when the plots are not up to date. In this case, the **Results** are not valid for the new *fine* mesh.

To determine the source of these warnings, proceed as follows.

11. In the Simulation manager tree, right-click the **FINE Mesh (-Default-)** study name and from the pull-down menu, select **What's wrong?...** The **What's Wrong** window opens, as shown in Fig. 29, and displays two warning messages.

Figure 29 – Warning descriptions associated with the current Study.

Read all statements adjacent to each warning in the **What's Wrong** window shown in Fig. 29. In brief, both warnings are caused by the fact that the mesh was altered. As such, **Results** that were *duplicated* from a prior study, which was based on a different mesh, are no longer valid. Thus, these warnings serve to remind users that a new Solution must be run corresponding to the new mesh.

12. Click **[Close]** to exit the **What's Wrong** window.

13. To eliminate the above warnings, simply right-click the Study name, **FINE Mesh (-Default-)** and from the pull-down menu, select **Run**. Observe the slightly increased time required to complete this solution (8 to 10 seconds).

*[Record: max. von Mises stress, max. Sigma-X, and max. Displacement1 in Table 1]***** An image of the solution for σ_x appears in Fig. 30.

Study Using High Quality Elements and MESH CONTROL

Perhaps the *most important* approach to refining mesh size is that of applying *mesh control*, which is investigated in this section. By this point in the example it is evident that a smaller mesh results in improved approximations of stress in a model. However, the approach of using a progressively smaller and smaller mesh size results in significant

Figure 30 – "Boxed" areas denote regions where *inefficient* use is made of a **Fine** size mesh because stress is nearly uniform in these regions of the model.

computational inefficiency during the solution process. For example, when the **Fine** mesh in Fig. 30 is applied to the entire model, consider the large number of equations solved in "boxed" regions of the model where stress is nearly uniform. A fine mesh is *un*necessary where *stress variation is minimal*.

Use of *mesh control* allows the user to manage element size on selected entities of the model, such as **Faces**, **Edges**, **Vertices**, or **Reference Points**. Controlling mesh size makes it possible to specify a smaller mesh only in selected regions of high stress *gradient*, such as near the notch, while simultaneously using a significantly larger mesh in regions where stress distribution is relatively uniform such as the boxed regions on the model in Fig. 30. Locating local regions of high stress at the start of an analysis is easily accomplished by using a default size mesh or even a draft quality mesh.

For the above reasons, the Notched Bar example is solved again. However, this time *mesh control* is applied only in the vicinity of the "notch." To most effectively demonstrate the true power of this method, **MESH CONTROL** is used in conjunction with a **COARSE** mesh. Although any of the three previous methods can be used to produce this study, it is most informative to use the *duplicate* method. When using this approach, however, it is important to note that **MESH CONTROL** must be applied to the *desired "original" mesh*. Thus, in the following steps a **COARSE** mesh is selected as the starting point for this analysis. The procedure below outlines steps for applying *mesh control* to selected parts of the model.

1. At bottom of the screen, right-click *only* the Simulation Study tab named **COARSE Mesh**. In the pop-up menu choose **Duplicate** as shown in Fig. 31.

2. In the **Define Study Name** window, delete the old name and type: **MESH CONTROL**, then click **[OK]**. The new study appears in the Simulation manager tree and a new tab is created beneath the graphics screen.

Figure 31 – Duplicating an entire Study.

Because everything in this new Study, except the mesh, is to remain as previously defined, the following steps introduce use of *mesh control*.

3. Right-click the **Mesh** folder and from the pull-down menu, select **Apply Mesh Control...** The **Mesh Control** property manager opens as illustrated in Fig. 32.

As noted above, an advantage of using mesh control is that it can be applied to local regions on a model. In the following steps, only portions of the model in the vicinity of the "notch" are selected due to the high stress gradient existing there.

4. In the **Selected Entities** dialogue box, the **Faces, Edges, Vertices, Reference Points, Components for Mesh Control** field is highlighted (light blue) indicating it is active.

Figure 32 – Selections made in the **Mesh Control** property manager.

5. Move the cursor onto the model and *at both the top and bottom notches*, select the two curved **Edges** and one **Face** at each notch as illustrated in Fig. 33. **Edge<1>**, **Edge<2>**, **Edge<3>**, **Edge<4>**, and **Face<1>**, **Face<2>** appear in the highlighted field of Fig. 32 in the order selected by the user.

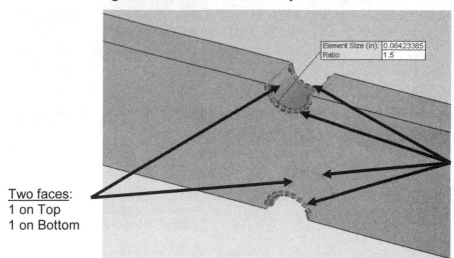

Figure 33 – Edges and faces selected for application of **mesh control** at top and bottom notches. Mesh control symbols appear on the selected entities.

At this point, no changes are made to default values in the **Mesh Parameters** dialogue box. However, the three fields in this dialogue box are explained below.

Unit: The ⌷ **Unit** field should be set to **in** (if not already selected).

Element Size: Initial element size (0.08423385 in) corresponds to the system default mesh size as verified by the pointer location on the **Mesh Factor** slider-scale. However, because the **COARSE** mesh study was duplicated, the software applies a **COARSE** mesh to all regions of the model *except* where mesh control is applied. Mesh control is based on a default size mesh. *Thus, do **not** change the slider setting.*

Ratio: a/b = 1.5 This value controls the increase of element size from one layer of elements to the next as elements radiate away from the selected entities. EXAMPLE: if "E" = the default element size, then subsequent layers of elements increase in size according to the progression: E, $E*(a/b)$, $E*(a/b)^2$, ... $E*(a/b)^n$ until $E \geq$ the default element size used on the remainder of the model.

Steps below complete the mesh definition process.

6. Click **[OK]** ✓ to close the **Mesh Control** property manager.

Unlike previous Studies, notice that a new mesh is not immediately generated on the model. Also notice that warnings symbols appear adjacent to the ⚠ Study name and on the ⚠ **Mesh** and ⚠ **Results** folders. Proceed as follows to update the mesh and run the solution.

7. Right-click the **Mesh** folder and from the pull-down menu, select **Mesh and Run**. Note the faster speed with which this solution is completed.

The model is re-meshed. An enlarged view of mesh and stress σ_x near the notches is shown in Fig. 34.

8. Click "+" adjacent to the **Mesh** folder and a **Mesh Controls** icon appears. Click the "+" adjacent to **Mesh Controls** and a Control-1 icon appears in the Simulation manager tree.

Figure 34 – View of mesh size altered by application of **Mesh Control** in the notch region.

Briefly examine plots in the **Results** folder.
[Record: max. von Mises stress, max. Sigma-X, and max. Displacement1 in Table 1]

To gain greater insight into factors affecting **Mesh Control**, make the mesh changes outlined below.

9. In the Simulation manager tree, right-click the Control-1 icon and from the pull-down menu select **Edit Definition…** The **Mesh Control** property manager opens as previously shown in Fig. 32. Notice that previously selected edges and faces remain unchanged.

10. In the **Mesh Parameters** dialogue box change the **a/b Ratio** value to **1.2**.

This action results in a smaller mesh adjacent to the notch and a decrease of size changes from one element layer to the next. Simultaneously the number of layers between the smallest and largest elements increases as is illustrated in Fig. 35.

11. Click **[OK]** ✓ to close the **Mesh Control** property manager.

Figure 35 – **Mesh Control** using a smaller **Ratio a/b = 1.2** results in a more gradual transition from small to large mesh size.

Because the mesh is being changed again, observe the *Warning* symbols adjacent to the Study name ⚠ **MESH CONTROL (-Default-)**, the ⚠ **Mesh** folder, and the ⚠ **Results** folder in Fig. 36. To determine the source of these warnings, proceed as follows.

12. Right-click the **MESH CONTROL (-Default-)** Study name in the Simulation manager tree and from the pull-down menu, select **What's wrong?...** The **What's Wrong** window opens, as shown in Fig. 37, and displays all three warnings.

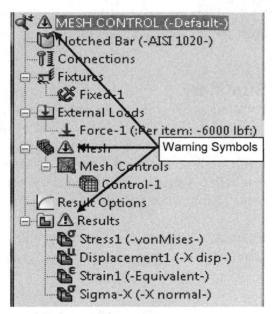

Figure 36 - SolidWorks Simulation Manager tree showing two errors and a warning.

Read statements adjacent to each warning in the **What's Wrong** window. Because all warning statements are related to a change of the mesh control **Ratio** to **a/b = 1.2**, results of the previous Solution, based on the **a/b = 1.5** ratio, are rendered invalid and a new Solution must be run.

Type	Feature	Description
⚠ Warning	🔲 Mesh	Mesh information is not current. Model might have been updated or mesh element size/tolerance was modified.
⚠ Warning	📖 Results	Results may not be valid due to the following changes to this study: Mesh information has been changed.
⚠ Warning	⚡ MESH CONTROL (-Default-)	There are some errors with this study due to following problems: Mesh information has been changed. Results may not be valid.

✓ Show errors ✓ Show warnings   [Help] [Close]

Figure 37 – Error and warning descriptions associated with the current study.

Thus, it is only necessary to run a new Solution, corresponding to the revised *mesh control*. Proceed as follows.

13. Click **[Close]** to dismiss the **What's Wrong** window.

14. In the Simulation manager, right-click the **Mesh** folder and from the pull-down menu, select **Mesh and Run**. Once again notice the faster speed with which this solution is completed.

The model is re-meshed automatically and a new solution is run. This new Solution corresponds to the revised *mesh control* previously shown in Fig. 35.

Summary

By using *mesh control*, a small mesh can be created in user selected areas of high stress gradient while a larger mesh is used in other regions of the model. Thus, mesh control results in efficient use of computational facilities, while simultaneously yielding good results in user specified regions. It is interesting to note that, although *mesh control* resulted in a smaller mesh near the notch for the most recent study, a larger stress was actually found for a **Ratio** of **a/b = 1.5**.

Examine stress and displacement values recorded in Table 1. What trends are noticed for changes in stress magnitude as mesh size decreases? Are these results expected?

Table 1 – Comparison of Stress and Displacement Results for Various Meshes

Mesh Type & Size	Maximum vonMises Stress (psi)	Maximum Sigma-X (psi)	Maximum Displacement X-Direction (in)
DRAFT Mesh DEFAULT size			
HIGH Quality Mesh COARSE size			
HIGH Quality Mesh DEFAULT size			
HIGH Quality Mesh FINE size			
High Quality Mesh MESH CONTROL **a/b=1.5** on COARSE size mesh			

Results Analysis

Now that the Notched Bar model has been evaluated using five different meshes, the significance of the resulting solutions is investigated below. Begin by creating a *simultaneous* display of results from the Draft quality mesh and from the three Studies for which high quality, *global* element sizes were changed. In other words, ignore *mesh control* solutions at this time. To open multiple viewports, proceed as follows. SolidWorks users may be familiar with this software feature and are encouraged to proceed on their own. However, all necessary steps are outlined on the following pages.

Create Multiple Viewports

1. In the Main menu, at top of screen, click **Window**, circled in Fig. 38. This figure also shows the pull-down menu and the options available for displaying multiple window configurations.

2. Move the cursor onto **Viewport** and from the second-level pull-down menu, select **Four View**. See Fig. 38.

Figure 38 – Menu selections used to open multiple viewports.

The graphics area immediately displays **Front**, **Left**, **Trimetric**, and **Top** views of the current screen image, Fig. 39, (clockwise starting at the top left). This image is altered in the following steps to enable side-by-side comparisons of the four solutions.

Figure 39 – The default display shows the currently active model in Front, Top, Trimetric, and Top views.

Various plots can be displayed in these viewports in keeping with user preferences. To facilitate the discussion below, it is suggested that the following order be used to place images in the four viewports. Begin by placing a plot of vonMises stress found using the **DRAFT** quality mesh in the upper left-hand viewport. The following steps outline this procedure.

3. Click anywhere in the upper left-hand viewport (labeled "**A**" in Fig. 40). This action activates the viewport.

4. Select the Simulation Study tab labeled **DRAFT Mesh-DEFAULT Size**. This action displays its contents in the Simulation manager tree.

Figure 40 – Multiple viewports facilitate comparison of results from multiple different studies or different aspects of a model within a single study

5. Next, click "+" adjacent to the **Results** folder to display its contents (if not already displayed).

6. Finally double-click **Stress1 (-vonMises-)** and the contents of that plot are displayed in viewport "**A**" as illustrated in Fig. 40. Proceed to following steps.

NOTE 1: As you proceed below do not be concerned if your *view* of the model differs from that shown. Desired views can be adjusted later based upon user preferences.

NOTE 2: Viewport labels **A**, **B**, **C**, **D** are added to Fig. 40 to facilitate discussion. These letters do not appear on the SolidWorks screen image.

7. Click in viewport **B** and repeat steps 3 to 6 for the von Mises stress plot of the **COARSE Mesh** size.

8. Click in viewport **C** and repeat steps 3 to 6 for the von Mises stress plot of the **DEFAULT Mesh** size.

9. Finally, click in viewport **D** and repeat steps 3 to 6 for the von Mises stress plot of the **FINE Mesh** study. This display may take longer to appear due to more data associated with the fine mesh.

Now that results of the four global element size studies are displayed in individual viewports, the screen images can be adjusted according to user preferences. Typically the choice of view depends upon those aspects that are of primary importance to a study. For example, a close-up view of the notch might be used to replace one, or all, of the views shown in Fig. 40. Viewports **A**, **B**, **C**, and **D** show trimetric views of each meshed model. To obtain these views, repeat step 10 as necessary.

10. Click inside each viewport and select the Trimetric icon. Then use the pan, and zoom options to best display desired results. A trimetric view is selected because it provides a good overview of mesh size, boundary conditions, and stress magnitudes important to this analysis.

When finished, your graphics screen should look *similar* to Fig. 40.

What Can Be Learned From This Example?

Most of the primary goals of this analysis were encountered and mastered as you worked through the example itself. Those goals included: (a) knowing 'when,' 'how,' and 'why' a model should be *defeatured*, (b) using the *copy* or *duplicate* feature to quickly create new plots and/or entire new studies; (c) using multiple *viewports* to facilitate results comparisons, and, (d) most important, using *global mesh refinement* and *local mesh control* as analysis refinement tools. One final topic, the importance of *verifying convergence to a solution* is discussed in the following "Analysis Insight" section.

Other Uses of the Copy Feature

The *copy* feature within SolidWorks Simulation is not limited to creating new studies in which mesh size change is the only analysis variable. In fact, any variable of a finite element analysis can be the central focus in a multiple solution study. For example, other variables that could be altered include, but are not limited to: material properties, loads, fixtures, part-to-part contact conditions, or modifications to model geometry.

Analysis Insight – Solution Convergence

The importance of mesh refinement and mesh control as part of a complete finite element analysis cannot be overstated! A single solution to a finite element analysis provides only one snapshot of what a possible solution to a problem might be. *One primary reason for performing multiple analyses is to determine whether or not a study converges to an acceptable solution.*

To determine *convergence*, it is possible to examine either displacement results or stress results. From the Introduction to this text, recall that displacements within the model are the primary unknowns in a finite element analysis. Next, strains are calculated from displacements, and finally, stresses are computed from strains. Because displacements are the first link in the solution chain, they are usually a better indicator of convergence to a solution as element size is altered. For the sake of brevity, only vonMises stress results and X-displacement results corresponding to changes of *global* mesh size are compared when testing for convergence.

To relate this discussion to the Notched Bar, **Table 2** summarizes results of all analyses developed in this example. These results should compare well with results you recorded in **Table 1**. Von Mises stress and X-displacement data in **Table 2** are obtained from Fig. 40 and various mesh plots created throughout this study.

Information about the number of nodes and elements in each mesh is obtained by right-clicking each **Mesh** folder and selecting **Details…** This procedure was first demonstrated in Chapter 1.

In **Table 2**, focus attention only on von Mises stress and X-displacement results corresponding to COARSE, DEFAULT, and FINE mesh sizes highlighted in the middle three rows of the table. These three rows show how stress magnitude increases as mesh size varies from 'coarse' to 'default' to 'fine.' Casual observation of magnitudes listed in the von Mises stress column reveals an increase of stress as the number of elements increases. This result is expected due to the ability of smaller elements to better model stress magnitudes in increasingly smaller regions of high stress gradient. High stress gradients typically occur around geometric discontinuities in a part and result in stress concentrations.

This finding might lead one to expect that as element size gets smaller and smaller, the stress magnitudes will continue to grow larger and larger. *However, in a properly constructed study quite the opposite is true!* In an analysis that is *converging* to a solution, stress results should tend to *level off* and approach some limiting value. That limiting value represents the best approximation to maximum stress in the model. Thus, the reason that *multiple solutions* should be a standard part of every finite element analysis is to determine whether or not results *converge to a solution.*

Analysis Insight (continued)

TABLE 2 – Summary of Results from the Notched-Bar Study

Mesh	No. Nodes	No. Elements	vonMises Stress (psi)	Sigma-X (psi)	Displacement X-Direction (in)
DRAFT Quality DEFALT size	1,606	6,444	15,403	15,761	0.001874
HIGH Quality COARSE size	1,902	1,027	20,914	23,119	0.001894
HIGH Quality DEFAULT size	10,627	6,444	22,694	24,637	0.001897
HIGH Quality FINE size	80,860	54,689	24,473	25,736	0.001899
HIGH Quality MESH CONTROL	8,888	5,531	24,472	25,355	0.001897

In Fig. 41, von Mises *stress* magnitudes are plotted against an increasing number of elements applied to the model. A logarithmic cure fit was used with an R-squared coefficient of $R^2 = 0.9981$, which indicates a very good fit to the data. The graph reveals that as the number of elements increases, maximum stress magnitude begins to level off. And, when stress magnitudes approach a limiting value, this is an indicator that the FEA solution is converging to a good approximation of the actual value.

Figure 41 – Convergence check using vonMises stress as a measure.

If analysis were stopped after using only the 'default' size mesh, then maximum von Mises stress would have been underestimated by at least (24,473 – 22,694) = 1,779 psi. Do you think a higher stress would be attained with further mesh refinement?

Analysis Insight (continued)

Displacement versus the number of elements is examined next to determine whether or not it provides a better indication of convergence to a solution than does the von Mises stress. Data in the displacement column of **Table 2** reveals an upward trend as the number of elements increases (i.e., as global mesh size gets smaller).

When plotted, axial displacement versus number of elements yields the graph shown in Fig. 42. Once again a logarithmic curve fit was applied to the data resulting in the curved line shown. In either case, a "leveling off" of results (i.e., convergence to a maximum displacement value) is indicative that the solution is converging.

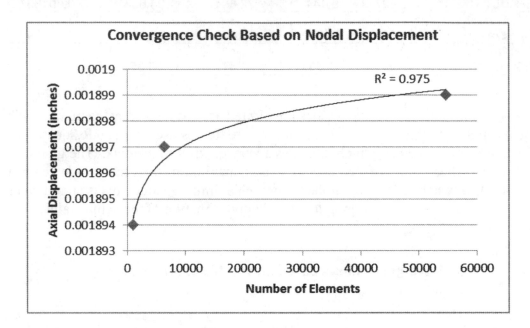

Figure 42 – Convergence check using displacement as a measure.

Summary:
The *need* to conduct more than a single finite element analysis is demonstrated in this example. The *reason* for conducting more than one analysis is to determine whether or not an analysis is approaching a limiting value. This is known as a convergence check.

Aside #1:
Results of the **Draft** quality mesh are *excluded* from the above discussion because it is most revealing to compare results obtained using the same *type* of mesh while only varying mesh size. All meshes used in the above comparison used **High** quality elements, i.e., solid tetrahedral elements with mid-side nodes.

Aside #2:
Comparison of displacement results for **Draft** quality and **High** quality meshes of the *same* size (i.e., default size), shown in **Table 1** and **2**, confirm that a **Draft** quality mesh is "stiffer" than a **High** quality mesh because a smaller displacement results for the **Draft** quality mesh.

Aside #3:

Despite the emphasis on *global* mesh size refinement in this example (i.e., changing the size of *all* elements), perhaps the most important means for controlling mesh size is use of *mesh control*. Mesh control can be applied to a specific area of interest on a *local* basis and yet provides accurate results at significantly lower computational overhead. For example, comparing values in **Table 2** reveals that the mesh control approach uses approximately 9.8 times fewer elements than does a globally **Fine** mesh, yet maximum von Mises stress results differ by less than 1.5%. Consider the computational savings realized by using *mesh control* in an extremely large and complex model.

Comparison of Classical and FEA Results

The importance of checking finite element results is emphasized throughout this text. Therefore, in keeping with this premise, it is appropriate to conclude this example with a classical analytical check. The notched bar model of Fig. 2 is repeated below.

R = notch radius = 0.25 in.

h = height (top to bottom) = 1.50 in

d = h – 2*R = 1.50 – 2*0.25 = 1.00 in (dimension at the reduced cross-section)

t = bar thickness = 0.50 in

F = applied force = 6000 lb

Figure 2 (repeated) – Dimensioned image of notched bar.

Nominal stress at the reduced cross-section in the Notched Bar:

$$\sigma_x = \frac{F}{A} = \frac{F}{d*t} = \frac{6000}{1*0.5} = 12000 \; psi$$

Geometric stress concentration factor: where: R/d = 0.25/1.00 = 0.25
                                                    h/d = 1.50/1.00 = 1.50

$K_t = 2.1$ (approximate) ←   From stress concentration factor chart found in a standard machine design textbook.

<u>Maximum stress in the Notched Bar:</u>

$(\sigma_x)_{max} = K_t * \sigma_x = 2.1 * 12000 = 25200$ psi

<u>Percent difference compared to the FINE Mesh:</u>

% Difference = [(SolidWorks Simulation – Classic)/ (SolidWorks Simulation)] * 100

% Difference = [(25736 – 25200)/(25736)] * 100 = 2.08%

Note that Sigma-X (σ_x) is used for comparison purposes since stress concentration factor charts depend upon axial stress as opposed to vonMises stress. The above calculations provide a good check of finite element results. Note that resultant stress ($\sigma_x)_{max}$ predicted by the *mesh control* model yields a 0.61 % difference.

Logging Out of the Current Analysis

This concludes analysis of a notched bar model where the effect of varying mesh size upon stress magnitude was investigated. It is suggested that this file *not* be saved. Proceed as follows.

1. On the **Main Menu**, click **File** followed by choosing **Close**.

2. The **SolidWorks** window opens in Fig. 43, and provides the options of either saving the current analysis or not. Select **[Don't Save]**.

Figure 43 – **SolidWorks** window prompts users to either save changes or not.

EXERCISES

End of chapter exercises are intended to provide additional practice using principles introduced in the current chapter plus capabilities mastered in preceding chapters. Most exercises include multiple parts. In an academic setting, it is likely that parts of problems will be assigned or modified to suit specific course goals.

╫ *Designates problems that introduce new concepts. Solution guidance is provided for these problems.*

EXERCISE 1 – Effect of Mesh Size at Hole Location

A rectangular bar with a centrally drilled hole is illustrated in Fig. E3-1. The bar is supported **(Fixed/immovable)** at its left-end and subject to an axial, tensile force of 370 kN applied normal to its opposite end. The bar is made from 2018 aluminum alloy. Open the file: **Plate With Hole 3-1**.

Figure E3-1 – Aluminum bar with central hole subject to an axial force. A geometric discontinuity is present in the form of the 40 mm diameter hole. **(All dimensions in mm)**

- Material: **2018 Alloy** aluminum (Use S.I. units)

- Mesh: In the **Mesh** property manager, select a ⊙ **Standard mesh**. High quality tetrahedral elements are to be used. Use three different meshes as specified in parts (a, c, and d) below.

- Fixture: **Fixed (**Immovable) restraint applied to left end of the model.

- External Load: **370 kN** applied normal to the right-end causing tension in the bar.

Develop a finite element model that includes: material specification, fixtures, external loads, mesh generation, and solution as specified below. For this analysis use high quality meshes of the sizes specified below.

Determine the following:

a. Using a *default* size mesh, create a plot of the *most appropriate stress* to permit comparison of stress magnitude adjacent to the hole with that predicted by classical equations for stress computed at the same location. See part (e) for calculation of classical results. Include fixtures, external load, and the mesh on this plot.

b. Use the **Probe** feature to produce a graph of the *most appropriate stress* from the top (or bottom) edge of the bar to the closest edge of the central hole. Because a straight path may not be available, choose both corner and mid-side nodes in as straight a line as possible. Include a descriptive title, axis labels, and your name on this graph.

c. Repeat part (b) after resetting the mesh size to *fine*. Use the copy or duplicate feature to save time creating this study.

d. Repeat part (b) a third time after resetting the mesh size by applying *mesh control* around both edges and the inner surface of the hole. Use a mesh control setting: **Ratio a/b = 1.5**. Also use the copy or duplicate feature to save time creating this study.

e. Use classical equations and available stress concentration factor charts to manually compute maximum stress at the hole.

f. Compare maximum stress results predicted using the three different meshes with that predicted by classical stress equations. Compute the percent difference for each comparison using equation [1].

$$\% \text{ difference} = \frac{(\text{FEA result - classical result})}{\text{FEA result}} *100 = \qquad [1]$$

g. Comment upon which FEA results are in best agreement with predictions of the classical equations? Which method of mesh refinement is usually preferred and why?

h. Based upon results for the maximum *appropriate stress* in the model, is the material Yield Strength exceeded? If "yes," what does theory predict will be the outcome in a ductile material such as Aluminum used in this example? When answering this question, also consider the magnitude of nominal stress computed using classical equations applied at the hole in part (e) above, but *without* applying the stress concentration factor.

EXERCISE 2 - Effect of Mesh Size at Shaft Fillet

A cylindrical rod changes diameter at the fillet shown in the Fig. E3-2. It is well known that generous fillets are beneficial in reducing stress concentration at changes of cross-section. This is particularly important because the bar in question is made from a relatively brittle material, gray cast iron, and the fillet radius is not very large. As such, the rod may be subject to significant effects of stress concentration at the geometric discontinuity. Consider the rod supported **(Immovable/Fixed)** at its left-end and subject to a 1,200 lb tensile force applied to its opposite end.

Open the file: **Shaft with Fillet 3-2**.

- Material: **Gray Cast Iron** (Use English units)

- Mesh: In the **Mesh** property manager, select a ⊙ **Standard mesh**. High quality tetrahedral elements result. Use three different meshes as specified below.

- Fixture: **Fixed/ Immovable** applied to left end of shaft.

- External Load: 1,200 lb applied normal to the right-end causing tension in the bar.

Figure E3-2 – Gray Cast Iron cylindrical rod subject to an axial tensile load of 1,200 lb. **(Dimensions shown in inches)**

Determine the following:

Develop a finite element model that includes: material specification, fixtures, applied external load, mesh generation (as specified below), and solution.

NOTE: This example is one where it is *not* appropriate to defeature the model because deleting the fillet radius would cause a dramatic increase of stress at the change of shaft diameter. In fact, a sharp fillet would probably result in stress values continuing to increase as the mesh size gets smaller. A sharp fillet would result in a solution where *divergence* from a solution rather than *convergence* to a solution would occur.

    a. Develop a finite element model using a default size, high quality mesh. For this mesh, perform the following:

- Create a stress contour plot of the *most appropriate stress* to permit comparison of maximum stress magnitude in the vicinity of the fillet with that predicted by classical stress equations computed at the same location. Include a mesh on this plot. See part (d) for classical stress calculations.

- Use the **Probe** feature to produce a graph of the *most appropriate stress* commencing approximately ¾-in to the right of the fillet and progressing along the surface of the model, in as near a straight-line as possible, through the fillet area up to the outside diameter (large diameter) of the left segment of the shaft. Choose both corner and mid-side nodes. Include your name, a descriptive title, and axis labels on this graph.

b. Repeat part (a) after resetting the mesh size to fine. Use the copy or duplicate feature to save time creating this study.

c. Repeat part (a) a third time beginning with the default size mesh. Use the copy or duplicate feature to save time creating this study. Then, alter the mesh by applying mesh control on the fillet. Use a mesh control ratio setting of: **Ratio a/b = 1.15**. Zoom in on the mesh when using the **Probe** feature to select nodes.

d. Use classical equations and available stress concentration factor charts to compute maximum stress at the fillet.

e. Compare results predicted using the three different meshes with that predicted by classical stress equations; clearly label each calculation. Compute the percent difference for each comparison using equation [1] (repeated below).

$$\% \text{ difference} = \frac{(\text{FEA result - classical result})}{\text{FEA result}} * 100 = \qquad [1]$$

f. Determine the Safety Factor, or lack thereof at the change of cross-section (i.e., at the fillet). Create a plot showing regions (if any) of the model with a Safety Factor less than two. NOTE: Cast iron, being a brittle material, has an ultimate strength rather than a yield strength. Account for this fact when selecting safety factor failure criteria. Name the failure criteria that was used.

g. Comment upon which FEA results are in best agreement with predictions of the classical equations? Based on your comparison, which method of mesh refinement is preferred and why?

h. For users conversant with modifying solid models in SolidWorks, proceed to alter the fillet radius at the change of cross-section to a radius "r" equal to half the difference of the two shaft sizes [where: r = (D – d)/2] and repeat parts assigned by your instructor. Report the amount by which stress at the fillet is reduced.

⫟ EXERCISE 3 - Stress in a Lawn Mower Blade due to Centrifugal Force (Special Topics: Custom Material, Centrifugal Force, Soft Spring Supports)

Dimensions of a typical steel lawn mower blade are shown in Fig. E3-3. The density used for steel is 0.282 lb/in³. For simplicity, the blade is modeled as having a uniform cross section with a centrally drilled 0.50 inch diameter hole. The goal is to determine maximum stress in the blade in the vicinity of the central hole. The blade rotates at 2800 rpm and, hence, is subject to centrifugal force. Due to the highly variable nature of "mowing forces" acting on the blade (caused by different grass heights, rocks, small branches, or other debris), mowing forces normal to cutting edges are to be neglected.

Develop a finite element model that includes: material specification, applied centrifugal force, mesh generation *(use mesh control)*, and solution. Solution guidance is provided relative to the application of a *centrifugal load* and the need for *soft spring* supports.

Open the file: **Lawn Mower Blade**

- Material: Steel properties not found in the Material table (use properties below).
  See ***Custom Material Specification**, p# 2-41.*
  Elastic Modulus: **E = 30 000 000** psi
  Poisson's Ratio: **v = 0.292**
  Mass Density: **0.282** lb/in³
  Yield strength: **S$_y$ = 40 000** psi

- Mesh: In the **Mesh** property manager, select a ⊙ **Standard mesh**. High quality tetrahedral elements result. Use the default size mesh.

- Fixture: **Soft Spring** See Solution Guidance section below for application details.

- External Load: None. Load is due to internal centrifugal forces caused by the 2800 rpm rotational speed.

Figure E3-3 – Basic dimensions of a typical lawn mower blade.

Three aspects of the current exercise are unique. First, the blade is made from a custom material that is not available in the SolidWorks material library. Second, a centrifugal force is applied to load the model. Centrifugal force is not an *external* force. Instead it is a load caused due to the mass of the blade rotating at high speed. Guidance on these two topics is provided below. Third, no **Fixtures** are applied to this model. Therefore, **Soft Springs** must be applied to maintain equilibrium. [See Chapter #1, pg. 1-37 (bottom) and pg. 1-38].

Solution Guidance

<u>**Custom Material Specification**</u> (It is assumed that the user has started a Study in SolidWorks Simulation.)

The recommended way to create a custom material definition is to begin with a *similar* existing material and then change material properties as outlined below.

- Open the **Material** window by right-clicking the part folder named **Lawn Mower Blade**, then select **Apply/Edit Material...**

- Because the steel mower blade is similar to other steels, select **Plain Carbon Steel** by *right*-clicking it in the list of available steels. Then from the pop-up menu, select **Copy**.

- Continue to scroll down the materials list and *right*-click **Custom Materials**. From the pop-up menu, select **New Category**. A new file folder is opened.

- Right-click the **New Category** folder and from the pop-up menu, select **Paste**. This action opens a copy of the **Plain Carbon Steel** sub-folder beneath the **Custom Materials / New Category** folder. Click the **Plain Carbon Steel** folder to open it in the right half of the **Material** window.

- On the **Properties** tab, select **Units:** as **English (IPS)**.

- Change **Name:** to **Custom Mower Blade Steel** and ignore remaining fields in the upper portion of the window. The **Description:** and **Source:** fields also can be left blank.

- Within the **Property** column of the lower table notice that red, blue, and black colors are used to indicate different **Property** names. Red lettering indicates information *required* for a stress solution. Blue lettering indicates *desirable, but unnecessary* information. And, property names appearing in black *are not required* for the current solution. Replace red values with values listed beneath "Material" in the problem statement. Ignore blank fields and values listed in black type.

- Click **[Apply]** followed by **[Close]** to exit the **Material** window. A check "✓" appears on the **Lawn Mower Blade** part folder and the **Name:** assigned above appears adjacent to the part folder.

Solution Guidance (continued)

Centrifugal Force Specification

- Right-click **External Loads** and from the pull-down menu select **Centrifugal...** The **Centrifugal** property manager opens as shown in Fig. E3-4.

- In the **Selected Reference** dialogue box the **Axis, Edge, Cylindrical Face for Direction** field is highlighted (light blue). Select the *inside* cylindrical *surface* of the hole.

Figure E3-4 – Specifying a **Centrifugal** force on a mower blade rotating at 2800 RPM.

- Convert the blade rotation speed of 2800 rpm to **Hz** (i.e., cycles/second or rev/sec).

- In the **Centrifugal Force** dialogue box, verify that **Unit** is set to **English (IPS)** and in the **Angular Velocity** dialogue box, type the rotational speed calculated in the previous step *(the value shown in Fig. E3-4 is intentionally incorrect)*. After typing this value and pressing **[Enter]**, a red arrow appears at the hole to indicate the direction of rotation. If rotation is not in the direction of the cutting edges of the blade (sides with tapered edges), then check ☑ **Reverse Direction**. If rotation direction does not change, open the **Symbol Settings** dialogue box and toggle the ☑ **Show preview** check box 'on' and 'off.'

- Click **[OK]** ✓ to close the **Centrifugal** property manager. A **Centrifugal-1** symbol appears beneath the **External Loads** folder.

Rigid Body Motion Prevention (Soft Springs)

As noted above, **Soft Springs** must be applied to the model prior to running the solution. The lawn mower blade of this exercise is analogous to the model in Exercise #3 of Chapter 1. Therefore, follow the general discussion and procedures for applying **Soft Springs** beginning near the bottom of page 1-38 and forward, and apply them to this example.

Determine the following:

Develop a finite element model that includes: material specification, soft springs, applied external load (centrifugal force), mesh generation, and solution.

a. After running the solution and obtaining the **Results** folder, edit the **Stress1 (-vonMises-)** plot by doing the following.
    - In the ☑ **Deformed Shape** dialogue box, select ⊙ **True Scale**. You will know when the deformed shape is turned off because the centrifugal force arrow will again appear at the central hole.
    - Display **Discrete** fringes on the model
    - Display the **Mesh** on the model (use *mesh control* at the hole).
    - Turn on ☑ **Show max annotation**
    - Next, *copy* the **Stress1 (-vonMises-)** plot. Then change the copied plot to display **P1: 1st Principal Stress**. Also, re-name this plot to reflect its true identity.
    - Repeat the preceding steps, except create a plot of **SX: X Normal Stress**.

b. Zoom in on the central hole of the mower blade that displays a plot of **P1: First Principal Stress**. Then, use the **Probe** tool to select all corner and mid-side nodes beginning at the top or bottom inner edge of the hole and proceeding outward to the *nearest* edge of the blade. When selecting nodes, traverse the model in the straightest line possible. Create a graph of this data. Include a descriptive title, axis labels, and your name on the graph.

c. Repeat step (b) to produce a graph showing the variation of **SX: X Normal Stress** at the same location on the model.

d. Manually calculate the nominal tensile stress at the center of the blade caused by blade rotation. Include a labeled free-body diagram used as the basis of this calculation. Also, show the calculation used to determine maximum stress at the hole location. Include a reference to the stress concentration factor chart used to make this calculation. Label each calculation. Simplify the analysis as follows. *HINT:* For the manual calculation *only*, create a free-body diagram of half of the mower blade as shown in Fig. E3-5. Assume half of the blade mass is located at the center of mass "**G**."

Figure E3-5 – Suggested ½ model to be used as a free-body diagram for manual calculations *only*. Do *not* use the above model for finite element analysis.

e. Use equation [1], repeated below, to compare percent differences between manually calculated maximum stress value and **P1: First Principal Stress** and **SX: X Normal Stress** calculated using the finite element approach. Which of these finite element results is in best agreement with manually calculated results? Why?

$$\% \text{ difference} = \frac{(\text{FEA result - classical result})}{\text{FEA result}} * 100 = \qquad [1]$$

Textbook Problems

In addition to the above exercises, it is highly recommended that additional problems involving stress concentration and/or significant changes of part geometry be worked from a design of machine elements or mechanics of materials textbook. Textbook problems provide a great way to discover errors made in formulating a finite element analysis because they typically are well defined problems for which the solution is known. Typical textbook problems, if well defined in advance, make an excellent source of solutions for comparison.

NOTES:

CHAPTER #4

THIN AND THICK WALL PRESSURE VESSELS

This chapter investigates modeling of thin and thick wall pressure vessels. More importantly, however, the use of *shell* elements is introduced and guidelines are provided regarding their use as opposed to *solid* tetrahedral elements. When taken alone, thin and thick wall pressure vessel problems are solvable in a rather straight forward manner using classical stress equations. Therefore, advantages of the Finite Element Analysis approach are realized most when investigating stresses in more geometrically complex regions of a pressure vessel. These regions include, but are not limited to, nozzles, pipe connections, flanges, transition regions, and saddles or other support structures associated with pressure vessel design and installation. Many of these special situations can be handled by application of principles outlined in preceding chapters. Thus, the two examples of this chapter focus on introducing additional capabilities of the SolidWorks Simulation software rather than on pressure vessels per se'.

Learning Objectives

Upon completion of this example, users should be able to:

- Convert a solid model to a part modeled using *shell* elements, and use a *shell* mesh to model thin-wall parts (whether or not the part is a pressure vessel).

- Change *system default* settings to simplify analyses with common characteristics.

- Recognize geometry and load *symmetry* and use it to reduce model size, solution size, and computation time. Know when and how to apply *symmetry restraints*.

- Apply *section clipping* to enhance viewing of results.

- Apply uniform *pressure* loading.

THIN-WALL PRESSURE VESSEL (Using Shell Elements)

Thin-wall pressure vessels are found in many common applications. Included among them are carbonated beverage containers (aluminum cans and plastic bottles), aerosol cans used to dispense everything from paint to hair spray, hydraulic cylinders, SCUBA tanks, steam boilers, and water towers that provide pressure to public water systems.

Problem Statement

This example is based on a thin-wall cylindrical pressure vessel closed on both ends with hemispherical heads as illustrated in Figs.1 (a) and (b). Wall thickness t = 3 mm and inside diameter of the cylinder d_i = 144 mm. The vessel is made of **AISI 1045** cold drawn steel and is subject to internal pressure **P = 1.4 MPa**. Other dimensions are included in Fig. 1(a). Fig. 1(b) shows a typical application where a similar vessel serves as a propane gas supply tank for a remote building not served by natural gas.

Figure 1(a) – Basic dimensions of a thin-wall pressure vessel closed with hemispherical ends.

Figure 1(b) – Pressurized cylindrical fuel tank outside a garage/storage building.

The dividing line between thin and thick wall pressure vessels is defined differently in various machine design[1] and mechanics of materials texts. If wall thickness "t" falls in the range where $t \leq r_i/20$ to $t \leq r_i/5$, (where, r_i = cylinder inside radius) then the cylinder is considered a thin-wall pressure vessel. This determination must be made at the outset of any pressure vessel problem because choice of the appropriate set of classical equations depends upon whether wall thickness is classified as "thin" or "thick." By either of the above definitions, the current model can be considered a thin-wall pressure vessel since the minimum criteria yields: t = 3 mm ≤ (72 mm)/20. Another assumption applied to thin-wall pressure vessels is that the magnitude of tangential stress (σ_t), also known as "hoop" stress or "circumferential" stress is assumed *uniform* through the wall thickness.

Primary stresses in the cylindrical pressure vessel walls are given by:

Tangential stress:
$$\sigma_t = \frac{p * d_i}{2 * t} = \frac{(1.4e6 \frac{N}{m^2})(0.144 \, m)}{2(0.003 \, m)} = 33.6e6 \text{ Pa} \qquad [1]$$

Longitudinal stress:
$$\sigma_\ell = \frac{p * d_i}{4 * t} = \frac{1}{2}\sigma_t = \frac{1}{2}(33.6e6 \text{ Pa}) = 16.8e6 \text{ Pa} \qquad [2]$$
(for a closed-end cylinder)

Where: p = pressure (N/m^2) = 1.4 MPa
                 t = wall thickness (m) = 0.003 m
                 d_i = inside diameter (m) = 0.150 m – 2*0.003 m = 0.144 m

Note that $\sigma_t = 2 * \sigma_\ell$.

---

[1] Budynas, R.G., Nisbett, J.K., Shigley's Mechanical Engineering Design, use: $t \leq r_i/20$.
Collins, J.A., Mechanical Design of Machine Elements, uses: $t \leq 10\% * d = (.1)(2*r) = r_i/5$.

These two stresses are perpendicular to sides of a stress element aligned with and perpendicular to the longitudinal axis of the cylinder shown in Fig. 2. Because no shear stresses act on sides of the element shown in Fig. 2, σ_t and σ_ℓ are principal stresses. Finally, all stresses on the hemispherical ends are tangential stresses, but their magnitude is half of that in the cylindrical portion of the vessel, thus, this stress is denoted as σ'_t.

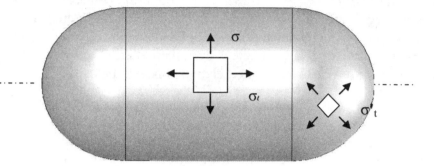

Figure 2 – Stress elements showing orientation of σ_t and σ_ℓ on the pressure vessel surface and on the hemispherical end. ($\sigma'_t = \frac{1}{2}\,\sigma_t$)

According to St. Venant's principle, normal stresses depicted in Fig. 2 are only valid at locations well removed from the junction between the cylindrical section and the hemispherical ends where end-conditions exist. Thus, to permit comparison with results of equations [1] and [2], the following finite element analysis focuses on stresses near the mid-section of the cylinder and on the hemispherical heads.

The next decision to be made is whether to use *solid* or *shell* elements for the finite element model. The guideline for this decision is quite different for a finite element analysis than that used to determine what set of classical equations should be used. For the current model, it is possible to use either *solid* or *shell* elements. Both would produce valid results. However, the selection of element type has a significant influence on the number of elements in a model, and hence upon solution time and memory requirements. Draft and high quality *shell* elements are pictured in Figs. 3 (a) and (b).

Figure 3 (a) – First-order (draft quality) triangular shell element.

Figure 3 (b) – Second-order shell element includes three additional mid-side nodes.

Shell elements are typically used for sheet metal and other thin parts. The principle used to decide what element type to use is that *shell* elements are applied when the thickness to span ratio is less than 0.05 (i.e., when one dimension is much smaller than the other two). For the current model, if the cylinder were laid out flat, the wall thickness (3 mm) divided by the lesser of the cylinder circumference ($\pi d_i^2/4 = \pi(144)^2/4 = 16286$ mm) or cylinder length (160 mm) yields: Span Ratio = 3 mm/160 mm = 0.01875 which is < 0.05.

A "rule of thumb" guideline to decide what element type to use is that *solid* elements are applied when two default size elements fit across the thickness of the part (i.e., across the part's minimum dimension). This guideline was applied to the curved beam in Chapter 2.

Shell elements look somewhat similar to solid elements except they are represented graphically as a single layer of elements, as if the mesh were drawn on a thin sheet of paper or the shell of an egg. Later images in this chapter will illustrate actual shell elements. However, because parts modeled using shell elements must have a finite thickness, a corresponding thickness is assigned as described later. The finite element analysis of a thin-wall pressure vessel using shell elements begins below.

1. Open SolidWorks by making the following selections. (*NOTE:* ">" is used to separate successive menu selections.)

Start>All Programs>SolidWorks 2013 (or) Click the **SolidWorks** icon on your screen.

2. From the main menu within SolidWorks select **File > Open...** Then browse to where your files are saved and open the SolidWorks Simulation file named **Thin Wall Pressure Vessel**. *It is strongly suggested that this model file be used for the current example rather than a user created pressure vessel model.*

Understanding System Default Settings

This section digresses from the problem solution to investigate methods of changing system default settings. Changing system default settings at the start of a Study can be advantageous because it can save time throughout the remainder of an analysis. For example, earlier problems required frequent specification of items such as mesh quality, units, and other attributes of an analysis. However, if these attributes are specified one time at the start of an analysis, they remain constant throughout the remainder of the problem. To practice altering some of these parameters, proceed as follows.

1. In the main menu, at top of screen, click **Simulation** to open a pull-down menu.

2. Near the bottom of this menu, select **Options...** The **Systems Options – General** window opens, a portion of which is shown in Fig. 4.

In this window, the **Systems Options** tab is initially selected as illustrated in Fig. 4. In the list at left of this window, the word General is highlighted to denote what settings are currently displayed. Because this Study focuses on use of a shell mesh, in the right half of this window, observe the default color scheme used to denote the bottom surface of shell elements. The text **Shell bottom face color** appears next to the system default color, orange, indicated adjacent to the arrow in Fig. 4. Before proceeding, observe other system default settings in this window. In particular, note that items such as ☑ **Show errors** and ☑ **Show warnings** are checked. These two items were introduced in the example of the previous chapter. Also, notice that ☑ **Show yield strength marker for vonMises plots** is checked thereby establishing it as a default display item on von Mises stress plots. Recall that this feature was used in the Safety Factor analysis of Chapter 2.

Figure 4 – Default settings beneath the **System Options** tab.
Default color of the bottom surface of a shell mesh is shown here.

3. At the top-left of this window, click the **Default Options** tab. Within this tab **Units** is highlighted (gray) to indicate it is selected in the list of options within the window. Only the right-half of this window is illustrated in Fig. 5. Within this window, the settings should appear as listed below; if not, change to the settings shown. Note that SI units are default within SolidWorks Simulation.

- Beneath **Unit System**, set default units to ⊙ **SI [MKS]**, if not already selected.

- Beneath **Units**, the unit of **Length/ Displacement**: should be set to **m** (meters).

- Adjacent to **Pressure/Stress:**, default units should be set to **N/m^2**. Other units do not pertain to this analysis and can be ignored.

Figure 5 – Selecting units to be applied throughout the analysis.

Specifying units as outlined above establishes a common set of units for an entire analysis. If, for example, your company or future employer uses English units exclusively, it would be a time-saver to reset default units accordingly. This could have been done for English unit examples worked in Chapters 1 and 2.

4. Return to the list of **Default Options** at the left of this window and click to select **Load/Fixture**, the **Default Options – Load/Fixture** window is displayed.

Brief examination of the right-half of the window (not shown) reveals that the **Symbol size** and **Symbol colors** for various types of loads and restraints can be specified here. Although no changes are made in this window, color-blind users may find it beneficial to alter default **Symbol colors** to suit their personal preferences.

5. Next, from the list of **Default Options** at the left of the window, click to select Mesh and verify that the system default settings in the right half of the window appear as shown in the list below.

Knowing the system default settings shown in this window and understanding that they remain unchanged unless altered by you, makes unnecessary many of the often repeated steps included in previous examples. For this reason, a brief explanation of each setting is included below. Reset any different settings to the default values listed below.

o **Mesh Quality** set to ⊙ **High**. *Reason*: A high quality mesh is recommended for most analyses and for models with curved surfaces. A draft quality mesh is typically used only for an initial Study where quick, approximate results are adequate.

o **Jacobian check** set to **[4 points]**. *Reason*: This option sets the number of integration points used when checking distortion levels in tetrahedral elements. The **4 points** selection is adequate for most analyses. Although **4** is the standard value, **6** points are automatically used for a shell mesh. Thus no change is necessary.

o Under **Mesher Settings**, clear the check mark from ☐ **Remesh failed parts with incompatible mesh**. *Reason*: This option is used where meshing difficulty occurs between bonded, solid parts by attempting to use incompatible mesh types. These instances are not encountered in this text.

o Set mesher type to ⊙ **Curvature based**. *Reason*: Beginning in 2011, a **Curvature based** mesh became the new default mesher within SolidWorks Simulation. It is somewhat slower, but is more accurate than a **Standard Mesh**. A Standard Mesh has been used thus far only because a more "orderly" mesh results.

o Clear the check mark from ☐ **Automatic transition**. *Reason*: This option automatically reduces element size at *every* change of geometry (fillets, rounds, holes, corners, etc.). Although this feature is nice, it unnecessarily complicates complex models by adding numerous nodes and elements in regions of little or no interest. It is preferable to apply **Mesh Control** (see Chapter 3) only in regions of interest.

o Clear the check mark from ☐ **Automatic trials for solids**. *Reason*: This option is primarily used in complex models where meshing difficulty is encountered. Its use is not demonstrated in this text.

o Check to select ☑ **Automatic re-alignment for non-composite shells**. *Reason*: This option causes the software to automatically reorient top and bottom surfaces of shell elements so that they are consistent within a model.

Ignore remaining options within this window.

6. Next, from the **Default Options** list at left of screen, select Results. Verify that the **Default solver** is set as ⊙ **FFEPlus**. *Reason:* **FFEPlus** is currently the fastest solver available in SolidWorks Simulation.
       •

7. Other options in this window direct analysis results to system default folders within SolidWorks. Unless other guidelines for file storage exist within your organization (university or company), use the default settings and ignore other settings in this window.

8. Return to the **Default Options** list and select Plot. The **Default Options - Plot** window opens. The right-half of this window is shown in Fig. 6.

9. Within this window, set **Fringe options:** to **Discrete**. This is a user preference, but is typically selected as **Discrete** in this text due to enhanced image characteristics when printed in black, white, and gray tones.

10. Adjacent to **Boundary options:** select **Model** to show a black outline of the model. *Reason:* This option helps identify model boundaries when stress contour plots are viewed on complex shapes or where "clipping" is used. This selection is also a user preference.

11. Another user preference is whether or not to display results on the deformed or undeformed shape of the model. Although this text typically elects display of the undeformed model, accept the default choice ⊙ **Show results on deformed shape**. Changes will be made on a case by case basis.

Familiarize yourself with other settings within this window. Other settings should remain set to system defaults.

Figure 6 – The **Plot** window is used to specify display options for all plots.

12. Next, in the **Default Options** list, click Color Chart and briefly observe items the user can control regarding display characteristics of the color chart including its placement on the screen, its size, and the format of numbers listed adjacent to the chart. In the **Number format** box, select ⊙ **Scientific** and set **No. of decimal places:** to **3**. Make no other changes to default settings.

A nice feature about using the above capabilities is that every plot in the current and future studies can be produced with the same set of user selected settings. Pre-setting these parameters for all plots saves considerable time when a consistent set of plot characteristics is desired. However, using these capabilities does not preclude a user from altering characteristics of a particular plot at any point during a Study.

We next investigate default settings of all plots created during a Study.

13. Click the "+" sign adjacent to **Default Plots** (if not already selected) and a listing of system default plots appears as shown on the *left*-side of Fig. 7.

14. At the left of the screen, below the **Static Study Results** folder, click to highlight the *name* **Plot1**. As of this writing, selecting the icon adjacent to **Plot1** does not activate this selection. The current screen image appears in Fig. 7.

15. In the right-half of the window, beneath **Results type:** select **Nodal Stress** (if not already selected). This selection is most typical because it gives stress magnitudes at specific locations (i.e., at each node) on the model.

Figure 7 – Individual plots are pre-defined to indicate items and components to be plotted.

16. Observe that the default stress plot listed beneath **Results component:** is **VON: von Mises stress**. As noted in Chapter 2, von Mises stress represents the most complex state of stress as a single value. As such, its value is easily compared to material yield or ultimate strength to give an indication of the safety, or lack thereof, in a part. This reason alone justifies it as worthy of being designated a default plot.

17. Return to the list of plots at the left of the screen and click the *name* **Plot2**. In the right-half of the screen observe the **Results type:** is set to **Displacement** and the **Results component:** is set to **URES: Resultant Displacement**.

18. Finally, click the *name* **Plot3** and observe the default definition for the **Results type:** is **Elemental Strain** and **ESTRN: Equivalent Strain** is listed in the **Results component:** field. Strain results might prove useful for comparison with experimentally determined strain gage readings. This plot is rarely referenced in this text.

Contents of the three default plot folders are based on the assumption that most users are interested in magnitudes of vonMises stress, model displacement, and strain in the model. Although this is a logical assumption, this text focuses primarily on stress results.

If additional default plots are desired, they can be added now or in the future. To add an additional default plot, proceed as follows.

19. Right-click **Static Study Results** and from the pop-up menu, select **Add New Plot** as shown in Fig. 8. Immediately **Plot4** is added to the bottom of the current list. Define the contents of this new plot as follows.

20. In the right-side of the window, beneath **Results type:**, select **Nodal Stress** from the pull-down menu (if not already selected).

21. Beneath **Results component:**, select **P1: 1st Principal Stress**.

Figure 8 – Adding a new plot and including user information on all printed plots.

OBSERVATION:

Because the current Study involves analysis of stresses in the walls of a cylindrical pressure vessel, it is known in advance that tangential and longitudinal stresses will result. Further, it is well known that tangential stress (σ_t) and longitudinal stress (σ_ℓ) correspond to the first and second principal stresses (σ_1 and σ_2) respectively. Therefore, *if* a user were dealing with pressure vessel analysis on a routine basis, it would make sense to add plots of the first and second principal stresses to the *default* set of plots produced at the conclusion of every study. However, since that is not the case for future examples in this text, **Plot4** is deleted in the following step.

---

22. Right-click the *name* **Plot4** and from the pop-up menu, select **Delete**.

23. Click the **[OK]** button to close the **Default Options** window.

The above overview should provide sufficient insight so that users can access the **Default Options** window at the start of a Study to define characteristics they wish to apply.

CAUTION: As of this writing (SolidWorks Simulation 2013, Service Pack 2) *only some* of the above features function as described above. Some changes to the default settings may not take effect despite their being altered in the **Default Options** window.

Creating a Static Analysis Using Shell Elements

Because *shell* elements require special preparation of the model within SolidWorks, this section begins with a brief overview of the basic methods of creating models to which a *shell* mesh can be applied followed by a walk-through of the actual steps.

The process begins by creating the part model within SolidWorks. For the thin wall pressure vessel, the line sketch, shown in Fig. 9, provides a starting point. This sketch is revolved about the X-axis at which time a wall thickness of 3 mm is specified. Figs. 1(a), 2 and 10 show the completed model.

Figure 9 – Line sketch used to generate the solid model.

The three basic ways to create a *shell* model are described briefly below.

a. First, by definition parts created as sheet metal parts are considered 'thin' by their very nature. These parts are automatically modeled as *shell* elements as demonstrated in several end-of-chapter problems.

b. Second, solid models can be converted to *shell* elements by defining a "mid-surface" located between the inner and outer surfaces of a solid model. This method is illustrated in the current example; it is the most challenging method.

c. Finally, a solid body can be converted to a sheet metal part and then to a shell model. This approach is best adapted to moderately thick parts that contain multiple bends between adjacent surfaces. This method is relatively straight forward and interested users are referred to Simulation **Help** for information.

The numerous references to "sheet metal" above do *not* imply that parts must be made of sheet metal. Instead, "sheet metal" refers to specific capabilities within the drafting portion of SolidWorks that allow bends and other metal forming operations to be incorporated into the design of sheet metal parts. But, in SolidWorks *Simulation*, do not let the words, "sheet metal," be misleading. In Simulation, these words refer to how the part is modeled in SolidWorks rather than the material of which a part is made. Consider for example the outer surface of a cell phone or a lap-top computer case. Although made of plastic, these thin wall items can be modeled in SolidWorks as sheet metal, plastic parts, thin parts, or surface parts. Each of these modeling techniques can be converted to shell elements. One caution, however, is that a shell mesh does not apply to thin models made of *composite* materials. As implied by its name, a composite material is made of multiple different materials. These materials are typically fabricated in multiple layers, and hence their properties are not uniform through their thickness.

Converting a Solid Model to a Shell Model

The model on your screen should appear similar to Fig. 10. Notice that the process for converting from a solid model to a shell model begins within SolidWorks, not in the Simulation portion of the program.

However, before converting the solid model into a shell model, the model is simplified by making use of *symmetry*. The thin-wall, cylindrical pressure vessel pictured in Fig. 10 is clearly a theoretical, "textbook" model. The rationale for this statement is quite obvious because no visible means of support are shown for the model as are no openings to permit fluids to enter or exit the container. However, this somewhat artificial geometry permits examination of methods to deal with *symmetry* when it occurs in a problem.

Figure 10 – Thin wall pressure vessel. Only one axis of symmetry is shown.

Because vessel shape is symmetrical (geometric symmetry) *and* because the internal pressure is uniform (symmetric loading), it is possible to analyze only a portion of the model. The sketch in Fig. 9 and solid model in Fig. 11 reveal that the current model was intentionally centered about the coordinate system origin when it was built. The front, right, and top sketch planes, included in Fig. 11, aid in visualizing that the model can be divided into eight symmetrical pieces. Model symmetry can be used to save computer memory and computation time. Because this is a rather simple model, significant savings are not realized. However, consider the computational savings realized if symmetry is used to model half of a complete aircraft fuselage (a pressure vessel when in flight). The current example demonstrates how symmetry can and should be used in other finite element solutions. Also, *symmetry* boundary conditions are introduced in this example.

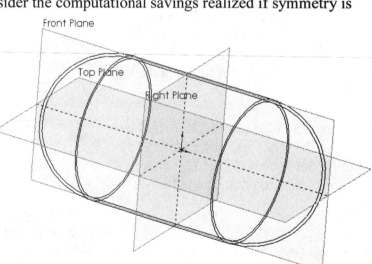

Figure 11 – Front, right, and top sketch planes introduced to show division of the model into symmetrical portions.

4-11

The following discussion outlines steps to convert a solid model into a shell model.

1. If **Axis1** does not appear on the model, from the main menu select **View**. Then, from the pull-down menu, select ⟨ Axes ⟩. **Axis1** should appear on the model as shown in Fig. 10.

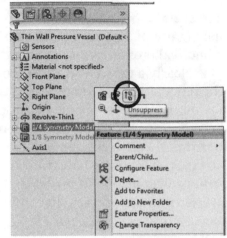

2. Near the bottom of the SolidWorks Feature manager tree, right-click the grayed-out **1/4 Symmetry Model**. This action causes the pop-up menu, shown in Fig.12, to open.

3. Above this menu select the **Unsuppress** icon circled in Fig. 12. Immediately ¼ of the model is displayed in the graphics area.

4. Repeat steps 2 and 3, but this time select the grayed-out **1/8 Symmetry Model** and **Unsuppress** it.

Figure 12 – **Unsupressing portions of** the symmetrical model in the SolidWorks feature manager.

The portion of the model selected for analysis should now appear as shown in Fig. 13. Note that virtually any fraction of the model could be selected, but the 1/8 model is useful for reasons described later.

Also, notice how the use of descriptive names in the SolidWorks feature manager facilitated identification and selection of desired model attributes in the preceding steps.

The next step is to create a mid-surface between the inner and outer faces of the solid model shown in Fig. 13. This new surface is used to create a shell mesh.

Figure 13 – A 1/8 model of the thin-wall pressure vessel. Symmetry is used to reduce analysis time and computer memory requirements.

5. From the main menu, select **Insert** and from the next two pull-down menus, select **Surface** ▶ followed by **Offset...** The **Offset Surface** property manager opens as shown in Fig. 15.

6. Placing the cursor in the light blue field of the **Offset parameters** dialogue box reveals the message, **Surface or Faces to Offset**.

7. Move the cursor onto the *inner surface* of the model and *right*-click. In the pop-up menu, choose **Select Tangency** and immediately a ghost image of an offset surface appears inside the model, see Fig. 14. Also, **Face<1>** and **Face<2>** appear in the highlighted field. **Face<1>** and **Face<2>** refer to the cylindrical and hemispherical surfaces. Both surfaces are selected because they are tangent to one another and because **Select Tangency** was activated earlier in this step.

8. If the offset surface is not clearly visible, increase the **Offset Distance** by typing **10** or **15** mm in the box located at the bottom of the **Offset parameters** dialogue box.

NOTE: It is also acceptable to select outside surfaces of the model. The only difference is that the offset surface appears outside of the model and locations of the surface in the steps below will be reversed.

Figure 14 – An **Offset Surface** appears inside the pressure vessel model.

9. Because a shell is to be located at the mid-surface of the model, in the **Offset Distance** field, shown in Fig. 15, type **1.50** mm, which is half of the 3 mm wall thickness. Click anywhere in the graphics screen to implement the 1.5 mm offset.

10. To visualize where the offset surface is located zoom in on any segment of the wall edge and toggle (i.e., multiple click) the ⬈ **Flip Offset Direction** button. When the surface appears midway *between* the inside and outside walls it is correct. NOTE: Due to its light color, the mid-surface may be very difficult or impossible to see when located *between* the surfaces.

11. Click **[OK]** ✓ to close the **Offset Surface** property manager. A line representing the mid-surface should appear on the model.

Figure 15 – Selecting offset surfaces and specifying the **Offset Distance**.

12. Near the top of the SolidWorks feature manager tree, click the "+" sign adjacent to **Solid Bodies(1)**. This reveals the **1/8 Symmetry Model** as the original *solid* body.

13. Immediately below the preceding selection, click the "+" sign adjacent to **Surface Bodies(1)**. This action reveals **Surface-Offset1**, which was created in steps 5 to 11.

CAUTION: In the following step do *NOT* select the **1/8 Symmetry Model** located near the bottom of the SolidWorks feature manager tree.

14. Next, return to **Solid Bodies(1)** and beneath it right-click on **1/8 Symmetry Model**. This action opens a pull-down menu. In the menu select ⊠ Delete Body…

15. The **Delete Body** property manager opens and shows **1/8 Symmetry Model** in the **Bodies to Delete** dialogue box.

16. Click **[OK]** ✓ to close the **Delete Body** property manager and the following things occur:

- The **Solid Bodies(1)** folder is removed from the SolidWorks Feature manager tree.

- The model appears as a thin surface (i.e., a *shell*) shown in Fig. 16.

- ⊠ **Body-Delete1** appears at the bottom of the SolidWorks feature manager.

The preceding steps appear to delete the original **Solid Bodies(1)** folder and its contents from the Feature manager tree. However, **Delete Body** is simply a feature in the SolidWorks tree and it can be restored as follows.

Figure 16 – The 1/8 symmetry model shown as a thin *shell*. (Compare with Fig. 13).

17. At the bottom of the SolidWorks Feature manager tree, right-click ⊠ **Body-Delete1** and from the icons located just above the pull-down menu, select the **Suppress** ⬇ icon. The solid body model is again displayed in the graphics area and in the SolidWorks Feature manager tree.

Because it is desired to complete this analysis using a shell model, un-do the preceding step as follows.

18. Once again right-click ⊠ **Body-Delete1** and, from the icons located just above the pull-down menu, select the **Unsuppress** ⬆ icon. The shell model reappears in the graphics area.

This concludes one of the three different procedures for converting a solid model to a shell model. The next section outlines the remainder of the shell analysis process.

Open a New Simulation Study

1. In the main menu, select **Simulation** and from the pull-down menu choose **Study...** Alternatively, on the **Simulation** tab, open the ▼**Study Advisor** and select the 🔍 **New Study** icon. A partial view of the **Study** property manager is shown in Fig. 17.

2. In the **Name** dialogue box, type **Pressure Vessel-Shell Study** as a descriptive name for the Study.

3. Verify that the **Type** dialogue box is set to **Static**.

4. Click **[OK]** ✓ to close the **Study** property manager. A warning ⚠ appears adjacent to the Study name. On your own, check **What's wrong?...**

Figure 17 – **Study** property manager showing Study **Name** and Study **Type** (**Static**).

Assign Material Properties

1. In the Simulation manager tree, right-click the ◇ **Thin Wall Pressure Vessel (-Thickness: not defined-)** folder and from the pull-down menu select **Apply/Edit Material...** The **Material** window opens. Observe that the part icon appears as a thin surface rather than the original solid part.

2. Beneath **SolidWorks Materials**, click the "+" sign adjacent to **Steel** and from the list of materials, select **AISI 1045 Steel, cold drawn.** Verify that **Units:** should be set to **SI – N/m^2 (Pa)**. Recall changing default units to **SI** and units of length to meters **m** at the beginning of this example. *If necessary, change **Units:** to **SI**.*

3. Click **[Apply]** followed by **[Close]** to close the **Material** window. A "✓" appears on the ◇ **Thin Wall Pressure Vessel** surface icon.

Define Shell Thickness

The software recognizes that the pressure vessel is modeled as a "thin" part due to the **Revolve-Thin1** command circled in the SolidWorks feature manager tree, Fig. 18. Wall thickness was specified when the original *solid* model was created in SolidWorks. However, because the solid model was converted to a shell model, the software requires the user to specify its thickness again because (a) the solid part along with its thickness was "deleted," and (b) because it might be desired to specify a different thickness for analysis. Also, if you checked the meaning of the warning ⚠ symbol in step 4 above, you discovered it was due to a missing thickness specification. To specify shell thickness, proceed as follows.

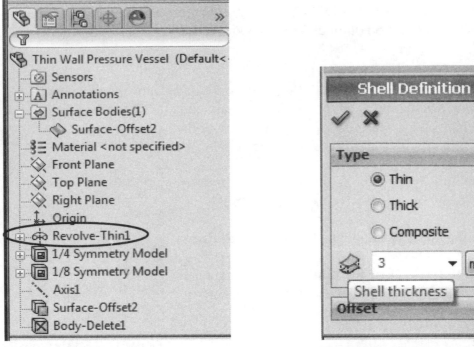

Figure 18 – SolidWorks Feature manager tree.

Figure 19 – Shell thickness is specified In the **Shell Definition** property manager.

1. Right-click [⌀ Thin Wall Pressure Vessel (-Thickness: not defined/Material: AISI 1045 Steel, cold drawn-)] in the Simulation manager. *Pass the cursor over this folder to display its entire name.* From the pop-up menu select **Edit Definition…** The **Shell Definition** property manager opens as shown in Fig. 19.

2. In the **Type** dialogue box, select ⊙ **Thin** (if not already selected).

3. Verify **Units** are set to **mm** and type **3** into the **Shell Thickness** box in Fig. 19.

4. Click **[OK]** ✓ to close the **Shell Definition** property manager. The error symbol ⚠ is removed from the Study name because shell thickness is now defined.

Assign Fixtures and External Loads

Symmetry Restraints Applied

As noted earlier, the pressure vessel is a symmetrical model as far as both geometry and loads are concerned. This section introduces symmetrical loading and fixture boundary conditions as outlined next. What is different, however, is that shell elements restrict both *translation* and *rotation* at node locations. This differs from solid tetrahedral elements that restricted only *translations* at node locations. The next step is to define restraints along "cut" edges of the model and loads (pressure) applied to its interior.

1. Right-click the **Fixtures** folder and from the pull-down menu select **Advanced Fixtures...** The **Fixture** property manager opens, but initially it will *not* look like Fig. 20 until step 4 is performed.

Before proceeding to the next step, observe *possible* movement of the generic rectangular model displayed in the **Example** dialogue box. This animation illustrates that two translations parallel to a selected reference plane are possible and one translation perpendicular to the same plane is also possible. However, for a *shell* model, restricting appropriate *edge* movement is essential to defining proper symmetry restraints.

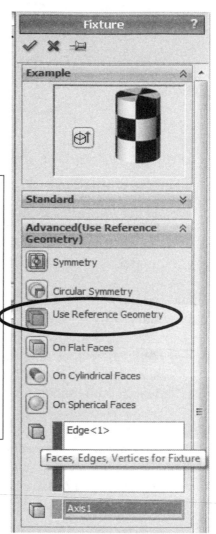

Figure 20 – The **Advanced** dialogue box is used to select edges for symmetry restraints.

> **Aside:**
> General guidance for applying restraints (fixtures) to either solid or shell models is explained below.
>
> a. **For Solid Models** – Every *face* that is coincident with a plane of symmetry should be prevented from translating in its *normal* direction.
>
> b. **For Shell Models** – Every *edge* that coincides with a plane of symmetry should be prevented from translating in the *normal* direction and from rotating in the other two perpendicular directions.

However, before defining restraints, it is necessary to identify those edges of the model on which restraints are to be applied.

Refer to the partial view of the **Advanced** dialogue box, shown in Fig. 20, and the part model in Fig. 21 while implementing the following steps. Work carefully when selecting edges or surfaces.

2. Near the bottom of the **Advanced (Use Reference Geometry)** dialogue box the **Faces, Edges, Vertices for Fixture** field is highlighted (light blue) to indicate it is active and awaiting user selection of *edges* to which symmetry restraints are to be applied.

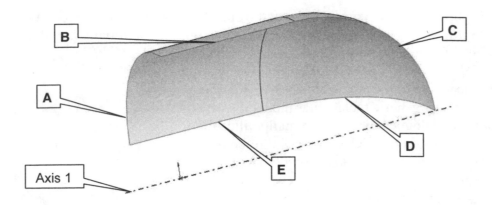

Figure 21 - Identification of shell edges to which symmetry restraints are applied.

3. Zoom-in on the model to select the ¼ circular edge, labeled **A** in Fig. 21. Do *not* select other edges, faces, or vertices. The selected edge, **Edge<1>** appears in the **Faces, Edges, Vertices for Fixture** field (see Fig. 20) and is highlighted on the model.

4. At the bottom of the **Advanced** dialogue box click to activate (light blue) the **Face, Edge, Plane, Axis for Direction** field. Then, if **Axis1** is visible on the model, click to select it. Otherwise, click **Axis1** in the SolidWorks flyout menu. **Axis1** now appears in the active field *and* the animated model changes to that shown in Fig. 20. This step establishes **Axis1** as an axis of symmetry along the length of the model.

Next, apply the principle stated in item (b) of the previous page, which states: *"Every **edge** that coincides with a plane of symmetry should be prevented from translating in the normal direction and from rotating in the other two perpendicular directions."* To do this, proceed as follows.

Figure 22 – Displacements set to zero on model edge.

5. In the **Fixture** property manager, scroll down to the **Translations** dialogue box shown in Fig. 22. Then select the **Axial** icon. Ensure that **0** appears in the value box. This selection sets to zero model translation along **Axis1** on edge **A**.

6. Next, scroll down to the **Rotation** dialogue box and set both **Radial** and **Circumferential** rotations to zero by clicking their icons, (i.e., rotation is prevented in both of these directions).

7. Click **[OK]** ✓ to close the **Fixture** property manager.

Next, repeat the above procedure, but select all edges **B**, **C**, **D**, and **E** of Fig. 21and apply appropriate restraints. Try this on your own, or follow the steps outlined below.

8. Right-click the **Fixtures** folder and from the pull-down menu select **Advanced Fixtrures…** The **Fixture** property manager opens.

9. In the **Advanced** dialogue box and select **Use Reference Geometry**, circled in Fig. 23. Also, the **Faces, Edges, Vertices for Fixture** field is highlighted (light blue) to indicate it is active.

10. On the model, select edges **B**, **C**, **D**, and **E** labeled in Fig. 21. **Edge<1>** through **Edge<4>** appear in the **Faces, Edges, Vertices for Fixture** field and are highlighted on the model. Refer to Fig. 23.

11. At the bottom of the **Advanced** dialogue box click to activate (light blue) the **Face, Edge, Plane, Axis for Direction** field. Again either click **Axis1** in the SolidWorks flyout menu or on the model. **Axis1** now appears in the active field.

12. Set the **Translations** and **Rotation** restraints to zero (0) as shown at the arrows in Fig. 23.

Figure 23 – **Translations** and **Rotation** settings for edges **B**, **C**, **D**, and **E**.

13. Click **[OK]** ✓ to close the **Fixture** property manager.

The resulting symmetry restraints are shown on the model in Fig. 24.

Figure 24 – An internal view of the model showing **Symmetry** restraints applied to all cut edges.

Zoom in and carefully observe the symbols used to indicate symmetry boundary conditions. All previous examples used solid tetrahedral elements for which **Immovable** restraints were appropriate. **Immovable** restraints prevent translations in the three coordinate directions X, Y, Z and are pictured in Fig. 25 (a). **Fixed** restraints are illustrated in Fig. 25 (b) where the added "disk" on the tail of each vector represents an added rotational restraint. Finally, the **Symmetry** restraint is pictured in Fig.25 (c). It prevents translation in a direction normal to the restrained face or edge (arrow shaped vector) *and* prevents rotation about the other two axes associated with the restrained edge ("thumb-tack" shaped vectors). When fully restrained, shell elements restrict three translations in X, Y, Z directions *plus* they prevent rotations specified above. Restraint symbols on edges of your model should resemble those shown in Fig. 24 (c).

(a)   (b)   (c)

Figure 25 – (a) **Immovable** restraint symbol; (b) **Fixed** restraint symbol only applies to shell elements, however it is only used where appropriate; (c) **Symmetry** restraint applied to shell elements on cut surfaces of the thin-wall pressure vessel.

Pressure Load Applied

Loading of the thin-wall cylinder is completed by the addition of an internal pressure as outlined next.

1. Right-click the **External Loads** folder and from the pull-down menu select **Pressure...** The **Pressure** property manager opens (not shown).

2. In the **Type** dialogue box, choose ⊙**Normal to selected face** (if not already selected).

3. The **Faces for Pressure** field is highlighted (light blue) to indicate it is active. Select the *inside* surfaces of both the cylindrical and hemispherical portions of the model. **Face<1>** and **Face<2>** appear in the **Faces for Pressure** field and both surfaces are highlighted to indicate their selection.

Figure 26 – Uniform pressure distribution acting on internal surfaces of the model.

4. Within the **Pressure Value** dialogue box, verify that **Units** are set to **N/m^2**. Also, in the ⊞ **Pressure Value** field, type **1.4e6** for the applied internal pressure. Units of **N/m^2** appear adjacent to this field.

Pressure vectors are displayed on interior surfaces of the model shown in Fig. 26. These arrows should be directed *toward the inner surface*; if not check **Reverse direction**.

5. Click **[OK]** ✓ to close the **Pressure** property manager.

The 1/8 model is now properly restrained using fixtures that restrict model translations and rotations in the appropriate directions. No additional restraints are needed. However, if the model were not fully restrained, a warning would appear during the Solution and additional restraints to prevent "rigid body motion" would be required. The need for rigid body restraint is demonstrated in the second half of this chapter.

Mesh the Model

The meshing process outlined below is considerably shortened because the system default mesh is used.

1. In the Simulation manager tree, right-click the **Mesh** folder and from the pull-down menu select ▥ **Create Mesh…** The **Mesh** property manager opens.

2. Check "✓" to open the ☑ **Mesh Parameters** dialogue box and select ⊙**Curvature based mesh** (if not already selected).

This is the first time the system default mesh is used. However, be aware that a curvature based mesh is *not* being used because a shell model is to be meshed. Rather it is used to acquaint users with this alternate mesh type and to show differences between it and the **Standard mesh** used in earlier examples.

3. Accept the default mesh size and click **[OK]** ✓ to close the **Mesh** property manager.

Meshing proceeds automatically and Fig. 27(a) shows an image of the thin-wall pressure vessel displayed with a **Curvature based** *shell* mesh. Also shown are all applied loads and fixtures. Recall that a curvature based mesh is more accurate, hence the reason it is the default mesh applied within SolidWorks Simulation. Also, notice that the model appears as a "paper-thin" shell.

Figure 27(b), on the other hand, shows the thin-wall pressure vessel with a **Standard mesh** displayed on its surface. Although solutions that accompany a standard mesh execute slightly faster than the curvature based mesh, the resulting solutions are not quite as accurate. The primary reason a standard mesh has been specified for problems up to this point is that a *more orderly* mesh results. Such a mesh is advantageous when selecting nodes in a straight line across an area of interest on a model. Carefully examine the shape of each mesh in Figs. 27(a) and (b). You should only have the mesh shown in Fig. 27(a) on your model. The "bottom" (orange) surface is also labeled in Fig. 27(a).

Orange indicates "bottom"

Figure 27 (a) – **Curvature based mesh** displayed on a shell model of the thin-wall pressure vessel.

Figure 27 (b) – **Standard mesh** displayed on a shell model of the thin-wall pressure vessel. Notice that a **Standard mesh** is more orderly than the **Curvature based mesh**.

Recall the system default conventions adopted at the beginning of this example. There the color orange denotes the "bottom" surface of shell elements. Assuming the inner surface of the model is considered as the "bottom," then this surface should appear orange. If it is not orange, then model surfaces must be reversed (i.e., "flipped"). Read the following steps because they may be required for some end of chapter Exercise problems. *However, only perform these steps if top and bottom surfaces need to be interchanged.*

4. Click to select the cylindrical surface on either the inside or outside of the model. Then, while pressing the **[Shift]** key, select the adjacent hemispherical surface.

5. Right-click the **Mesh** icon and from the pull-down menu select **Flip Shell Elements**. This action should reverse locations of the top and bottom surfaces.

NOTE: In earlier versions of SolidWorks Simulation it may be necessary to repeat steps 4 and 5 to cause the desired changes to take effect.

Colors of the top and bottom surfaces should now reverse, (orange moves to the inside [bottom] and gray is switched to the outside [top] surface). The last two steps are not mandatory. They simply illustrate how a model can be altered to conform to the user's preference. The model is now complete and ready to be solved as outlined below.

Solution

1. Right-click **Pressure Vessel-Shell Study (-Default-)** and from the pull-down menu select **Run**. Or, click the **Run** icon on the **Simulation** tab.

After the Solution is complete, three default plots, **Stress1 (-vonMises-)**, **Displacement1 (-Res disp-)**, and **Strain1 (-Equivalent-)** are listed below the Simulation manager tree.

Results Analysis

Because the emphasis of this example is on mastering basic techniques for working with shell elements, only stress results are examined below.

1. Right-click the **Results** folder and from the pull-down menu select **Define Stress Plot...** The **Stress Plot** property manager opens as seen in Fig. 28.

2. In the **Display** dialogue box, click to open ▼ the **Component** pull-down menu and select **P1: 1st Principal Stress** at upper arrow in Fig. 28. Also verify that **Units** appear as **N/m^2**.

3. Next, in the **Display** dialogue box of Fig. 28, notice that the **Shell Face** field indicates the stress plot is pre-set to display stresses on the **Top** surface of the model.

Figure 28 – **Stress Plot** property manager.

4. Click **[OK]** ✓ to close the **Stress Plot** property manager and a plot of first principal stress, like that shown in Fig. 29, appears in the graphics area. Also, **Stress2 (-1st principal-)** is listed beneath the **Results** folder.

P1 (N/m^2)

34,571,056.0
32,910,394.0
31,249,730.0
29,589,066.0
27,928,404.0
26,267,740.0
24,607,076.0
22,946,412.0
21,285,750.0
19,625,086.0
17,964,422.0
16,303,759.0
14,643,096.0

Figure 29 – First principal stress distribution over the TOP surface of the thin-wall pressure vessel. **Fixtures** and **External Loads** are hidden.

To easily identify these results as occurring on the top surface of the model, change the name of the **Stress2 (-1st principal-)** folder as follows.

5. At the bottom of the Simulation manager tree, click-pause-click on the name **Stress2 (-1st principal-)** and type: **1st Principal Stress-TOP** and press **[Enter]**. This new name, shown in Fig. 30 identifies the current plot shown in Fig. 29.

Figure 30 – Re-naming the stress plot using a descriptive name.

For convenience viewing results, turn off the **External Loads** and **Fixture** symbols. Try this on your own or use the following steps.

6. Right-click the **Fixtures** folder and from the pop-up menu select **Hide All**. Repeat this step for the **External Loads** folder.

7. If the model appears deformed, click the ▣ **Deformed Result** icon. The model should now look like Fig. 29.

Unlike solid, tetrahedral elements for which stress variation is shown *through* the model, results plotted for *shell* elements correspond to stress on either the *top* or the *bottom* surface. We next investigate the magnitude of σ_1 on the bottom surface of the model.

8. Repeat steps 1 to 7 above, except:
   - In step 3, select the **Bottom** shell surface to stress display σ_1.

   - In step 5, change the plot name to indicate **1st Principal Stress-BOTTOM**.

- Next, alternately double-click on **1st Principal Stress-TOP** and then **1st Principal Stress-BOTTOM** to display the plots. Compare the two *different* values of σ_1 on each surface. Note value changes in the stress legend.

Commencing in SolidWorks Simulation 2013, a new option to view stress, displacement, and strain results on both surfaces of a 3D representation of a shell model is offered. To use this option, proceed as follows.

9. Right-click the **Results** folder and from the pull-down menu, select **Define Stress Plot...** The **Stress Plot** property manager opens.

10. In the **Display** dialogue box pull-down menu, select **P1: 1st Principal Stress**.

11. In the **Advanced Options** dialogue box, check ☑**Render shell thickness in 3D (slower)**. Note that the **Shell Face** field is grayed out to indicate it is inactive.

12. Click **[OK]** ✓ to close the **Stress Plot** property.

13. Finally, right-click the **Stress4(-1st principal-)** and from the pull-down menu, select **Probe**. Clicking anywhere on the model yields an information "flag" that indicates stress values on both top *and* bottom surfaces. These same results also appear in the **Results** dialogue box of the **Probe Result** property manager.

14. Click **[OK]** ✓ to close the **Probe Result** property manager.

Results Comparison (Tangential Stress = σ_1 on Cylindrical Surface)

To obtain a representative value of first principal stress, σ_1, on the cylindrical pressure vessel, an area well removed from the cylindrical to hemispherical head transition region is selected. Proceed as follows.

1. Double-click **1st Principal Stress-TOP (-1st principal-)** to display this plot in the graphics area.

2. Right-click **1st Principal Stress-TOP** and from the pull-down menu, select **Probe**. The **Probe Result** property manager opens.

3. In the **Options** dialogue box, select ⊙**At location** (if not already selected), and proceed to select two or three points *near* or *on* the circular edge of the model as depicted in Fig. 31.

Figure 31 – Stress **Probe** on **Top** surface of cylindrical area.

4. Values will vary at points selected. For the three points selected in Fig. 31, the average value of stress is computed as σ_1 = 33,086,957 N/m^2. (numbers will vary) Using this average value yields the following percent difference. (rounded values used)

$$\% \text{ difference} = \left[\frac{\text{FEA result} - \text{classical result}}{\text{FEA result}}\right]100 = \left[\frac{3.309e7 - 3.36e7}{3.309e7}\right]100 = 1.5\% \qquad [3]$$

Equation [3] yields good agreement between classical and FEA results. Notice that it would *not* be appropriate to compare classical values with the maximum stress displayed on the model and at the top of the stress legend. Maximum stress is ignored because it occurs in the cylindrical to hemispherical *transition region* where effects attributed to St. Venant's principle occur.

To further explore comparison of stress results, consider comparing the magnitude of tangential stress, $\sigma_1 = \sigma_t$, on the entire cylindrical *surface*. Proceed as follows.

5. In the **Options** dialogue box of the **Probe Result** property manager, choose ⊙**On selected entities**. All displayed values are cleared from the model and from the property manager.

6. In the **Results** dialogue box the **Faces, Edges or Vertices** field is highlighted (light blue). Move the cursor onto the cylindrical end of the model and click to select it. **Face<1>** appears in the **Faces, Edges or Vertices** field.

7. Near the middle of the **Results** dialogue box, click the **[Update]** button, circled in Fig. 32. The table is automatically populated with stress magnitudes at all nodes on the cylindrical surface.

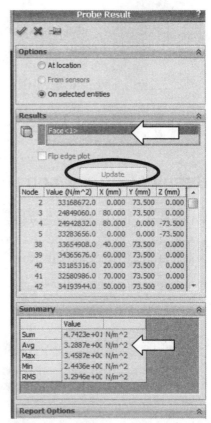

Figure 32 – **Probe Results** on the *entire* cylindrical surface of the pressure vessel.

8. In the **Summary** dialogue box, near bottom of the property manager, observe the average (**Avg**) value of stress $\sigma_1 = \sigma_t$ on this surface is 3.2887e+007 N/m^2,

in Fig. 31 (numbers may vary). Be aware that this value includes a portion of both higher (dark red) and lower (orange, yellow, and light green) stresses near the hemispherical to cylindrical transition region.

When compared to the same classical result used above, the following percent difference is obtained. (rounded values used)

$$\% \text{ difference} = \left[\frac{\text{FEA result} - \text{ classical result}}{\text{FEA result}} \right] 100 = \left[\frac{3.289e7 - 3.36e7}{3.289e7} \right] 100 = 2.2\% \qquad [4]$$

This result is also in good agreement with classical results.

9. Click **[OK]** ✓ to close the **Probe Result** property manager.

Other Meaningful Results Comparisons

Two additional comparisons would be useful to verify stress results for the thin wall pressure vessel analyzed using shell elements. Those comparisons include FEA results for longitudinal stress σ_ℓ in the cylindrical segment of the vessel and tangential stress in the hemispherical head, where -

$$\sigma'_{t(Hemispherical)} = \frac{1}{2}\sigma_{t(Tangential)} = \frac{1}{2}\sigma_1 \qquad [5]$$

Either of these stresses can be investigated using steps similar to those outlined above.

If, however, stress magnitudes on the hemispherical head are to be investigated, the following additional guidance is essential. Briefly, zoom in on the hemispherical head and notice the more blotchy, medium and dark blue, appearance of this region. Because greater stress variation is observed on this surface, a larger number of **Probe** points should be selected when used to determine an *average* stress magnitude in this region.

Guidance for Determining Symmetry Fixtures

The key to determining **Fixtures** for symmetrical *shell* or *solid* models is to begin by identifying edges of the model that satisfy the previously stated guideline (paraphrased below):

> "Every *surface* or *edge* that coincides with a plane of symmetry should be prevented from <u>translating</u> in the *normal direction . . .*"

Once the *normal direction* is identified on a symmetrical model, then its **Translation** fixture can be selected and set equal to zero (0). Next, **Rotation** fixtures are selected by choosing the *other two remaining* **Fixtures** from the **Rotation** fixture dialogue box.

Because symmetry and its associated **Fixtures** can be puzzling to first time users, the following example is provided. Hopefully the example will clarify, using word and images, what might be confusing in the preceding paragraph.

EXAMPLE:
Figure 33 (a) shows a symmetrical vessel subject to zero internal pressure. Similarly, Fig. 33 (b) shows a deformed view of the same vessel when subject to a significant internal pressure (model deformation is exaggerated). The dashed vertical line represents one plane of symmetry that divides the vessel into equal left and right halves. Also shown are three infinitesimal stress elements of the type encountered in a basic mechanics of materials course (not to be confused with *finite elements*). Figure 33 (a) shows these elements located at a distance **x** to the left and right of a central element, which is located on the axis of symmetry.

Begin by considering the question: *"Why is <u>translation = 0</u> on a symmetrical surface or edge?"*

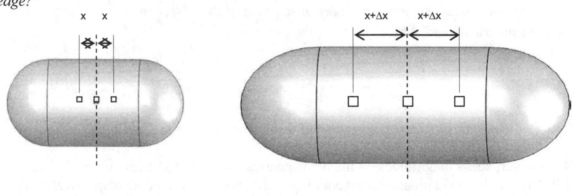

Figure 33 (a) – Undeformed pressure vessel.   Figure 33 (b) – Deformed pressure vessel showing stress element *deformation* and *translation*.

After the vessel is pressurized, two things happen. First, *all elements change size* due to strain and the resulting stress. Second, stress elements to the left and right of the symmetry plane also undergo *translation* (Δx) due to deformation (elongation) of the pressure vessel. However, although the center element also deforms due to strain, it does *not* undergo translation because it is located *on* an axis of symmetry. This then is the reason why *translation* **Fixtures** are set equal to zero *normal* to the plane of symmetry.

The next question is: *"After the **Translation Fixture** is defined, how are **Rotation Fixtures** defined?"*

Refer to Figs. 21 and 22 repeated on the following page. The answer to the above question is quite simple. In Fig. 22 notice that **Radial, Circumferential,** and **Axial** fields appear in the same order from top to bottom in both the **Translations** and the

Rotation dialogue boxes. Thus, whatever **Fixture** is set equal to zero in the **Translations** dialogue box (bottom field), the *other two* **Fixtures** are set equal to zero in the **Rotation** dialogue box (top two fields).

The above discussion focused only on **Fixtures** applied edge **A** of the symmetrical model in Fig. 21 below.

Figure 21 (repeated) - Identification of shell edges to which symmetry restraints are applied.

Figure 22 (repeated) - Displacements set to zero on model edge.

Although slightly more confusing for *translations* along symmetry edges **B**, **C**, **D**, and **E**, where circumferential **Fixtures** are set equal to zero in the **Translations** dialogue box, you will notice that the *other two* **Fixtures** are set equal to zero in the **Rotation** dialogue box as shown in Fig. 23 (not repeated here). Think through this set of **Fixtures** and make sketches like Figs. 33 (a) and (b) to better understand how they were determined.

Closing Observations

1. SolidWorks Simulation applies a linear interpolation across the model thickness when determining results (stress, displacement, or strain) on the **Top** and **Bottom** surfaces of shell models.

2. Maximum stress magnitudes may occur on the **Bottom** (inside) or **Top** (outside) surface of shell elements depending upon part loading. This observation is valid for all thin *shell* models, not just for pressure vessels.

Analysis of Machine Elements Using SolidWorks Simulation

Logging Out of the Current Analysis

This concludes analysis of a thin wall pressure vessel using *shell* elements. It is suggested that this file *not* be saved. Proceed as follows.

1. On the **Main Menu**, click **File** followed by choosing **Close**.

2. The **SolidWorks** window in Fig. 33 opens and provides the options of either saving the current analysis or not. Select **[Don't Save]**.

Figure 34 – **SolidWorks** window prompts users to either save changes or not.

THICK WALL PRESSURE VESSEL

In the second-half of the current chapter, analysis of a thick-wall pressure vessel is performed. Thick-wall pressure vessels are found in numerous applications including high pressure piping, gun and cannon barrels, some hydraulic cylinders, and related uses. Thick-wall pressure vessels are classified as such in applications where wall thickness "t" exceeds $t > r_i/20$, where r_i = inside radius. For these applications, assumptions related to thin-wall pressure vessels are no longer valid. Primary among these differences are: (a) radial stress, which is neglected in thin-wall formulations, is known to vary through the wall thickness; and (b) tangential (a.k.a., hoop or circumferential) stress may vary significantly through the wall thickness. Much of thick-wall cylinder theory is also relevant to analysis of press and shrink fits, which are investigated in the next chapter.

Problem Statement

Thick-Wall Pressure Vessel

This example is based on a thick-wall cylindrical pressure vessel that is closed on one end, but attached to a rigid pipe connection at the opposite end as illustrated in Fig. 35. This vessel is made of Alloy Steel and is subject to an internal pressure $P_i = 16.0$ MPa and an external pressure that approximates standard atmospheric pressure $P_o = 0.101$ MPa. Cylinder dimensions, necessary to apply classical stress equations, are also included in Fig. 34. The goal is to determine tangential and radial stress variation through the cylindrical wall of this pressure vessel.

Figure 35 – Basic dimensions and geometry of the thick-wall pressure vessel.

1. *Skip to step 2 if SolidWorks is already open.* Otherwise open SolidWorks by making the following selections.

Start>All Programs>SolidWorks 2013 (or) Click the **SolidWorks** icon on your screen.

2. From the SolidWorks main menu, select **File > Open…** Then use procedures common to your computer environment to open the SolidWorks Simulation file named **Thick Wall Pressure Vessel**.

Defining the Study

Because tetrahedral elements are used to create a solid model of the pressure vessel, the majority of procedural steps employed to create this study are familiar to users who have worked the examples in preceding chapters. However, all necessary steps are included below. This study again uses symmetry restraints, but of a different type, and also introduces new methods for viewing results.

1. On the **Simulation** tab click the ▼ **Study Advisor** icon and from the pull-down menu select **New Study**. Or, in the main menu, click **Simulation** and from the pull-down menu, select **Study…** The **Study** property manager opens.

2. In the **Name** field, type: **Thick Wall Pressure Vessel-YOUR NAME**.

3. Select a **Static** study and click **[OK]** ✓ to close the **Study** property manager.

Due to symmetry differences (left and right ends of the model differ) and to introduce the concept of *rigid body* motion, a ½ model, rather than a 1/8 model, is selected for the thick-wall example. Prior to commencing a finite element analysis, the model is defeatured; also, half of the model is suppressed. For purposes of illustration, the small fillet at the pipe connection is selected to be defeatured. Proceed as follows. NOTE: It may be necessary to drag down the bottom of the SolidWorks Feature manager tree to view the **Pipe Connector Fillet** and **Half-Model of Cylinder** referenced in step 4.

4. At the bottom of the SolidWorks Feature manager, right-click **Pipe Connector Fillet** and select the **Suppress** icon. This action removes the fillet at the junction between the cylinder and pipe joint in Fig. 36. Is this really necessary? On this simple model, probably not. Also, it could *introduce* a significant stress concentration at this location. The fillet is only removed to remind users to defeature a model when possible.

Figure 36 – Half-section of the thick-wall pressure vessel after defeaturing.

5. Also near the bottom of the SolidWorks Feature manager, right-click **Half-Model of Cylinder** and from the pop-up menu, select the **Unsuppress** icon.

The model changes to a half-cylinder representation shown in Fig. 36. Notice how assigning descriptive names to folders facilitates identifying their function. Prior to renaming the **Half-Model of Cylinder** folder, its generic name was "Cut-Extrude2."

Assign Material Properties

1. Right-click the **Thick Wall Pressure Vessel** folder *(not the Study name)* and from the pull-down menu, select **Apply/Edit Material...** The **Material** window opens.

2. Because users should be familiar with this window, on your own select **Alloy Steel (SS)**. Verify that units are set to **SI-N/m^2 (Pa)**, then click **[Apply]** followed by **[Close]**. A check "✓" appears on the **Thick Wall Pressure Vessel** folder and the material designation is listed adjacent to the part name.

Define Fixtures and External Loads

1. Right-click **Fixtures** and from the pull-down menu choose **Advanced Fixtures...** The **Fixture** property manager opens.

2. In the **Advanced** dialog box, select the Symmetry icon. Next, select the cut surface highlighted in Fig. 37. **Face<1>** is listed in the **Planar Faces for Fixture** field and **Fixtures** *normal to the plane of symmetry* appear. As a reminder that symmetry is specified, a ghost image of the other half of the model also appears.

3. Click **[OK]** ✓ to close the **Fixture** property manager.

Restraint symbols appear on the model *normal* to the cut face. Restraints act in the Z-direction. Physically this means that these symmetry restraints permit axial displacements (along the length of the cylinder) and radial displacements (change of cylinder diameter) when the cylinder is subject to internal or external pressure. These displacements are consistent with the half-model selected. At present, however, both X and Y *rigid body* displacements of the model are still possible because the model is currently restrained in the Z direction only.

Figure 37 – Half-model of pressure vessel with symmetry restraints applied in the Z-direction.

Because symmetry fixtures only restrain the model in the Z-direction, it is necessary to apply additional restraints in the X and Y directions to prevent what is called "rigid body" motion. The type of restraints selected depends heavily upon the nature of actual operating conditions. Because the pipe connection on right end of the cylinder is considered attached to a rigid (i.e., immovable) pipe, not shown, the remaining restraints are applied at that location. Fortunately, this immovable restraint does not interfere with finite element results in the thick-wall portion of the pressure vessel.

Analysis Insight

Although not part of this example, consider the following two scenarios:

A different set of fixtures results if, in addition to being attached to a rigid pipe at its right end, the left end of the cylinder is mounted against a fixed surface (e.g., an immovable wall or support bracket). That additional restraint would alter stress distribution within the cylinder because longitudinal deformation of the model would then be prevented at both ends.

Consider yet one additional design/analysis scenario in which the model, restrained as described in the preceding paragraph, is subsequently subjected to a significant temperature change. This condition would add temperature induced deformation (expansion or contraction) associated with the coefficient of thermal expansion for the model material. This scenario would require a separate thermal analysis to determine deformations and stresses caused by a temperature change.

Continue to define remaining restraints and loads in the following steps.

4. Right click the **Fixtures** folder and from the pull-down menu select **Fixed Geometry...** The **Fixture** property manager opens.

5. Within the **Standard (Fixed Geometry)** dialogue box, select ⌐ **Fixed Geometry** (if not already selected).

6. Zoom in on the right-end of the pipe extension, shown in Fig. 38, and click to select the cut surface. Immovable restraint symbols (shown dark) in the X, Y, and Z directions are added to the model and **Face<1>** appears in the **Faces, Edges, Vertices for Fixture** dialogue box.

7. Click **[OK]** ✓ to close the **Fixture** property manager. The model is now restrained in all directions.

Figure 38 – The **Fixed/Immovable** restraint is added to the attachment surface associated with a rigid pipe connection.

The next step is to apply an internal pressure $P_i = 16.0$ MPa to all internal surfaces of the pressure vessel. Proceed as follows.

8. Right-click **External Loads** and from the pull-down menu select ⊞ **Pressure...** The **Pressure** property manager opens.

9. In the **Type** dialogue box, verify that ⊙**Normal to selected face** is chosen.

10. The **Faces for Pressure** field is highlighted (light blue) to indicate it is active and awaiting user input.

11. Move cursor onto the model and click to select *all interior* surfaces (both cylinder ends, both internal fillets, and cylindrical surfaces of the cylinder and the pipe extension). A total of six faces **(Face<1>, Face <2>, ... Face<6>)** should be listed in the **Faces for Pressure** field.

12. Beneath **Pressure Value**, verify that **Units** are set to **N/m^2** and type **16.0e6** in the ⊞ **Pressure Value** field.

Figure 39 – Internal pressure applied to six faces within the thick-wall pressure vessel.

13. Click **[OK]** ✓ to close the **Pressure** property manager. The model should appear as shown in Fig. 39.

Next apply atmospheric pressure $P_o = 0.101$ MPa to all external surfaces of the model. Try this on your own or follow steps below.

14. Repeat steps 8 through 13 with the following two exceptions.

    a. In step 11, select *all exterior* surfaces. Once again, a total of six faces should be chosen.

    b. In step 12, type **0.101e6** N/m^2 in the ⊞ **Pressure Value** field.

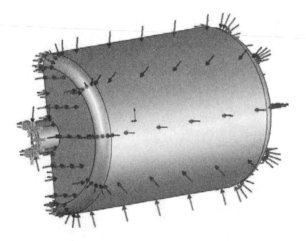

Figure 40 – Atmospheric pressure applied to exterior of the thick-wall pressure vessel.

The exterior of the pressure vessel should now appear as shown in Fig. 40.

Create a Duplicate Study

Because it is desired to model the thick-wall pressure vessel with two different meshes, a duplicate study is created *before* the model is meshed. Either duplicate the study on your own or follow steps 1 through 3 outlined below.

1. Beneath the graphics area, right-click the **Thick Wall Pressure Vessel-YOUR NAME** Study *tab* and from the pop-up menu, select **Duplicate**. The **Define Study Name** window opens.

2. In the **Study Name:** field, replace the existing name with **Thick Wall Pressure Vessel-FINE Mesh**.

3. Press **[OK]** to close the **Define Study Name** window.

Mesh the Model – Default Size Standard Mesh

1. Return to the original Study named **Thick Wall Pressure Vessel-YOUR NAME** by selecting its tab beneath the graphics area of the screen.

2. Right-click the **Mesh** folder and from the pull-down menu select **Create Mesh...** The **Mesh** property manager opens.

Because an *orderly* mesh is desired for this analysis, a **Standard Mesh,** rather than the system default **Curvature based mesh** is used. Proceed as follows.

3. In the **Mesh Density** dialogue box accept the default mesh size (pointer located at the middle of the **Coarse** to **Fine** slider-scale).

4. Open the ☑ **Mesh Parameters** dialogue box and select ⊙ **Standard Mesh**. Also verify that **Units** are set to **mm**. This selection results in creation of an orderly mesh on the model.

5. Click **[OK]** ✓ to close the **Mesh** property manager.

The meshed model along with its boundary conditions is shown in Fig. 41.

Figure 41 – Default size **Standard Mesh** applied to the thick-wall pressure vessel.

Analysis Insight

Examination of mesh size on the *cut surface* of the pressure vessel in Fig. 41 reveals that a *single* element spans the entire wall thickness. However, near the beginning of this chapter, a general guideline for determining when *solid* elements can be used stated that, "…the minimum number of elements recommended across the thickness of a part (i.e., across the part's minimum dimension) should be *at least two elements.*"

Mesh the Model – Fine Size Standard Mesh

Given the guideline in the **Analysis Insight** above, it is appropriate to reduce element size so that at least two elements span the pressure vessel wall thickness. This change is easily made as follows.

1. Beneath the graphics area of the screen, select the **Thick Wall Pressure Vessel-FINE Mesh** Study *tab*. This action switches to the duplicate Study.

2. Right-click the **Mesh** folder and from the pull-down menu select **Create Mesh…** The **Mesh** property manager opens

3. In the **Mesh Density** dialogue box, click-and-*drag* the pointer on the **Mesh Factor** slider-scale from its default, mid-range position, to the **Fine** position.

4. Check ✓ to open the ☑ **Mesh Parameters** dialogue box and select a ⊙ **Standard Mesh**. Also verify that **Units** are set to **mm**.

5. Click **[OK]** ✓ to close the **Mesh** property manager and initiate re-meshing the model. Note the increased time required to mesh the model. The model now appears as shown in Fig. 42 with two elements across the cylinder wall thickness. NOTE: Exterior pressure symbols are hidden to reduce clutter on Fig. 42.

Figure 42 – Pressure vessel showing mesh size reduced to half of the default mesh size so at least two elements span the cylinder wall thickness.

Analysis Insight

Based on the stress concentration example of Chapter 3, where variation of mesh size was investigated, it was found that moving the pointer on the mesh size slider-scale to either the left or right extreme position had the effect of doubling or halving the default mesh size.

The default mesh size for the model shown in Fig. 41 is **20.06035261 mm**. Thus, changing element size to **Fine** reduces its nominal size to **10.0301763 mm**, or exactly half the previous size. As a consequence, two elements now span the thick-wall portion of the pressure vessel as illustrated in Fig. 42.

Although two elements span the thick-wall portion of the model, only one element spans the thickness in the pipe connector neck. Zoom in to examine the neck area. This outcome might be considered acceptable because tangential and radial stresses in the thick-wall portion of the pressure vessel are of primary importance in this study.

When compared to the original model, however, a dramatic increase in the number of nodes and elements is observed for the fine mesh model. These changes are summarized in Table 1.

Aside:

The default mesh size would yield adequate results for this model. However, because stress through the cylindrical wall thickness is to be examined in greater detail, the additional nodes and elements will prove helpful.

Table 1 – Comparison of Finite Element Model Size

	Original Model (Default Mesh Size)	Revised Model (Fine Mesh Size)	Increase in Model Complexity
No. of Nodes	16,132	88,246	Approx. 5.5 times larger
No. of Elements	9,399	56,002	Approx. 6 times larger

In this instance, following the general guideline, which suggests at least two solid elements across a part's minimum thickness, results in a significant increase in mesh density with a corresponding increase in solution time. This is a logical cause-and-effect consequence of changing global mesh size.

Solution

Having defined material properties, fixtures, loads, and a mesh, the thick-wall model is subjected to analysis as outlined below.

1. Either click the **Run** ⏷ icon on the **Simulation** tab or right-click the **Thick Wall Pressure Vessel-FINE Mesh (-Default-)** study folder and from the pull-down menu, select **Run**. Solution time for the **Fine** mesh is only slightly longer. To view actual "run time" at the end of the Solution, right-click the **Results** folder and from the pop-up menu select **Solver Messages...** In the **Solver Message** window the **Total solution time** is listed as **00:00:02** seconds (more or less). Click ⊠ or **[OK]** to close the **Solver Message** window.

2. Computed results, in the form of plots, are listed beneath the **Results** folder. Notice that plots contained in these folders revert to the system default plots.

Results Analysis

Displacement Analysis

To gain some insight into deformation of the thick-wall pressure vessel subject to internal and external pressures, attention is first directed to the **Displacement1 (-Res disp-)** folder.

1. Right-click the **Displacement1 (-Res disp-)** folder and from the pull-down menu select **Show**. A displacement plot of the model is shown in Fig. 43.

2. *If* the pressure vessel does not appear deformed, click on the [Deformed Result] **Deformed Result** icon in the Simulation toolbar.

3. Click **[OK]** to close the **Displacement Plot** property manager.

4. In the Simulation manager tree, right-click **Fixtures**, and from the pull-down menu select **Hide All**. This action hides all restraints acting on the model.

5. Repeat step 4 for the **External Loads** folder.

6. Orient the model in a front view 🔲.

7. To compare the deformed and undeformed model shapes, right-click **Displacement1 (Res-disp)** and from the pull-down menu select **Settings**. In the **Deformed Plot Options** dialogue box, check ☑ **Superimpose model on the deformed shape** and drag the **Transparency:** slider to the left to "**0**."

Figure 43 – Image of the model with symmetry and pressure boundary conditions "hidden." **Fixtures** are also hidden. The un-deformed model shape is superimposed on the image.

A comparison of the displacement plot (color image) with the un-deformed shape (gray image) of the pressure vessel reveals the following, common sense, observations.

  a. All axial displacements are *away* from the immovable pipe-end.

  b. Bulging of both the left and right ends of the model contributes to longitudinal (axial) deformation *away* from the immovable end.

  c. Longitudinal deformation (axial stretch) of the cylindrical section also contributes to overall axial deformation.

  d. Slight radial deformation (bulging) of cylindrical walls is observed.

  e. Virtually zero displacement occurs in the pipe connection.

8. Clear the check mark from ☐ **Superimpose model on the deformed shape** and click **[OK]** ✓ to close the **Settings** property manager.

Analysis Insight

Taking into account the fact that displacements depicted in Figs. 43 and 44 are greatly exaggerated, approximately 42.0229 times larger than actual (see bottom line of text on the plot title), briefly consider how different boundary conditions (such as supports or a fixed wall at the left-end of the pressure vessel) described in an earlier **Analysis Insight** section, would impact results of the current example.

The significant effect of correct or incorrect boundary conditions (i.e., loads and fixtures) on finite element analysis results cannot be overemphasized!

---

von Mises Stress Analysis

The next topic for investigation is interpretation of stresses occurring within the model.

    1. Double-click the **Stress1 (-vonMises-)** folder to display the plot shown in Fig. 44.

Figure 44 – Regions of high vonMises stress on the thick-wall pressure vessel model.

Regions of high vonMises stress at fillet radii on both ends of the cylinder and in the vicinity of the pipe-to-cylinder connection are circled on Fig. 44. All von Mises stress magnitudes are less than the yield strength listed beneath the color coded stress chart.

Tangential Stress Analysis

The next focus of this study is on tangential and radial stress distributions typically associated with analysis of pressurized thick-wall cylinders. However, before examining stress plots, it is helpful to have some expectation of magnitudes associated with these two stresses. Therefore, solutions based on Lame's equations for values of tangential and radial stresses at both the inside and outside surfaces of a thick-wall cylinder are included below.

Tangential stress at outside surface:

$$(\sigma_t)_o = \frac{p_i r_i^2 - p_o r_o^2 - r_i^2 r_o^2 (p_o - p_i)/r_o^2}{r_o^2 - r_i^2}$$

$$= \frac{16.0e6(0.15)^2 - 0.101e6(0.175)^2 - (0.15)^2(0.101e6 - 16.0e6)}{(0.175)^2 - (0.15)^2} = 87.9 \text{ Mpa}$$

[6]

Tangential stress at inside surface:

$$
(\sigma_t)_i = \frac{p_i r_i^2 - p_o r_o^2 - r_i^2 r_0^2 (p_o - p_i)/r_i^2}{r_o^2 - r_i^2}
$$

$$
= \frac{16.0e6(0.15)^2 - 0.101e6(0.175)^2 - (0.175)^2(0.101e6 - 16.0e6)}{(0.175)^2 - (0.15)^2} = 103.8 \text{ Mpa}
$$

[7]

Radial stress at inside surface:

$$
(\sigma_r)_i = \frac{p_i r_i^2 - p_o r_o^2 + r_i^2 r_0^2 (p_o - p_i)/r_i^2}{r_o^2 - r_i^2} = \frac{p_i r_i^2 - p_o r_o^2 + p_o r_o^2 - p_i r_o^2}{r_o^2 - r_i^2}
$$

$$
= \frac{-p_i (r_o^2 - r_i^2)}{(r_o^2 - r_i^2)} = -p_i = -16.0 \text{ Mpa} = \text{ (internal pressure)}
$$

[8]

Radial stress at outside surface:

$$
(\sigma_r)_o = \frac{p_i r_i^2 - p_o r_o^2 + r_i^2 r_0^2 (p_o - p_i)/r_o^2}{r_o^2 - r_i^2} = \frac{p_i r_i^2 - p_o r_o^2 + p_o r_i^2 - p_i r_i^2}{r_o^2 - r_i^2}
$$

$$
= \frac{-p_o (r_o^2 - r_i^2)}{(r_o^2 - r_i^2)} = -p_o = -0.101 \text{ MPa} = \text{ (external pressure)}
$$

[9]

So that we can learn more about how to use the software to our advantage, two alternative ways of viewing these results in SolidWorks Simulation are investigated on the following pages. We begin with what might be considered the most intuitive method of viewing stress results and then proceed to a second method that makes use of the *Section Clipping* capability of the software. Begin by adding a plot of first principal stress within the **Results** folder. Try this on your own or follow the steps outlined below.

1. Right-click the **Results** folder and from the pull-down menu, select **Define Stress Plot...** The **Stress Plot** property manager opens.

Central portion of cylinder

P1 (N/m^2)

529,947,616.0

483,439,776.0

436,931,936.0

390,424,096.0

343,916,256.0

297,408,416.0

250,900,560.0

204,392,720.0

157,884,880.0

111,377,040.0

64,869,204.0

18,361,364.0

-28,146,476.0

Figure 45 – Plot of 1st principal stress distribution throughout the thick-wall pressure vessel.

2. In the **Display** dialogue box, click to open the 🖿 **Component** pull-down menu and from the list of available stresses, select **P1: 1st Principal Stress**.

3. Verify that 📏 **Units** are set to **N/m^2**.

4. Click **[OK]** ✓ to close the **Stress Plot** property manager.

Figure 45 shows a front view of 1st principal stress distribution (σ_1) throughout the model. Once again observe regions of high stress at both end fillets where the cylinder and flat ends join. Unfortunately, the figure above does not provide good delineation of stress variation through the central, thick-wall portion of the cylinder labeled in Fig. 45. That is to say, the mid-section of the cylinder appears a fairly uniform shade of light blue.

Analysis Insight

Regions of high principal stress and maximum vonMises stress are typically most important to a designer whose focus is on product safety. However, because a primary objective of this example is to investigate stresses associated with thick-wall pressure vessel theory and to learn different ways to display those results, the following section describes how better to examine these stresses while simultaneously discovering additional software plotting capabilities.

Adjusting Stress Magnitude Display Parameters

A quick review of previous calculations for tangential stress variation from the inside to the outside cylindrical surfaces of the model, equations [6] and [7] above, reveals:

Tangential stress at inside: $(\sigma_t)_i = 103.8$ Mpa

Tangential stress at outside: $(\sigma_t)_o = 87.9$ MPa

Comparing the above values with the range of 1st principal stress magnitudes displayed in the color-coded stress legend adjacent to the model (currently displayed on your screen) reveals that the above stresses occupy only a small portion of the full range of stress values displayed on the model; see circled portion of the stress legend in Fig. 45. Thus, if it is desired to verify values of 1st principal stress between 87.9 MPa to 103.8 MPa, in the cylinder wall, then the stress display can be adjusted to bracket these stress values. The following steps outline one procedure to accomplish this.

1. Beneath the **Results** folder right-click **Stress2 (-1st principal-)** and from the pull-down menu select **Chart Options…** A portion of the **Chart Options** property manager opens as shown in Fig. 46.

Figure 46 – Controlling the range of stresses displayed using the **Defined** option.

2. At the bottom of the **Display Options** dialogue box, select ⊙**Defined:** This option provides a means of setting user defined upper and lower bounds for stress magnitudes to be displayed. In the upper box, type **85.0e6**, which is slightly lower than the *minimum* 1st principal stress value of $(\sigma_t)_o = 87.9$ MPa expected at the outside surface.

3. Similarly, in the bottom box, type **107.0e6**, which is slightly higher than the *maximum* 1st principal stress value of $(\sigma_t)_i = 103.8$ MPa expected at the inside surface of the cylinder.

4. Click **[OK]** ✓ to close the **Chart Options** property manager. Figure 47 (a) displays 1st principal stress magnitudes throughout the model.

5. Next, zoom-in on the boxed region, shown in Fig. 47 (a), to obtain a close-up view of stress variation through the cylinder wall as illustrated by the multiple color fringes in Fig. 47 (b). Notice that the center of the cylinder is well removed from effects of end-conditions caused by fillets at both ends of the cylinder.

(a)   (b)

Figure 47 – (a) 1st principal stress plot after magnitudes are restricted to the range: 85.0 MPa < σ_1 < 107.0 MPa; (b) close-up of tangential stress distribution (σ_1) through the thick-wall.

The **Probe** feature is used next to determine actual values of 1st principal stress at various nodes across the wall thickness.

6. Right-click **Stress2 (-1st principal-)** and from the pull-down menu select **Probe**. The **Probe Result** property manager opens as shown in Fig. 48 (a). *Initially no values appear in the table.*

7. Begin at the inside of the cylinder wall, as near as possible to the middle of the cylinder; see "**START**" label on Fig. 47 (b). Then successively click and move the cursor slightly upward (moving in as straight a line as possible) and repeat until five node points are selected across the wall thickness. Stress values at each node point are simultaneously displayed on the model [also shown in Fig. 47 (b)] and in the **Results** dialogue box, Fig. 48 (a). *If difficulty selecting nodes is experienced, see the Aside section below.*

Aside:

If difficulty is experienced selecting the *unseen* nodes, temporarily close the **Probe Result** property manager by clicking ✖ and turn "on" the mesh display as follows.

    a. Right-click **Stress2 (-1st principal-)** and from the pull-down menu select **Settings…**

    b. Within the **Settings** property manager, click to open the pull-down menu beneath **Boundary Options** and select **Mesh**. Click **[OK]** ✓.

A mesh displayed on the model should facilitate selecting corner *and* mid-side nodes on each element across the wall thickness. Repeat steps 6 and 7 with the mesh displayed.

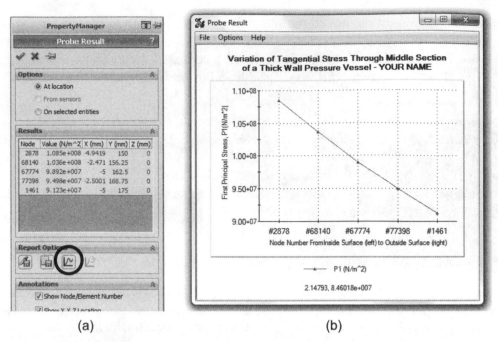

(a)   (b)

Figure 48– (a) **Probe** window displays values of $\sigma_1 = \sigma_t$ at node locations across the cylinder thick-wall; (b) the **Probe Result** window shows a graph of tangential stress variation from the inside surface (high stress) to the outside surface (lower stress) of the thick-wall pressure vessel.

8. After using the **Probe** feature to select nodes, click the **[Plot]** button (circled in Fig. 48 (a) at bottom of the **Probe Result** property manager) to display a graph of tangential stress variation through the wall thickness as shown in Fig. 48 (b). Note the addition of a descriptive title, including your name, and axis labels.

9. After examining the graph, click ⊠ to close the **Probe Result** graph.

10. Click **[OK]** ✓ to close the **Probe Result** window.

11. If the mesh is still displayed on the model, right-click **Stress2 (-1st principal-)** and from the pull-down menu select **Settings…** In the **Boundary Options** dialogue box, open the pull-down menu and select **Model**.

12. Click **[OK]** ✓ to close the **Settings** property manager.

A quick comparison of classical results found using Lame's equations, and finite element results for tangential stress magnitudes at the inside and outside wall surfaces yields the following.

For tangential stress at the inside surface:

$$\% \text{ difference} = \left[\frac{\text{FEA result} - \text{classical result}}{\text{FEA result}}\right]100 = \left[\frac{108.5e6 - 103.8e6}{108.5e6}\right]100 = 4.3\% \quad [10]$$

Tangential stress at the outside wall surface:

$$\% \text{ difference} = \left[\frac{\text{FEA result} - \text{ classical result}}{\text{FEA result}}\right]100 = \left[\frac{91.24e6 - 87.9e6}{91.24e6}\right]100 = 3.7\% \quad [11]$$

Both these percent difference values are low enough that the analyst should have reasonable confidence in the finite element analysis results.

This concludes examination of tangential stress variation through the cylinder wall by conventional methods. The next section examines an alternate means of viewing these same results by using **Section Clipping** plots.

Using Section Clipping to Observe Stress Results

Use of *Section Clipping* is introduced in this section. Section plots are used where it is desirable to view stresses interior to a solid model, such as in an assembly of multiple parts, or at various sections within the pressure vessel for this example. Steps below outline use of the *Section Clipping* feature.

1. If the previous close-up view of the pressure vessel wall, appearing in Fig. 47 (b) remains on the screen, use the **Zoom to Fit** icon ⊕ to restore the graphic display to a full image of the model. Then click the **Trimetric** view icon to orient the model in an view like that shown in Fig. 49.

2. Activate *Section Clipping* by right-clicking **Stress2 (-1st principal-)** and from the pull-down menu select **Section Clipping...** The **Section** property manager opens as shown in Fig. 50.

3. In the **Section1** dialogue box, notice that **Front Plane** is selected as the default viewing plane. Also, the **Distance** field, located immediately below **Front Plane** in Fig. 50, is set at **0.00 mm**, thereby indicating that the section view is currently displayed *on* the front surface of the model.

Section Clipping drag-handle.

Figure 49 – Trimetric view of model showing 1st principal stress and the **Section Clipping** drag-handle.

4. In the **Options** dialogue box, clear the "✓" from ☐ **Show contour on the uncut portion of the model**. Immediately the interior and exterior surfaces of the model are shaded the default model color (typically gray). This makes for easier viewing stress contours on cut sections.

5. Next, click-and-drag the *Section Clipping* drag-handle shown in Fig. 49. This action permits dynamic viewing of stresses within the model at any depth from the **Front Plane**.

6. Undo step 4 by checking ☑ **Show contour on the uncut portion of the model**, and again move the *Section Clipping* drag-handle.

A similar effect to that created in step 4 can be obtained as outlined next.

7. In the **Options** dialogue box, check to select ☑ **Plot on section only**. This action restricts plotted stresses to the **Front Plane** *at* the current depth. Once again, move the *Section Clipping* drag-handle and observe the resulting display.

8. To display stress distribution on a mid-plane through the model, type **0** in the **Distance** field of the **Section 1** dialogue box as shown in Fig. 50, and press **[Enter]**. This action creates the display shown in Fig. 51.

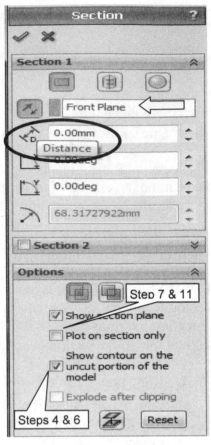

Figure 50 – The **Section** property manager is used to control display of stress contours *within* a model.

P1 (N/m^2)

1.070e+008
1.052e+008
1.033e+008
1.015e+008
9.967e+007
9.783e+007
9.600e+007
9.417e+007
9.233e+007
9.050e+007
8.867e+007
8.683e+007
8.500e+007

Section Clipping options demonstrated in steps 4 through 8 are convenient for masking stress contours which otherwise might make it difficult to differentiate between desired stress contours and other nearby colored fringes.

Figure 51 – Image of tangential stresses in the cylinder wall with the ☑ **Plot on section only** option active.

9. Within the **Section1** dialogue box, experiment by clicking the down arrow ▼adjacent to **0.00mm** in the **Distance** spin box. The down arrow moves the section away from the front plane in the negative z-direction and into the model. Conversely, if the up arrow ▲ is selected, the section viewing plane moves away from the model (+ z-direction). For values greater than **0.00mm**, the section plane is located *in front* of the model, thus the model is not sectioned and no

stresses are visible. It is also possible to examine stress at a particular depth within the model by typing any desired location into the **Distance** spin-box.

10. Also experiment by clicking ▲ and ▼ arrows in the **Rotation X** and **Rotation Y** spin boxes located in the **Section 1** dialogue box and observe the display.

11. Reset **Distance** to **0.00** mm and clear the check-mark "✓" from ☐ **Plot on section only**.

As a final demonstration of the *Section Clipping* feature, tangential stress variation through the cylinder wall is viewed by sectioning the cylinder perpendicular to its length as outlined below.

12. Either rotate the model to display its right-side view or, from the SolidWorks toolbar select the right-side view icon. A right-side view, looking down the axis of the cylinder from the pipe connection-end, appears in Fig. 52.

13. In the **Section 1** dialogue box, click to activate (highlight light blue) the **Reference entity** field (top field that currently shows the words "**Front Plane**").

14. Next, click + to open the **SolidWorks** flyout menu, at top-left of the graphics screen. Then select the **Right Plane**.

Figure 52 – Right-side view of model prior to taking a section view.

15. Notice that **Right Plane** now appears in the highlighted **Reference entity** field and, because the origin of the Cartesian coordinate system is located at the middle of the model, the right plane bisects the model at its mid-section. As a result, tangential stress variation through the wall thickness is shown as illustrated in Fig. 53. Rotate the model to verify this view.

Figure 53 – Section view taken at the right plane.

16. Once again, to aid in examining stresses in the wall only, in the **Options** dialogue box, click to check ☑ **Plot on section only**. The resulting display is shown in Fig. 54.

Figure 54 shows stresses on the cut section only. The section clipping drag-handle is also shown. The model is rotated to reveal the section location on an outline of the model.

Figure 54 – Tangential stress display on mid-section of the model.

17. In the **Section 1** dialogue box, experiment by clicking the up ▲ or down ▼ arrows on the **Distance** spin box to observe the effect on stresses displayed in the model. Also experiment using the **Rotation X** and **Rotation Y** spin boxes.

18. Click **[OK]** ✓ to close the **Section** property manager.

Analysis Insight

Section Clipping is most advantageous for heat transfer and fluid flow problems where temperature or pressure variation throughout a model is of primary importance. It finds less use for stress analysis problems because maximum stresses always occurs on part surfaces. It is also possible to use the **Probe** feature in combination with any of the *Section* plots to investigate stress *within* a model.

This concludes the analysis of thin and thick-wall pressure vessels using both *shell* and *solid* elements, respectively. Alternate ways to examine results were also explored.

19. Close the model without saving results.

Design Insight

When engaged in the design of any sort of pressure vessel, ASME Boiler and Pressure Vessel Codes[2] must be consulted. The Premium version of SolidWorks Simulation contains a Study type aligned with ASME codes. See the 🔲 Pressure Vessel Design icon in the **Type** dialogue box of the **Study** property manager.

---

[2] The ASME Boiler and Pressure Vessel Code, B31.3-1013 American Society of Mechanical Engineers, New York, NY, 2013.

EXERCISES

EXERCISE 1 – Thick Wall Pressure Vessel

The cylinder in Fig. E4-1 allows three separate pipe connections. The connection on top of the cylinder is considered **Fixed** due to its rigid external attachment (not shown). However, both pipes on the flat, right end are connected to flexible pipe segments (also not shown) that permit movement in the X (axial) and Y (vertical) directions. Movement in these directions is permitted to accommodate axial and circumferential expansion when the tank is pressurized. In other words, movement is only restricted in the Z-direction at these pipe connections. Perform a finite element analysis of this cylinder subject to the following guidelines. Open the file: **Pressure Vessel 4-1**. (Use SI units)

Figure E4-1 – Cylindrical pressure vessel with three pipe attachments. Wall thickness t = 25 mm.

- Material: **AISI Type 316L stainless steel** (Use S.I. units)

- Mesh: In the Mesh property manager, select a ⊙ **Standard Mesh**. (NOTE: Determine whether $t \le r_i/20$ to ascertain if thin or thick wall classical stress equations should be used to calculate stress in the cylinder walls.

- External Loads: **P = 950 kN/m^2**, internal pressure. External pressure is negligible.

- Fixtures: The pipe connection on top of the cylinder is **Fixed/Immovable**.

    Pipes on right end of the tank restrain movement in the **Z**-direction only. This restraint and its direction are somewhat arbitrary, but are included to demonstrate how alternative restraints might be applied.

    Assistance dealing with these pipe restraints is included in the **Solution Guidance** *box below.*

    Apply **Symmetry** restraints on cut surfaces of the cylinder.

Solution Guidance

Begin by reducing the model to half of the tank geometry as follows.

- In the SolidWorks Feature manager locate **Half-Model of Cylinder** and **Unsuppress** it.

- Do *not* remove fillets at each pipe connection since their removal will cause a significant increase in stress at these locations.

To apply restraints in the Z-direction on end surfaces of the horizontal pipe connections, proceed as follows.

i. Right-click **Fixtures** and from the pull-down menu, select **Fixed Geometry...**

ii. In the **Advanced** dialogue box, select **Use Reference Geometry**.

iii. Click the *end faces* of both pipe extensions located on the right-side of the cylinder. **Face<1>** and **Face<2>** appear in the **Faces, Edges, Vertices for Fixture** field.

iv. Activate (highlight) the **Face, Edge, Plane Axis for Direction** field. Then, in the SolidWorks flyout menu, select **Right Plane** (it is oriented in the Z-direction).

Figure E4-2 -Restraints applied to prevent motion in the Z-direction.

v. In the **Translations** dialogue box, select the **Along Plane Dir 1** icon. The field is highlighted (white) and "**0**" appears. This value indicates zero translation is allowed in the selected Z-direction. See Fig. E4-3

vi. Click **[OK]** ✓ to close the **Fixture** property manager.

Figure E4-3 – Restraint symbols in Z-direction.

Vectors displayed on the model should be oriented in the Z-direction, see Fig. E4-3. Either the ± Z-direction is acceptable since displacement = 0.

Develop a finite element model that includes: material selection, fixtures, external loads, mesh the model (two elements are required across the cylinder wall thickness; one element thickness is permitted on pipe extensions), and a solution.

Determine the following:

   a. Create a stress contour plot of von Mises stress in the cylinder and all its connecting entities. Include all fixtures, external loads, and automatic labeling of maximum von Mises stress on this plot. Does the maximum von Mises stress exceed material yield strength?

   b. Use classical equations to calculate magnitudes of tangential and radial stresses at both the inside and outside surfaces of the cylinder. Label calculations. Assume these calculations are made in a region well removed from the cylinder ends and pipe connections.

   c. Use finite element analysis to determine tangential stress in the cylinder wall *opposite* the top pipe connection. When determining this stress, reduce the range of stress values plotted to magnitudes slightly above and slightly below tangential stress magnitudes anticipated on the inside and outside surfaces. Plot the *appropriate stress* contour to show tangential stress distribution through the cylinder wall.

   d. Use the **Probe** feature to produce a graph of tangential stress variation through the cylinder wall from inside to outside. Choose both corner and mid-side node points at the middle of the cylinder (i.e. midway between its left and right ends.) Add a descriptive title, axis labels, and your name to this graph.

   e. Repeat step (c), but replace "tangential" stress with "radial" stress.

   f. Repeat step (d), but replace "tangential" stress with "radial" stress.

   g. Compare the percent difference between FEA results and results obtained from classical pressure vessel calculations determined in part (b). Results to be compared include the tangential stresses at inside and outside surfaces of the cylinder and also radial stresses at inside and outside surfaces. Use the following equation to compute the percent difference between results.

$$\% \text{ difference} = \frac{(\text{FEA result - classical result})}{\text{FEA result}} * 100 = \qquad [1]$$

   h. Comment upon the "goodness" of agreement between results of part (g). If classical and FEA results differ by more than 8%, explain why.

EXERCISE 2 – Analysis of a Sheet Metal Bracket Using Shell Elements

The bracket shown in Fig. E4-4 is one of two brackets used to attach a cargo case to the rear of a motorcycle frame. **Chrome Stainless Steel** is used for the bracket to enhance appearance and to provide corrosion resistance. Bolts attach the bracket to the frame through three holes on the vertical (left) leg as illustrated in Fig. E4-4. A downward design load of 14 lb is applied at the hole on tab **A**. This load represents a portion of load carried by tab **A** in a fully loaded cargo case. Perform a finite element analysis of this part using *shell* elements applied at the mid-surface of the part.

Figure E4-4 – Bracket used to attach a cargo case to a motorcycle frame.

Open the file: **Bracket 4-2**.

- Material: **Chrome Stainless Steel** (Use English units)

- Mesh: Use the default ⊙ **Curvature based mesh** and default mesh size. Mesh using *shell* elements defined on the mid-surface. NOTE: When using the **Shell mesh using mid-surface** option, thickness of the elements is automatically extracted from the SolidWorks model geometry for this example.

- Fixtures: Apply a **Fixed** restraint to the three bolt holes. This fixture can be applied to either the hole edge or to its inner surface.

- External Load: **14-lb** vertical load applied to the hole edge or inner surface of the hole on Tab A. This force is directed downward on the tab as shown in Fig. E4-4

This exercise is used to demonstrate application of shell elements to a sheet metal part. Recall from the chapter introduction that sheet metal parts are automatically treated as shell elements by the software. As such, this exercise provides insight into a second way of creating a shell model. Guidance used to create a shell model of the bracket using this second method is provided below.

How is it known that the current model is a sheet metal part? To answer this question, open the part file and examine the SolidWorks Feature manager tree. In the tree, **Sheet-Metal1** is listed along with several SolidWorks features that pertain exclusively to sheet metal parts. Also, in the Simulation manager tree observe that **Bracket 4-2** is represented by a "thin sheet" icon ◇ Bracket 4-2 rather than by the solid body icon ▭ Bracket 4-2.

Solution Guidance

1. Apply **Fixtures** to the three holes. **Fixed** restraints can be applied to either the hole edge or to surfaces within each hole. Restraints are automatically transferred to edges of a shell element model.

2. Applying a downward force on tab **A** is similar to that of applying a directed force on a split-line. The 14-lb downward force can be applied to either an *edge* or the *inner surface* of the hole in tab **A**.

Method #2 for Defining a Shell Model

1. Right-click **Bracket 4-2 (-Chrome Stainless Steel-)** (or) choose whatever filename was specified by you. From the pull-down menu, select **Edit Definition…** The **Shell Definition** property manager opens as seen in Fig. E4-5.

2. In the **Type** dialogue box, choose ⊙ **Thin** and set **Unit** to **in**. The grayed-out number appearing in the **Shell Thickness** field **0.1046** corresponds to the sheet metal thickness specified in SolidWorks. This step permits the user to view the part thickness.

3. Click **[OK]** ✓ to close the **Shell Definition** property manager.

4. Right-click **Mesh** and select **Create Mesh…** The **Mesh** property manager opens.

5. Open the ☑ **Mesh Parameters** dialogue box, verify that ⊙ **Curvature based mesh** is selected.

Figure E4-5 – Checking Shell thickness as specified in the original SolidWorks drawing file.

6. Accept remaining default settings and click **[OK]** ✓ to close the **Mesh** property manager.

Note the small number of steps required to create a shell mesh on this sheet metal bracket [three steps (1) to (3) above] as compared to approximately twenty steps required to specify the mid-surface and then shell mesh the thin wall pressure vessel example. This streamlined procedure is realized because the original model was defined as a sheet metal part and the software automatically recognizes this fact. Models classified as "surface parts" are equally simple to convert to a shell mesh.

Develop a finite element model that includes: material specification, fixtures, external loads, mesh generation, and solution.

Determine the following:

a. Plot von Mises stress on the top surface of the shell face; include the applied load and fixtures on this plot. Consider the top surface to be that shown facing upward in Fig. E4-4 (i.e., the top side of the model is the side to which the external 14-lb load is applied). Include automatic labeling of maximum and minimum von Mises stress on this plot.

   NOTE: If the "top" surface, as defined in (a) above, appears orange in color (recall orange denotes the "bottom" surface), then **Flip Shell Elements** as outlined in the example problem. However, remember to hold the **[Shift]** key while selecting *all* surfaces on one side of the model.

b. Repeat part (a) for the "bottom" surface of the bracket. By what percent do the maximum von Mises stresses on the top and bottom surfaces differ? On what surface does the maximum von Mises stress occur? (top or bottom)

c. Questions: Where on the model does maximum stress occur? Does this stress exceed the material yield strength? Describe factors, such as part geometry, location of the applied load, and other influencing factors that cause the maximum stress to occur where it does on the model.

EXERCISE 3 – Joist Hanger Analysis Using Shell Elements

"Joist" is the name commonly applied to beams used to support floors in residential and commercial construction. So called "joist hangers" are often used to connect the ends of joists to a "header beam." For individuals unfamiliar with floor joists, header beams, and joist hangers, these items are labeled in Fig. E 4-6. Common nails are used to fasten joist hangers, beams, and joists. However, this exercise is simplified to examine only loads transferred to a joist hanger by a single floor joist. Also, nails used to fasten a joist to the joist hanger are not explicitly modeled. The joist hanger to be analyzed is shown in Figs. E4-7 (a) and (b).

Open the File: **Joist Hanger**

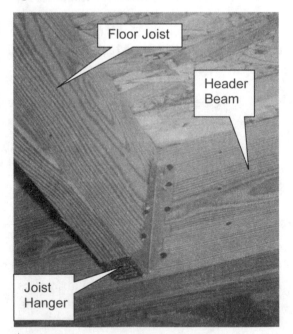

Figure E4-6 – A joist hanger and related beams are identified in the image above.

(a)	(b)

Figure E4-7 – Typical joist hanger used to support 2"x10" floor joists. A load of 140 lb is distributed over the bottom surface indicated by the arrow in the figure.

- Material: **Galvanized Steel** (Use English units) Galvanized steel is used because joist hangers are also used under porches, decks, and in other exposed exterior environments.

- Mesh: **Shell Mesh** – Traditionally used to model sheet metal parts. Use the default **Curvature based mesh** and default mesh size.

- Fixture: **Fixed** restraints are applied *only* to nail holes at locations **A, A′, B, B′,** and **C, C′** in Fig. E4-7(b). Nails passing through these holes connect the joist hanger to a header beam like that labeled in Fig. E4-6.

- External Load: A **140** lb downward load is applied normal to the bottom surface of the joist hanger. This load accounts for lumber weight plus the weight of furnishings, appliances, and people on the floor above. It is *uniformly distributed* over the bottom of the joist hanger.

Develop a finite element model that includes: material specification, fixtures, external load, mesh generation, and solution as specified below. See Solution Guidance for Exercise 2 to determine thickness of the joist hanger.

Determine the following:

a. Before creating any plots, ensure that the "top" side of the meshed model corresponds to the inside of the "U" shaped joist hanger. Recall that *all* surfaces that share the same *side* of the model must be specified as the same surface (i.e., top and bottom surfaces cannot be mixed together on the same surface). It may be necessary to imagine the part flattened out to help identify surfaces common to one side of the model. Next, create a von Mises stress plot showing the stress distribution on the top surface of the joist hanger. For this plot, turn on the **Show max annotation** feature. Adjacent to this image, show a manual calculation of the uniform load applied to the bottom of the joist hanger.

b. On the plot created in part (a), identify all regions of high stress by circling them. Also, on the plot, answer the question: "Is the material yield strength exceeded at any of these high stress locations?" If "yes" label these locations as "FS < 1."

c. Repeat parts (a) and (b), but create a plot of von Mises stress on the bottom surface of the joist hanger. On this plot, state whether the largest von Mises stresses occur on the top or bottom surface of the shell model.

d. Assume that lack of attention to detail, carelessness, rushing to finish the job, or just plain laziness, results in fewer than all nails being driven through holes **Fixed** to the header beam at locations **A, A′, B, B′,** and **C, C′.** On your own create two additional scenarios. In scenario 1, omit one nail from *each side* of the joist hanger where it is attached to the header beam. In scenario 2, omit two nails from *each side* of the joist hanger. Do this by editing the **Fixtures** folder as follows.

    • In the Simulation manager tree, select **Fixture-1** and from the pull-down menu, select **Edit Definition...**

    • In the **Standard (Fixed Geometry)** dialogue box right-click the nail fixtures to be eliminated and then from the pull-down menu, select **Delete**.

    • Click **[OK]** ✔ to close the **Fixture** property manager.

e. For both scenarios 1 and 2, repeat parts (a) and (b) of this problem. Does the joist hanger become unsafe for either of these two scenarios? If "yes" identify the unsafe scenario(s) and label areas where the safety factor is "FS < 1."

Textbook Problems

In addition to the above exercises, it is highly recommended that additional problems involving pressure vessels and/or thin parts be worked from a design of machine elements textbook. Textbook problems provide a great way to discover errors made in formulating a finite element analysis because they typically are well defined problems for which the solution is known. Typical textbook problems, if well defined in advance, make an excellent source of solutions for comparison.

CHAPTER 5

INTERFERENCE FIT ANALYSIS

This chapter examines modeling of an interference fit between two mating parts. For purposes of discussion the generic term "interference fit" is considered synonymous with the terminology "force fit" or "shrink fit." In SolidWorks Simulation, however, all these fit types are referred to as "shrink fits." Interference fits are often used to join two members together without the need for other fastening devices such as pins, set-screws, or keys, key seats, and keyways. Interference fit analysis is often considered together with thick wall pressure vessel analysis since the internal member exerts the equivalent of an outward pressure on the part into which it is force fit. And, conversely, the external member exerts the equivalent of an external pressure onto the part it surrounds.

Although this example solves an interference fit problem for a single set of part dimensions, it is important to recognize that, in practice, maximum and minimum stress levels occur due to dimensional variations of mating parts. For example, a minimum level of interference must be ensured in order to transfer a desired torque between mating components. This case results when the smallest shaft is inserted into the largest hole. Conversely, when tolerances are such that the largest shaft is inserted into the smallest hole then maximum interference results. Stress levels correspond directly to the amount of interference. Another factor to consider occurs when different materials are used for mating parts. In these instances the effects of differential dimension changes due to thermal expansion or contraction may also have to be considered. The above scenarios are cited to alert the user to some additional factors that affect interference fits. However, because the emphasis of this text is on mastering use of SolidWorks Simulation, these additional factors are not considered in this example.

Learning Objectives

Upon completion of this example, users should be able to:

- Set-up and analyze an *interference fit* in an assembly.

- Define and use a *cylindrical* coordinate system.

- Examine results in a *local (cylindrical)* coordinate system.

- Generate a *report* summarizing Study results.

- Apply alternative means of *controlling rigid body motion*.

Problem Statement

A partially dimensioned section view of a wheel and its axle is shown in Fig. 1. The wheel is part of an overhead traveling crane used to transport heavy materials from point-to-point on a factory floor. The 2.5041 inch diameter shaft is shrink fit into a wheel-hub with inside diameter of 2.5000 inches resulting in a 0.0041 inch diametral interference.

This example is the first to include analysis of an *assembly* involving more than one part. Analysis of this model begins below.

Figure 1 – Maximum shaft size and minimum hole size (minimum bore) for an interference fit between a shaft and crane wheel.

1. Open SolidWorks by making the following selections. (*NOTE:* ">" is used to separate successive menu selections.)

Start>All Programs>SolidWorks 2013 (or) Click the **SolidWorks** icon on your screen.

2. When SolidWorks is open, select **File > Open…** and open the file named **Wheel Shaft Assembly**. The model opens and the **Assembly** tab appears at the top left of your screen. *(If the Assembly menu is to be opened, simply click its tab.)*

Interference Check

Before beginning an analysis of this assembly, confirm that interference does indeed exist between the shaft and wheel. Check for interference as follows.

1. In the Main menu, click **Tools** and from the pull-down menu select ⬚ Interference Detection... A partial view of the **Interference Detection** property manager is shown in Fig. 2.

2. In the **Selected Components** dialogue box observe that the **Wheel Shaft Assembly.SLDASM** is pre-selected as the assembly to be checked for interference. Also notice that the **Results** dialogue box currently indicates that interference is **Not calculated**.

3. In the **Selected Components** dialogue box, click the **[Calculate]** button. Immediately the *volume* of interference between the shaft and wheel is calculated and listed in the **Results** dialogue box as **0.06 in^3**. Also, the interference region between the shaft and wheel is highlighted as seen in Fig. 2. Interference is thus verified.

4. Click **[OK]** ✓ to close the **Interference Detection** property manager.

Figure 2 – The interference fit region is highlighted during an Interference Check of parts in the shaft and wheel assembly.

Create a Static Analysis (Study)

1. In the main menu, select **Simulation** and from the pull-down menu choose **Study...** Alternatively, click the **Simulation** *tab* to activate it. Next, beneath the **Study Advisor** icon, click ▼, then select **New Study**. A partial view of the **Study** property manager is shown in Fig. 3.

2. In the **Name** dialogue box type "**Force Fit Analysis-YOUR NAME**" as a descriptive name for this Study.

3. In the **Type** dialogue box select **Static** as the analysis **Type** (if not already selected).

4. Click **[OK]** ✓ to close the **Study** property manager.

5. The Simulation manager opens at left of the graphics area.

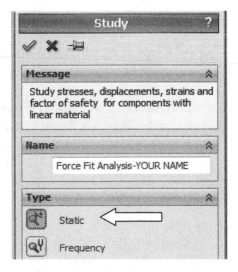

Figure 3 – Initial steps to create a Study in SolidWorks Simulation.

Assign Material Properties to the Model

Unlike previous examples, materials for the **Shaft** and **Wheel** were *pre-assigned* within SolidWorks.

1. Click the "+" sign adjacent to the **Parts** folder. This action reveals that material for **Shaft-1** is listed as (-[SW]Alloy Steel-) and for **wheel-1** material is listed as (-[SW]Cast Alloy Steel-) shown above the vertical arrow in Fig. 4. The [SW] designation indicates material properties were assigned in SolidWorks and are automatically transferred into SolidWorks Simulation.

Before proceeding, verify material properties are specified using English units as outlined below.

Figure 4 – Simulation manager tree showing that materials for the Shaft and Wheel assembly are pre-selected in SolidWorks.

2. Right-click **Shaft-1(-[SW]Alloy Steel-)** and select **Apply/Edit Material…** In the **Materials** window set **Units:** to **English (IPS)**; then select **[Apply]** and **[Close]**.

3. Repeat step 2 for **wheel1(-[SW]Cast Alloy Steel-)**.

SolidWorks Default Connection Definition

Before proceeding, examine the **Connections** defined between the wheel and shaft.

1. Click the "+" sign to open the **Connections** folder. Then, within this folder click the "+" sign to open the **Component Contacts** sub-folder.

2. Observe that **Global Contact (-Bonded-)** is initially defined between the shaft and wheel. A **Bonded** contact indicates that parts act as if they are permanently "glued" together, which is *not* the case in this example.

Analysis Insight

- It is possible to *change* the material specified within SolidWorks at any time. Simply follow the procedure outlined in step 2 before the Solution is run.

- The **Global Contact (-Bonded-)**, which appears beneath the **Component Contacts** folder, is the software default setting for parts in direct contact. Because the intent is to investigate a "Force Fit" between the wheel and shaft, this contact setting is changed later in this example.

Defeature and Simplify the Model

An enlarged view of the shaft and wheel assembly is shown in Fig. 5. Careful observation reveals numerous small fillets and rounds on various edges of the model. Knowing in advance that the current assembly is to be analyzed using finite element methods, the original SolidWorks model was created to facilitate the defeaturing process by creating all small fillets and rounds in a single step. Therefore, the defeaturing steps outlined below are very efficient.

NOTE: Larger fillets at the four "corners" of the spoke cut-outs are *not* removed from the model because, if removed, they might be a source of significant stress concentration. This insight is based upon engineering judgment. Proceed as follows to defeature the model.

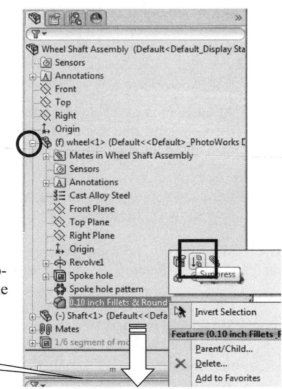

Figure 5 – Observe multiple fillets and rounds on various edges of the model.

1. If necessary, click-and-drag the lower boundary of the SolidWorks feature manager tree downward to reveal its full contents. See arrow at bottom of Fig. 6.

2. Click the "+" sign adjacent to the **wheel<1>** folder, circled in Fig. 6, to display steps used to create the wheel model in SolidWorks.

3. Right-click "**0.10 inch Fillets & Rounds**" highlighted near the bottom of the feature manger in Fig. 6. A pop-up menu also appears to the right of the feature manager tree in Fig. 6.

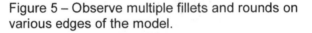

Click here to drag.

Figure 6 – Selections in the SolidWorks feature manager tree to simplify wheel geometry (i.e., to defeature it).

4. Within the pop-up menu, select the **Suppress** icon boxed in Fig. 6. This action removes all small fillets and rounds from the wheel as shown in Fig. 7. The model is simplified (defeatured) prior to meshing.

The model is further simplified by making use of model symmetry as outlined next.

Apply Fixtures

Reduce Model Size Using Symmetry

Examination of the defeatured model, shown in Fig. 7, reveals symmetry in the repeated pattern of spokes and holes on the crane wheel. Once again, it is possible to reduce model size and speed up the solution process if model symmetry is used to our advantage. Because there are six spokes and six openings, it is obvious that 1/6th of the model (or a $360^{o}/6 = 60^{o}$ "slice" or "wedge"), is the smallest symmetrical segment that can be used. It is possible to select other fractions of the assembly provided geometric symmetry is preserved. Other convenient model segments would be 1/3 (a 120° slice),1/2 (a 180° slice), or 2/3 (a 240° slice). Proceed as follows.

Figure 7 – Observing symmetry of the defeatured shaft and wheel assembly.

1. At the bottom of the SolidWorks manager tree, right-click the grayed-out "**1/6 segment of model**" icon highlighted in Fig. 8.

2. From the pop-up menu, select the **Unsuppress** icon shown at the arrow on Fig. 8.

The result of steps 1 and 2 produces a 1/6th segment of the shaft and wheel assembly shown in Fig. 9.

3. Click-and-drag the upper boundary of the Simulation manager tree *upward* to provide more room to view its contents. CAUTION: Do *not* use the "rollback" bar pictured here as it is associated with the SolidWorks manager tree.

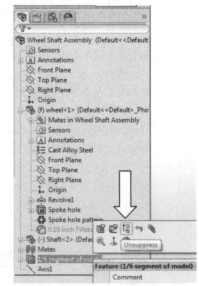

Figure 8 – Unsuppressing the 1/6th model of the shaft and wheel assembly.

Analysis Insight

Due to model symmetry, it is possible to select a "slice" of the model that either intersects openings between wheel spokes (as illustrated in Fig. 9) or one that intersects spokes on both sides of an opening.

The decision to model using the segment shown in Fig. 9 is based on an understanding that a full picture of stresses in a single spoke is more revealing than a split image of the stress distribution in a half-spoke on either side of an opening. While this is the preferred selection, FEA results are *not* affected by this choice.

Figure 9 – Symmetry applied to yield a 1/6th segment of the shaft and wheel assembly.

Define Symmetry Restraints (Fixtures)

Symmetry restraints were first introduced in the previous chapter where segments of thin and thick-wall pressure vessels were considered. Symmetry restraints serve the purpose of making the cut portion of a symmetrical model behave *as if* the entire model were still present. Therefore, symmetry restraints must be applied to all surfaces created when the model is cut. Figure 9 shows one surface (#1) on the shaft and two surfaces (#2 and #3) on the hub and outer rim of the wheel, respectively. Of course, three duplicate surfaces exist on the opposite side of the "slice." Therefore, symmetry restraints must be applied to a total of six surfaces. Proceed as follows to apply symmetry restraints.

1. In the Simulation manager tree, right-click **Fixtures** and from the pull-down menu select **Roller/Slider...** The **Fixture** property manager opens.

2. Observe motion of the "generic" model in the **Example** dialogue box. In essence this image shows that the block is able to move (translate) left or right and up or down on the plane, but it cannot translate in normal to the fixed plane.

Figure 10 – **Roller/Slider** Fixture applied to all cut surfaces of the shaft and wheel assembly.

3. The **Faces for Fixture** field is active (highlighted light blue) and awaits selection of surfaces to which symmetry restraints are to be applied. Move the cursor over the model and select the three numbered surfaces shown in Fig. 9. Also select their counterparts on the opposite side of the model. Rotate the assembly as necessary to select all cut faces.

With each selection, a new surface is highlighted and is listed as **Face<1>@wheel-1** (or **@Shaft-1** etc.), **Face<2>@...**, up to ... **Face<6>** in the **Faces for Fixture** field. Also, restraint symbols appear on the model as illustrated in Fig. 10.

4. Click **[OK]** ✓ to close the **Fixture** property manager. ⌂ **Roller/Slider** appears beneath the **Fixtures** folder in the Simulation manager tree.

Analysis Insight

Prior versions of SolidWorks Simulation permitted application of the ▣ **Symmetry** fixture to solve the current model. However, commencing with SolidWorks Simulation 2013, SP-1 (Service Pack update) the ▣ **Symmetry** fixture has been redefined to apply only to1/2, 1/4, or 1/8 models or models having true orthogonal symmetry. Recall application of the ▣ **Symmetry** fixture to the $1/8^{th}$ model of a thin wall pressure vessel (see Figs. 11 & 13 in Chapter 4). This same fixture was also applied to the ½ model of a thick wall pressure vessel (Fig. 35, Chapter 4). Because the 1/6 "slice" of the wheel-shaft assembly does not exhibit the required orthogonal symmetry, different fixtures must be used. NOTE: If, however, ½ of the wheel-shaft assembly were used, then the ▣ **Symmetry** fixture could be applied.

Nevertheless, there remain at least three different **Fixtures** that can be applied to a symmetrical model that is reduced in size by cutting it into *non*-orthogonal "slices" or "wedges." Those three **Fixtures** are described below.

Roller/Slider – ⌂ Roller/Slider
This restraint is a good option because it allows translation in two directions along a plane, but restricts motion *normal* to the plane. A **Roller/Slider** restraint is demonstrated in this example.

On Flat Faces – ▣ On Flat Faces
Although cut faces of the wheel-shaft assembly "slice" are *not* orthogonal, they are *flat*. Therefore, like the above restraint, the **On Flat Faces** fixture permits translations in two direstions along a cut face, but no translation *normal* to the face. Thus, this restraint could also be applied to the current example.

Use Reference Geometry – ▣ Use Reference Geometry
This option requires the user to specify which of three translations (two along the plane and one normal to the plane) are set to zero. Obviously, translation *normal* to the plane must be set equal to zero. When solid and shell elements occur in the same model, separate **Use Reference Geometry** fixtures must be specified for each.

Analysis Insight (continued)

Circular Symmetry – [Circular Symmetry]
If given a choice, many users might choose the **Circular Symmetry** fixture for the wheel-shaft assembly based simply on its icon shape. The icon depicts a slice of a generic circular model. However, this is one **Fixture** that *absolutely cannot* be applied to the current model. *Why?* Use of this restraint is limited to cases where loads or displacements are present in the circumferential direction. An example of such a load might be caused by a belt drive, chain tension, or gear forces acting tangent to the circumference of a circular pulley or sprocket.

Rigid Body Motion -
As noted in the thick-wall pressure vessel example, while assignment of symmetry boundary conditions applies proper restraints to account for missing portions of the model, those same boundary conditions may not provide sufficient restraint to prevent "rigid body motion" of the model.

For this example, note the following two facts: (a) All restraints shown in Fig. 10 are applied normal to cut surfaces of the 1/6th model; and (b) *If* each restraint vector were broken into components, then each vector could be replaced by its X and Y force components. Rotate the model to a front view to convince yourself of these two facts. Therefore, an obvious conclusion is that model translations are restrained in the X and Y directions, but *no restraint* exists in the Z-direction (axial direction). Thus, rigid body motion of the model is *not* currently restrained in the axial direction.

Because rigid body motion is not allowed in finite element studies, additional restraints must be added to the model as outlined next.

Apply Fixtures to Eliminate Rigid Body Motion

Because the assembly consists of two parts, the shaft and the wheel, both parts must be restrained properly. The need to restrain both parts may seem counter-intuitive since a shrink fit is defined between the shaft and wheel and a shrink fit is considered to be a semi-permanent connection. However, this seeming contradiction provides an opportunity to note that shrink fit contact is considered frictionless by default within SolidWorks Simulation. Therefore, proceed as follows to apply restraints to prevent rigid body motion.

1. Right-click **Fixtures** and from the pull-down menu, select **Fixed Geometry...** The **Fixture** property manager opens as shown on the left side of Fig. 11.

2. Open the **Advanced** dialogue box and select **Use Reference Geometry**. The reason for selecting **Reference Geometry** will be apparent in a future step.

3. In the **Advanced** dialogue box the **Faces, Edges, Vertices for Fixture** field is active (light blue). Proceed to select two *vertices* on the model (one on the shaft center-line and the other on the wheel). Selected vertices are shown circled on Fig. 11. After selecting these vertices, **Vertex<1>@Shaft-1** and **Vertex<2>@ wheel-1** appear in the active field. The actual number within **Vertex< >** depends on the order of selection. *Any other vertices could have been selected.*

Figure 11 – **Fixture** property manager and selections of vertices and reference geometry needed to prevent rigid body motion of the shaft and wheel assembly.

4. Next, click to activate (light blue) the second field from top in the **Advanced** dialogue box. The identifier **Face, Edge, Plane, Axis for Direction** appears when the cursor is passed over this field as illustrated in Fig. 11.

5. Select **Axis1** either on the model or near the bottom of the SolidWorks flyout menu (circled in Fig. 11). **Axis1** is selected because it is oriented in the Z-direction, the direction in which rigid body translation is to be prevented. After making this selection, **Axis1@Shaft-1@Wheel Shaft Assembly** appears in the highlighted field.

6. Open the **Translations** dialogue box (if not already open) and set ▤ **Unit** to **in**. Then, at the bottom of this dialogue box (see bottom arrow in Fig. 11), select the **Axial** icon and accept the zero value shown. This value indicates that *no* translation is permitted in the **Axial** (Z) direction.

7. Click **[OK]** ✓ to close the **Fixture** property manager. **Reference Geometry-1 (:0 in:)** appears beneath the **Fixtures** folder in the Simulation manager tree. Also, restraint symbols appear on the model at the two locations circled in Fig. 11.

8. Right-click **Fixtures** and from the pull-down menu select **Hide All**. This action temporarily hides restraint symbols to reduce clutter on the model.

The preceding steps ensure that the assembly is restrained against rigid body translation in the axial Z-direction.

Aside:

The focus of this example is on modeling and analyzing an interference fit. Therefore, no *external* loads or *reactions* are applied to the model. In real life, external loads and reactions would be due to wheel-to-rail contact and shaft support reactions.

As a consequence, only forces due to an interference fit are included in this analysis. These forces are equal and opposite between contacting surfaces. In brief, forces caused by interference fits are internally balanced.

Use Contact Sets to Define a Shrink Fit

Because the wheel inside diameter is smaller than the shaft outside diameter, an interference/shrink fit exists. When analyzing shrink fits in SolidWorks Simulation you are cautioned that the amount of interference should be greater than 0.1% of the larger diameter at the interface between mating parts (here: 0.001*2.5041 = 0.0025041 < 0.0041). Because the 0.004- in interference is greater than 0.0025041in shaft size, the above restriction is satisfied thus a valid solution is expected. This restriction is imposed because the amount of overlap between mating parts must be sufficiently large to overcome approximations introduced during meshing. If the amount of interference is too small, inaccurate solutions may result.

To establish a shrink fit between the shaft and wheel, it is necessary to specify the surfaces where interference occurs. To facilitate selecting these surfaces, components of the assembly are separated by creating an exploded view as follows.

1. From the Main menu select **Insert**. Then from the pull-down menu select **Exploded View...** A portion of the **Explode** property manager is illustrated in Fig. 12.

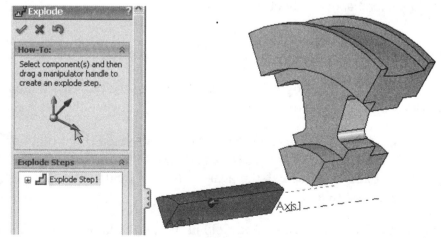

Figure 12 – Manually creating an exploded view of the shaft and wheel assembly.

Read instructions in the yellow **How-To:** dialogue box at top of the **Explode** property manager and proceed as follows.

2. For this example, move the cursor onto the graphics screen and click to select the *shaft*. Immediately, an X, Y, Z coordinate triad appears to "float" near the shaft. Click-and-drag the vector aligned with the direction of the shaft axis and drag the shaft away from the wheel as illustrated in Fig. 12. This action is recorded in the **Explode Steps** dialogue box as **Explode Step1**.

3. Click **[OK]** ✓ to close the **Explode** property manager. NOTE: Either component could be moved in any direction to create an acceptable exploded view.

4. Within the Simulation manager, right-click the 🔩 **Connections** folder. A pull-down menu appears. *NOTE: This is the first time the **Connections** folder is used.*

5. From the pull-down menu select **Contact Set…** The **Contact Sets** property manager opens, but it initially appears different than illustrated in Fig. 13.

Figure 13 – Defining faces where a shrink fit occurs between the shaft and wheel. For this example the **Target** and **Source** faces can be interchanged without consequence.

6. In the **Contact** dialogue box, choose ⊙ **Manually select contact sets**.

7. At top of the **Type** dialogue box, click ▼ to open the pull-down menu and select **Shrink Fit** as the type of contact to be modeled between the shaft and wheel.

8. The **Faces, Edges, Vertices for Set 1** field is activated (light blue) and awaits input. Rotate the model as necessary and select the *inside surface* of the hole as the **Set 1**. **Face<1>@wheel-1** appears in the top field of Fig. 13. **Set 1** entities are also referred to as the "source."

9. Next, click to activate the second field in the **Type** dialogue box. This is the **Faces for Set 2** field. Move the cursor over the model and select the *cylindrical*

surface of the shaft as the **Set 2** surface, also shown in Fig. 13. **Face<2>@Shaft-1** appears in the active field. **Set 2** is also referred to as the "target." NOTE: In this example either surface can be designated as **Set 1** or **Set 2**. However, this observation is not valid in all cases. See item (c) in the Analysis Insight section below for important details about "source" and "target" designations.

Analysis Insight:

a) Refer to the **Contact Sets** property manager in Fig. 13 and note the **Properties** dialogue box at the bottom of this property manager. As noted earlier, interference fits are considered frictionless by default. However, if our goal were to investigate torque transmitted by an interference fit joint, then friction between mating surfaces would be defined here. Note that the friction value is "grayed out" (inactive). This example does not examine **Friction** effects.

b) Also before closing the **Contact Sets** property manager, briefly revisit the pull-down menu that lists the various types of connections available. Understanding these criteria and a built-in hierarchy that accompanies them is essential to proper modeling a variety of design and analysis situations. For example, in *assemblies* of multiple parts, SolidWorks Simulation applies a system default assumption that all contacting surfaces are **Bonded** together. This assumption treats all contacting faces of different components in an assembly as if they are permanently "glued" together. As such, the **Bonded** condition is applied *Globally* to all contacting parts. This assumption is applied unless one of the other contact conditions, such as the **Shrink Fit** used in this example, is specified *locally* (i.e., limited to contact between specific contacting entities in an assembly). Contact conditions defined in the **Contact Set** property manager have higher priority than do Global or component contact definitions.

   To pursue this topic further, the interested reader is referred to **Help** located on the main menu. From the **Help** pull-down menu, select **SolidWorks Simulation** followed by **Help Topics** and in the [Search Web Help 🔍] field, type "source and target." Review discussion under **Types of Contact**. Virtually all types of contact sets found there are excellently described and illustrated by animated examples.

c) The use of "source" or "target" is interchangeable in this example since both contacting surfaces are *faces*. However, the true definition of **Set 1** "source" entities refers to faces, edges, vertices, points, or beam joints. Whereas the definition of a **Set 2** "target" *only* refers to a face. Thus, in terms of the shrink fit modeled here, contacting faces satisfy the criteria for both a "source" and a "target." On the other hand, if a specific contact were to be defined between the surface of the shaft and the *edge* of the wheel hub, then the shaft *face* must be **Set 2**, the "target," while an *edge* of the wheel hub must be **Set 1**, the "source."

---

10. Finally, click **[OK]** ✓ to close the **Contact Sets** property manager. **Contact Set-1 (-Shrink Fit<wheel-1, Shaft-1>-)** appears beneath **+ Contact Sets**.

Mesh the Model and Run the Solution

Although a correct solution is obtained with the model in either the exploded or unexploded state, return it to its *un*exploded state before meshing. This is done to permit observation of node alignment, or lack thereof, between nodes on the shaft and wheel after meshing. One way to *un*explode the model is outlined below.

1. Click the **Configuration Manager** icon shown circled at top of the SolidWorks Feature manager in Fig. 14.

2. Next, click the "+" signs adjacent to + **Wheel Shaft Assembly Configuration(s)** (if not already selected) and also adjacent to + **Default [Wheel Shaft Assembly]**.

3. Next, right-click **ExplView1**. Then, from the pull-down menu shown in Fig. 14, select **Collapse** to return the model to its assembled view.

4. Toggle back to the **SolidWorks Feature Manager** icon shown boxed in Fig. 14.

Figure 14 – Accessing the **Configuration Manager** tree to "collapse" (*un*explode) the shaft and wheel assembly.

5. In the Simulation manager tree, right-click the **Mesh** icon and from the pop-up menu select **Create Mesh…** The **Mesh** property manager opens.

6. Check ☑ **Mesh Parameters** to open this dialogue box. In this box verify that ⊙**Curvature based mesh** is selected and ⫞ **Units** are set to inches (**in**).

7. The default mesh size is considered acceptable for this analysis. However, before meshing, click ⟱ to open the **Options** dialogue box. One of the options listed there is ☐ **Run (solve) the analysis**. *If* this option is selected, the software proceeds directly to the Solution after meshing the model. While this action eliminates one step in the solution process, it is typically *not* recommended. Why? Because, if an error occurs, the user does not know if it is due to a failure to mesh the model or due to an error in the solution process. Therefore, click **[OK]** ✓ to close the **Mesh** property manager and mesh the model.

8. Finally, right-click the Study name, **Force Fit Analysis-YOUR NAME (-Default-),** and from the pull-down menu select **Run**. The solution process takes slightly longer when solving for an interference fit (typically <10 seconds).

9. If the mesh is not displayed after the solution, right-click the **Mesh** icon and from the pull-down menu, select **Show Mesh**.

The meshed model appears in Fig. 15. NOTE: The system default **Curvature based mesh** was used in this example for the simple reason that it provides a more accurate solution. Also, an orderly mesh is not needed in subsequent steps.

Zoom in to examine nodes on the edge between the contacting surfaces circled in this figure. Notice that nodes on the shaft and wheel are not necessarily aligned with one another. This is called an "incompatible mesh."

Figure 15 – Meshed model of the shaft and wheel assembly. Approximately nine corner nodes exist along the contacting surfaces.

Examination of Results

Default Stress Plot

Begin by examining the vonMises stress plot to gain an overview of results. Desired appearance attributes for this plot are defined below so that they can be copied when producing additional plots.

1. If necessary, click the "+" sign adjacent to the **Results** folder to display a list of the three default plots, **Stress1**, **Displacement1**, and **Strain1**.

2. If necessary, double-click **Stress1 (-vonMises-)** to display this plot. Zoom-in on the model to observe deformation between the shaft and wheel hub in the interference fit region. If the deformed model does *not* appear or if units on the stress legend are *not* psi, follow steps 3 to 5. Otherwise skip to step 6.

3. Right-click **Stress1 (-vonMises-)** and from the pop-up menu, select **Edit Definition...** The **Stress Plot** property manager opens.

4. In the **Display** dialogue box, change 📏 **Units** to **psi**.

5. Check "✓" to open the ☑ **Deformed Shape** dialogue box (if not already selected). Within this dialogue box, select ⊙ **Automatic**. Then click **[OK]** ✓ to close the **Stress Plot** property manager. The system default, exaggerated deformation scale, is applied to an exploded view of the model.

After examining the deformed model, return it to its un-deformed shape as follows.

6. On the **Simulation** tab, located above the graphics area, click the **Deformed Result** icon.

YOUR NAME - vonMises Stress in a Force Fit
Model name: Wheel Shaft Assembly
Study name: Force Fit Analysis-YOUR NAME
Plot type: Static nodal stress Stress1

von Mises (psi)

53,837.5
49,361.5
44,885.6
40,409.6
35,933.6
31,457.7
26,981.7
22,505.8
18,029.8
13,553.8
9,077.9
4,601.9
126.0

Figure 16 – vonMises stress plot incorporating modified display characteristics outlined in this section.

Next, adjust appearance of the von Mises plot so that, at the conclusion of this process, the plot appears as shown in Fig. 16. Proceed as follows.

7. Right-click **Stress1 (-vonMises-)** and from the pop-up menu, select **Edit Definition...** The **Stress Plot** property manager opens.

8. Click ⌄ to open the **Advanced Options** dialogue box. Then, click to *clear* the check from ☐ **Average results across boundary for parts**. This action is important because parts of this assembly are made of two *different materials*. Also, the shaft is loaded in radial and circumferential compression while the inside of the wheel is subject to radial compression and circumferential tension. Therefore, it is not appropriate to average stress results across these two different parts. The resulting values would be meaningless.

9. Also within the **Stress Plot** property manager, click ⌄ to open the **Property** dialogue box. In this dialogue box, click to "check" ☑ **Include title text** and in the empty field, type your name followed by a descriptive title for the plot.

10. Click **[OK]** ✓ to close the **Stress Plot** property manager.

11. Once again, right-click **Stress1 (-vonMises-)** and from the pop-up menu select **Settings...** The **Settings** property manager opens.

12. In the **Fringe Options** dialogue box, click the pull-down menu and select **Discrete** as the display mode for fringes.

13. Within the **Boundary Options** dialogue box, open the pull-down menu and select **Model** to display a black outline on the model.

14. Click **[OK]** ✓ to close the **Settings** property manager.

Observation of Fig. 16 reveals that stress levels in the vicinity of the shrink fit (53,837 psi) *exceed* Yield Strength of the wheel material, which is 35000 psi. Figure 17 shows a summary of properties for the wheel in the **Material Details** window. Material yield strength, **SIGYLD** = 34994 psi ≈ 35000 psi, is listed adjacent to the arrow. Another way to examine this fact is explored in the "Aside" section below.

Aside:

Recall that material information is available at any time by clicking the "+" sign adjacent to the **Parts** folder to reveal **Shaft-1** and **wheel-1**. Next, right-click **wheel-1 (-Cast Alloy Steel-)** and in the pull-down menu, shown in Fig. 17, and select **Details...** This action opens the **Material Details** window located at the right side of the Fig. 17.

Figure 17 – Accessing material property details for the wheel to permit comparison of material Yield Strength with resulting stress in the component.

Notice that material yield strength does not appear on the vonMises stress plot as occurred in earlier examples. The reason for this is that assemblies involve multiple parts, which are often made of different materials. Therefore, the potential for different material properties prohibits the display of a single yield strength value. Because of this, an alternative procedure to that of using the *Safety Factor* check can be applied to display regions where yield strength is exceeded. To apply this method, begin by making a *temporary* change in the **Chart Options** property manager outlined below.

a) If **Stress1 (-vonMises-)** plot is not displayed, double-click its name to display it.

b) Right-click **Stress1 (-vonMises-)** and from the pull-down menu select **Chart Options...** The **Chart Options** property manager opens.

c) Near the bottom of the **Display Options** dialogue box click to select **◉Defined:**. Then, in the bottom box (corresponding to maximum stress) type a value somewhat greater than the yield strength for the wheel as **38000** (or **3.8e4**) and click in the graphics area.

d) Do *not* close the **Chart Options** property manager at this time.

A new plot of vonMises stress within the shaft and wheel assembly is shown in Fig. 18. However, this plot highlights (in red) the entire region where stress due to the interference fit exceeds the yield strength. Examination of the colored stress chart reveals that stresses above approximately 34843 psi are shown in red. Therefore, the stress region above the yield strength (35,000 psi) is easily identified. Next, reset the plot to its original settings as follows.

von Mises (psi)

3.800e+004
3.484e+004
3.168e+004
2.853e+004
2.537e+004
2.221e+004
1.905e+004
1.590e+004
1.274e+004
9.580e+003
6.422e+003
3.264e+003
1.063e+002

Note enlarged
region shown in red

Figure 18 – Locating regions where yield strength is exceeded by re-defining chart **Display Options**.

e) Return to the middle of the **Display Options** dialogue box and select ⊙**Automatic**, which restores previous max. and min. stress values.

f) Click **[OK]** ✓ to close the **Chart Options** property manager. The image is reset to display the full-range of von Mises stress throughout the assembly.

The fact that yield strength of the wheel is exceeded is cause for redesign of the interference fit and/or selection of an alternative wheel material. However, since the goal of this example is to focus on defining interference fits and interpreting results related to those fits, a re-design of the shaft and wheel assembly is not pursued here. We now return to investigate more meaningful ways to display results.

Stress Plots in a Cylindrical Coordinate System

Tangential (Circumferential or Hoop) Stress

Tangential stress is one of two stresses easily calculated using classical stress equations for a shrink fit. However, because traditional stresses like σ_x, σ_y, σ_z, σ_1, σ_2, σ_3, τ_{xy}, τ_{yz}, τ_{zx}, etc., in a Cartesian (X, Y, Z) coordinate system are not conducive for representing circumferential stress in cylindrical parts, a cylindrical coordinate system is introduced below to facilitate the examination of results.

When establishing a cylindrical coordinate system, *any* axis can be used to define the axis of a local cylindrical coordinate system. However, this axis must be chosen wisely because once an axis is selected, stresses usually associated with SX = σ_x, SY = σ_y, and SZ = σ_z take on new meanings as summarized in Table 1.

In the following discussion, "reference axis" refers to an axis aligned with the centerline of a cylindrical coordinate system.

Table 1 – Correspondence between stresses in a Cartesian coordinate system and their equivalents in a cylindrical coordinate system.

Original Meaning of Stress	New Meaning in the Cylindrical Coordinate System
SX = stress in X-direction σ_x.	SX = stress in the *radial* direction (σ_r) relative to the selected reference axis.
SY = stress in Y-direction σ_y.	SY = stress in the *tangential* or *circumferential* direction (σ_t) relative to the selected reference axis.
SZ = stress in Z-direction σ_z.	SZ = stress in the *axial* direction (σ_a) relative to the selected reference axis.

In brief, no matter what axis is chosen to be the reference axis[1] of a cylindrical coordinate system, the correspondence between radial, circumferential, and axial stresses listed in Table 1 remains valid. Thus, a reference axis is selected consistent with the above criteria.

Before selecting an axis to define a cylindrical coordinate system, a *copy* of the existing vonMises stress plot is made. The primary reason for making a copy of the stress plot is to save the time it would take to recreate all of the graphic settings defined earlier. Copy the plot as follows.

1. Right-click **Stress1 (-vonMises-)** and from the pop-up menu select **Copy**.

2. Right-click the **Results** folder and from the pop-up menu select **Paste**. A plot named **Copy[1] Stress1 (-vonMises-)** is added to the list of plots beneath the **Results** folder.

3. Double-click **Copy[1] Stress1 (-vonMises-)** to display an *identical* plot of the vonMises stress including all previously defined display options.

Next, a cylindrical coordinate system is defined. **Axis1**, aligned with the shaft centerline, is the only logical choice for the axis of a cylindrical coordinate system. However, since the goal is to display tangential stress in the cylindrical coordinate system, two changes must be made to the *copied* plot. First, **SY** must be specified as the stress to be viewed in this plot because, according to Table 1, **SY** = *tangential* stress in a cylindrical coordinate system. And second, **Axis1** must be defined as the axis of a cylindrical coordinate system. Proceed as follows to alter the copied plot.

4. Right-click **Copy[1] Stress1 (-vonMises-)** and from the pop-up menu select **Edit Definition...** The **Stress Plot** property manager opens as shown in Fig. 19.

5. In the **Display** dialogue box, click ▼ to open the stress 📖 **Component** pull-down menu and change it to **SY: Y Normal Stress**. This action also opens the **Advanced Options** dialogue box shown in Fig. 19. Recall that according to Table 1, stress **SY** represents *tangential* stress in a cylindrical coordinate system.

---

[1] Reference axis refers to an axis aligned with the centerline of the cylindrical coordinate system.

6. Move the cursor over the top field in the **Advanced Options** dialogue box to identify it as the **Plane, Axis, or Coordinate System**. Click to highlight this field (light blue) to indicate it is active and awaiting user input.

7. In the graphics screen, either click to select the center-line of the shaft axis (or) click to select **Axis1** in the SolidWorks flyout manager tree shown circled in Fig. 19. Either selection establishes **Axis1** as the reference axis of a cylindrical coordinate system and the name **Axis1@ Shaft-1@Wheel Shaft Assembly** appears in the currently active field.

8. Verify that ⊙ **Node Values** is selected and click **[OK]** ✓ to close the **Stress Plot** property manager.

Figure 19 – Selections to define a cylindrical coordinate system and circumferential stress.

The tangential stress distribution, as it appears in a cylindrical coordinate system, is shown in Fig. 20. Most of the model is green except in the contact region.

Figure 20 – Illustration showing tangential stress distribution in the shaft and wheel in a cylindrical coordinate system.

9. Once again move the cursor onto **Copy[1] Stress1 (-Y normal-)** and click-*pause*-click to select this 'name.' Then within the name field, type "**Tangential Stress**" and press **[Enter]**. The plot name is changed to **Tangential Stress (-Y normal-)**.

Observations:

Figure 20 displays the tangential stress distribution in a cylindrical coordinate system. Tangential stress in the wheel hub is analogous to tangential (circumferential or hoop) stress induced in a thick-wall cylinder subject to internal pressure. In this example, however, an interference fit is the cause of internal pressure acting on the external wheel hub. In Fig. 20, and on your screen, notice that the Global X, Y, Z coordinate system triad is supplemented by a cylindrical coordinate system symbol.

Also, observation of stress magnitude reveals that maximum tangential stress is approximately 900 psi below the wheel material yield strength. However, recall that vonMises stress in Fig. 16 and given by equation [1], is made up of *all* components of principal stress at a point. For simplicity, consider only a two-dimensional state of stress within the wheel hub, then both circumferential *and* radial stress components contribute to von Mises stress (σ') as follows.

$$\sigma' = \sqrt{\sigma_t^2 - \sigma_t\sigma_r + \sigma_r^2} \qquad [1]$$

where - σ_t = tangential stress (circumferential or hoop stress)
σ_r = radial stress
σ' = von Mises stress

This brief digression emphasizes the need to consider the *appropriate* stress when reaching conclusions about part safety.

Radial Stress

The above observation leads to the conclusion that *radial* stress should also be examined in order to obtain a complete picture of stress due to the interference fit. Proceed as follows to produce a plot of radial stress.

1. Make a copy of the **Tangential Stress (-Y normal-)** plot by clicking and dragging it onto the **Results** folder. The new copy is listed as **Copy[1] Tangential Stress (-Y normal-)** beneath the **Results** folder.

2. Double-click **Copy[1] Circumferential Stress (-Y normal-)** to open this plot and make it active. The plot appears unchanged because they are identical.

3. Right-click the new **Copy[1] Circumferential Stress (-Y normal-)** and from the pull-down menu select **Edit Definition...** The **Stress Plot** property manager opens as shown in Fig. 21. Open the **Advanced Options** dialogue box.

Because the preceding steps copied a plot that already includes a cylindrical coordinate system, there is no need to repeat steps required to define that coordinate system. Verify this by observing that **Axis1@Shaft-1@Wheel Shaft Assembly** appears in the top field of the **Advanced Options** dialogue box shown at the arrow in Fig. 21.

4. In the **Display** dialogue box, click to open the ▐**Component** pull-down menu and from the stresses listed, select **SX: X Normal Stress** which, according to Table 1, represents the *radial* stress in a cylindrical coordinate system.

5. Click **[OK]** ✓ to close the **Stress Plot** property manager.

Before proceeding, change the name of the plot currently named **Copy[1] Circumferential Stress (-X normal-)** to reflect that it now contains a plot of *radial* stress. Try this on your own or use the following step.

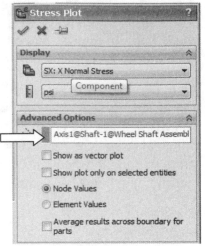

Figure 21 – Selecting SX: X Normal to display *radial* stress in the cylindrical coordinate system.

6. Click-*pause*-click the current folder and type **Radial Stress**. Then press **[Enter]**. The revised plot name should appear as **Radial Stress (-X normal-)**.

The resulting plot of radial stress is shown in Fig. 22. Radial stress represents stress normal to the two contacting surfaces. As such, radial stress represents the contact pressure between the shaft and wheel bore. Also observe the + and - signs of radial stress magnitudes shown in the color-coded stress scale. Virtually all radial stress magnitudes are negative within the model. Negative signs indicate compressive stresses acting on the outer surface of the shaft and on the inner surface of the wheel hub in the vicinity of the interference fit. This result is consistent with a general understanding of what happens in a shrink fit.

Figure 22 – Plot of *radial* stress distribution throughout the shaft and wheel assembly caused by the interference fit.

Verification of Results

Stress Predicted by Classical Interference Fit Equations

Consistent with previous examples, a check is made to determine the validity of results in the current analysis. However, classical equations for interference fits between mating parts are based on two assumptions. Those assumptions are that: (a) both components are of equal length, and (b) components are uniform thickness throughout their contact length. Both of these assumptions are violated in the current example, therefore, some differences between classical and FEA results are anticipated. The next paragraph describes two reasons for the expected differences.

First, the fact that both inner and outer members are not of equal length gives rise to higher stresses near both ends of the wheel hub at locations indicated in Fig. 23. These regions of high stress are caused by stress concentration effects due to pressure induced by the shrink fit combined with the geometric discontinuity where the shaft meets the hub. Higher tensile stress in this region of the hub was previously observed in Fig. 16. Second, a stiffening effect occurs in the central region of the hub, circled in Fig. 23, where the hub is thicker due to spokes and a built-up section located near its center. Stiffening in this region has the effect of altering magnitudes of all stresses examined thus far (tangential stress, vonMises stress, and radial stress).

Figure 23 – Geometric differences between the actual model and assumptions of classical interference fit equations.

Classical interference fit equations are applied below to determine tangential and radial stresses at the contact surface. Nominal part dimensions, given in Fig. 1, combined with SolidWorks material properties for the shaft and wheel, are used in equation [2] to determine the common contact pressure "p" between mating parts.

Solution for common contact pressure between force fit parts.

$$\delta = \frac{pR}{E_o}\left(\frac{r_o^2 + R^2}{r_o^2 - R^2} + v_o\right) + \frac{pR}{E_i}\left(\frac{R^2 + r_i^2}{R^2 - r_i^2} - v_i\right)$$

[2]

$$0.00205 = \frac{p(1.25)}{27.6e6}\left(\frac{(2.5)^2 + (1.25)^2}{(2.5)^2 - (1.25)^2} + 0.26\right) + \frac{p(1.25)}{30.5e6}\left(\frac{(1.25)^2 + 0^2}{(1.25)^2 - 0^2} - 0.28\right)$$

Solving equation [2] for contact pressure "p" between the wheel and shaft yields p = 17,530 psi = radial stress at the contact surface = σ_r.

Where: δ = radial interference = 0.0041/2 = 0.00205 in
p = the *unknown* contact pressure between mating parts
R = common radius at contacting surfaces = 1.25 in
r_i = inside radius of inner member (r_i = 0 for a solid shaft)
r_o = outside radius of external member (wheel hub radius is used)
where, r_o = 2.5000 in (not shown on Fig. 1)
E_i = modulus of elasticity for inner member (shaft)
E_o = modulus of elasticity for outer member (wheel)
v_i = Poisson's ratio for inner member (shaft)
v_o = Poisson's ratio for external member (wheel)

Next, using the contact pressure "p" that exists between the shaft and wheel hub, radial stress at the inner surface of the outer member (i.e., on the inner surface of the wheel hub) is computed in equation [3]. Logically, this value should equal the contact pressure.

$$(\sigma_r)_o = -p\frac{r_o^2 - R^2}{r_o^2 - R^2} = -17530\left(\frac{(2.50)^2 - (1.25)^2}{(2.50)^2 - (1.25)^2}\right) = -17,530\,psi$$

[3]

Finally, the tangential stress at the inner surface of the outer member (i.e., tangential stress on inner surface of the wheel hub) is given by equation [4].

$$(\sigma_t)_o = p\frac{r_o^2 + R^2}{r_o^2 - R^2} = 17530\left(\frac{(2.5)^2 + (1.25)^2}{(2.5)^2 - (1.25)^2}\right) = 29,200\,psi$$

[4]

Stress Predicted by Finite Element Analysis

Radial Stress Comparison

Given the prior observations about obvious differences between classical equation assumptions and the actual model, it is logical to expect differences between results predicted by classical equations and the finite element analysis (FEA). This section focuses on comparing results at contact locations predicted by classical equations [2] through [4]. Proceed as follows to determine radial stress (i.e., the contact pressure) between the shaft and wheel. Begin by reproducing the exploded view as follows.

*As of this writing, second time access to the **Explode** feature of SolidWorks (service pack 2.0) is not working properly. Thus, follow steps 1 through 4 below to turn exploded views "on" or "off".*

1. Click the **Configuration Manager** icon at top of the Feature manager tree. Click successive "+" signs until ⊞ 🔩 ExplView1 appears.

2. Right-click **ExplView1** and from the pull-down menu, select **Explode**. (NOTE: Although **Axis1** may move away from the model, the explode action is not executed until step 4 below.)

3. Return to the **Radial Stress (-X normal-)** and double click its name. The **Stress Plot** property manager opens.

4. Click **[OK]** ✓ to close the **Stress Plot** property manager and the model appears as an exploded view.

Now back to our investigation of radial stress on the contacting surfaces.

5. In the Simulation manager, right-click **Radial Stress (-X normal-)** and from the pull-down menu choose **List Selected**. The **Probe Result** window opens as shown in Fig. 24.

6. In the **Options** dialogue box, choose ⊙ **On selected entities** (if not already selected).

7. In the **Results** dialogue box the **Faces, Edges, or Vertices** field is highlighted (light blue) and awaits selection of the item for which results are to be displayed. On the graphics screen, rotate and zoom-in on the inner surface of the wheel hub shown "boxed" in Fig. 24, then click to select it. **Face<1>@wheel-1** appears in the active field.

8. Next, in the **Results** dialogue box, click the **[Update]** button.

Immediately the table is populated with data occurring at each node on the selected surface. The **Value (psi)** column contains values of *radial* stress at all nodes on the inside surface of the wheel hub. Also included are node numbers and X, Y, Z coordinates of each data point on the selected surface, and a column identifying the **Components**, in this case **wheel-1**, to which the data applies. NOTE: To accurately view tabulated data it may be necessary to click-and-drag the right margin of the manager tree as well as column-edges within the table to increase their width.

Figure 24 – Inside of the wheel surface is selected to examine results of all radial stresses acting on that surface. Results are summarized in the **Probe Result** table.

In the **Summary** dialogue box, located near the bottom of the **Probe Result** property manager, observe that radial stress values on the selected surface are summarized in several different forms (**Sum**, **Avg**, **Max**, **Min**, and **RMS**). For this example, consider only the **Avg** value listed as **-19447 psi** for the radial stress (values may vary). Using this value, a comparison with the result of classical equation [2] above yields-

$$\% \text{ difference} = \frac{\text{FEA result - classical result}}{\text{FEA result}} * 100 = \frac{-19447 - (-17530)}{-19447} * 100 = 9.9\%$$

[5]

Although the percent difference found in equation [5] exceeds desired expectations, it is a reasonable value given the differences between assumptions associated with use of classical equations and the actual model geometry. This larger than desired difference is another case where St. Venant's principle influences results near a discontinuity.

9. Select the **[OK]** ✓ to close the **Probe Result** property manager.

Tangential Stress Comparison

Next return to the **Tangential Stress (-Y normal-)** plot and repeat the above procedure, except this time determine the *tangential* stress on the inner surface of the wheel hub. Try this on your own. If needed, follow the steps outlined below.

1. Right-click **Tangential Stress (-Y normal-)**, then from the pull-down menu select **Show**.

2. Right-click **Tangential Stress (-Y normal-)** and from the pull-down menu choose **List Selected**. The **Probe Result** property manager opens.

3. In the **Options** dialogue box, choose ⊙ **On selected entities**.

4. On the graphics screen, select the inner surface of the wheel hub shown "boxed" in Fig. 24.

5. In the **Results** dialogue box, click the **[Update]** button.

Compare the **Avg** value for the tangential stress from the finite element analysis with that predicted by equation [4] above. The comparison is shown in equation [6] below.

$$\% \text{ difference} = \frac{\text{FEA result - classical result}}{\text{FEA result}} *100 = \frac{28749 - 29200}{28749} *100 = 1.6 \% \quad [6]$$

6. Click **[OK]** ✓ to close the **Probe Result** property manager.

These findings represent much better agreement the between Finite Element Analysis stress prediction and classical equation results. It might appear that the next logical step would be to compare finite element results for tangential and radial stresses on the outer surface of the *shaft* with results predicted by equation [3]. However, because the process outlined above selects data at *all* nodes on the cylindrical shaft surface, poor agreement is expected. Why? Because considerable area, on both ends of the shaft surface, lies outside of the contact area, results on this surface would be unduly influenced by stress in those regions. For this reason, these results are not compared here. However, if desired, *Split Lines* could be added to the shaft to limit comparison to the contact region only.

Quantifying Radial Displacements

Through additional application of the **List Selected** feature, SolidWorks Simulation provides a convenient means to verify the interference fit imposed on the mating parts. NOTE: Because the shaft and wheel hub are of different lengths, results obtained from the following analysis are expected to differ from those predicted by classical equations, which assume inner and outer members are equal in length. However, in instances where inner and outer members are of the same length, as in some end-of chapter exercises, excellent agreement of results is obtained (often < 1% difference). Our goal here is to learn how to make this comparison. Proceed as follows to determine part deformation.

1. In the Simulation manager, right-click the **Displacement1 (-Res disp-)** plot icon, and from the pull-down menu, select **Show**. The **Displacement** plot is displayed.

2. Again, right-click **Displacement1 (-Res disp-)** and from the pull-down menu, select **Edit Definition…** The **Displacement Plot** property manager opens as shown in Fig. 25.

3. In the ⬛ **Component** field of the **Display** property manager, select **UX: X Displacement**. According to Table 1, **UX: X Displacement** corresponds to *radial* displacement in a cylindrical coordinate system.

4. Also in the **Display** dialogue box, verify that ⊞ **Units** are set to **in** and that ⊙ **True scale** is selected in the ☑ **Deformed Shape** dialogue box.

5. Click ⬛ to open the **Advanced Options** dialogue box. Click to activate (light blue) the **Plane, Axis or Coordinate System** field. It now awaits selection of an axis to define a cylindrical coordinate system.

6. On the model, select **Axis1** on the shaft centerline as the reference axis for a cylindrical coordinate system. Alternately, near the bottom of the SolidWorks flyout manager tree, select **Axis1**. **Axis1@Shaft-1@Wheel Shaft Assembly** should appear in the highlighted field.

7. Click **[OK]** ✓ to close the **Displacement Plot** property manager.

8. If the plot produced in the preceding step does not appear on the graphics screen, double-click **Displacement1 (-X disp-)** to display the plot.

Figure 25 – Set-up of the **Displacement Plot** property manager to produce a plot of radial displacement.

9. Right-click **Displacement1 (-X disp-)** and from the pull-down menu choose **List Selected**. The **Probe Result** property manager opens.

10. In the graphics area, click the inner surface of the wheel hub shown "boxed" in Fig. 24. Then in the **Results** dialogue box, click the **[Update]** button.

The preceding step causes radial displacements at every node on the selected surface to be listed in the table of the **Results** dialogue box. Once again it may be necessary to click-and-drag to adjust column widths so that complete numerical values of displacement can be observed.

Of primary importance to this analysis is the **Avg** value of displacement listed in the **Summary** dialogue box. The value shown there corresponds to *radial* displacement of the inner surface of the wheel hub after the interference fit is accomplished. The **Avg** value of deformation on the inside surface of the wheel is listed as **0.0015101 in** (values may vary).

Without exiting the **Probe Result** property manager, proceed to examine deformation on the shaft surface as follows.

11. In the **Options** dialogue box, click ⊙ **On selected entities**. This action clears all values in the **Results** dialogue box.

12. Next, rotate the model so that the *cylindrical* surface on top of the shaft is visible and click to select it. **Face<2>@Shaft-1** appears in the active field.

13. Once again, click the **[Update]** button in the **Results** dialogue box. The table is now populated with values of the *radial* displacement on the outer surface of **Shaft-1**.

14. The **Avg** value of radial displacement listed in the **Summary** table is **-0.00031838 in**. This value of radial deformation is smaller than expected because both ends of the shaft extend outside the wheel hub where little or positive (swelling) deformation occurs due to the force fit.

15. Exit from the **Probe Result** property manager by clicking **[OK]✓**.

To determine total radial interference between the shaft and wheel, the absolute values of the above two **Avg** radial displacements are added together in equation [7]. The sum of these two values provides a reasonable (but smaller) approximation of the original radial interference specified in the opening statement of this example.

$$\text{Total radial interference} = |0.0015101| + |-0.00031838| = 0.001828 \text{ in} \qquad [7]$$

And, from the given information on page 5-2 of this example,

$$\text{radial interference} = \tfrac{1}{2} * \text{diametral interference} = \tfrac{1}{2} * 0.0041 = 0.00205 \text{ in} \qquad [8]$$

The difference between total radial interference for equation [7], based on displacement plots, and the given interference from equation [8] is,

$$\text{Difference} = 0.00205 - 0.001828 = 0.00022 \text{ in (rounded values)} \qquad [9]$$

The difference should, of course, be zero. However, knowing that the *entire* shaft surface is selected, but only that portion of the shaft surface within the contact region *should* be considered, the above difference is not investigated further. The important lesson learned is the process used to check that final interference equals that specified for the shrink fit.

This concludes the analysis portion of the current example. The closing section describes a semi-automated method of generating a **Report** within SolidWorks Simulation. *Do not close SolidWorks Simulation at this time.*

Generating a Report

SolidWorks Simulation provides a pre-defined **Report** format for quickly generating and sharing information related to any Study. The **Report** folder contains an outline of items that the user can choose either to include or to exclude from a report. The report also provides a means for sharing information with others either via the internet (an HTML file) or in print (as a Word® file). The process for including or excluding items from a report is outlined below.

1. Before generating a report, adjust the model size and orientation on the screen to best display graphical characteristics of interest to the user. This is done because the orientation of *all* plots produced within the report is identical to the current screen image.

2. On the **Simulation** *tab*, select the **Report** 🖩 Report icon. Or, in the main menu, click **Simulation**. Then, from the pull-down menu select **Report…** Either action opens the **Report Options** window shown in Fig. 26.

At the top-center of this window the **Current report format:** is set to **Static Study Format**.

Immediately below the **Report sections:** caption is a listing of sections that the user can either check ☑ to include in a report or clear the check mark ☐ to exclude that section from a report.

Figure 26 – Initial window of the **Report** folder showing a list of possible items that can be included or removed from a sample report.

When each section name is highlighted in the left-hand column of Fig. 26 (see arrow), the user has the option of entering explanatory text into a comments box on the right-side of the window.

In the report generated below, several items are omitted for the sake of brevity.

3. Begin by highlighting ☑ **Description** at top of the **Report sections:** column. Then, in the right side of the window, enter a brief description of the current example problem in your own words.

4. Clear the check mark adjacent to ☐ **Assumptions**, thereby omitting this section.

5. Proceed down the list leaving virtually all sections of the report checked ☑. However, clear check marks from ☐ **Sensor Details**, ☐ **Resultant Forces**, and ☐**Beams** because these items were *not* included in this study. Beginning at the top of the **Report sections:** column, for each checked section, also check the ☑ **Comments:** box and type a brief description in the accompanying text-box. NOTE: By typing in the **Section name:** field, located just above the **Comments:** field, it is possible to change the name of any section to that which you would like included in the report.

6. In the middle of the window, beneath **Header information** check ☑ **Designer** and enter your name in the adjacent field. Do likewise for the ☑ **Company** name and enter either your company or university name. If you wish to experiment, check other boxes ☑ and enter information about yourself. All this information is placed at the top of each page of the report.

7. At the bottom of the **Report Options** window check ☑ **Show report on publish** and then press the **[Publish]** button. These settings automatically generate a Word® version of the report.

When the automatic report generation is complete, a Word® document opens on the screen. Take several minutes to scroll through the report and review the information you entered and the information automatically recorded within the report folder. Notice the variety of details relevant to the current example that are saved. Items such as the mesh type, mesh quality, and mesh size, are included along with data about the FEA solver used, material specifications, fixtures, and full color plots, etc. are *summarized* in the **Report**. While this file contains much useful data, it cannot replace the engineering insight that goes into evaluating results of a Study.

This concludes the present example. Unless instructed to save results of this example, proceed as follows to exit SolidWorks Simulation without saving the solution.

1. From the main menu select **File** and from the pull-down menu select **Close**.

2. A **SolidWorks** window opens and prompts: "**Save documents before closing.**" Select **[Don't Save]**.

EXERCISES

‡‡ *Designates problems that introduce new concepts. Solution guidance is provided for these problems.*

EXERCISE 1 – Interference Fit Between a Bushing and Machine Frame

A bronze bushing is to be force fit into a hole in the cast iron wall of a machine frame. A bushing of this type serves as a bearing in a journal bearing set. The journal (i.e., the shaft) and bearing are separated by a thin film of lubricant, typically oil. Only the bushing and a small, square *portion* of the machine frame are shown in Fig. E5-1; the shaft is not shown and is *not* part of this analysis. Important dimensions of the bushing and wall are included. The wall thickness and bushing length are equal. It is assumed that a sufficiently large segment of the machine frame is included in the model below so that boundary effects, due to influences of St. Venant's principle, are insignificant. Create a finite element analysis of the interference fit between these two mating parts.

Open the file: **Bushing and Frame 5-1**.

Figure E5-1 – Bushing and a portion of a machine frame wall. A comparison of the bushing outside diameter (o.d. = 40.064 mm) and the hole inside diameter (i.d. = 40.000 mm) in the machine frame reveals an interference fit between these mating parts.

- Material: Machine frame – **Gray Cast Iron** (Use S.I. units)
  Bushing – **Tin Bearing Bronze** (listed beneath "**Copper Alloys**")

- Mesh: Use system default size **Curvature based mesh**, tetrahedral elements.

- Fixture: Set **Connections > Contact Set** to **Shrink Fit** between the bushing and machine frame. If necessary, add restraints to prevent rigid body motion.

Solution Guidance

Discussion below provides general guidance (i.e., hints and reminders) for the solution to this problem. In particular instances where this solution differs from the example problem of this chapter, specific steps are provided.

Early in the solution process, defeature the model by removing chamfers from both the bushing and frame.

- Expand the SolidWorks Feature manager tree if necessary to view its contents.

- Click "+" to open the **Frame <1> (Default<<Default>_Display State 1>)** folder at the upper arrow in Fig. E5-2.

- Locate and **Suppress** the **Frame Chamfer** circled in Fig. E5-2.

- Similarly, beneath + **Bushing<2> (Default<<Default>_Display State 1>>)**, locate and **Suppress** the **Bushing Chamfer** (not shown in Fig. E5-2).

Also, use load and geometric symmetry to reduce the model to ¼ of the given assembly. (See lower arrow in Fig. E5-2).

- In the SolidWorks Feature manager tree, right-click **Quarter Model – Assembly** and from the pop-up menu select the **Unsuppress** 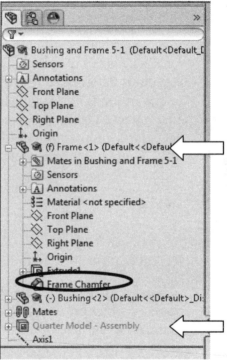 icon

Figure E5-2 – Menu selections used to defeature the Frame and unsuppress the **Quarter Model-Assembly**.

<u>HINT</u>:
When applying restraints to the model, consider carefully what restraint(s), if any, must be specified to prevent rigid-body-motion.

Develop a finite element model that includes: material specification, fixtures, a meshed model, and a solution. Defeature the model prior to analysis.

Determine the following:

a. Perform an interference check between the bushing and machine frame. Plot the resulting image.

b. In a separate image, show the ¼ model with symmetry and rigid body restraints (only if additional restraints are needed). This image is to show the defeatured model.

c. Using classical equations, compute circumferential and radial stresses at the inner surface of the machine frame and the outer surface of the bushing. It is common practice to use the *radius* of a circle tangent to the inside of the block that represents the machine frame as the outside "radius" of the outer member. Also determine the common contact pressure between these surfaces. Label each calculation.

d. In a cylindrical coordinate system, plot and compare circumferential stress at the inner surface of the machine frame with results calculated using classical equations determined in part (c). The value to be used for the finite element stress on the frame is the **Avg.** value of circumferential stress determined by using the **List Selected** feature applied to the inner surface of the hole in the frame. If necessary, click-and-drag to adjust column widths to show all digits of tabulated data. Compute the percent difference between classical and finite element analysis results using equation [1].

$$\% \text{ difference} = \frac{(\text{FEA result - classical result})}{\text{FEA result}} *100 = \qquad [1]$$

e. Repeat part (d) for circumferential stress at the outer surface of the bushing.

f. In a cylindrical coordinate system, plot and determine the average value of radial stress (contact pressure) between mating surfaces. Apply the **List Selected** feature to the inner surface of the hole and outer surface of the bushing. Although, theoretically, these values should be the same, some differences may occur. Therefore, determine the average of these two values and compare it with the classical result predicted for contact pressure determined in part (c). Then determine the percent difference by again using equation [1].

g. Because length of inner and outer members is equal, determine the *radial* displacement of the bushing (inner member) and machine frame (outer member) using the average **(Avg.)** value determined using the **List Selected** option. Determine the total radial interference and compare it with the given interference. Determine the percent difference using equation [1] above. If these values do not agree within 2% or less, determine the source(s) of the error and correct it/them. Comment upon whether or not the results agree, and if not, explain why.

╫ EXERCISE 2 – Force Fit Between a Bushing and Belt Sander Drive-Roll (Special Topic: Soft Spring supports)

A bronze bushing is force fit into a hole on the left end of a drive-roll for the industrial belt sander shown in Fig. E5-3. The drive-roll is supported by a stub shaft, not shown, inserted into the bushing from the left side and by a drive shaft on its right end as seen in Fig. E5-4. Only the force fit between the bushing and drive-roll, circled at the left end of the model in Fig. E5-4 is to be analyzed. Therefore, the affected parts can be modeled as a circular disk and bushing shown in Fig. E5-5. This model assumes that effects, due to St. Venant's principle caused by the hollow portion of the drive-roll, are insignificant and can be ignored. Important dimensions of the bushing and disk are shown in the figure below. The disk thickness and drive-roll hole outside diameter are equal (0.6250-in). Create a finite element analysis of the interference fit between these two mating parts.

Figure E5-3 – Industrial belt sander and drive-roll showing force fit bushing at left end.

Figure E5-4 – Geometry of belt sander drive-roll assembly.

- Material: Sander Disk - **2014-T4 Aluminum**
  (Use English units)
  Bushing – **Tin Bearing Bronze**
  (listed beneath "**Copper Alloys**")

- Mesh: Use system default size **Curvature based mesh**, tetrahedral elements.

Figure E5-5 – Simplified model of
left end of the belt sander drive- roll.

- Fixture: Set **Connections > Contact Set** to **Shrink Fit** between the bushing and belt sander disk. If necessary, add **Soft-Spring** restraints (see bottom of page 1-38 and forward) to prevent rigid body motion.

Open the file: **Belt Sander Disk and Bushing 5-2**

Develop a finite element model that includes: material specification, fixtures, a meshed model, and a solution.

Determine the following:

a. Perform an interference check between the bushing and belt sander disk. Plot the resulting image and list volume of interference value.

b. Use classical equations to compute circumferential and radial stresses at the inner surface of the belt sander disk and the outer surface of the bushing. Also determine the common contact pressure between these surfaces. Label each calculation.

c. In a cylindrical coordinate system, plot and compare the finite element value of circumferential stress at the inner surface of the belt sander disk with results calculated using classical equations determined in part (b). For this comparison use the **Avg.** value of circumferential stress determined using the **List Selected** feature applied to the appropriate surface of the model. If necessary, click-and-drag to adjust column widths to show all digits of tabulated data. Compute the percent difference between classical and finite element analysis results using equation [1].

$$\% \text{ difference} = \frac{(\text{FEA result - classical result})}{\text{FEA result}} * 100 = \qquad [1]$$

d. Repeat part (c) for circumferential stress at the outer surface of the bushing.

e. In a cylindrical coordinate system, plot and determine the average value of radial stress (contact pressure) between mating surfaces. Apply the **List Selected** feature to the inner surface of the hole and outer surface of the bushing. Although, theoretically, these values should be the same, some differences may occur. Therefore, determine the average of these two values and compare it with the classical result predicted for contact pressure determined in part (b). Then determine the percent difference by again using equation [1].

f. Because length of inner and outer members is equal, determine the *radial* displacement of the bushing (inner member) and belt sander disk (outer member) using the average **(Avg.)** value determined using the **List Selected** option. Then, determine the total radial interference and compare it with the given interference. Determine the percent difference using equation [1] above. If these values do not agree within 2% or less, determine the source(s) of the error and correct it/them. Comment upon whether or not the results agree, and if not, explain why.

EXERCISE 3 – Interference Fit Between a Gear and Shaft

To realize greater economy in manufacturing and assembly, the means of attaching a spur gear to its shaft is to be simplified. Originally, the gear was mounted to a hub by two screws at **A** shown Figs. E5-6 (a) and (b). The hub, in turn, was keyed to a shaft to prevent relative rotation between itself, the gear, and the shaft. An initial analysis revealed that a shrink fit between the gear and its shaft is adequate to transmit the required torque thereby eliminating the need for four parts (hub + two screws + key). Also eliminated are the operations of drilling two holes in the gear, drilling and tapping two holes in the hub, and broaching and milling the keyway and keyseat in the hub and shaft respectively. Finally, additional costs associated with producing the hub and associated machining operations, material, and inventory/handling are also eliminated.

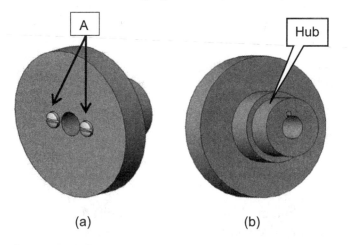

(a) (b)

Figure E5-6 Schematic representation of gear and hub assembly before simplification

Figure E5-7 Simplified geometry of spur gear and shaft using force fit.

The 96 tooth spur gear in Fig. E5-7 is to be shrink fit onto an **Alloy Steel** shaft. As noted above, contact pressure between the shaft and gear was determined to be sufficient to transmit the desired power at the design rpm. However, a finite element study is proposed to determine tangential and radial stress in both the shaft and gear due to the shrink fit. Also, stress due to stress concentration is known to occur where the shaft exits the gear due to the change of geometry at this location. A simplified model of the gear and shaft is shown in Fig. E5-8 along with dimensions of the gear (hole) inside diameter and shaft outside diameter.

Figure E5-8 – Dimensions necessary to perform analyses. All dimensions in mm.

Open the file: **Spur Gear and Shaft Assembly 5-3**

- Material: Shaft – **Alloy Steel** (Use SI units)
              Spur Gear – **1046 Steel, cold drawn**

- Mesh: a. Use system default size **Curvature based mesh**, tetrahedral elements when determining tangential and radial stresses in the shaft and gear.

     b. Refine *mesh size* and/or use *mesh control* in the contact region to better determine stress due to stress concentration where the shaft exits the gear.

- Fixture: Set **Connections > Contact Set** to **Shrink Fit** between the gear and shaft. If necessary, add restraints to the right (free) end of the shaft to prevent rigid body motion.

Develop a finite element model that includes: material specification, fixtures, a meshed model, and a solution. Defeature the model prior to analysis.

Determine the following:

a. Perform an interference check between the gear and shaft. Plot the resulting image and report the volume of material interference.

b. Use classical equations to compute tangential and radial stresses at the inner surface of the gear blank and the outer surface of the shaft. Also determine the common contact pressure between these surfaces. Label each calculation.

c. In a cylindrical coordinate system, plot and compare tangential stress at the inner surface of the gear with results calculated using classical equations determined in part (b). The value to be used for the finite element stress in the gear is the **Avg.** value of tangential stress determined by using the **List Selected** feature applied to the inner surface of the gear hole. If necessary, click-and-drag to adjust column widths to show all digits of tabulated data. Compute the percent difference between classical and finite element analysis results using equation [1].

$$\% \text{ difference} = \frac{(\text{FEA result - classical result})}{\text{FEA result}} * 100 = \qquad [1]$$

d. Repeat part (c) for tangential stress at the outer surface of the shaft.

e. In a cylindrical coordinate system, plot and determine the average value of radial stress (contact pressure) between mating surfaces. Apply the **List Selected** feature to the inner surface of the gear hole and outer surface of the shaft. Although, theoretically, these values should be the same, differences may occur. Compare the separate values determined for the gear and shaft with the classical result predicted for contact pressure determined in part (b). Which of these values, for the gear or the shaft, is in best agreement with the classical result? State the reason for differences, if any, between results in best agreement and the reason why results differ more for those in worst agreement. Determine the percent difference for each by again using equation [1].

f. Next, pay particular attention to the region where the shaft exits the gear. And, using a method of your own choosing, refine the mesh size to obtain a more accurate determination of stress in this region. For the model using a refined mesh, apply *Section Clipping* to cut both the gear and shaft in half, along the shaft centerline, to examine stress in this region. Produce a section clipping plot of half of the entire model *and* a zoomed-in plot of stress in the contact region.

g. Questions: What stress did you choose to display on the model plotted for part (f) above? State reason(s) why you choose the particular stress displayed on the model for part (f). Can the stress magnitude plotted in part (f) be compared with a manual calculation for stress at the juncture between the gear and shaft? If the answer to the previous question is "yes," include a manual calculation of stress beneath the plot and reference the stress concentration factor chart used to make your calculation. If the answer is "no," then explain why a comparison cannot be made. Finally, if classical and finite element results are compared, compute the percent difference between stress magnitudes determined using these two methods; label this calculation.

⫤ EXERCISE 4 – Stress Variation in a Saw Blade due to Centrifugal Force (Special Topics: Centrifugal Force, Soft Spring Supports)

A saw blade of the type used on table saws, miter saws, and portable power saws is shown in Fig. E5-9. This part is considered to be a thin rotating disk provided (a) its thickness is constant, (b) its outside radius is large compared to its thickness, and (c) stresses are constant through its thickness. Blades of this type are labeled with a maximum rotational speed limit, which in this case is 5500 rpm. Additional external loads, due to cutting forces between the saw blade and work-piece, are not considered in this exercise. Despite the hole at the center of the saw blade, both stress concentration and interference fits are *ignored* in this exercise.

Figure E5-9 – Front and side views of a typical circular saw blade used in wood cutting applications. (All dimensions in inches)

Develop a finite element model that includes material specification, applied centrifugal force, mesh generation, and solution. Because *centrifugal loading* and use of *soft springs* to support the part are not topics of the current chapter, guidance is provided to deal with these two aspects of the solution.

Open the file: **Circular Saw Blade**

- Material: **Chrome Stainless Steel** (English units) density $\rho = 0.282$ lb/in^3

- Mesh: Specify a default size **Standard mesh**

- Fixture: **Soft Springs**. See Solution Guidance section below.

- External Load: None. Load is due to centrifugal force caused by rotational speed of 5500 rpm.

Solution Guidance

Guidance is provided below regarding (a) the use of soft springs to restrain the model, and (b) the application of a centrifugal force to load the model. Steps below presume that the **Circular Saw Blade** file is open and a Simulation Study has been initiated.

<u>Rigid Body Motion Prevention</u>

As noted above, **Soft Springs** must be applied to stabilize the model. Model stabilization is necessary because (a) **Fixed** or other common restraints are not appropriate for a part that is considered to be rotating, and (b) the centrifugal force applied to the blade does not provide restraints in the X, Y, or Z directions. Simply stated, static restraints are not consistent with assumed rotation of the saw blade.

For additional discussion about soft springs, see Chapter 1, pages 1-38 (bottom) to 1-40 (bottom). Soft springs can be assigned any time before the solution is run.

- Right-click the Study name at top of the Simulation manager tree (not to be confused with the name at top of the SolidWorks Feature manager tree). A pull-down menu appears as shown in Fig. E5-6. From the pull-down menu, select **Properties...** The **Static** window opens as shown in Fig. E5-7.

- Within the **Options** tab, select ☑ **Use soft spring to stabilize model**. Also select ⊙ **Direct Sparse** as the equation solver method. This solver must be used in conjunction with the soft spring option.

- Click **[OK]** to close the **Static** window.

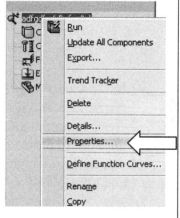

Figure E5-6 – Accessing the Study level pull-down menu to assign **Soft Spring** support to the model.

Figure E5-7 – Selecting **Soft Spring** support in the **Static** window.

Solution Guidance (continued)

<u>**Centrifugal Force Specification**</u>

- Right-click **External Loads** and from the pull-down menu select **Centrifugal...** The **Centrifugal** property manager opens. See Fig. E5-8.

- In the **Selected Reference** dialogue box the **Axis, Edge, Cylindrical Face for Direction** field is highlighted (light blue). Select the *inside* cylindrical *surface* of the hole.

Figure E5-8 – Specifying a **Centrifugal** force on a saw blade rotating at 5500 RPM.

- In the **Centrifugal Force** dialogue box, type the rotational speed into the **Angular Velocity** field. Convert 5500 rpm to **Hz** (i.e., cycles/second = rev/sec). After typing this value, click in the graphics area and a red arrow appears inside the hole to indicate the direction of rotation. If the arrow is opposite the direction in which the saw teeth are "leaning," then select ☑ **Reverse Direction** and click **[OK]** ✓ to close the **Centrifugal** property manager. *NOTE: Value shown above for Hz is not correct.*

- The notation **Centrifugal-1** appears beneath the **External Loads** folder.

Determine the following:

Develop a finite element model that includes: material specification, soft springs, applied load (due to centrifugal force), mesh generation, and solution.

a. After running the solution and obtaining the **Results** folder, edit the **Stress1 (-vonMises-)** plot by doing the following.

- Turn off the ☐ **Deformed Shape**. You will know when the deformed shape is turned off because the centrifugal force arrow will again appear at the central hole.

- Display **Discrete** fringes on the model

- Display the **Mesh** on the model

- Turn on ☑ **Show max annotation**

- Next, *copy* the **Stress1 (-vonMises-)** plot. Then change the copied plot to display **P1: 1st Principal Stress**. Also, re-name this plot to reflect its true identity. HINT: Does the 1st principal stress represent *tangential* or *radial* stresses caused by rotation?

- Repeat the preceding step, except create a plot of **P2: 2nd Principal Stress**. HINT: Does the 2nd principal stress represent *tangential* or *radial* stresses caused by rotation?

b. Zoom in on the saw blade that displays a plot of **P1: 1st Principal Stress**. Then, use the **Probe** tool to select all corner and mid-side nodes beginning at the edge of the center hole and proceeding outward to as near as possible to the tip of any tooth. When selecting nodes, traverse the model in the straightest line possible. Create a graph of this data. Alter the graph title and axes labels to better describe information contained on the graph. Include you name in the graph title.

c. Repeat step (b) to produce a graph showing the variation of **P2: 2nd Principal Stress** at the same location on the model.

d. Either write a computer program or set up a spreadsheet to calculate both the tangential and radial stress variation from the central hole outward to the blade tip. Calculate the two stress magnitudes at 0.20 inch increments beginning at the hole inside radius and proceeding outward to the 5.00 inch outside blade radius. Also, within this computer program or spreadsheet, plot and label graphs of stress variation for both stress types. Use the following classical equations to compute tangential and radial stresses.

Tangential stress in a rotating disk.

$$\sigma_t = \rho\omega^2\left(\frac{3+v}{8}\right)\left(r_i^2 + r_o^2 + \frac{r_i^2 r_o^2}{r^2} - \frac{1+3v}{3+v}r^2\right) \qquad [2]$$

Radial stress in a rotating disk.

$$\sigma_r = \rho\omega^2\left(\frac{3+v}{8}\right)\left(r_i^2 + r_o^2 - \frac{r_i^2 r_o^2}{r^2} - r^2\right) \qquad [3]$$

Where,
ρ = mass density of the saw blade = density/(386 in/sec^2)
v = Poisson's ratio
r_i = inside radius (inches)
r_o = outside radius (inches)
r = radius to the point of interest, a variable value (inches)
ω = angular velocity in cycles/sec = rev/sec

e. Use equation [1], repeated below, to compare percent differences between maximum stresses calculated using equations [2] and [3] with maximum stress values **P1: 1st Principal Stress** and **P2: 2nd Principal Stress** calculated using the finite element approach. Based on comparisons of calculated values and graphs, identify which finite element stress (**P1** or **P2**) corresponds to the tangential stress in the saw blade. Does the other finite element stress correspond to the radial stress in the saw blade? If "yes," state the basis for this conclusion. If "no," state why not.

$$\% \text{ difference} = \frac{(\text{FEA result - classical result})}{\text{FEA result}} * 100 = \qquad [1]$$

Textbook Problems

In addition to the above exercise, it is highly recommended that additional problems involving interference fits between mating parts be worked from a design of machine elements textbook. Textbook problems provide a great way to discover errors made in formulating a finite element analysis because they typically are well defined problems for which the solution is known. Typical textbook problems, if well defined in advance, make an excellent source of solutions for comparison.

CONTACT ANALYSIS

Examples up to this point have included models for which various preliminary steps, such as suppressing or un-suppressing certain model features, were pre-planned so that examples could proceed quickly to introduce new finite element principles and techniques. However, a real analysis is not often delivered in such a "ready to go" condition unless the user, or a CAD technician, plans ahead to prepare a model in the desired format. Thus, to better prepare FEA users for a more realistic scenario, this example includes many of the necessary preparatory steps thereby creating a more realistic example from beginning to end. In addition, contact conditions existing between mating parts under load and iso clipping are also explored.

Learning Objectives

Upon completion of this example, users should be able to:

* Assign loads to a *non-flat surface* in *specified direction*(s)

* Define *Contact/Gap* conditions with *no penetration*

* Use *Animation* to understand deformation and stress development as load(s) are applied

* Apply *Iso Clipping* to view model stresses

* Display *Contact Pressure* plots

Problem Statement

A trunion mount, of the type used to attach hydraulic or pneumatic cylinders to a fixed surface, is shown in Fig. 1. Both the trunion and pin are made of **Alloy Steel**. The pin is subject to an 800 lb force acting upward to the right at 60° from the horizontal as shown in a right-side view in Fig. 2. The goal of this analysis is to determine maximum von Mises stress and its location on the trunion mount and to determine contact pressure distribution between the pin and holes in the trunion.

Figure 1 – Typical trunion mount.

Contacting surfaces occur where the pin passes through holes in the side-plates of the trunion and where the mid-portion of the pin is acted upon by a cylinder. For this reason, it is necessary to create separately identifiable contacting surfaces on the pin. *Split Lines* are used to divide the pin surface. Figure 31, pg. 6-23 shows an assembled view of a trunion mount and cylinder base.

F = 800 lb
at 60° angle

(right-side view)

Trunion
mount

Pin

Figure 2 – Right-side view of trunion mount and pin showing direction of applied force.

The procedure outlined below is not the only way to apply *Split Lines* to the pin. It is, however, deemed simpler to demonstrate this aspect of model preparation on the pin alone, before joining it with the trunion base to form an assembly. Proceed as follows. *(Because a personal goal should be to develop independent competence using SolidWorks Simulation, some steps below are abbreviated where prior experience should be sufficient).*

Preparing the Model for Analysis

1. Open **SolidWorks 2013**.

2. Select **Files > Open…** and open the part file named "**Trunion Pin**."

All steps related to locating and creating *Split Lines* occur within SolidWorks, therefore a new Study is not started at this time. Three *Split Lines* are to be added to the trunion pin at locations illustrated on Fig. 3. It is important to know that the origin of the coordinate system is located at the center of the pin and that the pin is centered in the trunion mount. Given this information, those who are comfortable in their ability to locate the necessary reference planes and *Split Lines* are encouraged to proceed on their own. These individuals can skip the next two sections, titled "Add Reference Planes" and "Insert Split Lines." However, all necessary steps are provided below if guidance or review is desired.

3.00

1.50

.75

.25

Split Line locations

Figure 3 – Location of *Split Lines* at the intersection of the pin and side supports of the trunion mount and at the center of the pin.

Add Reference Planes

1. From the main menu select **Insert**.

2. In the pull-down menu, highlight **Reference Geometry** ▶ and from the subsequent pop-up menu, select **Plane…** The **Plane** property manager opens.

3. Click "+" or , circled in Fig. 4, to open the SolidWorks flyout menu.

4. In the **First Reference** dialogue box the field is active (light blue). In the SolidWorks flyout menu, select **Right Plane**. See arrow **#1** in Fig. 4. The **Right Plane** appears at the center of the model.

Figure 4 – Selecting the **Right Plane** as a starting point, the first **Reference Plane** is located 0.75 in to its right.

5. In the **Offset Distance** spin box, at arrow **#2**, type **0.75** as the distance from the **Right Plane** to the location of the first **Reference Plane**. Left-click in the graphics area and a "ghost" image of the **Reference Plane** appears at the proper location. *Do NOT right-click to accept this plane because the property manager will close.*

By coincidence, a second reference plane is located 0.75 in. to the right of the first. This is due to the fact that each vertical side of the trunion support is 0.75 inches thick (confirm this by examining dimensions on Fig. 3). Because the second reference plane is to be located the *same* distance from the first, proceed as follows to locate it.

6. In the **Number of planes to create** field, at arrow **#3**, click the up arrow ◢ on the spin box to increase the number of planes to **2**. Immediately a second "ghost" reference plane appears as shown in Fig. 4.

7. Click **[OK]** ✓ to close the **Plane** property manager and accept both of these reference planes. **Plane1** and **Plane2** are labeled on the pin and added to the bottom of the SolidWorks feature manager tree.

A model of the pin and its two **Reference Planes** is shown in Fig. 5.

Figure 5 – Two **Reference Planes** are created to denote locations where *Split Lines* are to be added to the pin.

Insert Split Lines

Intersections of **Plane1** and **Plane2** with the pin are used to locate *Split Lines* on the model as outlined below.

1. In the Main menu select **Insert** and from the pull-down menu highlight **Curve ▶**. Then from the pop-up menu, select **Split Line…** The **Split Line** property manager opens as shown in Fig. 6.

2. Because **Split Lines** are to be located where each plane intersects the pin, in the **Type of Split** dialogue box, choose ⊙ **Intersection**.

3. Click to activate the upper field of the **Selections** dialogue box. The **Splitting Bodies/Faces/Planes** field is highlighted. Either select each of the planes appearing on the pin or click **Plane1** and **Plane2** in the SolidWorks flyout menu. Names of the two planes are listed in the upper field in the order selected.

Figure 6– The **Split Line** property manager is used to determine locations of *Split Lines* on the model.

4. Move the cursor onto the second field; its name appears as **Faces/Bodies to Split**. Click to activate this field (light blue). Then, move the cursor into the graphics area and select anywhere on the *cylindrical* surface of the pin. **Face<1>** appears in the active field.

5. In the **Surface Split Options** dialogue box, the setting should appear as ⊙ **Natural**. If not, select it.

6. Click **[OK]** ✓ and two *Split Lines* appear on the pin as shown in Fig. 7. Also, **Split Line1** is listed at the bottom of the SolidWorks feature manager.

Figure 7 – *Split Lines* located on the trunion pin surface at intersections with the two **Reference Planes**.

Because symmetry exists between left and right halves of the trunion and pin assembly, only the right-half of the pin is used for analysis. Therefore, no additional *Split Lines* need be added to the other half of the model. Save this file as outlined below.

7. From the main menu, select **File** followed by **Save As...**

8. In the **Save As** window, name the part "**Pin with Split Lines**" and **[Save]** the file to a PC, or to network file space. It is *not* recommended to save the file to a temporary storage device such as a USB drive for reasons described in the Introduction.

9. Close the file by selecting **File > Close**. *(Do not close SolidWorks.)*

Create the Assembly Model

It is assumed that most SolidWorks Simulation users are familiar with the SolidWorks work environment and the process of creating an *assembly* composed of two or more *parts*. Those individuals can proceed on their own to join the **Trunion Base** and the **Pin with Split Lines** to form an assembly and proceed to the section titled **Create a Finite Element Analysis (Study)**. The pin should be centered between sides of the trunion base. However, for users who are new to both SolidWorks and SolidWorks Simulation, a step-by-step procedure to create the assembly follows.

In the assembly the pin is located concentric with holes in the trunion base and extends ¼ inch outside of the two side supports as shown in Fig. 3. This location will be replicated in the assembly created in the following steps.

1. In the main menu, click **File > New…** The **New SolidWorks Document** window opens.

2. Click the **Assembly** icon and then click **[OK]**. The **Begin Assembly** property manager opens as shown in Fig. 8.

3. Click to activate the **Keep Visible** push-pin circled at top-center of the property manager. This action keeps the property manager open during several steps. Also read the upper sentence in the yellow **Message** dialogue box.

4. At the bottom of the **Part/Assembly to Insert** dialogue box, select the **[Browse…]** button. The SolidWorks **Open** window appears. Scroll down the list of files to the location where the **Trunion Base** file is stored. If not found, browse to the file location you set up.

5. From the list of files, select **Trunion Base** and click **[Open]**.

Figure 8 – The **Begin Assembly** property manager used to bring *parts* into an *assembly*.

6. The cursor and part appear and move together in the graphics area. Move the cursor to the top of the **Begin Assembly** property manager and click **[OK]** ✓. The trunion base automatically moves to the coordinate system origin. If the cursor is moved back into the graphics area a second trunion base appears on the screen. ***Do not click again!***

Ignore the second trunion base that appears and proceed directly to the next step.

7. Move the cursor into the **Part/Assembly to Insert** dialogue box and again select the **[Browse…]** button. The SolidWorks **Open** window appears.

8. In the **Open** window, select the **Pin with Split Lines** and click **[Open]**. The cursor and pin appear and move together on the graphics screen.

9. Move the pin to a position above and to the left of the trunion base as illustrated in Fig. 9 and click to place it there. NOTE: *It may be necessary to roll the middle mouse button to down-size the screen image.* A small image of a mouse should appear with a green check-mark "✓" on the right mouse button, click the right mouse button to accept this position and simultaneously close the **Begin Assembly** property manager. *(The actual pin location is arbitrary, but first time users will gain greater insight into the assembly process if the pin and base do not initially intersect).*

The next task is to assemble the pin into holes on the trunion base. This requires use of a **Mate** definition between the parts to be joined. Because we are currently working in the *assembly* mode, the **Assembly** tab and its tool bar, shown in Fig. 10, should be displayed near the top of the screen.

10. If the **Assembly** tab does not appear, apply steps 11 and 12 below. Otherwise skip to step 13.

11. Right-click *any **tab*** at top-left of the graphics area, shown boxed in Fig. 10.

12. From the pull-down menu, check "✓" to select ✓ **Assembly** and the **Assembly** *tab*, like that shown in Fig. 10 appears.

13. Open the **Assembly** toolbar by clicking its *tab* shown at the arrow in Fig. 10.

Figure 9 – Trunion base and pin (in an arbitrary position) prior to assembly.

Figure 10 – **Assembly** toolbar with large buttons and text.

CAUTION #1: In the steps that follow the **Mate** icon 📎 is a single paper clip. It is *not* to be confused with the two paperclips labeled **Mates** located at the bottom of the SolidWorks feature manager.

CAUTION #2: Make sure system units are set to **IPS (inch, pound, second)** before proceeding. Make the following menu selections: **Tools > Options… >**, then select the **Document Properties** tab > and in the left column select **Units >**. On right side of the window select ⊙ **IPS (inch, pound, second)**, and click **[OK]** to close the window.

The **Mate** icon circled is circled in Fig. 10. The **Mate** property manager is used to define geometric relationships (i.e., locations) of one part relative to another.

14. On the **Assembly** tab click the **Mate** 📎 icon. A portion of the **Mate** property manager opens as seen in Fig. 11.

15. The **Mate Selections** dialogue box is active (highlighted light blue). Passing the cursor over this field indicates it is to be filled with the **Entities to Mate**.

The first step in creating a mate is to position the pin so that it is concentric (aligned) with holes in the trunion base. To accomplish this, the two parts are selected as described next. NOTE: Because *Split Lines* are defined on the pin, its surface is effectively subdivided into segments at each *Split Line*. However, as described in the next step it is necessary to select *only one* cylindrical segment on the pin.

16. Click to select *any* cylindrical surface on the pin and the *cylindrical* surface *inside* either hole as highlighted in Fig. 12. The Pin moves to align its cylindrical surface with that of the Trunion Base. Names of the two selected faces appear in the **Mate Selections** dialogue box. The software is "smart" enough to guess that a concentric mate is probably desired, but this is not confirmed until the next step.

Figure 11 – Initial selection of surfaces to be specified as concentric is made in the **Mate** property manager.

A small pop-up icon bar appears as shown in Fig. 12. It shows icons of several possible mates that might be defined between the two cylindrical surfaces.

17. It is suggested that new users select the **Concentric** icon in the **Standard Mates** dialogue box because its name is listed adjacent to its icon. However, both icons are circled in Fig. 12 and either can be selected.

Figure 12 – Defining a **Concentric** mate between the pin and trunion base holes results in alignment between the two parts.

After selecting **Concentric**, the name **Concentric1** appears at the top of the property manager (see arrow in Fig. 12) and names of the two selected faces are listed in the **Mate Selections** dialogue box.

18. Click **[OK]**✓ to close the **Concentric1** property manager. *(Do NOT click [OK] twice; see next step).*

The property manager remains open, but its name changes back to **Mate**. Proceed as follows to further define pin location within the holes

19. Click the right *end* of the pin *and* the right-face of the trunion support shown highlighted in Fig. 13. The pin-end aligns itself flush with the trunion face.

However, because the 3.5 inch long pin is to be centered between the two supports (whose outside dimension is 3.00 in, see Fig. 3), final pin location is altered as follows.

20. Click the **Distance** ⊢⊣ icon and type **0.25** into the **Distance** spin box. See arrow **#1** in Fig. 13. Verify units appear as **in**. Then, click anywhere in the graphics screen. This value ensures that the pin is offset 0.25 inch from the two selected surfaces. *See next step.*

Figure 13 – Two faces are selected so that the appropriate **Distance** between them can be defined to center the pin between holes on the trunion base.

21. If the pin appears recessed within the right-side hole, it is necessary to check ☑ **Flip Dimension** located at arrow **#2** below the **Distance** spin box. The assembly should now appear as shown in Fig. 2, repeated below.

22. Click **[OK]** ✓ *twice* to close the **Distance1** and then the **Mate** property managers.

23. To protect the work invested in this example thus far, from the main menu select **File > Save As...** and in the **Save As** window, name the assembly "**Trunion and Pin Assembly**" then click **[Save]** to save the file.

Figure 2 – (Repeated) Shows the pin centered between two trunion sides.

Cut Model on Symmetry Plane

This example makes use of model symmetry to realize computational efficiencies associated with a smaller assembly and to provide additional practice using this powerful software feature. Steps below lead the user through one of several possible procedures to create a symmetrical half-model.

1. Rotate a front view of the model into the plane of the screen by clicking ▼ on the **View Orientation** icon. Then select the **Front** view icon. See Fig. 14.

2. Next, in the SolidWorks Feature manager, click to select **Front Plane**; see arrow in Fig. 14. A **Front Plane** is shown on an image of the model in Fig. 14.

NOTE: Additional top, front, and right planes exist for both the trunion base and for the pin. Although consistency of plane location was carefully coordinated for this example, it is important to realize that individual parts are created in their own *local* coordinate system. These individual local coordinate systems may be oriented differently once parts are brought together into the *global* coordinate system of an assembly.

Figure 14 – The **Front Plane** is selected as the plane to sketch on as part of the process of cutting the model in half.

3. Switch to sketch mode by clicking the **Sketch** *tab* near the top of the screen; the **Sketch** toolbar opens. Within the **Sketch** toolbar select the **Sketch** icon to open a sketch on the front plane. If the **Sketch** tab is not available, follow steps 11 and 12 of the previous section to add it, but replace the word **Assembly** with **Sketch**.

4. In the **Sketch** toolbar, select the **Line** icon and move the cursor onto the graphics screen. The cursor changes to a pencil symbol with a line adjacent to it.

5. Move the cursor above (or below) the *middle* of the assembly and a vertical dashed line appears to indicate alignment with the coordinate system origin. Click at this location and move the mouse to create a vertical line that extends completely through the model and beyond its opposite border, then click again to

end the line. Press **[Esc]** to terminate line drawing and click the close sketch icon if it appears at top right of the graphics screen.

A screen image of the assembly should appear as shown in Fig. 15.

6. In the **Features** toolbar, select the **Extrude Cut** 🔲 icon and the **Cut-Extrude** property manager opens. NOTE: If the **Features** toolbar does not appear, right-click the main menu and from the pull-down menu, select the 🌐 **Features** icon. A portion of the **Cut Extrude** property manager is illustrated in Fig. 16.

Figure 15 – Vertical line drawn on the **Front Plane** at center of the trunion and pin assembly. Also shown is the warning window that appears when closing a sketch.

7. The **From** dialogue box should indicate **Sketch Plane** and the **Direction1** dialogue box should indicate **Through All**.

8. If necessary, rotate the model so the surface created by extending the vertical line into a cutting plane is visible slicing through the model as shown in Fig. 17.

Three arrows appear on the plane. They point in directions in which the model is cut and material is removed. Carefully observe the direction of the arrow *normal* to the plane. It should point *away* from the right-half of the model. Recall that the right-half of the pin was modified by the addition of *Split Lines*. Thus, the right-half of the model is to be saved.

9. *Only if* the normal arrow is directed toward the right half of the model, click to change its direction by selecting ☑ **Flip side to cut**. See arrow in Fig. 16. When the normal arrow is directed toward the left-side of the assembly, proceed to the next step.

Figure 16 – **Cut-Extrude** property manager used to define direction for the portion of the assembly that is removed by the sketch plane.

Direction of
material to be
removed.

Right side
of model.

Figure 17 – The cutting plane created by extending the vertical line into a plane is
shown along with arrows indicating the direction in which material is to be removed.

10. Click **[OK]** ✓ to close the **Cut-Extrude** property manager. After cutting, the
    assembly should appear as shown in Fig. 18.

This concludes the somewhat lengthy process of
preparing a model for finite element analysis.
Although these, or similar steps, were done for you
in previous problems, one goal of the current
example is to develop a comprehensive picture of
typical tasks involved in formulating a complete
analysis. The following sections define and solve
the finite element model.

Figure 18 – Assembly after cutting it in half
to make use of geometric symmetry.

Create a Finite Element Analysis (Study)

1. In the main menu, click **Simulation** and from the pull-down menu, select **Study…** The **Study** property manager opens.

2. In the **Name** field, type **Trunion and Pin Contact Analysis – Your Name** to identify this study.

3. Verify that a **Static** analysis is selected then click **[OK]** ✓ to close the **Study** property manager. The Simulation manager appears on the left of the screen.

4. In the main menu, click **Simulation** and from the pull-down menu select **Options…** The **Systems Options - General** window opens.

5. Under the **Default Options** tab, select Units and set the following options:

   • In the right-half of the window under **Unit system**, select ⊙ **English (IPS)**

   • Under **Units** set **Length/Displacement:** to **in** and **Pressure/Stress:** to **psi** (if not already selected). Ignore remaining options.

6. Click **[OK]** to close the **Default Options - Units** window.

Assign Material Properties

1. In the Simulation manager tree right-click the **Parts** folder and select **Apply Material to All…**

2. In the left half of the **Material** window, beneath **SolidWorks Materials**, open the **+ Steel** folder. And, from the list of materials, select **Cast Alloy Steel**.

3. In the right-half of the **Material** window, **Units:** *should* appear as **English (IPS)** as defined above. If not, change units at this time.

4. Click **[Apply]** followed by **[Close]** to exit the **Material** window.

Assign Fixtures and External Loads

The following section includes subtitles to identify specific restraint types applied to the model. Individuals are encouraged to use subtitles to guide their application of restraints on their own. However, complete instructions are provided if desired.

Symmetry and Immovable Restraints

In the following steps, **Fixed** (immovable) and **Symmetry** restraints are applied at bolt holes on the trunion base and at cut (symmetrical) surfaces respectively.

1. Right-click the **Fixtures** folder and from the pull-down menu, select **Fixed Geometry…**

2. In the **Standard (Fixed Geometry)** dialogue box, ensure the **Fixed Geometry** ⊠ icon is selected (gray highlight) and the **Faces, Edges, Vertices for Fixture** field is active (highlighted light blue).

3. Move the cursor over the model and zoom in, as necessary, to select the *inside surface* of each bolt hole on the trunion base. Restraint symbols appear inside each hole as illustrated in Fig. 19.

Figure 19 – **Fixed** restraints are applied to bolt holes and **Symmetry** restraints are applied to cut surfaces of the pin and trunion base.

4. Click **[OK]**✓ to close the **Fixture** property manager.

5. Again, right-click the **Fixtures** folder and from the pull-down menu select **Fixed Geometry…** The **Fixture** property manager opens.

6. Click to open the **Advanced** dialogue box and select the **Symmetry** ▦ icon from the list of available fixture types.

7. Apply this restraint by selecting both *cut surfaces* on the pin and trunion base highlighted in Fig. 19. An outline of the left-half of the model appears to visually confirm that symmetry modeling is active. **Symmetry** restraints appear normal to the cut surface, thereby preventing displacement in the X-direction.

8. Click **[OK]** ✓ to close the **Fixture** property manager.

Connections Define Contact Conditions

In the Simulation manager tree in Fig. 20, open the **Connections** folder and all its sub-folders. This folder is always present, but it becomes important any time an *assembly* is analyzed so that interactions (i.e., contact conditions) between mating parts can be defined. The **Connections** folder was also encountered in Chapter 5, where a Shrink Fit was analyzed. The following steps outline how **Connections** are used to define a local contact condition between the pin and inner surface of the hole in the trunion base. Notice the default condition assumes all surfaces are bonded.

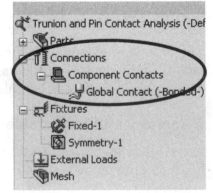

Figure 20 – **Connectors** folder in the Simulation manager tree.

To facilitate selection of the contacting surfaces, begin by creating an exploded view of the assembly. Proceed as follows.

1. In the main menu click **Insert** and from the pull-down menu select **Exploded View…** The **Explode** property manager opens with the message, "**Select component(s) and then drag the manipulator handle to create an explode step.**"

2. Click to select the pin. Then *drag* the manipulator arrow in the direction of the +X-axis (this direction corresponds to the pin axis) to move the pin away from the model as shown in Fig. 21.

3. Click **[OK]** ✓ to close the **Explode** property manager.

Figure 21 – Explode the assembly to facilitate selection of contacting surfaces.

4. In the Simulation manager tree, right-click the **Connections** folder and from the pull-down menu, select **Contact Set…** The **Contact Sets** property manager opens as shown in Fig. 22.

5. In the **Contact** dialogue box, select ⊙ **Manually select contact sets**.

6. In the **Type** dialogue box, select **No Penetration** from the pull-down menu. This action defines the type of contact between the pin and hole surfaces.

7. The upper field of the **Type:** dialogue box should be active (light blue). Select the *inner surface* of the hole, highlighted in Fig. 22, and **Face<1>@ Trunion Base-1** is listed in the **Faces, Edges, Vertices for Set 1** field.

Figure 22 – Selecting surfaces between which the **Contact/Gaps** restraint is applied.

8. Next, click inside the **Faces for Set 2** field (second field from top) to activate it. Then, on the pin, select the corresponding surface, also highlighted in Fig. 22. **Face<2> @Pin with Split Lines-1** appears in the **Faces for Set 2** field.

9. Click **[OK]** ✓ to close the **Contact Sets** property manager. Beneath the **Connections** folder appears an icon labeled + **Contact Sets**. Click the "+" sign to reveal: **Contact Set-1 (-No Penetration<Trunion Base-1, Pin with Split Lines-1>-)**." Place the cursor over this text to reveal its entire name.

Apply a Directional Load

This section outlines steps to apply a directional load to the round pin. In previous examples, force components in the X, Y, or Z directions were applied to parts with flat surfaces. Using that approach, the 800 lb force applied to the pin at a 60° angle from the horizontal in Fig. 1 should be represented by its Y and Z force components. However, this example demonstrates application of these force components in a way not used in earlier problems. Further, because only half of the model is being analyzed, only half of the 800 lb force is applied to the pin. First, however, the model is re-assembled (un-exploded) as follows.

1. Select the **Configuration** manager icon ⊞ located at top of the SolidWorks feature manager tree.

2. At top of the **Configuration manager**, click the "+" sign adjacent to **Default [Trunion Pin and Assembly]** to display an additional sub-folder.

3. Next, right-click ⊞ ⟲ ExplView1 and from the pull-down menu, select **Collapse**.

After the model is re-assembled, proceed as follows to apply the load.

4. In the Simulation manager, right-click the **External Loads** folder, and from the pull-down menu select **Force...** The **Force/ Torque** property manager opens; see Fig. 23.

5. In the **Force/Torque** dialogue box, select the **Force** icon. It appears shaded dark gray.

6. Also in the **Force/Torque** dialogue box, choose ⊙ **Selected direction**. The property manager changes to look like that shown in Fig. 23.

7. Click to highlight the **Faces, Edges, Vertices, Reference Points for Force** field. Rotate the model as necessary and click the cylindrical pin surface highlighted in Fig. 24. **<Face1>@Pin with Split Lines-1** is listed in the upper field.

Figure 23 – Selecting faces to define force component direction in the **Force/Torque** property manager.

8. Also in the **Force/Torque** dialogue box, click to activate the **Face, Edge, Plane, for Direction** field (second field from top) and proceed to select the trunion support face highlighted in Fig. 24. **Face<2>@Trunion Base-1** appears in the active field.

Aside: It is also possible to select any other face, edge, plane or axis that is aligned with the direction of the applied force components. Other *surfaces* that could be selected include: the cut-end of the pin; the cut-face of the trunion base; or the **Right Plane** in the SolidWorks flyout menu (the plane selected *must* be at the assembly level, *not* at the component level) Also, edges in the Z-direction can be used.

Figure 24 – Selecting the surface for force application and a face to define its direction.

The bottom portion of the **Force/Torque** property manager is shown in Fig. 25. In the **Force** dialogue box, three choices are available for defining magnitude and direction of a force. Icons adjacent to the top two fields show two different directions for applying forces parallel to the selected face while the bottom field indicates a force applied perpendicular to the selected face.

9. In the **Force** dialogue box, move the cursor over the top field. Its name appears as **Along Plane Dir 1**. Click the icon adjacent to this field to activate it. Immediately, force vectors are displayed on the center segment of the pin. *(Ignore their direction for now.)*

10. These vectors are parallel to the trunion face selected above. Use the coordinate system triad to verify that these vectors lie in the Z-direction. This direction corresponds to the horizontal component of the 400 lb force[1]. Therefore, in the top field, type **200**, which is determined from:

$$F_Z = 400 * \cos 60° = 200 \text{ lb}$$

Figure 25 – Specifying magnitude and direction of force components.

---

[1] Recall, only half the total force of 800 pounds, or 400 pounds, is applied to the half-model.

Figure 1 (repeated below) shows geometry related to the above calculation. Also observe the on-screen "flag" that displays direction, units, and magnitude of the force component.

11. If force vectors are oriented in the incorrect direction, check ☑ **Reverse direction**. Refer to Fig. 26 for proper directions of force components.

F = 800 lb
at 60° angle

(right side view)

Figure 1 (repeated) – Right-side view of trunion mount and pin showing direction of applied force.

12. Enter the Y-component of force on your own and verify that its direction is upward as shown on Fig. 26. Use a force magnitude of:

$$F_Y = 400*\sin 60° = 346.4 \text{ lb}$$

13. Make certain the force **Normal to plane** is deselected (i.e., the bottom field in the **Force** dialogue box should be "grayed" out).

14. Click **[OK]** ✓ to close the **Force/Torque** property manager.

Y and Z force components applied to the pin should now appear as shown in Fig. 26. If force component directions differ from those shown, right-click the **Force-1** or **Force-2** and select **Edit Definition…**; then select ☑ **Reverse direction**. **Symmetry** and **Fixed** restraints are temporarily hidden to reduce clutter in Fig. 26.

Figure 26 – To improve visibility, the Y and Z components of force applied to the pin are illustrated to a somewhat enlarged scale. (Left-side view).

Mesh the Model and Run the Solution

1. Right-click the **Mesh** folder and from the pull-down menu select **Create Mesh...**

2. Open ☑ **Mesh Parameters** and accept the default mesh size. Also, select ⊙**Standard Mesh**. Click **[OK]** ✓ to close the **Mesh** property manager and mesh the model.

3. On the Simulation tab, click the **Run** 🖼 icon. *If the analysis fails in an error, click [OK] to close error windows and repeat step 3.*

Notice the longer time required for this solution (approx.. 12 seconds). This is due to the **Solving contact constraints:** portion of the analysis. NOTE: Meshing the model must occur *after* **No Penetration** is specified as the contact mode between mating parts.

Results Analysis

A primary goal of this example is to introduce tools used to observe contact pressure (stress) between mating components. Also, because the resulting state of stress is rather complex to model using simple classical stress equations, little attention is focused on other stress results in the current model. However, because von Mises stress is widely used to compare stress magnitude against material Yield Strength, its results are examined briefly below.

Von Mises Stress

1. If von Mises stress is not displayed on the model, double-click **Stress1 (-von Mises-)** located beneath the **Results** folder. An image of von Mises stress distribution in the model is displayed in Fig. 27 and on your screen.

2. If the model does not appear as a deformed view, right-click **Stress1 (-vonMises-)** and select **Edit Definition...** Within the **Stress Plot** property manager, verify that a check appears adjacent to ☑ **Deformed Shape** and select ⊙ **Automatic** as the scaling method.

Figure 27– von Mises stress contours displayed on the deformed shape of the trunion and pin assembly.

3. Click **[OK]** ✓ to close the **Stress Plot** property manager. The image should appear similar to that shown in Fig. 27; if not, double click **Stress1 (-vonMises-)**.

Observe the maximum von Mises stress of 2679.1 psi (values may vary) is well below the material Yield Strength (34,994 psi). Yield Strength is *not* typically displayed on assembly plots because dissimilar materials might be used for different components. However, in this example all materials are the same, thus Yield Strength is shown.

Iso Clipping

Unlike **Section Clipping** that permits stepping through a model at user specified increments of *distance* to view stresses on different "slices" of the model, **Iso Clipping** aids interpretation of results by permitting a variety of display options *based on stress magnitude*. These options are investigated below.

1. Right-click **Stress1 (-vonMises-)** and from the pull-down menu select **Iso Clipping…** An initial view of the **Iso Clipping** property manager is illustrated in Fig. 28.

The **Iso 1** dialogue box contains a sliding scale whose two extreme values correspond to the minimum and maximum values of the quantity displayed on the color-coded stress scale appearing on the graphics screen. In the present case, von Mises stress magnitudes are displayed.

Figure 28 – Sliding stress scale in the **Iso Clipping** property manager.

2. In the **Iso 1** box, click-and-*drag* the sliding scale pointer and observe stress *levels* change on the model. Simultaneously, a moving arrow, adjacent to the color-coded stress scale, indicates the magnitude of stresses currently being displayed. Sliding the pointer from left-to-right results in lower stress levels being peeled away such that only areas of high stress remain. The *current value* of stress magnitude also appears in the **Iso value** box in the **Iso 1** dialogue box.

3. By clicking the **Reverse clipping direction** icon ⬚, circled in Fig. 28, and then moving the sliding scale pointer from left-to-right, increasing levels of stress are displayed on the model.

4. Next, in the **Options** dialogue box, located at bottom of the **Iso Clipping** property manager in Fig. 28, check ☑ **Plot on iso surface only** and once again move the sliding scale pointer. This time observe that *only* stress of a certain magnitude is plotted. This result is *not* pictured on the model in Fig. 29. Return **Iso Clipping** to its original setting by again clicking the **Reverse clipping direction** icon ⬚

The option demonstrated in step 4 permits easy identification of regions where stress is *at* a certain magnitude.

5. Before proceeding, clear the check mark from □ **Plot on iso surface only**.

Figure 29 – **Iso Clipping** is set to display stresses *between* values set in the **Iso 1** and **Iso 2** dialogue boxes.

6. Next, check ☑ **Iso 2** to open a second dialogue box in the **Iso Clipping** property manager and click the **Reverse clipping direction** icon ⬈ for **Iso 2**. See Fig. 29.

7. Use the sliding scale in each dialogue box to set a lower bound and an upper bound for stress magnitudes to be displayed. In Fig. 29 **Iso 1** is set at **403.8** psi and **Iso 2** is set at **1881.7** psi. *Any approximations of these values are acceptable.*

The corresponding plot, shown at the right side of Fig. 29, displays stress values *between* approximately 403 psi to 1882 psi. Also observe two arrows adjacent to the color-coded stress scale. These arrows mark the lower and upper bounds of stress magnitudes currently displayed. NOTE: If an error was made in the steps above, it may be necessary to click the **Reverse clipping direction** icons ⬈ to properly set upper and lower bounds.

Analysis Insight

Iso Clipping permits easy identification of regions where stress levels are *above or below* a given value.

Iso Clipping also permits isolating and displaying stresses *at* a specific level or *between* specified lower and upper limits.

Before proceeding, return the full display of von Mises stress contours to the model as follows.

8. Clear the check-mark "✓" from the □ **Iso 2** dialogue box.

9. In the **Iso 1** dialogue box, slide the scale pointer to the extreme left position to display the full range of stress contours on the model. If they do not appear, click the **Reverse clipping direction** icon ▣.

10. Click **[OK]** ✓ to close the **Iso Clipping** property manager.

Animating Stress Results

SolidWorks Simulation **Animation** capability permits dynamic viewing of a model due to applied loads provided ☑ **Deformed Shape** was checked, as specified in steps 2 and 3 of the "**von Mises Stress**" section. During animation the model is cycled from no load to maximum load while stress, displacement, or strain is displayed. Insight gained by viewing these variations can be valuable in determining whether or not the model is behaving as expected based on applied loads and restraints. Proceed as follows to animate the von Mises stress results.

1. Right-click **Stress1 (-vonMises-)** and from the pull-down menu select ▶**Animate…** The **Animation** property manager opens as shown in Fig. 30.

2. If the model is animated, click the **Stop** ▣ button at top of the **Basics** dialogue box.

3. Within the **Basics** dialogue box, the upper field controls the number of **Frames** (i.e., the number of still images that are played back in sequence to simulate continuous motion). Set the **Frames** spin-box value to **10**. This value is a user preference. Higher values create smoother, but slower, animations.

Figure 30 – A portion of the **Animation** property manager showing the **Frames** and **Speed** controls.

4. The slide-scale, located at the bottom of the **Basics** dialogue box, controls the **Speed** of animation. Moving the slide to the left slows the animation and, conversely, movement to the right increases animation speed.

Experiment with these capabilities on your own. The model can be rotated to view it from different angles while animation is proceeding. Observe the model in a front view an note that planes of symmetry do *not move* in the X-direction. Use the **Start** ▷, **Pause** ‖, and **Stop** ▣ buttons, located from left to right across the top of the **Basics** dialogue box, to control animation. If desired, an animated sequence can be saved as an AVI file.

5. After experimenting with this capability, click **[OK]** ✓ to close the **Animation** property manager.

Animation of stress variation in the trunion mount corresponds to each power stroke of a cylinder. Although not studied here, cycling of stress from minimum to maximum should emphasize the need to conduct fatigue analysis of any machine component.

Displacement Results

Displacement or **Strain** results can be displayed and examined in like manner to that described above for the von Mises stress plot. Users are encouraged to examine the displacement display and animate it on their own.

Analysis Insight

For those familiar with the actual hardware used in a trunion mounted pneumatic or hydraulic cylinder, the deformed model should raise questions about the validity of loads applied to the pin. A photograph of a complete trunion mount, shown in Fig. 31, reveals that the central portion of the pin passes through a *close fitting* hole on the cylinder base. As such, it is highly unlikely that the pin deforms (bends) like the image currently displayed. A better model of the trunion mount and pin assembly should include a more rigid **Contact Set** definition applied on the center portion of the pin.

Figure 31 – Close-up view of a trunion mount attached to the base of a pneumatic cylinder.

This insight is introduced to emphasize, once again, the significant influence of using *proper boundary conditions* to obtain accurate finite element results. On your own, consider whether or not the accuracy of boundary conditions (i.e., **Loads** and **Fixtures**) applied to this model could be further improved. For example, knowing that the trunion mount is to be bolted down, should another restraint be applied to the bottom surface of the trunion mount to prevent deflection/penetration *into* a rigid surface beneath it? Also consider how additional restraints applied to the bottom surface of the trunion depend on the stiffness of the surface to which it is fastened.

Proper finite element analysis requires its users to carefully consider numerous factors that directly influence the validity of results. The ability to easily create and model these alternate design scenarios is clearly one of the strengths of the finite element approach.

Contact Pressure / Stress

The final section of this example explores the **Contact Pressure** plot. This plot displays, in a unique graphical format, the contact pressure developed between mating parts for which **Contact Set** conditions are specified. Proceed as follows to display this plot.

1. Begin by turning off the display of loads and restraints on the model. Right-click the **Fixtures** folder and from the pull-down menu, select **Hide All**. Do the same for the **External Loads** folder.

2. Next, right-click the **Results** folder and from the pull-down menu, select **Define Stress Plot...** The **Stress Plot** property manager opens.

3. Within the **Display** dialogue box, click to open the stress **Component** pull-down menu and from the list of options, select **CP: Contact Pressure**.

4. Click **[OK]** ✓ to close the **Stress Plot** property manager. A new plot named **Stress2 (-Contact pressure-)** is listed beneath the **Results** folder.

5. If the contact pressure plot is not displayed, double-click **Stress2 (-Contact pressure-)**. *Rotate the model and carefully examine the results. The default display of contact pressure is relatively small.*

The following steps outline how to adjust the contact pressure plot to appear as illustrated in Figs. 32 (a) and (b).

(a)   (b)

Figure 32 – (a) Left-side view of **Contact pressure** between the pin and hole in the trunion mount; (b) view showing the three-dimensional nature of **Contact pressure** between mating surfaces.

6. Right-click **Stress2 (-Contact pressure-)** and from the pull-down menu select **Vector Plot Options...** The **Vector plot options** property manager opens as shown in Fig. 33.

7. In the **Options** dialogue box, type **600** in the **Size** field to enlarge the contact pressure vectors displayed on the current plot. The value chosen for the **Size** field is a user preference and should be selected to create a meaningful display. (Maximum **Size** = 1000 %).

8. Make certain that ⊙ **Match color chart** is selected. This option adds color to the vector plot such that, in addition to vectors indicating the magnitude and direction of contact pressure, the vector color also corresponds to that displayed in the color-coded legend.

9. Click **[OK]** ✓ to close the **Vector plot options** property manager. Your display should now appear similar to that shown in Figs. 32 (a) or (b).

Figure 33 – Magnitude of the vector display is controlled within the **Vector plot options** property manager.

10. Rotate and zoom-in on the model to gain a better appreciation of the three-dimensional nature of contact pressure variation between the pin and hole in the trunion mount. Observe that higher contact pressure exists toward the loaded side of the pin.

A **Contact Pressure** plot is somewhat unique because it displays both magnitude and direction of pressure between the contacting surfaces. Existence of this plot is dependent on the *No Penetration* **Contact Set** condition defined earlier in this example.

This concludes analysis of contact pressure developed between the trunion base and a pin subject to an external load. This example file can be closed without saving. If file space is at a premium, delete the file.

11. In the main menu, select **File > Close**. Then in the SolidWorks window, select **Don't Save**.

Analysis Insight – How Contact Pressure relates to previous examples.

In closing, consider how methods of this chapter could have been applied to the pin used to attach a roller to the cam follower in the example of Chapter #1 or to determine contact stress in the vicinity of the pin hole in the curved beam model of Chapter #2. Likewise, it could have been used to reveal a plot of contact pressure caused by the interference fit between the wheel and shaft assembly of Chapter #5.

EXERCISES

EXERCISE 1 – Contact Pressure Between a Clevis and Pin

At the push-rod end of a hydraulic or pneumatic cylinder (opposite end from the trunion mount) is a part that connects the cylinder push-rod to a driven component. This connector, commonly called a "clevis," takes many different forms, one of which is illustrated in Fig. E6-1. A clevis is typically threaded onto the end of a cylinder push-rod. It then is connected to a driven device by means of a pin. The figure below shows the geometry of a typical clevis with a reaction force, F = 8600 N, applied to its clevis pin. As in the example problem of this chapter, open the part files **Clevis Pin 6-1** and **Clevis 6-1** to create an appropriate assembly **Mate** after defining *Split lines* on the pin. Then perform a finite element analysis to determine the items requested below.

F = 8600 N
@ 20° from the
horizontal

Figure E6-1 – Top, front, and isometric views of a clevis and pin assembly. A force of 8600 N is applied to the pin as shown in the front view. (Use SI units)

- Material: **1045 Steel, cold drawn** for both the clevis and pin. (Use S.I. units), consider steel to be ductile.

- Mesh: Use system default size **Curvature based mesh**, tetrahedral elements.

- Fixtures: **Fixed (immovable)** - Appropriate for a push-rod threaded into the hole
  Symmetry - as instructed below
  Contact Set - Specify **No penetration** between the clevis pin surface and the clevis hole.

- External Load: Apply appropriate force components to model the load applied to the pin.

Assumptions:

> ➢ The pin (40 mm long) is centered between sides of the clevis (clevis height = clevis width = 36 mm, square).

> ➢ Use symmetry to model half of the clevis and pin assembly.

Determine the following:

Develop a finite element model that includes: material specification, fixtures, external load(s), mesh, and a solution. Defeature the model if needed and delete the "cosmetic threads" as outlined below. *Reminder: Assuming the example of the current chapter was worked, recall that system default units were changed to English at the outset of that example. Refer to section* **Create a Finite Element Analysis (Study),**" *page 6-13 (steps 4 to 6) to define SI units for the current exercise.*

Cosmetic Threads

So called "cosmetic threads" are included on the Clevis model to provide insight into its means of attachment to a cylinder push-rod end. Cosmetic threads are a symbolic representation of screw threads rather than actual geometric shapes cut into the model. As such, they serve their intended purpose of conveying information, but do not affect results. For example, they do not cause stress concentration due to thread profiles cut into the model. It is often desirable to **Delete** cosmetic threads because, if not deleted, they cause a circle and/or dashed lines to appear on various views of the model as shown in top, front, and isometric views in Fig. E6-1. Although this remnant of the thread profile does not affect results, it may be found bothersome by some individuals. *At the start of this exercise*, delete cosmetic threads as follows.

1. Open the file **Clevis 6-1**.

2. Contents of the SolidWorks feature manager are shown in Fig. E6-2.

3. Near the bottom of the SolidWorks feature manger, click the "+" sign adjacent to **Threaded Hole Cut-Extrude2**.

Beneath this icon, right-click **Cosmetic Thread 4** and from the pull-down menu select **Delete**.

4. Return to the problem solution.

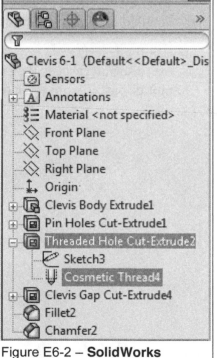

Figure E6-2 – **SolidWorks** feature manager used to **Delete** the **Cosmetic Threads**.

a. Create a plot showing all restraints and loads applied to half of the assembly model. This image might be thought of as the finite element equivalent of a free-body diagram. Do not show stresses or a mesh on this plot. Adjacent to the image, hand write calculations used to determine the X and Y force components acting on the pin. Also, on a small sketch oriented the same as the model, draw and label magnitudes of the X and Y force components applied to the model.

b. Create a plot showing **Contact Pressure** between the pin and clevis. Enlarge the vector size to make them easily visible, but in reasonable proportion to the overall image. Select a view that clearly shows the three dimensional nature of contact pressure variation within the clevis.

c. Create a plot of von Mises stress contours displayed on a deformed image of the pin and clevis assembly. Show the deformed model by checking ☑ **Deformed Shape** and select ⊙ **Automatic** as the scaling method. Also, incorporate automatic labeling of the maximum von Mises stress.

d. Create a safety factor plot based on von Mises stress. Identify region(s) of the assembly that have a safety factor less than 2.0 (if any) based on the material yield strength.

e. Use **Iso Clipping** to create a plot that shows regions of the model where von Mises stress exceeds the material yield strength (if any such regions exist). Include automatic labeling of the maximum von Mises stress on this plot.

f. Discuss **Fixtures** you applied to the clevis and pin model. Provide sound reasoning and justification for restraints applied at the threaded clevis attachment location. If you believe the suggested restraints are incorrect or can be improved, provide a detailed discussion that justifies your opinion.

g. Briefly describe the procedure used to plot the stress magnitudes for part (e) of this exercise and discuss the correspondence, or lack thereof, between the safety factor plot of part (d) and the Iso Clipping plot of part (e).

EXERCISE 2 – Contact Pressure in a Hip Prosthesis

Hip replacement joints are frequently used for individuals who suffer from severe arthritis or hip bone fractures. Fig. E6-3 illustrates the stem and cup for a typical hip prosthesis. The femur (upper leg bone) is prepared by removing its upper portion and by reaming an appropriate size cavity into which the prosthesis stem is cemented. To further distribute upper body weight to the femur and relieve shear forces in the bone cement between the stem and femur, a lip labeled in Fig. E6-3 (b), transfers a compressive load to the upper end of the femur. Similarly, the cup is fixed to the hip bone by bone adhesive and projections that protrude into receiving holes drilled into the hip bone. These protrusions stabilize the cup and prevent cup rotation relative to bone tissue. A screw connector is also provided. Specific surface areas of the stem and cup are porous (not illustrated below). Re-growth of natural bone tissue into these porous areas promotes development of a stronger bond between the prosthesis and bone. The cup liner provides a low friction wear surface between the ball and cup.

Open File: **Stem and Cup Assembly**

Figure E6-3 – Figure (a) shows a hip prosthesis as it would appear implanted in the human body.[2] Figure (b) is an exploded view showing the three main components of the **Stem and Cup Assembly**.

Disclaimer
Actual part dimensions and materials are considered proprietary information. Therefore, dimensions and part materials used in this exercise are *not* representative of actual data.

---

[2] Photo [Fig. E6-3 (a)] courtesy of Zimmer Inc., Warsaw, Indiana

- Material[3]:
  - o **Cup Liner** - Locate under **Plastics**, then choose **PA Type 6**
  - o **Stem** - Locate under **Titanium Alloys** then choose **Commercially Pure CP-Ti UNS R50700 Grade4 (SS)**
  - o **Cup Outer** - Same material as **Stem**

- Mesh: Use system default size **Curvature based mesh**, tetrahedral elements.

- Fixture: To be specified by the user based on experience gained in previous exercises and an understanding of the hip replacement process described above. Carefully consider how and where restraints are applied to the model relative to how and where external loads are applied.

- External Load: Person's weight = **145** lb. You may decide to use a different external load. If so, include the reason for your decision in part (a) of the exercise listed below.

Determine the following:

Develop a finite element model that includes: material specification, realistic fixtures, external load(s), mesh generation, and solution.

a. On the upper half of one page, create a plot showing all fixtures and loads applied to the stem and to the cup assembly. Manually label vectors representing **Fixtures** to differentiate them from vectors representing **External Loads**. This image represents the finite element equivalent of a free-body diagram. Do not show stresses or a mesh on this plot. On the lower half of the page, provide:

   - good reason(s) and justification for fixtures and/or external load(s) applied to the cup outer. Discuss items such as magnitude(s) and direction(s).

   - good reason(s) and justification for fixtures and/or external load(s) applied to the stem. Discuss items such as magnitude(s) and direction(s).

   - If an external load other than the person's given weight is used, provide insight into the reasoning used to determine and recommend an alternate load.

b. Create a plot of von Mises stress contours displayed on a deformed image of the stem and cup assembly. Show the deformed model by checking ☑ **Deformed Shape** and select ⊙ **Automatic** as the scaling method. Also, incorporate automatic labeling of the maximum von Mises stress.

c. Create a plot showing **Contact Pressure** between the "ball" (located at top of the Stem) and the Cup Liner (located between the ball and Cup Outer). Enlarge contact vector size to make vectors easily visible, but in reasonable proportion to

---

[3] Materials and their associated properties shown here in *no way* reflect actual manufacturer's specifications.

the overall image. Select a view that clearly shows the three dimensional nature of contact pressure variation.

d. Question: Based on your understanding of fatigue in metals, does the maximum von Mises stress determined in part (b) place this Stem and Cup Assembly in danger of failure? Discuss practical reasons for your answer in terms of stress repetitions expected for the assembly. Also discuss the engineering reasons for your answer. Consider topics such as stress magnitude, type of stress (tensile versus compressive), and material characteristics of the general class of titanium steels.

EXERCISE 3 – Stress Concentration Analysis using Part Symmetry

Exercise No. 1 of Chapter 3 is repeated here. However, make use of model symmetry discussed in the **Analysis Insight** section on pages 5-8 and 5-9 of Chapter 5 and techniques mastered in the current chapter to reduce the size of the **Plate With Hole** model. For your convenience, all necessary parts of the previous exercise are repeated here. NOTE: The previous exercise need *not* have been worked.

Open the file: **Plate With Hole 3-1**.

Figure E6-4 (Figure E3-1 repeated) – Aluminum bar with central hole subject to an axial force **F**. A geometric discontinuity is present in the form of the 40 mm diameter hole.

- Material: **2018 Alloy** aluminum (Use S.I. units)

- Mesh: In the **Mesh** property manager, select a ⊙ **Standard mesh**; high quality tetrahedral elements are used. Use three different meshes as specified in parts (a, c, and d) below.

- Fixtures: Determined by user.

- External Load: **F = 370 kN** acts normal to right-end causing tension in the bar.

Develop a finite element model that includes: material specification, symmetry restraints, external load, mesh generation, and solution as specified below. For this analysis use high quality meshes of the sizes specified below and perform the following.

Solution Guidance

• To simplify application of model symmetry, refer to the SolidWorks Simulation manager tree.

When applying **Fixtures** to the model, open the **Advanced** dialogue box and select the **Symmetry** [icon] Symmetry icon. Apply **Symmetry** restraints to all cut surfaces of the model.

Determine the following:

a. Using a *default* size mesh, create a plot of the *most appropriate stress* to permit comparison of its magnitude adjacent to the hole with that predicted by classical equations for stress computed at the same location; see part (e) for calculation of classical stress results. Include fixtures, symmetry restraints (if any), external load(s), and mesh on this plot. On the plot, specify the magnitude of the applied load. Also on this plot answer the question: Is it necessary to apply any additional restraints on the symmetry model? If so, specify its/their direction.

b. Use the **Probe** feature to produce a graph of the *most appropriate stress* from the top edge of the bar to the upper edge of the central hole. Note that a straight path should be available for this model because nodes must lie on the cut edge; use both corner and mid-side nodes. On this graph, include a descriptive title, axis labels, and your name.

c. Repeat part (b) after resetting the mesh size to *fine*. Use the copy feature to save time creating this study.

d. Repeat part (b) a third time after resetting the mesh size by applying *mesh control* around both edges and the inner surface of the hole. Use a mesh control setting of: **Ratio a/b = 1.2**. Also, use the copy feature to save time creating this study.

e. Use classical equations and available stress concentration factor charts to manually compute maximum stress at the hole.

f. Compare results predicted using the three different meshes with that predicted by classical stress equations. Compute the percent difference for each comparison using equation [1].

$$\% \text{ difference} = \frac{(\text{FEA result - classical result})}{\text{FEA result}} * 100 = \qquad [1]$$

g. For the three different meshes, comment upon which FEA results are in best agreement with predictions of the classical equations? Which method of mesh refinement is usually preferred and why?

h. If Exercise 1 of Chapter 3 was worked, compare magnitudes of the maximum *appropriate stress* at the hole location. Compare magnitudes *only* for the case when *Mesh Control* is used. Then answer the question, "Which FEA model (i.e., the *complete* model or the *symmetrical* model) is in best agreement with calculation of stress at the hole location determined using classical equations and stress concentration factor charts? If differences exceeding 4% are obtained, explain the reason for this difference.

i. Symmetry is used to reduce model size and computation time, especially for large, complex models. At the start of this exercise, a decision was made regarding what you believe to be smallest symmetric model segment that could be used to solve this problem. In retrospect, do you think it is possible to further reduce model size through the application of symmetry principles? If "yes," sketch the reduced model and show all restraints (symmetry included) acting on that model. Apply **Fixture** vectors to the model showing their correct direction and label them using "S" to denote *symmetry* restraints (if any) and "**RB**" to denote *rigid body* restraints (if any). Also show and label **External Loads**.

Textbook Problems
In addition to the above exercises, it is highly recommended that additional problems involving contact between mating parts be worked from a design of machine elements textbook. Textbook problems provide a great way to discover errors made in formulating a finite element analysis because they typically are well defined problems for which the solution is known. Textbook problems, if well defined in advance, make an excellent source of solutions for comparison.

NOTES:

CHAPTER #7
BOLTED JOINT ANALYSIS

Machine screws, bolts, and/or nuts and bolts in combination, are some of the most frequently used means of joining mechanical components. Bolted joints are commonly used in non-permanent connections where access to components for repair or replacement is essential. This example examines steps involved to successfully model bolted connections. Bolted connections are but one of many connection types available in SolidWorks Simulation. Other connector types contained within the software, but not examined here, include: springs, rigid, pins, links, spot welds, edge welds, and bearing connections between components.

Learning Objectives

Upon completion of this example, users should be able to:

- Specify *bolt connectors*

- Define *custom material properties* for bolt connectors

- Identify when mesh refinement is necessary based on a *high stress gradient*

- Define *contact sets* between parts without the use of Split Lines (see Exercise 1)

Problem Statement

An angle bracket is attached to a long, rigid support plate as illustrated in Fig. 1. Both the support plate and angle bracket are made of **ANSI 1020 Steel**. For purposes of this example, the support plate is shortened by arbitrarily cutting it in the vicinity of the two dashed lines on either side of the angle bracket. Four **M 12 x 1.75** bolts with nuts (i.e., 12 mm diameter metric bolts with a thread pitch = 1.75 mm) fasten the two parts together

through the four holes shown. Bolts and nuts are not shown in the accompanying figure. All bolts are tightened to a preload of **24000** N. The goal is to determine bolt loads when the joint is loaded by a force of **5000** N acting normal to the top surface of the tab at the right end of the angle bracket. Force **F** can act either toward or away from the tab surface shown on Fig. 1, but is not a cyclic load.

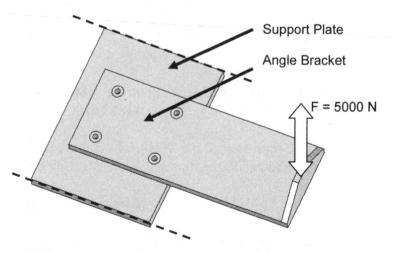

Figure 1 – Basic geometry of the angle bracket and support plate, showing bolt hole locations.

1. Open SolidWorks by making the following selections. (*NOTE:* ">" is used to separate successive menu selections.)

Start>All Programs>SolidWorks 2013 (or) Click the **SolidWorks** icon on your screen.

2. When SolidWorks is open, select **File > Open…** Then use procedures common to your computer environment to open the file named "**Support Plate and Angle Bracket**." The screen image should look similar to Fig. 1.

Create a Static Analysis (Study)

1. In the main menu, select **Simulation** and from the pull-down menu select **Study…** Alternatively, select 🔍 **New Study** found beneath the ▼ **Study Advisor** icon on the **Simulation** tab. Either action opens the **Study** property manager.

2. In the **Name** dialogue box, type "**Bolted Joint-DOWNWARD Load-YOUR NAME**."

3. Verify that a **Static** analysis is selected and click **[OK]** ✓ to close the **Study** property manager. A Study outline appears in the Simulation manager.

Assign Material Properties to the Model

Material properties of the support plate and angle bracket are assigned in this section. Because both components are the same material, this procedure is quite straightforward. Try it on your own using **AISI 1020** steel and select **SI – N/m^2 (Pa)** units. Steps are provided below if guidance is desired.

1. Right-click the **Parts** folder and from the pull-down menu, select **Apply Material to All…** The **Material** window opens.

2. In the **Material** window, open the **+ Steel** folder (if not already open) and from the list of materials, choose **AISI 1020**.

3. In the right-half of the **Material** window, verify that **Units:** are set to **SI – N/m^2 (Pa)** and verify the material Yield Strength is **351571000** N/m^2.

4. Click **[Apply]** followed by **[Close]** to close the **Material** window.

Notice that bolt material is *not* specified at this time. Bolt material is specified independently when other bolt characteristics are defined.

Apply External Load and Fixtures

Traditional Loads and Fixtures

This section outlines the application of restraints and an external load using procedures similar to those encountered throughout this user manual. Those wishing to apply fixed/immovable restraints to top and bottom cut edges of the support plate and a 5000 N load normal to the tab on the right end of the angle bracket are encouraged to proceed on their own. However, steps are provided below if guidance is desired.

1. In the Simulation manager, right-click the **Fixtures** folder and from the pull-down menu, select **Fixed Geometry...** The **Fixture** property manager opens.

2. In the **Standard (Fixed Geometry)** dialogue box, select the ☒ **Fixed Geometry** icon (if not already selected).

Figure 2 – Application of restraints to cut-surfaces at top and bottom of the support plate.

3. The **Faces, Edges, Vertices for Fixture** field is active (highlighted light blue). Move the cursor into the graphics screen and rotate and zoom-in on the model as necessary to select the two cut surfaces of the support plate shown in Fig. 2. **Face<1>** and **Face<2>@Support Plate-1** appear in the highlighted field.

4. Click **[OK]** ✓ to close the **Fixture** property manager. ☒ **Fixed-1** appears beneath the **Fixtures** folder.

Next apply a downward force on top of the tab at the right-end of the angle bracket.

5. Right-click the **External loads** folder and from the pull-down menu, select **Force...** The **Force/Torque** property manager opens as illustrated in Fig. 3.

6. In the **Force/Torque** dialogue box, verify that the ⬇ **Force** icon is selected (gray highlight) and that force direction is selected as ⊙ **Normal**.

7. The **Faces and Shell Edges for Normal Force** field is highlighted (light blue) and awaits input. Select the top surface of the angle bracket shown in Fig. 3.

Figure 3 – Application of a downward force normal to top surface of the tab located at the right-end of the angle bracket.

8. From the ▣ **Unit** pull-down menu, select **SI** as the desired units.

9. In the **Force Value** field, type **5000** N and select ⊙ **Per item**. The force should act downward, if not check ☑ **Reverse Direction**.

10. Click **[OK]** ✓ to close the **Force/Torque** property manager.

Define Bolted Joint Restraints

Individual bolted fasteners used to join the angle bracket and support plate are defined next. Discussion below assumes the bolt head is located on top of the angle bracket while the nut is located against the bottom surface of the support plate as identified in Fig. 4. Definition of bolted joints takes place within the **Connections** folder located in the Simulation manager tree.

Carefully and sequentially work through the following steps to define *one bolt at a time*. NOTE: If all bolt clamping surfaces are selected in a single step, software ability to isolate *individual* bolt reactions is lost. Also, while proceeding through the following steps, place the cursor onto each field or icon to reveal its name. This approach enhances insight into understanding the function of each option.

Angle Bracket
(top surface)

Support Plate
(bottom surface is
out of view)

Figure 4 – Angle bracket and support plate showing bolt holes numbered from 1 to 4 in counterclockwise order.

1. Right-click **Connections** and from the pull-down menu select **Bolt…** The **Connectors** property manager opens; a partial view is shown in Fig. 5. Carefully note the **Message** highlighted in yellow.

2. To avoid having to re-open the **Connectors** property manager for every bolt, click the **Keep Visible** "push-pin" circled in Fig. 5.

3. At top of the **Type** dialogue box, click ▼ to open the pull-down menu and examine the various connector types listed. Then, from the list of possible connectors, select **Bolt** (if not already selected).

4. Select the **Standard or Counterbore with Nut** fastener shown boxed in Fig. 5. Move the cursor over the remaining icons to get an overview of other connector types available within the **Bolt** connector sub-group.

Within SolidWorks Simulation there exist multiple ways to define bolted connectors. The most direct method is outlined below. In order to define a nut and bolt, the parameters listed in Table 1, on the next page, are needed. Table 1 shows values applicable to metric grade 5.8, **M 12 x 1.75** bolts and nuts used in this example. Information shown in Table 1 is readily available in most design of machine elements texts.

Figure 5 – Partial view of the **Connectors** property manager with the **Keep Visible** push-pin and connector type selected.

Table 1 – Data required to define nut and bolt characteristics.

PARAMETER	VALUE
Bolt shank diameter	12 mm
Bolt head diameter	18 mm
Nut diameter	18 mm
Bolt Elastic Modulus	207e9 N/m^2
Bolt Poisson's Ratio	0.292
Bolt Pre-load	24000 N

The following steps proceed from top to bottom of the **Connectors** property manager. To ensure selection of the correct field, move the cursor over each field to reveal its name. Also recall that the bolt head is located on the angle bracket, considered to be the top of the model, and the nut is located in contact with the support plate (bottom side of the model) in Fig. 8.

5. Click to activate (light blue) the **Circular Edge of The Bolt Head Hole** field (if not already selected). Then zoom-in on the *top* of the angle bracket and click to select the *top edge* of bolt hole #1; see Fig. 8. **Edge<1>@Angle Bracket-1** is listed in the active field as shown in Fig. 6. An information "flag" should appear attached to the selected bolt hole. This flag summarizes all bolt parameters as they are defined. Neglect initial values shown in the flag. Click and drag the information flag to a convenient location on the screen.

6. Next, in the **Type** dialogue box, click to activate (highlight) the **Circular Edge of The Bolt Nut Hole** field labeled in Fig. 7. *CAUTION: This step is easily missed in the repetitive process outlined below.*

Figure 6 – The **Connectors** property manager after selecting **Bolt** as the connector type.

7. Rotate the model and zoom-in on the *bottom* of the support plate to select the corresponding bottom *edge* of bolt hole #1. **Edge<2>@ Support Plate-1** is listed in the active field.

8. Immediately beneath this field, check ☑ **Same head and nut diameter**. This step matches the nut and bolt head diameters, which is common practice for standard bolt connections.

9. To the right of the **Bolt Head** diameter field, click to open the **Unit** pull-down menu and select **mm**. *Units must be specified prior to entering the bolt head diameter.*

10. To the left of the **Unit** field, type **18** mm in the **Head Diameter** field.

11. Next, adjacent to the **Nominal Shank Diameter** field, click to change **Unit** to **mm**.

12. In the **Bolt Shank Diameter** field, type **12** mm.

13. If necessary, clear the check mark "✓" from ☐ **Tight Fit**. This option does not pertain to bolts inserted through clearance holes such as are used in this example.

Figure 7 – Top portion of the **Connectors** property manager showing selections used to define bolts and nut contact faces.

Bolt Head Diameter

Nominal Shank Diameter

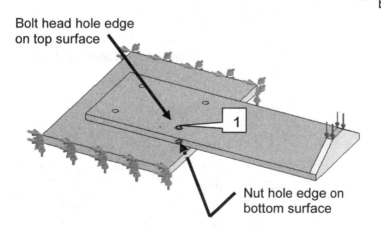

Bolt head hole edge on top surface

Nut hole edge on bottom surface

Figure 8 – Model showing selection of hole edges for the bolt head and nut contact faces for bolt #1.

Next, direct your attention to the **Material** dialogue box. In this dialogue box it is possible to select bolt material from the **Material** window, as has been done in all previous examples, or to specify custom material properties as outlined below.

14. Scroll down to the **Material** dialogue box shown in Fig. 9, select ⦿ **Custom**. The bolt information "flag" expands to display additional information to be specified by the user.

15. In the **Unit** ▤ dialogue box, verify that **SI** is selected.

16. Adjacent to the **Young's Modulus** E_x field, type **207e9** N/m^2 to identify the bolt modulus of elasticity.

17. In the **Poisson's Ratio** field ⬍, type **0.292**.

18. Leave the **Thermal expansion coefficient** α blank. Temperature is not a factor in this bolt joint.

Figure 9 – Specifying custom material properties for bolts in the **Material** dialogue box.

Figure 10 – Bolt preload specified as an axial (tensile) force in the bolt.

19. Scroll to the bottom of the **Connectors** property manager where the **Pre-load** dialogue box appears as shown in Fig. 10. Open the ▤ **Unit** pull-down menu and from the list, again select **SI** (if not already selected).

20. Next, select ⦿ **Axial**. This selection indicates that the bolt preload is expressed by an axial (tensile) load in the bolt caused when the nut is tightened.

21. In the **Axial load** field, type **24000** N.

22. Return to the top of the **Connectors** property manager and click **[OK]** ✓ (green check mark). This action applies all of the above settings to bolt #1.

As specifications are entered for each remaining bolt and nut, symbols representing bolt connectors appear at each hole location as illustrated in Fig. 11.

Figure 11 – Bolt connector symbols appear at locations of the Head and Nut Contact Faces. Rotate the model to view symbols on bottom of the support plate.

Because the **Keep visible** push-pin was selected, the **Connectors** property manager remains open and all values entered to describe the first bolt are retained. Unless changed by the user, the software assumes that additional identical bolts are used. Thus, it only remains to select the top and bottom hole-edges for the remaining bolts and nuts in the counterclockwise order shown numbered in Fig. 11. *NOTE: Keeping track of the order in which bolts are specified is only necessary to identify bolt locations during the analysis portion of a solution.* Proceed as follows.

23. Return to the top of the **Type** dialogue box and click to select the **Circular Edge of the Bolt Head Hole** field to highlight it. On the *top* surface of the angle bracket, select the *edge* of hole #2. The hole edge is highlighted.

24. Beneath the above field, click to activate the **Circular Edge of the Bolt Nut Hole** field. Rotate the model and zoom-in on the *corresponding* hole on the *bottom* of the support plate. Click to select the edge of this hole and bolt connector symbols appear on the model. In the property manager, scroll down and notice that all other data entries remain as previously defined.

25. Return to the top of the **Connectors** property manager, and click **[OK]** ✓. This action applies the previous settings to the bolt at location 2.

Repeat steps 23 through 25 for *each* remaining bolt. Follow the numerical order shown in Fig. 11. *See step 26 after defining bolt #4.*

26. After defining bolt #4 (and clicking **[OK]** ✓ in step 25), select **Cancel** ✖ to close the **Connectors** property manager.

At this point, **Bolt Group-1** appears beneath the **Connectors** folder. Click the "+" sign adjacent to **Bolt Group-1** to reveal **Counter Bore with Nut-1** through **Counter Bore with Nut-4** listed beneath this folder in the Simulation manager tree as illustrated in Fig. 12.

NOTE: If all bolts had been specified using the **Hole Series** feature in SolidWorks, then Simulation would have asked "**Do you want to add bolt connectors to all holes in the Hole Series?**" Selecting **Yes** would have automatically applied the selected bolt to all holes in the same series.

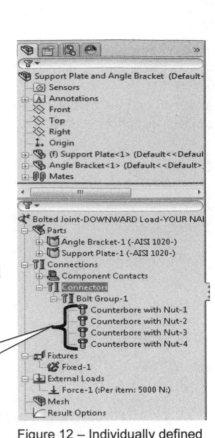

Bolt Connector Icons

Figure 12 – Individually defined bolt connectors listed beneath the **Load/ Restraint** folder.

Analysis Insight

Instead of specifying bolt preload as an **Axial** force, in the **Pre-load** dialogue box, it is also possible to specify bolt preload in terms of torque applied to tighten the nut as shown in the **Pre-load** dialogue box of Fig. 13.

When bolt ⊙**Torque** is specified, the software uses a re-arranged form of equation [1], see next page, to compute the axial preload F_i. Notice that the torque coefficient **K**, listed as "**Friction Factor (K)**" at the bottom of the **Pre-load** dialogue box, can be changed to account for specific joint conditions.

Friction Factor (K) is affected by a variety of joint and bolt characteristics, such as: surface finish (painted, plated, clean, etc.); alignment (parallelism of surfaces and/or flatness under the bolt head and nut); and thread condition (dry, lubricated, coated, etc.).

Pre-load	⌃
🔲	SI ⌄
	◯ Axial
	⊙ Torque
🔩	57.6 ⌄ N-m
↔	0.2 ⌄
	Friction Factor(K)

Figure 13 – **Preload** dialogue box showing specification of bolt **Torque** rather than an axial preload value.

The relationship between bolt preload and bolt torque is typically defined in design of machine elements texts by the following equation.

$$T = KF_i d \qquad\qquad [1]$$

Where: F_i = desired bolt preload (the initial axial tensile force in the bolt)
T = applied torque required to develop a desired preload F_i
K = torque coefficient (K = 0.20 is a generally accepted value)
d = nominal bolt diameter

For this example, if ⦿ **Torque** were selected rather than ○ **Axial** preload, then the torque used to tighten the bolt is given by:

$$T = KF_i d = (0.20)(24 \text{ kN})(0.012 \text{ m}) = 57.6 \text{ N-m}$$

See the entry typed into the **Torque** field in Fig. 13.

This completes the definition of individual bolt connectors. However, because we are dealing with an assembly, it is also necessary to define contact conditions between the two members that are bolted together. This task is addressed in the next section.

Define Local Contact Conditions

Contact between the angle bracket and support plate must also be defined. Because there are only two components in this assembly, it would be possible to define contact between mating surfaces by applying a *Global* contact. Specifying *Global* contact applies the same contact condition to all contacting surfaces in an assembly. However, it is more instructive to define contact in a *Local* sense (i.e., specific to the two contacting surfaces). This approach provides the user with greater control when defining contact between two specific parts and prepares the user to deal with more unique situations should they be encountered in other modeling applications. Begin by switching to an exploded view.

1. In the main menu, select **Insert** and from the pull-down menu choose **Exploded View...** The **Explode** property manager opens.

2. Click to select the angle bracket (top part) in Fig. 14. A coordinate system triad appears on the part. Drag the Y-axis of the triad upward. Release the mouse button when the figure looks similar to Fig. 14. (Alternatively, drag the support plate downward).

Figure 14 – Exploded view prior to defining contact conditions.

3. Click **[OK]** ✓ to close the **Explode** property manager.

4. In the Simulation manager tree, right-click the **Connections** folder and from the pull-down menu select **Contact Set…** The **Contact Sets** property manager opens as shown in the middle of Fig. 15.

5. In the **Contact** dialogue box, choose ⊙ **Manually select contact sets**.

6. In the pull-down menu at top of the **Type** dialogue box, select **No Penetration**.

7. The **Faces, Edges, Vertices for Set 1** field is highlighted (light blue) and awaits input. Move the cursor into the graphics screen and rotate the model to select the bottom, left-end of the angle bracket shown with dark highlight in Fig. 15 (a). A *Split Line* is provided to facilitate selecting only the contact surface. **Face<1>@Angle Bracket-1** is listed in the active field.

(a) Select bottom of Angle Bracket. (b) Select top of Support Plate.

Figure 15 – Selection of equal and opposite faces defined to be in contact with **No Penetration**.

8. Click to highlight (light blue) the **Faces for Set 2** field, located at the bottom of the **Type** dialogue box. Then, proceed to select the contact face in the vicinity of bolt holes on top of the support plate. See highlighted face in Fig. 15 (b). **Face<2>@Support Plate-1** is listed in the active field. Once again *Split Lines* are provided to permit selection of only the contact surface. NOTE: Exercise 1, at end of this chapter, outlines steps to *automatically* find contact sets *without* use of Split lines.

Analysis Insight:

In the **Properties** dialogue box, notice that it is possible to define **Friction** between the contacting surfaces. This option is typically applied when the potential for movement is investigated between mating parts. Since friction is not pertinent to this example, clear the ☐ **Friction** check-box (if necessary) before proceeding.

---

9. Click **[OK]** ✓ to close the **Contact Sets** property manager. Highlighting disappears from the model and beneath the **Connections** folder appears an icon labeled **Contact Sets**. Click the "+" sign to reveal the full name: "**Contact Set-1 (-No Penetration<Angle Bracket-1, Support Plate-1>-).**"

Before proceeding, return the model to its original, un-exploded, state as follows.

10. Toggle to the **Configuration Manager** by clicking its icon 🔳 at top of the SolidWorks manager tree.

11. Click the "+" sign adjacent to **Default [Support Plate and Angle Bracket]**.

12. Right-click ⊞ 🔳 ExplView1 and from the pull-down menu, select **Collapse**.

13. Toggle back to SolidWorks by clicking the **SolidWorks** 🔳 icon.

Mesh the Model and Run Solution

1. In the Simulation manager right-click the **Mesh** folder and from the pull-down menu select **Create Mesh...** The **Mesh** property manager opens.

2. Check "✓" to open the ☑ **Mesh Parameters** dialogue box, set 🔳 **Unit** to **mm**, accept the default mesh size, and select ⊙ **Curvature based mesh**.

3. Click 🔳 to open the **Advanced** dialogue box and verify that **Jacobian points** is set to **[4 Points]**, the default setting. This setting indicates a high quality mesh.

4. Click **[OK]** ✓ to close the **Mesh** property manager and mesh the model. WARNING: Do *not* select ☐ **Run (solve) the analysis**.

The above warning is included because there is a reasonable likelihood that the solution could fail. Recall an earlier warning that indicated it is *not* recommended to use the "☐ **Run (solve) the analysis**" option available in the **Options** dialogue box of the **Mesh** property manager. The reason for this recommendation is that, if a solution fails to run, the user does not know whether the model failed to mesh properly or whether the solver failed to run the analysis. By keeping these two steps separate, the user is better able to pin-point the source of failure. And, knowing the source of a failure facilitates correcting the problem as outlined below.

*Before proceeding to the next step, be forewarned that the solution might fail. The solution below **assumes failure occurs** in the equation solver. Thus, whether or not the solver fails, proceed as if it fails to learn more about software capabilities. Therefore, after starting to **Run** the solution in step #5, proceed immediately to step #6 and the following steps up to and including step #8. It is suggested to pre-read these steps.*

5. On the Simulation tab, select 🖼 **Run**. Alternatively, in the Simulation manager tree right-click the Study name, **Bolted Joint-DOWNWARD Load (-Default-)**, and select **Run**.

6. Immediately after starting the solution, the **Bolted Joint-DOWNWARD Load-YOUR NAME** solution window opens. This window tracks the percent of the solution completed as a bar-graph shown in Fig. 16.

Figure 16 – Window used to track progress toward a Solution.

7. Within this window select the **[More>>]** button, circled in Fig. 16. This action expands window size to that shown in Fig. 17.

Figure 17 shows a second bar-graph. This graph tracks progress of individual components of the overall solution. Observe the **Current Task:** caption circled in Fig. 17, which changes from:

a. **Establishing stiffness matrix** – The first step sets-up equations based on material stiffness, and corresponding displacements caused by loads applied to the model.

b. **Decomposition of stiffness matrix** – Iterates equations of part (a) multiple times seeking convergence to a solution that satisfies *consistent* displacements throughout the model.

c. **Solving contact constraints** – Because **No Penetration** is specified between the two *different* parts, it is more difficult to establish consistent displacements at nodes in this area of the model. Gaps also might occur between mating parts. Most solution time is devoted to solving contact constraints. The Solution alternates between steps (b) and (c).

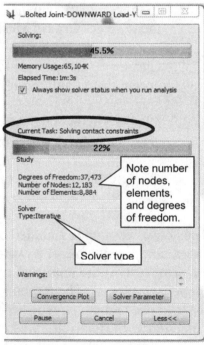

Figure 17 – The expanded solution window permits viewing computation time devoted to different aspects of the Solution.

8. After about two minutes, depending on computer speed and other programs running in the background, the solution *may* stop in a state of error. In that case, the **Linear Static** window shown in Fig. 18 (a) announces that "**The Iterative Solver stopped. Status code: 8 FILE_ERROR No result saved.**"

9. Click **[OK]** to close the **Linear Static** window. A second window, Fig. 18 (b) opens and directs the user to "**Use the Direct Sparse solver**" as an alternate solution method.

(a) (b) (c)

Figure 18 – Error and warning windows displayed upon termination of a failed analysis.

10. Click **[OK]** to close the second **Linear Static** window. Next, the **Simulation** window, shown in Fig. 18 (c) opens. This window informs the user that the current Study **Failed**. Due to the long File and Study names used for this example, the last part of the message, which indicates the Study **Failed**, is not visible. Click **[OK]** to close the **Simulation** window.

Analysis Insight

Notice the increase in time required to solve this problem. The primary time increase occurs during multiple iterations required to solve the contact constraints portion of the solution where contact conditions between nodes on mating parts are determined. The following paragraph provides a non-technical description of the solution process.

To help understand the reason for this time increase, consider that deformation of one part (the angle bracket) causes or transfers that deformation to the mating part (the support plate) where the surfaces are in contact, but cannot penetrate one another. Also, imagine the parts starting from an un-deformed state and gradually transitioning to a fully deformed state. Throughout this incremental deformation process, the governing equations between mating parts must be satisfied at all times (i.e., consistent deformations must exist throughout the model *and* across the contact area). Thus, each small change of deformation is accompanied by new calculations that begin where the previous deformation (displacement) ended. Therefore, the governing equations are solved and satisfied multiple times as the deformation "grows" step-by-step to its final maximum displaced condition.

Solving contact constraints is further complicated by the fact that very small separations, or gaps, may occur between the originally contacting surfaces. Hence the solver must also deal with discontinuities (i.e., gaps) in the displacement field that initially was consistent (i.e., no gaps). This, in part, explains why so much computation time is devoted to the **Solving contact constraints** portion of the solution. Can you guess where these gaps might occur in the current model? What display technique, introduced in an earlier chapter, might be used to reveal such gaps?

Whether or not your solution failed, proceed as follows.

The error shown in Fig. 18 (b) prompts the user to apply the **Direct Sparse** Solver to the solution of this problem. Details about this solver are beyond the scope of this text. However, problems involving **No Penetration** tend to result in longer solutions for reasons cited in the **Analysis Insight** section. Techniques incorporated into the **Direct Sparse** solver are better suited to solve this type of problem. Thus, *the solution is repeated below* using this alternate solver. Proceed as follows.

11. Right-click to select the Study name, **Bolted Joint-DOWNWARD Load-YOUR NAME (-Default-)** listed at top of the Simulation manager. From the pull-down menu select **Properties...** The **Static** window opens.

12. Near the bottom of the **Options** tab, click to select ⊙ **Direct sparse** as the solver type. Notice the previous solver was ○ **FFEPlus**.

13. Click **[OK]** to close the **Static** window.

14. In the Simulation manager tree, right-click the Study name, **Bolted Joint-DOWNWARD Load-YOUR NAME (-Default-)**, and select **Run**.

15. As the solution runs, it is suggested that the **[More>>]** button in the Solution window again be selected. Note the **Solver Type:** is now listed as **Sparse**.

Observations:

- The solution time increases significantly.

- Most of the solution time, 65%, is still devoted to **Solving contact constraints** while 27% is devoted to **Decomposition of stiffness matrix** operations. Only 8% of solution time is devoted to **Forming stiffness matrix**.

After a successful solution is complete, proceed as follows.

Results Analysis for the Downward External Load

Von Mises Stress

Briefly examine a plot of von Mises stress to gain an understanding of the magnitude and distribution of this stress throughout the assembly.

1. Click the "+" sign adjacent to the **Results** folder (if not already selected).

2. If the von Mises stress plot is not already displayed, right-click **Stress1 (-vonMises-)** and from the pull-down menu, select **Show**.

3. Right-click **Stress1 (-vonMises-)** and from the pull-down menu select **Edit Definition…** The **Stress Plot** property manager opens.

4. In the **Display** dialogue box change **Units** to **N/m^2**, if necessary.

5. In the **Advance Options** dialogue box, clear the check mark from ☐ **Average results across boundary for parts** and verify that ⊙ **Node Values** is selected.

6. Check "✓" to open the ☑ **Deformed Shape** dialogue box and within this box, select ⊙ **Automatic** to apply the system default exaggerated deformation to the model display.

7. Click **[OK]** ✓ to close the **Stress Plot** property manager.

8. Double-click the color coded stress scale in the graphics screen. This is an easy to remember short-cut to open the **Chart Options** property manager.

9. In the **Display Options** dialogue box, check both ☑ **Show min annotation** and ☑ **Show max annotation**.

10. In the **Position/Format** dialogue box, select **scientific** as the **Number Format** and select **3** as the **No of Decimals** to be displayed.

11. Click **[OK]** ✓ to close the **Chart Options** property manager. A plot of von Mises stress on the deformed model should appear as illustrated in Fig. 19.

Observe that the maximum von Mises stress, indicated on the model and in the color-coded legend as 1.959e+008 N/m^2 is considerably less than the material Yield Strength of 3.516e+008 N/m^2. Values may vary from those shown in Fig 19.

Figure 19 – von Mises stress distribution as seen in a top view of the assembly corresponding to a downward acting load on the model.

Did you notice that the *same* numerical results were obtained using the **FFEPlus** and **Direct sparse** solvers?

Bolt Forces (for Downward Load)

A primary feature of a bolt analysis is the ability to determine forces acting at each bolt. In the assembly analyzed in this example, it is reasonable to expect similar bolt forces in bolts #1 and #2, which are equidistant from the applied load. Similarly for bolts #3 and #4, which are located a further, but at equal distance from the applied load. Axial force in each bolt is the algebraic sum of its preload, due to tightening the nut, plus effects due to external load(s) acting on the joint. Bolt forces are examined as follows.

1. Right-click the **Results** folder, and from the pull-down menu, select **List Pin/Bolt/Bearing Force…** The **Pin/Bolt/Bearing Force** window opens; see Fig. 20.

Examination of this window reveals the **Study name:** near the upper left corner.

2. Beneath the study name is the **Connector:** field where, in a pull-down menu, it is possible to select results for **All pins**, **All bolts**, **All bearings** or results for each individual bolt. From this pull-down menu, select **Counterbore with Nut-1**.

3. Adjacent to the **Connector:** field, verify that the current set of **Units:** is set to **SI**.

Finally, at the bottom of the window, the **X, Y, Z-**components and the **Resultant** values are listed for the **Shear Force (N)**, **Axial Force (N)**, and **Bending moment (N-m)** that act on bolt #1.

Figure 20 – The **Pin/Bolt/Bearing Force** window summarizes all Shear Force, Axial Force, and Bending moments that act on each bolt in the joint.

4. In the **Axial Force** row, observe the **Resultant** in the far right column. Its value is **24059** N. *NOTE: Values may differ slightly due to computational round-off.*

5. Click the **Connector:** pull-down menu again and from the list of connectors, select **Counterbore with Nut-2**. This bolt is positioned adjacent to bolt #1 on the model. Observe that the **Resultant** axial bolt force is **24073** N.

6. Next, display results for **Counterbore with Nut-3** and **Counterbore with Nut-4**. And again observe values of the **Resultant** axial bolt forces. For bolt #3, Resultant = **22810** N, and for bolt #4, Resultant = **22955** N.

7. Close the **Pin/Bolt/Bearing Force** window by clicking the **[Close]** button.

Observations:

a. Forces at both bolts in the same row differ by only 0.06% in bolts closest to the applied load and differ by 0.63% in the row furthest from the applied load.

b. Forces at bolts #1 and #2 differ at most by 0.3% from the specified bolt preload (24000 N) and both loads are slightly *higher* than the given preload.

c. Note the difference of 145 N between resultant axial forces in bolts #3 and #4 that are located in the row furthest from the applied load. These values differ by at most 0.60% from the specified bolt preload of 24000 N.

d. The bolted joint is well designed because most of the load is carried by the material clamped between the bolt head and nut. This observation is based on the fact that bolt axial load differs by at most only 24000 - 22810 = 1190 N from the bolt preload value of 24000 N.

e. Symmetry of results between bolts in the two different rows lends credence to the fact that the problem is formulated correctly. That is to say, loads on bolts #1 and #2 are within 14 N of each other while loads on bolts #3 and #4 differ by 145 N. However, as expected, loads on bolts at different distances from the applied load are observed to differ from one another.

Define a New Study with the Applied Force Acting Upward

Because the above analysis does not reveal significantly different bolt loads at the two rows of bolts, the example is next re-worked with an upward force applied to the angle bracket as shown in Fig. 22. To efficiently run a new analysis, a *duplicate* of the existing study is created (refer to Chapter 3). That duplicate Study will then be altered to reflect application of an upward load. Notice how easy it is to complete this new study! Try this on your own or follow steps outlined below.

1. Beneath the graphics area of the screen, right-click the Simulation Study *tab* labeled **Bolted Joint-DOWNWARD Load** and from the pop-up menu, select **Duplicate**. The **Define Study Name** window opens as shown in Fig. 21.

2. In the **Study Name:** field, type **Bolted Joint-UPWARD Load** and click **[OK]**. This action creates an exact duplicate of the former study and opens a new Simulation Study tab beneath the graphics screen. The new tab is now active.

Figure 21 – A *duplicate* of the existing study is assigned a new **Study Name**.

To differentiate this study from its predecessor, it is only necessary to reverse the load applied to the angle bracket using the three quick steps below.

3. If necessary, click the "+" sign adjacent to **External Loads** in the Simulation manager to reveal **Force-1 (:Per item: 5000 N:)** defined during the previous Study.

4. Next, right-click **Force-1 (:Per item: 5000 N:)** and from the pull-down menu select **Edit Definition...** The **Force/ Torque** property manager opens.

5. Just below the **Force Value** of **5000** N, click to check "✓" ☑ **Reverse direction**. Force vectors applied at the end of the angle bracket should now be directed upward as shown in Fig. 22.

Figure 22 – Bolted joint model with the applied force reversed so that it acts upward.

6. Click **[OK]** ✓ to close the **Force/Torque** property manager.

Because all aspects of the previous study were copied, nothing else need be done except to re-run the solution corresponding to the altered loading condition. Re-running the solution eliminates the warning symbols ⚠ and ⚠ adjacent to the **Results** folder and adjacent to the Study name **Bolted Joint-UPWARD Load (-Default-)**, respectively. Why do these warning symbols appear? HINT: What was changed in step 5?

7. On the **Simulation** tab, click the **Run** 🖾 icon.

NOTE: Because the duplicated Study already contains the **Direct Sparse** solver it is likely that this solution will run without an error. *(Run time approx. 1+ min).*

Results for the bolted assembly subject to an upward acting load are examined next.

Results Analysis for the Upward External Load

Von Mises Stress

Begin by examining von Mises stress.

1. If the von Mises stress plot is not displayed, click the "+" sign adjacent to the **Results** folder to reveal a list of available plots. Then right-click **Stress1 (-vonMises-)** and from the pull-down menu, select **Show**.

The vonMises stress plot corresponding to the upward acting load is shown in Fig. 23. Zoom in on the small circled area and note the *small area* of high stress near the **Max.** stress flag.

Figure 23 – von Mises stress distribution throughout the model corresponding to an *upward* acting load of 5000 N.

To obtain a good overview of stress distribution throughout the model, rotate the model to view all surfaces. Notice that, corresponding to an upward load, a maximum stress within the model of 4.705e+008 N/m^2 (*values may vary*) is observed. Also note that material yield strength is exceeded. Close examination reveals the region of maximum stress is located adjacent to bolt hole #2. The region of maximum stress is very small and some important implications of this finding are discussed in the **Analysis Insight** section below. Zoom in on the area of maximum stress to view the high stress gradient adjacent to bolt hole #2.

Analysis Insight

If the load is statically applied and the material is ductile, it can be argued that localized yielding will occur in regions of maximum stress if the material yield strength is exceeded (which is true in this example). A further argument is that localized yielding in a highly stressed area results in a lowering of that stress (due to local yielding) and increased strength. This increased strength is due to the phenomenon commonly referred to as "cold-working" of the material. On the other hand, if the material is brittle or if loads are repeatedly applied and released (or reversed) failure by fracture or fatigue will likely occur.

The most instructive way to investigate any high stress region is with the mesh displayed on the model. The reason for this is that the rate of change of stress magnitude, also known as "stress gradient," can be observed in relation to element size. Therefore, we next examine the region of high stress gradient on the *surface* of the angle bracket, circled in Fig. 23, to demonstrate its significance relative to mesh size.

Begin by zooming in to observe the small area of high stress adjacent to bolt #2, circled in Fig. 23. Also, observe the small area of high stress adjacent to bolt #1.

To further emphasize the stress gradient in this region, Fig. 24 shows an enlarged view of the area adjacent to bolt #2 with the default curvature based mesh superimposed on the model. On your own, create a view like that shown in Fig. 24. The following steps are provided in the event that guidance is desired.

2. Right-click **Stress1 (-von Mises-)**. From the pull-down menu, select **Settings...** The **Settings** property manager opens.

3. Verify that the **Fringe Options** dialogue box is set to **Discrete**; if not change it. This action further emphasizes the boundary of the high stress (red area) relative to mesh size.

4. Next, from the pull-down menu in the **Boundary Options** dialogue box, select **Mesh**. A mesh is superimposed on the model.

5. Click **[OK]** ✓ to close the **Settings** property manager.

6. Select a **Top View** and zoom-in on the high stress area circled on Fig. 23. The high stress area is outlined in black for emphasis in Fig. 24.

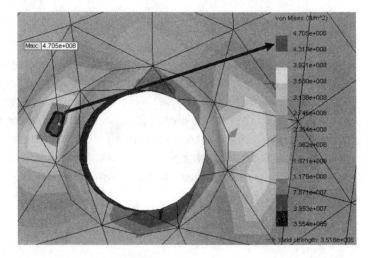

Figure 24 – Enlarged view showing the maximum stress region lies within a *portion* of the elements outlined in the figure. Stress magnitude is correlated to the color-coded stress scale.

Conclusion: Because the high stress region is *smaller than any individual element* (i.e., in Fig. 24 it occupies only a small portion of two adjacent elements), *a smaller mesh should be used in this region*. Why? Page I-9 and Fig. 15 of the Introduction noted that stress is calculated at Gauss points within each element. Thus, if high stress occurs *within a small region of any element*, that stress magnitude will be sorely *underestimated* in that element due to much lower stress magnitudes at the element's remaining Gauss points. Also, recall that a finer mesh reveals stress levels more accurately. Because this small area occurs adjacent to a geometric discontinuity (the bolt hole), use of *Mesh Control* outlined in Chapter 3, should be considered.

The above observation is of paramount importance in any analysis where a high stress gradient occurs. However, because determination of bolt forces is the primary goal of this example, and because mesh refinement was investigated in Chapter 3, we return to analyze the bolted joint results without applying mesh refinement at this time.

Bolt Forces (for Upward Load)

The effect of altering direction of the applied load upon bolt forces is examined next.

1. Right-click the **Results** folder, and from the pull-down menu, select **List Pin/Bolt /Bearing Force…** The **Pin/Bolt/Bearing Force** window opens.

Figure 25 – Forces at **Counterbore with Nut-1** corresponding to an upward load applied to the angle bracket.

2. Verify that **Units:** are set to **SI**. If not, change to **SI** units.

3. Open the pull-down menu adjacent to **Connector:** and from the list of connectors, select **Counterbore with Nut-1**. The **Pin/Bolt/Bearing Force** window should appear as shown in Fig. 25. (Alternatively, select **All Bolts** from the pull-down menu, and scroll through the results.)

4. For bolt #1 the **Axial Force (N)**, in the **Resultant** column at the far right of the table, is **30344** N (values may differ slightly). This value represents an increased axial (tensile) bolt load of 6344 N above that known to be the initial bolt pre-load of 24000 N.

5. Open the pull-down menu adjacent to **Connector:** and from the list of connectors, select **Counterbore with Nut-2**. In the **Axial Force** row, the **Resultant** force in this bolt is now **30473** N, which is within 129 N of the value obtained at bolt #1 in the previous step. (Axial loads at bolts #1 and #2 differ by only 0.43%).

Recall that bolts #1 and #2 are located adjacent to one another at the same distance from the applied load. Theoretically, identical bolt loads are expected at these two locations. However, due to differences of mesh geometry, inaccuracies, and round-off error, the reasonable differences noted above are considered acceptable.

6. Repeat steps 3 and 4 for **Counterbore with Nut-3** and **Counterbore with Nut-4**. Axial bolt forces at these two locations are **22933** N and **23054** N respectively. (Axial loads at bolts #3 and #4 differ by only 0.53 %).

A side view of the model in Fig. 26 supports the finding of larger bolt tensile forces at bolts nearest to the applied load due to the additional upward "pull" resisted by bolts #1 and #2. In this instance, a slight decrease below the bolt preload of 24000 N occurs at bolts #3 and #4, which are farthest from the applied load. Check these values on your own.

Location of bolts #3 & #4

Location of bolts #1 & #2

Figure 26 – Side view of the bolted joint with the angle bracket subject to an upward load at its right end.

Analysis Insight

Before closing the **Pin/Bolt Force** window, observe magnitudes of the **Shear Force** and the **Bending moment**. **Bending moment** is defined to act under the head of a bolt. Although **Bending** *moment* values appear quite small, bending *stress* in the bolts combines with axial stress and is quite high; it should be checked. The magnitude of Resultant **Shear Force** varies from a high of 1124 N at bolts #1 and #2 to a low of 923 N at bolts #3 and #4 respectively. Resultant **Shear Forces** are small compared to axial forces acting on the bolts. More importantly, however, shear stress in the bolt subject to the maximum shear force is small relative to bolt shear strength. The following calculation examines shear stress in the most heavily loaded bolt.

$$\tau = F_s/A_s = 1124.2 \text{ N}) / (0.0763 \text{ m}^2) = 14.7 \text{ k N/m}^2 = 0.0147 \text{ MPa} \qquad [2]$$

where:

F_s = maximum shear force at a bolt (see calculation of F_s below)

A_s = minor area of bolt thread (at root of thread profile) NOTE: For structural bolts, the nominal bolt diameter should be used.

τ = shear stress in bolt caused by maximum shear force

When compared to a conservative value of shear strength (S_{sy} = 234 MPa) for a Grade 5.8 metric bolt, the shear stress is only 0.006 % of bolt shear strength. For this reason, shear stress is not considered significant in this example.

However, for many structural applications, shear in bolts is the *primary* mode of loading. In those instances, shear load on bolts is of prime importance. An end-of-chapter exercise examines a bolted joint where shear in the joint is the governing factor.

NOTE: The shear force F_s in equation [2] is determined as follows from the maximum X and Z shear force components occurring at bolt #1 in shown Fig. 28.

$$F_S = \sqrt{F_x^2 + F_z^2} = \sqrt{(924)^2 + (-641)^2} = 1124N \qquad [3]$$

It may be possible to gain some insight into the origins of the X and Z components of shear force, by animating the model. Do this on your own, or proceed as follows.

7. Select **[Close]** to exit the **Pin/Bolt/Bearing Force** window.

8. If the von Mises stress plot is not displayed, double-click **Stress1 (-vonMises-)**.

9. Right-click **Stress1 (-vonMises-)** and from the pull-down menu, select **Edit Definition…** The **Stress Plot** property manager opens.

10. Check "✓" to open the ☑ **Deformed Shape** dialogue box and verify that ⊙ **Automatic** is selected. The distortion scale factor is **7.93634844** (values may differ). This value is altered below.

11. Click **[OK]** ✓ to close the **Stress Plot** property manager.

12. Right-click **Stress1 (-vonMises-)** and from the pull-down menu, select ▶**Animate…** If the model is animated, select the **Stop** ■ icon.

13. In the **Basics** dialogue box, increase the **Frames** to **10** and move the **Speed** control slide to the left. These actions smooth-out and slow the animation.

14. Click the **Start** ▶ icon.

15. Slowly rotate the model to examine its deformation due to the applied load. Pay particular attention to deformations in the region below bolts #1 and #2 where the angle bracket and support plate intersect. Does a "gap" appear between parts?

16. Click **[OK]** ✓ to close the **Animation** property manager.

Because it may be difficult to observe deformations that cause shear forces in bolt #1 and bolt #2, repeat steps 9 through 15 above, except replace step 10 with the following.

17. In the ☑ **Deformed Shape** dialogue box, select ⊙ **User Defined**. In the adjacent field, type **30**. Then continue at step 11. This action artificially increases the magnitude of deformation displayed in Fig. 27. Observe the separation (gap) that occurs between the plate and angle bracket in the boxed region.

Figure 27 – Using animation to visualize origins of shear forces in the X and Z-directions at bolts #1 and #2.

The deformed model should appear similar to that illustrated in Fig. 27. In the following discussion, particular attention is focused on deformations between mating parts in the vicinity of the bolts.

18. **Stop** ■ the animation and click **[OK]** ✓ to close the **Animation** property manager.

Figure 28, below, represents a top view of the bolted joint where bolt connectors are represented by circles. Shear force components, directed according to their ± signs listed in the **Pin/Bolt/Bearing Force** window, are shown at each bolt location. Using a combination of Fig. 28 and deformations viewed when animating the model, directions of the shear force components should begin to "make sense."

Figure 28 – Shear force components in the X and Z-directions developed in each bolt.

Bolt Clamping Pressure

Bolt preload is known to apply an equal and opposite clamping force on the joined members. Using software capabilities investigated in Chapter 6, contact pressure is investigated next. This analysis provides further insight into the intent of the bolted joint analysis capability within SolidWorks Simulation.

1. Right-click the **Results** folder and from the pull-down menu, select **Define Stress Plot...** The **Stress Plot** property manager opens.

2. In the **Display** dialogue box, click to open the pull-down menu adjacent to **VON: von Mises Stress** and from the pull-down menu select **CP: Contact Pressure**.

3. Verify that **Units** are set to **N/m^2**.

4. Next, in the **Advanced Options** dialogue box, clear the check-mark from ☐ **Average results across boundary for parts**.

5. Click **[OK]** ✓ to close the **Stress Plot** property manager. A new plot, labeled **Stress2 (-Contact pressure-)** is listed beneath the **Results** folder.

6. If not already displayed on the graphics screen, double-click **Stress2 (-Contact pressure-)** to display a contact pressure plot similar to that shown in Fig. 29.

Figure 29 – Contact pressure plot showing interaction between the angle bracket and the support plate when subject to the upward load.

Users are encouraged to alter the graphic display to appear like Fig. 29. Necessary steps are provided below if guidance is desired.

7. Right-click **Stress2 (-Contact pressure-)** and from the pull-down menu, select **Settings…** The **Settings** property manager opens.

8. Within the **Boundary Options** dialogue box, click to display the pull-down menu and from it select **Model**. The **Fringe options** dialogue box can be set to either **Discrete** (preferred) or **Continuous**.

9. Click **[OK]** ✓ to close the **Settings** property manager.

Because bolt restraint symbols might obscure other pertinent graphical information, temporarily remove them from the display as follows.

10. In the Simulation manger tree, right-click **Connectors** and from the pull-down menu select **Hide All**.

11. Repeat step 10 to temporarily hide **Fixtures** and **External Loads** (optional).

If the contact pressure vectors initially appear too small, which is often the case, increase their size as follows. Try this on your own or apply the steps listed below.

12. *If necessary*, double-click **Stress2(-Contact pressure-)** to again display the contact pressure.

13. Right-click **Stress2 (-Contact pressure-)** and from the pull-down menu select **Vector Plot Options…** The **Vector plot options** property manager opens.

14. In the **Options** dialogue box, type **600** in the **Size** field (upper spin-box) to enlarge the size of contact pressure vectors displayed. Vector **Size** is a user preference.

15. Accept other default settings in this property manager and click **[OK]** ✓ to close it. Your display should now appear similar to Figs. 29 and 30.

16. Rotate and zoom-in on the model to gain better insight into what is actually plotted.

Figure 30 shows three different views of contact pressure vectors in the vicinity of the bolt holes and throughout the assembly.

Top View   Trimetric View

Front (edge) View

Figure 30 – Various views showing distribution of contact pressure between mating parts in the bolted joint subject to an upward load.

Analysis Insight

Do graphical results in Fig. 30 (currently displayed on your screen) correspond with what you expected to see? The answer might surprise many users. However, it is valuable to understand what these plots reveal in order to ensure that results are interpreted correctly. Some additional questions that might be asked are:

   a. Is the contact pressure shown in Fig. 30 applied by the bolts onto the plates?
or
   b. Is the contact pressure shown in Fig. 30 the pressure that exists between the plates themselves?
or
   c. Do the plots represent the superposition of contact pressure due to bolt clamping forces (i.e., forces beneath the head of the bolt and nut) and due to plate contact?

The answer to question (a) is that, although bolt preload "grips" the parts together, a **Connections** condition was not specified between contacting faces of the bolt or nut and corresponding top and bottom surfaces on the parts. For this reason, contact pressure between the bolt or nut and the plate surface is *not* illustrated.

Based on the preceding observation, it should be clear that the answer to question (b) is that contact pressure between the mating parts (i.e., between the plates) *is shown* in Fig. 30. Verify this by observing the direction of pressure vectors shown in a front view of the contacting surfaces. All vectors originate at the contacting surface between each part and point away from the surface on which pressure acts. Also, in all views, notice that no contact pressure is shown to the right of bolts #1 and #2. This is consistent with Fig. 26, repeated below, which indicates a location where separation (i.e., a gap) between the plates may develop. This gap reduces or eliminates contact pressure between the structural members.

Region of downward bending occurs behind the first row of bolts.

Location of possible separation between parts.

Figure 26 – (repeated) Probable location for a **Gap** to develop between parts.

Fig. 30 also reveals a "footprint" of pressure to the left of and between bolts #1 and #2. This pressure distribution is due to the downward bending of the bracket to the left of bolts #1 and #2 caused by the upward deformation of the part to the right of these bolts.

Analysis Insight (continued)

Question (c) is already answered in response (a) above. However, it is worthy to note that even if no external load were applied to the angle bracket, contact pressure would still result in both plates in the vicinity of all four bolt connectors. In other words, the images show that bolt preload causes contact pressure between the parts that are gripped rather than between the bolt connectors themselves and the gripped members.

Bolts #3 and #4 are relatively unaffected by the upward load applied at the right end of the bracket. Therefore, notice the fairly uniform shape of contact pressure distribution both in terms of magnitude (front view) and geometry ("circular" shapes in the top view) around these bolt holes.

Summary

Based on this example, it is evident that bolt force determination is one of the primary outcomes of a bolted joint analysis. This capability is useful for predicting and verifying design or analysis of bolt connections under load. Also, application of the **Contact Pressure** capability permits an analyst to determine the contact pressure distribution between mating parts in the vicinity of connectors, such as bolts. This knowledge enhances understanding of factors such as bolt spacing when used to create "pressure tight" connections.

Exercises on the following pages outline a different method for defining contact between mating parts that does not require the use of Split Lines.

This concludes the study of bolted joints, their definition, resulting contact pressure(s), and bolt reaction forces.

It is suggested that this example file not be saved. Proceed as follows.

1. From the main menu, select **File > Close** (suggested) and select **Don't Save**.

Figure 31 – Close the current example file without saving results.

EXERCISES

⊥ EXERCISE 1 - Eccentrically Loaded Bolt Joint
(Special Topic: Automatically Find Contact Sets)

A steel plate is connected to a vertical column by means of four **M 16 x 2, Grade 8.8** steel bolts. Bolt material properties are: **E = 207 GPa** and **Poisson's Ratio = 0.292**. The column is a 254 mm x 76 mm structural steel channel. Both the column and plate are made of **ASTM A36 Steel**. The channel can be considered rigidly fixed (**immovable**) on cut surfaces above and below the connection location. Only a segment of the channel is shown in the figures below. The plate is subject to a vertical load of **16** kN applied to its top-right *edge* as shown in Fig. E7-1. Figure E7-1 shows the basic geometry of parts in this assembly. For simplicity, detailed images of the bolts are not shown. Open files **Column 7-1** and **Plate 7-1** and perform a finite element analysis to determine items requested below.

Figure E7-1 – Basic geometry of the column and plate. A 16 kN load is applied on the upper-right *edge* of the plate. Bolt numbers are shown in "call out" boxes.

- Material: **ASTM A36 Steel** (column and plate material properties)
  $E = 207e9$ **Pa**, and Poisson's ratio $v = 0.292$ (bolt properties)

- Mesh: Use system default size **Curvature based mesh**, tetrahedral elements.

- Fixtures: **Fixed** as necessary on top and bottom cut surfaces of the column.

  Connections with **No Penetration** between the column and plate. A simplified method of defining contact between these two parts is outlined in the **Solution Guidance** section below.

  Bolt connector with **Nut**, use a contact diameter = 30 mm under the bolt head and nut.

- External Load: **16 kN** downward at top-right *edge* of the plate.

- Assumptions: Bolts fit in clearance holes where $D_{Hole} = 17$ mm
  Bolts are field tightened to a torque $T = 226$ N-m
  Bolt torque coefficient $K = 0.20$

Determine the Following:

Begin by creating an assembly of the **Column 7-1** and **Plate 7-1** parts. If assistance creating the assembly is desired, see **Create the Assembly Model** on pg. 6-5 and foreword. Then develop a finite element model that includes: material specification, fixtures, external load(s), contact specification, bolt connectors, mesh, and solution.

Solution Guidance

This section outlines a simplified means for defining contact between mating parts *without* the need for *Split Lines*. *After* creating an assembly of the **Column** and **Plate** and after defining **Mates** between these two parts, then perform the steps below. The model should appear as shown in Fig. E7-2 prior to defining part contact.

Figure E7-2 – **Column** and **Plate** assembly prior to definition of contact conditions.

The following steps outline use of the **Automatically Find Contact Sets** software option when defining contact between mating parts. Despite the power of this option, it should be used with care because, in complex assemblies, it may find extra contact sets that are not intended or it may not find a contact set that the user wants. As a case in point, the **Automatically Find Contact Sets** option is applied *prior* to defining bolted connectors. This sequence is used because bolted connectors add the potential

---

Solution Guidance (continued)

for contact under the bolt head and nut and between the bolt shank and the inside surfaces of bolt holes. This sequence of steps eliminates the possibility of unwanted contact sets being defined. Proceed as follows to apply the simplified contact set capability. Steps below assume a Simulation Study has been started *and* proper **Mates** between the column and plate have been defined.

- In the Simulation manager, right-click the **Connections** and from the pull-down menu, select **Contact Set…** The **Contact Sets** property manager opens as shown in Fig. E7-3.

- In the **Contact** dialogue box, select ⊙ **Automatically find contact sets**. The property manager changes to look like Fig. E7-3.

- In the **Options** dialogue box, select ⊙**Touching Faces** (if not already selected).

- In the **Components** dialogue box, the **Select Components or Bodies** field is active (highlighted light blue). Move the cursor into the graphics screen and click to select *both* the **Column** and the **Plate**. Select parts in any order. Names of the selected parts, **Extrude1@Plate 7-1-1@Assem1** and **Cut-Extrude1@Column 7-1-1@Assem1** are listed in the active field; see Fig. E7-3.

- Next click the **[Find contact sets]** button and the software automatically identifies *any* contacting faces on these two parts. Within the **Results** dialogue box, names of the contacting faces are listed as **Contact Set-1 (-Plate 7-1-1, Column 7-1-1-)**. Word order maybe reversed.

- Also within the **Results** dialogue box, open the pull-down menu adjacent to **Type:** and select **No Penetration** to define the type of contact between the column and plate.

- Click **[OK]** ✓ to close the **Contact Sets** property manager.

- Click **[Yes]** in the pop-up **Simulation** window.

Figure E7-3 – The **Contact Sets** property manager facilitates definition of contact between mating parts.

Although a number of selections were involved in defining contact between the column and plate, use of the single **Contact Sets** property manager is much simpler than creating an exploded view; outlining contact areas using *Split Lines;* and then defining contact using the **Contact Sets** icon as yet another step. At this point, complete the definition of the finite element model and perform the analysis outlined below.

a. Create an isometric or trimetric plot showing all fixtures and external loads, including bolt connectors, applied to the model. This image is the finite element equivalent of a free-body-diagram. Do not show a mesh or stresses on this plot. This plot should fill at least half of an 8 ½ x 11 inch page. [See also item (c) below.] Manually label bolt numbers 1 through 4 on this figure. Bolt numbers should correspond to those shown on Fig. E7-1

b. Due to loading on this model, shear forces create the primary loads on each bolt. Using SolidWorks Simulation, determine the shear force components at each bolt location. Then, plot a front view of the model. On this plot sketch and label the magnitude and direction of each shear force component and the resultant shear force at each bolt.

c. Create a plot of contact pressure between the column and plate. Exaggerate the scale of contact pressure to best depict pressure distribution on the mating parts. Choose the best view or views to show the contact pressure plot(s).

d. Check the solution by manually calculating the shear force(s) at each bolt. Compare manually calculated results with finite element results and compute the percent difference between resultant shear forces at each bolt using equation [1]. Label calculations to correspond to the appropriate bolt number. Cut-and-paste copy(ies) of the **Pin/Bolt/Bearing Force** table from the finite element solution onto a page accompanying the manual solution. Be sure to correlate finite element results with the corresponding manual calculations of bolt shear force. Expect differences on the order of 12 to 15% between finite element and manual calculations. These differences may seem high, but there is a fundamental difference between assumptions applied to the manual calculations and to the finite element results. Questions: (1) State the assumptions applied to manual calculations of bolt shear force. (2) Based on your understanding of how FEA solutions are obtained, what is the difference in assumptions applied to these two methods of analysis?

$$\% \text{ difference} = \frac{(\text{FEA result - classical result})}{\text{FEA result}} * 100 = \qquad [1]$$

e. Question: Do directions of shear force components appearing in the **Pin/Bolt /Bearing Force** table correspond to shear forces acting on the bolt, or do they represent directions of shear forces exerted by the bolt on the members? Justify your answer in terms of sketches made in part (b).

EXERCISE 2 – Bolted Cylinder Head

A **Ductile Iron** "pipe-end" on a pressurized tank is sealed by an **Alloy Steel** cylinder head as shown in Fig. E7-4. The cylinder head is held in place by eight **5/8 inch-11 UNC, SAE Grade 8.2** steel bolts for which the modulus of elasticity, **E = 30e6 psi**, and

Poisson's ratio, **μ = 0.30**. The pipe-end is subject to an internal static pressure of 900 psi. A confined gasket seal (not shown) is located in the flange groove. Because the gasket is located in a confined groove rather than "sandwiched" between the cylinder head and the flange, its low stiffness relative to other components can be ignored. Figure E7-5 shows the basic geometry of parts in this assembly. Open files **Cylinder Head 7-2** and **Pipe End & Flange 7-2** and perform a finite element analysis to determine items requested below.

Figure E7-4 – Bolted joint closing a "stub-end" on a pressurized tank.

Figure E7-5 – Basic geometry of the cylinder head and flanged pipe end. Assume the pipe segment is sufficiently long to minimize the effect of fixtures applied to its bottom end.

- Material: **Alloy Steel** (cylinder head)
  Ductile Iron (pipe-end and flange)
  E = 30e6 psi, and Poisson's ratio **v = 0.30** (bolt material)

- Mesh: Use system default size **Curvature based mesh**, tetrahedral elements.

- Fixtures: Define as necessary on the cut (bottom) pipe-end

  Contact Set between cylinder head and pipe flange is to be specified as **No Penetration**. See **Solution Guidance** in Exercise 1 of this chapter for a simplified method of defining contact between the cylinder head and pipe flange.

  Bolt connector with **Nut**: Assume the outside diameter under the bolt head and nut is 15/16 inch (0.9375 in).

- External Load: Pressure = **900 psi** acts on all internal surfaces

- Assumptions: Bolts fit in clearance holes where D_{Hole} = 0.6875 in
  Bolts are field tightened to a torque T = 2540 lb*in
  Bolt torque coefficient K = 0.20

Determine the Following:

Begin by creating an assembly of the **Cylinder Head** and **Pipe End & Flange**. If assistance creating the assembly is desired, see **Create the Assembly Model** on pg. 6-5 and foreword. Then use the simplified **Automatically Find Contact Sets** procedure outlined in the **Solution Guidance** section of the Exercise 1 in this chapter as you develop the finite element model. The complete model should include: material specification, contact specification, fixtures, external load(s), bolt connectors, mesh, and solution.

a. Create a plot showing all restraints and loads applied to the model. This image is the finite element equivalent of a free-body-diagram. Do not show a mesh or stresses on this plot. This plot should fill at least half of an 8 ½ x 11 inch page. On this plot, write a brief statement that clearly identifies the type of fixture(s) applied to the cut-end of the pipe segment shown in Fig. E7-5.

b. Create a plot of contact pressure between the cylinder head and the pipe flange. Exaggerate the scale of contact pressure to best depict pressure distribution on the mating parts. What can be stated about the uniformity of contact pressure between the mating surfaces (i.e., between the cylinder head and pipe flange)? In your answer pay particular attention to pressure distribution in spaces *between* bolts on the bolt circle that joins these two parts together. Why is this pressure distribution important?

c. Due to loading on this model, each bolt is subject to its initial pre-load plus a portion of the load due to internal pressure. Use SolidWorks Simulation to determine the load in a representative number of bolts (at least four) by accessing results in the **Pin/Bolt /Bearing Force** window. Cut-and-paste screen images of four **Pin/Bolt/Bearing Force** windows onto an 8 ½ x 11 inch page. See also item (d) below.

d. Develop a set of manual calculations, based on bolt theory, to determine the resultant tensile load in a typical bolt. This bolt load should include both the bolt preload and the portion of external load carried by each bolt. Place these calculations on a page following the page created for item (c). Compare manually calculated results for the total axial bolt load with finite element results and compute the percent difference between resultant bolt tensile forces using equation [1].

$$\% \text{ difference} = \frac{(\text{FEA result - classical result})}{\text{FEA result}} * 100 = \qquad [1]$$

⫟ EXERCISE 3 – Bolted Trailer Hitch
(Special Topics: Application of Remote Loads, Automatically Find Contact Sets)

The trailer-hitch assembly shown in Fig. E7-5 is subject to both vertical and horizontal force components when towing a trailer. The vertical force component, or "tongue weight," (**W**) is defined as the downward force due to a *portion* of the trailer weight plus its cargo that acts on the hitch. Towing force (**F$_T$**) is the force required to pull the trailer, its reaction on the hitch "ball" is shown in Fig. E7-5. **F$_T$** is zero when the trailer is at rest; is reasonably steady when pulling a trailer at constant speed; and is maximum during acceleration or deceleration. NOTE: Hitch geometry shown in Fig. E7-5 is different than that in Exercise 5 of Chapter 2, therefore, do not use results or the model from that problem.

Figure E7-5 – Trailer hitch, ball, and channel assembly.

The goal of this exercise is to determine bolt forces and contact pressure between a 20-in long, 3x5 steel channel and the trailer hitch assembly shown in Fig. E7-6, (where: channel height = 3-in and weight = 5 lb/ft). Left and right *ends* of the **ASTM A36 Steel** channel are considered rigidly fixed (**immovable**) where it is welded to a truck frame (not shown). Two **1/2–13 UNC, SAE Grade 7** steel bolts attach the hitch to the channel through holes 1 and 2 labeled below. Because application of forces to the hitch "ball" is not the objective of this analysis, the problem can be simplified by defining applied forces using the **Remote Load/Mass** feature available in SolidWorks Simulation. Open file: **Hitch-Channel Assembly 7-3**.

Figure E7-6 – Trailer hitch and channel assembly showing bolt hole locations.

Assume the following.

- Material: **ASTM A36 Steel** (structural steel channel), English units: **IPS**
  Alloy Steel (trailer hitch)
  E = 30e6 psi, and Poisson's ratio **ν = 0.30** (bolt material)

- Mesh: In the **Mesh** property manager, select ⊙ **Curvature based mesh**
  and use the default mesh size.

- Fixture: Apply **Fixed** (immovable) restraints on both left and right ends of
  the 3x5 steel channel.

  The **Contact Set** between the channel and hitch is to be specified
  as **No Penetration**. See **Solution Guidance** in Exercise 1 of this
  chapter for a simplified method of defining contact between the
  channel and trailer hitch.

  Bolt connector with **Nut**: Assume the outside diameter under the
  bolt head and nut is 3/4 inch (0.750 in) and bolt diameter = ½ in.

- External Load: Apply force components using the **Remote Load/Mass** feature.
  Tongue weight **W = 220 lb** (vertical downward).
  Tow force **F$_T$ = 440 lb** (horizontal) in the -X-direction. This
  towing force component corresponds to maximum acceleration.

- Assumptions: Bolts are a "tight fit" in holes where D$_{Hole}$ = 0.5 in
  Bolts are tightened to a torque T = 1340 lb*in
  Bolt torque coefficient K = 0.20

Analysis Insight

Use of the **Remote Load/Mass** feature permits application of forces[1] at locations remote
from a model. The **Remote Load/Mass** feature is used primarily where modeling
simplification is realized. In this example, application of force components to curved
surfaces of the hitch ball can be accomplished by several methods. However, using the
Remote Load/Mass option is one of the more direct approaches. Also, understanding
this software capability enables you to use this feature in other situations.

To begin, a brief review of SolidWorks coordinate systems is in order. Each *part* created
within SolidWorks has its own local coordinate system. The channel origin is located
half-way between its upper and lower surfaces and midway between its left and right
ends shown circled in Fig. E7-7(a). The hitch origin is located at the bottom of the ball-
hole illustrated and circled in Fig. E7-7(b). These origin locations were specified when
dimensioning the original parts in SolidWorks **Sketch** mode.

---

[1] Additionally, moments, displacements, and (in the case of static, frequency, linear dynamic, or buckling
studies) model mass can be defined at locations remote from the model.

(a)   (b)

Figure E7-7 - Coordinate system origin locations for the Channel and Hitch as defined within SolidWorks sketch mode.

However, when the channel and hitch are joined to form an *assembly*, the first part brought into the assembly, is considered to be the *base component* and its origin becomes the default origin of the assembly[2]. In this example the channel is the base component. Thus, the **Global** coordinate system corresponds to that of the channel.

Furthermore, defining coordinates for force application at the **Remote Load/Mass** location (presumed to be at center of the hitch-ball) relative to the **Global** coordinate system (located on the channel) is somewhat tedious. However, Fig. E7-8 reveals that the center of the hitch-ball is located **1.616-in** above the ball shoulder. Thus, a **User defined** coordinate system will be defined at the base of the hitch-ball. Use of **Global** versus **User defined** coordinate systems will be clarified as this example proceeds.

Figure E7-8 – The original **Sketch** shows height of the ball center above the base of the hitch shoulder. Force components **W** and F_T are applied at the ball center.

Solution Guidance

It is assumed that the user has opened a Simulation file and started a Study. The following instructions serve as a guide; they are less detailed than step-by-step procedures found in example problems.

<u>Application of a Remote Load/Mass</u>
Because coordinate systems play an integral role in simplifying application of remote loads, begin by displaying the original *origins* on the model.

   a.   In the **Main Menu** select **View** followed by ✥ **Origins**. Origins of the Channel and Hitch are displayed on the model.

---

[2] The *base component* can be changed and along with it the assembly origin. However, that topic is best considered within SolidWorks and is not pursued here.

Solution Guidance (continued)

b. Next, from the **Main Menu**, choose **Insert > Reference Geometry > Point**. The **Point** property manager opens. In the **Selections** dialogue box, choose **Arc Center** and move the cursor onto the *top edge* of the ball-hole and click to select it. Click **[OK]** ✓ to close the **Point** property manager.

c. In the **Main Menu** select **Insert > Reference Geometry > Coordinate System**. A new origin appears at the **Point** specified in the preceding step. Observe directions of the X, Y, Z coordinate axes. Specifically, the +X axis is directed toward the front of the towing vehicle and +Y, and +Z directions are determined using the right-hand rule. Click **[OK]** ✓ to close the **Coordinate System** property manager. An image of the new coordinate system remains on the model.

Aside: Directions of the X, Y, Z axes can be changed while the **Coordinate System** property manager is open in step (c) above. Alternatively, directions of force components can be changed when they are defined in the **Remote Load/Mass** property manager. In this example the latter option is used.

When ready to apply **External Loads**, proceed as follows.

d. In the Simulation **Property Manager** right-click the **External Loads** folder, then select **Remote Load/Mass…**

e. In the **Type** dialogue box, select ⊙ **Load/Mass (Rigid connection)**. This option is used when stiffness of the part to be *replaced* by a remote load is significant relative to the rest of the model. It is also selected because it can be applied to a **Face**, **Edge**, or **Vertices** of the model as executed in the next step.

Aside: The O**Load (Direct transfer)** option could also be used, however, it is less accurate in this case because it can only be applied to **Faces** (i.e., entire surfaces) of a model. Doing so results in a less accurate depiction of actual forces on the "ball."

f. Next, in the **Type** dialogue box the **Faces, Edges, or Vertices, for Remote Load/Mass** field is active (highlighted light blue). Move the cursor onto the *top edge* of the ball-hole and click to select it.

g. In the **Reference Coordinate System** dialogue box, select ⊙ **User defined**. If **Coordinate System1** does not appear in the **Select a Coordinate System** field, then click to activate (light blue) the **Select a Coordinate System** field and move the cursor onto the model to choose the coordinate system defined at top of the ball hole. **Coordinate System1** should appears in the highlighted field.

Solution Guidance (continued)

h. In the **Location** dialogue box, verify that **Unit** ▯ is set to **in**. Then in the **Y-Location** field, type **1.616** and leave the **X** and **Z** coordinates equal to zero (**0**).

i. In the **Force** dialogue box, verify **Unit** ▯ is set to **lbf** and specify the **X-Direction** force as **670** lbf acting in the **–X** direction and specify the **Y-Direction** force component as **300** lbf acting downward. Select ☑ **Reverse direction** as necessary so that you model appears as shown in Fig. E7-9.

j. Click ✓ **[OK]** to close the **Remote Loads/Mass** property manager.

Figure E7-9 – Specifying **Location** coordiniates and **Force** magnitudes in the **Remote Loads/Mass** property manager.

HINT: If a solution is not obtained within 10 minutes it will probably end in a *Failure Error* after attempting to solve the defining equations for more than 30 minutes. Thus, terminate the solution after 10 minutes by clicking **[Cancel]** in the solver window. Then, in the **Stop Solver** window, select **[Yes]** to terminate the solution. Next, in the **Static Analysis** window, select **[No]** to "save results" followed by **[OK]** to close the next **Static Analysis** window. Finally, click **[OK]** to close the **Simulation** window.

To re-start a successful solution, *read the procedure* beginning at step #8, pg. 7-14 and begin by *performing* the procedure beginning at step #11, pg. 7-16. When using the **Direct Sparse** solver approach, solution time will run between 1.5 to 2 minutes on most computers.

Determine the following:

Begin by creating the SolidWorks Simulation model. If not already done, use the simplified procedure to **Automatically Find Contact Sets** between the hitch and channel. Steps to accomplish this task are outlined in the **Solution Guidance** section of Exercise 1 in this chapter. The complete model should include: material specification, contact specification, fixtures, remote external load(s), bolt connectors, mesh, and solution.

    a.   Create an isometric or trimetric plot showing all fixtures and remote external loads, including bolt connectors, applied to the model. This image is the finite element equivalent of a free-body-diagram. Do not show a mesh or stresses on this plot. This plot should fill at least half of an 8 ½ x 11 inch page. Manually label bolt numbers 1 and 2 on this figure to correspond to those in Fig. E7-6.

    b.   Create a plot of contact pressure between the channel and trailer hitch. Exaggerate the scale of contact pressure to best depict pressure distribution on the mating parts. Choose a *rear view* and a *left-side view* to show the contact pressure plot(s). Place the image on the lower half of the page containing the figure from part (a) of this exercise.

    c.   Due to loading on this model, each bolt is subject to its initial pre-load plus a portion of the load due to force components acting on the hitch ball. Use SolidWorks Simulation to determine the load in bolts #1 and #2 by accessing results in the **Pin/Bolt /Bearing Force** window. In the **Connector:** field of this window, select **[All bolts]**. Cut-and-paste a screen image of the **Pin/Bolt/Bearing Force** window onto an 8 ½ x 11 inch page. See also item (d) below.

    d.   Develop and label a set of manual calculations, based on bolt theory, to determine the resultant tensile load in a typical bolt. This bolt load should include both the bolt preload and the portion of external load carried by each bolt. Place these calculations beneath the **Pin/Bolt/Bearing Force** window on the page created for item (c). Compare manually calculated results for the total axial bolt load with finite element results and compute the percent difference between resultant bolt tensile forces using equation [1].

$$\% \text{ difference} = \frac{(\text{FEA result - classical result})}{\text{FEA result}} * 100 = \qquad [1]$$

    e.   Questions:
        • Do directions of shear force components appearing in the **Pin/Bolt /Bearing Force** table correspond to shear forces acting on the bolt, or do

they represent directions of shear forces exerted by the bolt on the hitch? Justify your answer by producing a sketch showing external loads acting on the hitch and shear forces acting at bolt holes 1 and 2.

- Is the hitch in equilibrium when considering shear forces? Show calculations to support your answer.

Textbook Problems

In addition to the above exercise, it is highly recommended that additional problems involving bolted connections be worked from a design of machine elements or a structural analysis textbook. Bolted assemblies can be loaded by axial loads, bending loads, shear loads, or a combination of all three. Textbook problems provide a great way to discover errors made in formulating a finite element analysis because they typically are well defined problems for which the solution is known. Typical textbook problems, if well defined, make an excellent source of solutions for comparison.

NOTES:

CHAPTER #8
DESIGN OPTIMIZATION

In keeping with current trends for faster, lighter, and more efficient designs, the Optimization Design feature within SolidWorks Simulation[1] should be a standard tool applied to all designs. Although the Optimization Design process performs much of the grunt work by iteratively seeking an optimum solution, control of the design process remains in the engineer's hands. This means that the designer still makes decisions regarding what *variables* of a machine part are allowed to be altered, what *constraints* are to be applied to the design, and what overall *goals* the design is to satisfy. Each of these aspects of the optimization design process is explored in the following example.

Learning Objectives
Upon completion of this example, users should be able to:

- Select and define *variables* to be optimized during the design process.

- Specify and limit *constraints* (sensors) applied to the optimization process.

- Define desired *goals* (sensors) for the optimization process.

- Set-up, run, and interpret results of the *Optimization Design* process.

- Plot and interpret *Local Trend Graphs*.

Problem Statement
An **Alloy Steel** part is comprised of a 180 mm long cylindrical rod joined perpendicular to a rectangular bar of length 100 mm. Except for a 2 mm fillet between the cylinder and rectangle, additional dimensions of this part are shown in Fig. 1. This part might be viewed as an "L" shaped cantilever beam fixed at its right end. The goal of this example is to minimize weight of the part while subject to restraints and loads shown in Fig. 2.

Fixed end of L-shaped cantilever beam

Figure 1 – Dimensioned view of the machine component named **L-Part**.

---

[1] The Optimization Design capability is available only in SolidWorks Simulation Professional and SolidWorks Simulation Premium. It is not included in basic SolidWorks Simulation.

A SolidWorks Simulation model of the **L-Part** and a portion of its Simulation Study are shown in Fig. 2. This example begins with a partially completed finite element model for two reasons. First, an *Initial Study* is *required* prior to initiating the optimization design process. And, second, beginning with a partially completed model allows us to focus attention on new topics rather than repeating subjects mastered in previous chapters. Figure 2 shows a **Fixed** restraint applied on end **A** of cylindrical rod **AB** and a downward force of **775** N acting on the surface at end **C** of rectangular segment **BC**. Other information to be satisfied by the optimization design is that stress in the part must not exceed one-half of the material yield strength (S_y = 620.422 e6 N/m^2) and the maximum allowable part deflection must not exceed 2.50 mm.

Figure 2 – Finite element model of the **L-Part** showing **Fixtures**, **External Loads** and the Simulation manager tree.

1. Open SolidWorks by making the following selections. *(NOTE:* ">" is used to separate successive menu selections).

   Start>All Programs>SolidWorks 2013 (or) Click the **SolidWorks** icon on your screen.

2. When SolidWorks opens, select **File > Open...** Then use procedures common to your computer environment to open the file named "**L-Part.**"

Complete and Run the Initial Study

Begin by completing the *Initial Study*. An initial study serves as the basis, or starting point, for a subsequent design optimization study. It does this by calculating finite element results for the current part "as is" before any changes are made. Open the initial Simulation Study as follows.

1. On the Simulation Study *tab* located beneath the graphics area, click the *tab* labeled **Initial Study L-Part**. This opens the partially completed Simulation Study. The model and Simulation manager tree should look like Fig. 2.

2. In the Simulation manager tree, verify that (a) the L-Part **Material** is specified as L-Part (-Alloy Steel-), (b) the **Fixtures** folder shows Fixed-1 and corresponding

restraints appear on end **A** of the cylinder; and (c) the **External Loads** folder shows `⊥ Force-1 (:Per item: -775 N:)` and downward vectors appear at end **C** of the rectangular beam.

3. Right-click the **Mesh** folder and from the pull-down menu, select **Details…** The **Mesh Details** window opens.

4. In the **Mesh Details** window, verify that a **Curvature based mesh** is specified as the **Mesher Used**. If not, re-mesh the model using this mesh specification.

5. On the Simulation tab near top of the screen, click the **Run** 🗔 icon. Or, in the Simulation manager tree, right-click **Initial Study L-Part (-Default-)** and from the pull-down menu select **Run…**

Upon completion of the run, the **Results** folder should list the three default plots [**Stress1 (-vonMises-)**, **Displacement1 (-Res disp-)**, and **Strain1 (-Equivalent-)**]. Before proceeding, a few alterations are made to the stress and displacement plots to set units and other display settings desired for these and future plots. Proceed on your own to incorporate SI units, discrete fringes, un-deformed model plots, label maximum stress, maximum displacement, and display legend values in scientific notation with three digits. If you make these changes on your own, skip to the **Observations- Design Optimization Considerations** text box (on page 8-5), otherwise follow the abbreviated steps below.

6. Right-click **Stress1 (-vonMises-)** and from the pull-down menu, select **Edit Definition…**

7. In the **Display** dialogue box change 📏 **Units** to **N/m^2** and turn off ☐ **Deformed Shape**.

8. Click **[OK]** ✓ to close the **Stress Plot** property manager.

9. Right-click **Stress1 (-vonMises-)** and select **Chart Options…**

10. In the **Display Options** dialogue box, check ☑ **Show max annotation**.

11. In the **Position/Format** dialogue box, click to open the ▼ **Number Format** `XXX.XX X.Xe2` box and select `XXX.XX X.Xe2` `scientific` **scientific** notation as the desired number format.

12. Immediately beneath the **Number Format** box, set the **No of Decimals** to **3**.

13. Click **[OK]** ✓ to close the **Chart Options** property manager.

14. Right-click **Stress1 (-von Mises-)** and select **Settings…**

15. In the **Settings** property manager change the **Fringe Options** dialogue box to **Discrete** as the fringe display type.

16. Click **[OK]** ✓ to close the **Settings** property manager.

The von Mises stress plot should now look like that shown in Fig. 3.

Figure 3 – Von Mises stress plot showing maximum stress occurs on the bottom surface near the fixed end. Results from the Initial Study.

The following steps are used to alter display of the displacement plot.

17. In the Simulation manager, right-click **Displacement1 (-Res disp-)** and from the pull-down menu select **Show**.

18. Repeat steps 6, 7, and 8 except update display characteristics for **Displacement1 (-Res disp-)** and in step 7 change units to **mm**.

19. Right-click **Displacement1 (-Res disp-)** and from the pull-down menu, select **Chart Options…**

20. In the **Display Options** dialogue box, check ☑ **Show max annotation** and only change to scientific notation if not already selected.

21. Click **[OK]** ✓ to close the **Chart Options** property manager.

22. Right-click **Displacement1 (-Res disp-)** and from the pull-down menu, select **Settings…**

23. In the **Settings** property manager change the **Fringe Options** dialogue box to read **Discrete** (if not already selected).

24. Click **[OK]** ✓ to close the **Settings** property manager.

The displacement plot should now appear as shown in Fig. 4.

Figure 4 – Displacement plot results for the Initial Study of the L-Part.

Observations – Design Optimization Considerations

1. Figure 3 reveals a maximum von Mises stress in the part of 193.9 MPa. This stress value is only about 31% of the material yield strength. This magnitude indicates that the part may be overdesigned relative to stress magnitude.

2. The maximum displacement shown in Fig. 4 is 1.917 mm. Although this displacement might be excessive in some situations, the problem statement indicates that a 2.50 mm maximum displacement is permissible in this application. This observation also leads to the conclusion that part size may be reduced thereby resulting in an increased deflection (displacement).

3. For simplicity, this example examines only the magnitude of **URES** (the maximum *resultant* displacement). However, in an actual machine application, examination of specific displacements in the **X**, **Y**, or **Z** directions would probably be more meaningful to examine.

As stated earlier, an Initial Study serves as the basis for an Optimization Design Study by providing a starting point (i.e., an estimate of initial values) for the iterative design process. Because magnitudes of both stress and displacement are found in the Study completed above, it is the only Initial Study needed. However, if thermal and vibration effects also influence the outcome of this part design, then two additional Initial Studies are needed. One study would be needed to establish *initial* thermal effects on the part (because expansion or contraction influence part displacement) and a second *Initial* Study would be required to determine a baseline natural frequency of the machine part.

Because neither of these two aspects are investigated in this text, they are not included in the current example. However, be aware that depending upon optimization goals, additional initial studies might be required.

After the Initial Study has been run, the next step is to set up an optimization Study. The following section introduces steps unique to the Optimization Design process.

Creating an Optimization Design Study

Because of its importance when determining the Variables, Constraints, and Goals needed to set up this problem, the optimization design goal is restated here.

DESIGN GOAL: To *minimize weight* of the **L-Part**.

1. Beneath the graphics area, right-click the Simulation Study *tab* labeled **Initial Study L-Part** and from the pop-up menu, select **Create New Design Study**. The lower portion of the graphics area changes to that shown in Fig. 5.

Figure 5 – Appearance of bottom of the screen upon launch of a Design Study. The current view shows contents of the **Variable View** tab.

2. Just below the **Variable View** tab, click to select the ☑ **Optimization** check box (if not already selected) shown boxed in Fig. 5. NOTE: Only the **Variable View** optimization tab is demonstrated in this example because it is the most commonly used approach for optimization design studies.

3. At the bottom of the screen, see arrow on Fig. 5, right-click the **Design Study 1** tab and from the pop-up menu, select **Rename**. Then type **Minimum Volume L-Part** and press **[Enter]**. This action creates a more descriptive study name.

4. Next, select the **Design Study Options** icon [icon] circled in Fig. 5. The **Design Study Properties** manager opens as shown in Fig. 6.

5. Within the **Design Study Quality** dialogue box, select ⊙ **High quality (slower)**. This approach selects a more refined iterative solver that takes more time to solve but yields better results.

Solution time depends on:
- Quality of the design study (selected in step 5).
- Complexity of model geometry.
- The number of variables, constraints, and goals to be optimized.
- The number of Simulation Studies to be run for each iteration. Each *initial* study requires its own optimization design study.
- The mesh size used in the Simulation Study.

6. Make no other changes in this property manager and click **[OK]** ✓ to close it.

Figure 6 – Specifying **quality** of the optimization scheme.

Understanding Optimization Design Terminology

Before setting up the Optimization Design it is helpful to develop an understanding of terminology associated with this type of Study. The terms to be defined include **Variables, Constraints, Goals,** and **sensors**. All of these terms, except **sensors**, are listed in the design study area located at the bottom of your screen and repeated in Fig. 7. A definition of terms and an overview telling how they apply to this example follows.

Figure 7 – Area of the optimization design table where variables, constraints, goals and sensors are defined.

- **Varaibles** – As implied by the name, variables are items that are changed within the software as it attempts to find an optimal solution to a problem.

EXAMPLE – **Variables** identified
For the current example it is assumed that lengths of the cylindrical rod **AB** and the rectangular segment **BC**, see Fig. 8, as well as the fillet radius and location of attachment between the cylindrical rod and the rectangular segment can*not* be changed. Thus, the only remaining dimensions that can be varied during the optimization process are: **width** = 15 mm and **height** = 30 mm of rectangular segment **BC** and the **diameter** = 20 mm of cylindrical rod **AB** in Fig. 8.

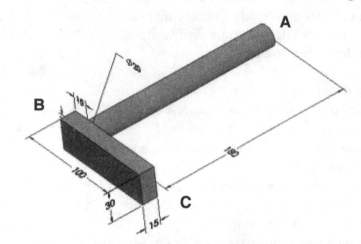

Figure 8 – Basic dimensuions applied to the **L-Part**.

- **Constraints** – Constraints are used to specify conditions that the final design must satisfy. As such, constraints are measurable quantities that are monitored during the optimization process. Each **Constraint** whose magnitude is monitored is assigned a **sensor** to track that item's value. (**Sensors** are defined last).

EXAMPLE – **Constraints** identified
The original problem statement included two constraints that are re-stated here. They are: (1) stress in the part must not exceed one-half of the material yield strength (S_y = 620.422e6 N/m^2), and (2) the maximum allowable part deflection must not exceed 2.50 mm. The final design must satisfy these two conditions.

- **Goals** – Goals are used to specify the objective(s) of an Optimization Design Study. As such, goals are also measurable quantities and therefore **sensors** are needed to monitor values specified for each goal.

EXAMPLE – **Goals** identified
The goal of the current example is to minimize weight of the part. Note, however, that because the entire part is made of the same material, minimizing part weight is analogous to minimizing part volume.

- **Sensors** – Sensors are *quantifiable* items, such as **Constraints** and **Goals**, that are calculated and assigned numerical values during each iteration of the optimization process. As such, **sensors** are applied to monitor these values to ensure that they remain within the limits defined for **Constraints** and **Goals**. **Sensors** described in the following paragraph must be applied to the current model.

EXAMPLE – **Sensors** identified
  o A **sensor** is required to monitor magnitude of vonMises stress so that it does not exceed one-half of the material yield strength.
  o A **sensor** is required to monitor part displacement (deflection) so that it does not exceed the maximum specified deflection of 2.50 mm.
  o A **sensor** is required to monitor part volume during each step of the optimization process to ensure that a minimum value is achieved.

Given an understanding of these definitions, the optimization design Study begins below.

Selecting and Specifying Design Parameters (Variables)

As previously noted the goal of this optimization design study is to minimize weight of the L-Part. This goal intuitively leads to determination of the variables that are altered during the optimization process. Because the entire part is made from the same material (Alloy Steel), it is reasonable to assume that part weight is proportional to part volume. Hence, *dimensions* of the part are selected as **Variables** to be minimized in this example.

The preceding statement would not be true if, for example, the part were made from two different materials (say steel and aluminum) where mass densities of the two different materials would play a role in minimizing overall part weight. In that case mass desnity rather than volume would be selected for minimization.

We begin by defining the **Variables** to be used in the optimization design process.

1. On the currently active **Variable View** tab, beneath **Variables**, open the pull-down menu labeled *Click here to add Variables* ▼ shown at the arrow in Fig. 9.

2. From the pull-down menu, select *Add Parameter...* This action opens the **Parameters** window shown in Fig. 10.

   Also notice that dimensions appear on the model after this selection is made. On the screen, position the L-Part and **Parameters** window so that both can be seen.

Figure 9 – Access to pull-down menus for adding **Variables**, **Constraints**, and **Goals**.

3. Within the **Parameters** window, click in the field beneath **Name** and type **Width**.

4. Also in the **Parameters** window, beneath **Category**, verify that **Model Dimension** appears. If not, open the pull-down menu ▼ and select it.

Figure 10 – Specifying a dimension as a **Variable** during the Optimization Design process.

5. Next, click within the box beneath the **Value** heading to activate this field. Then, in the graphics area, rotate and zoom-in on the model to select the **15** mm width dimension of the rectangular cross section shown at **#1** in Fig. 11. Immediately the **15** mm dimension is entered in the **Value** column and its dimensions (**mm**) appears beneath the **Units** heading.

*The **Dimension** property manager may also open. If so, ignore it until later.*

6. Click **[OK]** at bottom of the **Parameters** window to close it. The *Width* **Variable** now appears in the design table as circled and indicated by the arrow in Fig. 11.

Figure 11 – Selection of part dimensions as **Variables** and listing of the **Width** variable in the Optimization Design field.

7. Repeat steps 1 through 6, except in step 3 type **Height** into the *second row* beneath the **Name** column of the **Parameters** window. Also, after clicking to activate the corresponding **Value** field, proceed to select the **30** mm dimension labeled **#2** on the model in Fig. 11. Click **[OK]** to close the **Parameters** window.

8. Repeat steps 1 through 6 a third time, except in step 3 type **Diameter** into the *third field* beneath the **Name** column. Then, after clicking to activate the corresponding **Value** field, proceed to select the **Φ20** mm dimension on the model labeled **#3** in Fig. 11. Click **[OK]** to close the **Parameters** window.

At this point all three design **Variables** have been selected.

9. *If the **Dimension** property manager opened between steps 5 and 6, notice it is not used during the **Variable** definition process.* Thus, click **[OK]** to close it at this time.

The Optimization Design table should now appear as shown in Fig. 12. *If it does not*, a variation of the above procedure might have been used.[2] In that case, open the pull-down menu labeled **Click here to add Variables ▼**, and select the items listed there to display them in the design table.

Figure 12 – The **Width**, **Height**, and **Diameter Variables** as they originally appear in the Optimization Design field.

Several observations about the **Variables** section of the optimization design table are made on the following page. Refer to the image on your screen while reviewing these observations.

---

[2] It is also possible to enter all variables (**Width**, **Height**, and **Diameter**) one line at a time without exiting the **Parameters** window. If that approach is used, it is necessary to execute the step in the sentence following footnote number 2. However, to maintain correspondence with remaining steps outlined in this chapter, it is suggested that **Width**, **Height**, and **Diameter** be selected in the order listed.

Observations

Begin by opening ▼ any of the drop down menus shown boxed in Fig. 12. The menu is repeated in the figure at right. This menu reveals three different approaches that can be used to search for an optimum design. Of these, the **Range with Step** and **Discrete Values** approaches are described below along with examples of their use. The **Range** approach is later applied to the current Study.

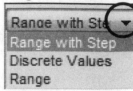

Range with Step -

- All variables are originally listed as **Range with Step**. The **Range with Step** approach is useful when seeking minimum, maximum, and mid-range values over a specified optimization range. The software automatically suggests **Min:**, **Max:**, and **Step:** values according to the following equations.

$$\text{Step} = \frac{(\text{original dimension})}{2}$$

$$\text{Min.} = (\text{original dimension}) - \text{Step}$$

$$\text{Max.} = (\text{original dimension}) + \text{Step}$$

However, the user is free to substitute other values for **Min:**, **Max:**, and **Step:** by typing new values into the appropriate fields shown in Fig. 12. For **Width** = 15mm, the default optimization study would be run for values of **Min:** = 7.5mm, **Max:** = 22.5mm, and **Step:** size = 7.5mm yielding optimization results corresponding to widths of 7.5mm, 15.0mm, and 22.5mm. *Only these three values would be evaluated.* Units must be included with all values. The designer is free to alter the **Step** size to investigate other discrete increments.

Discrete Values

- A second option in the drop-down menu is **Discrete Values**. For this option the user would type each value and its units separated by a comma. For example the following values might be entered as possible rod diameters to be investigated: 0.1875in, 0.250in, 0.3125in, 0.375in, . . ., etc. This approach is useful where a *standard size* steel bar is sought. NOTE: The above values differ by 1/16 inch increments.

Why might a user choose the **Discrete Values** option? Because steel bars are available in standard *discrete* sizes such as 1/16 inch increments for sizes from 3/16 inch diameter up to 5/8 inch diameter, at which point standard bar diameters increase by 1/8 inch increments for rods up to 1¼ inches in diameter. Thus, conducting a design optimization using **Discrete Values** is a useful approach in situations like that described here.

For the current example we apply use of the **Range** option as outlined next.

> 10. pen ▼ the pulldown menu adjacent to **Width** and from the pull-down menu select **Range**. The **Range** option allows *continuous* variable values (i.e., any value) between a specified minimum and maximum. It is not limited to a specific step size nor is it limited to discrete values as described in the **Observations** text box on the previous page.

When using the **Range** option, observe that the software-selected **Min:** and **Max:** values are initially the same as previously specified for the **Range with Step** approach. However, **Min:** and **Max:** values can be changed according to the designer's preference. Proceed as follows. Changing the **Min:** value is demonstrated in the next step.

> 11. Adjacent to **Width**, type **4.0mm** as the new **Min:** value and leave the **Max:** value as specified at **22.5mm**. Be sure to include units.

Design Insight

Why might a designer choose a lower value for **Width** of the rectangular segment of the L-Part? Recall the equation below for moment of inertia **I** for a rectangular cross-section such as occurs in segment **BC** of the L-Part.

$$I = \frac{bh^3}{12}$$ Where: **Height (h)** has a greater effect on I than does **Width (b)** of a rectangle.

Because the goal of this optimization is to minimize weight (volume) of the part. And, because a larger moment of inertia is associated with the **Height** dimension, relative to the 775 N downward force, it follows that little resistance to bending in the vertical plane is realized due to part **Width**. Therefore, a lower limit is selected for the **Min: Width** dimension with the hope that that part volume can be minimized smaller than would result corresponding to the software selected **Min:** value of 7.5mm.

> 12. Adjacent to the **Height** variable, select **Range** from the ▼ pull-down menu.

> 13. Next, change the **Min:** value to **14mm** and leave the **Max:** value as specified at **45mm**.

Why make this small change from 15mm to 14mm? Looking ahead to the **Diameter** variable, its **Min:** value is currently listed as 10mm. Therefore, *if* the optimization design process determines that cylinder diameter can be reduced to 10mm, then the smallest **Height** dimension should not be less than 14 mm based on the following calculation.

Min: Height = (10mm cylinder diameter) + (2mm fillet radius x 2) = 14mm

Thus, 14mm would correspond to the minimum **Height** allowable to permit a full 2mm fillet radius around the entire 10mm cylinder. Recall, fillet radius is *not* a design **Variable**.

14. For the **Diameter** variable, select **Range** from the ▼ pull-down menu. However, make no changes to either **Min:** or **Max:** values. The **Variable** table should now look like Fig. 13.

⊟ Variables					
Width	Range	▼	Min: 4mm	Max: 22.5mm	
Height	Range	▼	Min: 14mm	Max: 45mm	
Diameter	Range	▼	Min: 10mm	Max: 30mm	
Click here to add Variables		▼			

Figure 13 – Completed **Variable** table for the **L-Part** Optimization Design example.

Define Constraints and their Sensors

Although it is probably unnecessary, it is worth emphasizing that **Constraints** are *not* the same as **Restraints**. **Restraints** refer to **Fixtures** used to anchor or attach parts and assemblies to other segments of a machine, structure, hinge joint, base, etc. Whereas, **Constraints** are measurable quantities used to specify conditions that the final, optimized design must satisfy. The two constraints identified for the current example are (1) the maximum von Mises stress must not exceed ½ of the material yield strength, and (2) the maximum resultant displacement of any point on the model must not exceed 2.5mm. Proceed next to define these constraints.

Define the Stress Constraint and Sensor

1. On the **Variable View** *tab* in the optimization table, beneath **Constraints,** click to open the pull-down menu labeled ***Click here to add Constraints*** ▼. From the pull-down menu, select *Add Sensor...* The **Sensor** property manager opens as shown in Fig. 14, but does not initially look like Fig. 14

2. In the ☑? **Sensor Type** dialogue box, select **Simulation Data** from the pull-down menu.

3. Within the **Data Quantity** dialogue box, in the ☑? **Results** field, select **Stress** as the item to be monitored (if not already selected) and in the 🔲 **Component** field, select **VON: von Mises Stress** as the specific stress to be monitored (if not already selected).

Figure 14 – Defining the stress **Constraint** applied to the optimization design process.

4. In the **Properties** dialogue box under **Units** 🔳, select **N/m^2** and for the **Criterion** 🔳 field, choose **Model Max** (if not already selected).

5. Click **[OK]** ✓ to close the **Sensor** property manager. **Stress1** is listed beneath the **Constraints** section in the design optimization table.

Design Insight

You might be asking, "Why is **Simulation Data** selected as the **Sensor Type**?"

Because stress magnitude is to be no more than half of the material yield strength and because stress is calculated in SolidWorks Simulation, therefore **Simulation Data** is monitored as the source for this stress magnitude during the optimization process. The same is true of model displacement which is defined next.

Define the Displacement Constraint and Sensor

1. Beneath **Constraints,** click to open the pull-down menu labeled *Click here to add Constraints* ▼. From the pull-down menu, select *Add Sensor...* The **Sensor** property manager opens.

2. In the **Sensor Type** dialogue box, once again select 〽️ *Simulation Data* from the pull-down menu.

3. In the **Data Quantity** dialogue box, open ▼ the 〽️ **Results** pull-down menu and select **Displacement** as the item to be monitored. Also from the 🔳 **Component** pull-down menu, select *URES: Resultant Displacement* as the specific item to be monitored.

Aside: If only the vertical (Y-displacement) were important, then it could have been selected in the previous step.

4. In the **Properties** dialogue box under **Units** 🔳, select **mm** and for the 🔳 **Criterion** field, choose **Model Max** (if not already selected).

5. Click **[OK]** ✓ to close the **Sensor** property manager and **Displacement1** is listed beneath the **Constraints** section in the optimization table shown in Fig. 15.

We now return to the right half of the optimization table to define limiting values for these **Constraints**.

6. In the drop down menu adjacent to **Stress1**, shown boxed in Fig. 15, select **Is less than**. And, adjacent to **Max:** type *half* the value of the material yield strength. That value is -

$$\tfrac{1}{2} * S_y = \tfrac{1}{2} * 620422000 = 310211000 \ N/m^2$$

7. In the drop down menu adjacent to **Displacement1**, select **Is less than**. And, adjacent to **Max:** type **2.50mm**. The **Constraints** portion of the optimization table should now look like Fig. 15.

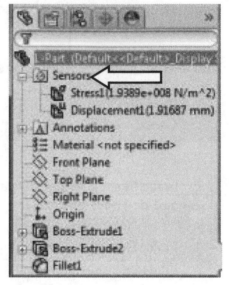

Figure 15 – Completed **Constraint** table for the **L-Part** Optimum Design example.

8. Near the top of the SolidWorks feature manager tree click the "+" sign adjacent to **Sensors**. In Fig. 16 and on your screen, notice that values adjacent to the **Sensors** for **Stress1** and **Displacement1**. These values were computed during the *Initial Study*. Values may vary slightly from those shown.

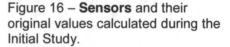

Figure 16 – **Sensors** and their original values calculated during the Initial Study.

Recall that values from the *Initial Study* form the starting point from which to run and track sensor values during subsequent optimization design studies.

Define a Goal and its Sensor

Although only a single **Goal** is specified in this example, it is important to note that multiple goals can be specified. When multiple goals are used, it is also possible to apply "weights" for each goal, where a higher weight assigns more importance to that goal during the optimization process.

The optimization design goal, namely to *minimize part volume*, has been stated several times throughout this example. Implementation of this step is outlined next.

1. At bottom of the design optimization table, within the **Goals** section, select *Click here to add Goals* ▼ and from the pull-down menu select *Add Sensor...* The **Sensor** property manager opens as shown in Fig. 17.

2. In the **Sensor Type** dialogue box, select **Mass Properties** from the pull-down menu (if not already selected).

3. Next, within the **Properties** dialogue box, select **Volume** from the pull-down menu. Part *volume* is synonymous with its weight.

Figure 17 – Defining the optimization design Goal and its sensor.

4. Finally, click within the **Entities to Monitor** field (highlighted light blue to indicate it is active). Move the cursor *anywhere* on the model image and click to select the **L-Part** as the item to be monitored for minimum volume.

Observe that **Fillet1** appears in the **Entities to Monitor** field. In this case, the fillet is selected by the software because it was the last feature added when the part was modeled in SolidWorks. Verify this by referring to the bottom of the SolidWorks feature manager, or flyout menu, where **Fillet1** is listed. This entry does *not* imply that only volume of the fillet will be monitored and/or minimized.

5. Click **[OK]** ✓ to close the **Sensor** property manager and **Volume1** is listed beneath the **Goals** section of the design optimization table.

6. Also beneath the **Goals** section, verify that **Minimize** appears next to **Volume1**. If not, select **Minimize** from the ▼ pull-down menu. Also, examine other optimization criteria available in the pull-down menu.

7. Within the SolidWorks feature manager observe that the total volume of the original (initial) **L-Part** appears as 101605.013 mm^3 is now listed beneath the **Sensors** folder. Clearly this is the entire part volume, not just the fillet volume.

Figure 18 – Select the **[Run]** button to begin the Optimization Design study.

The Optimization Design Study is completely defined and ready to execute. The **[Run]** button, located just beneath the **Variable View** tab, is now active (no longer grayed-out).

8. Click to select the **[Run]** button shown at the arrow in Fig. 18.

As the Design Optimization process executes, direct your attention to model images displayed on the screen. Then, continue reading below.

The optimization process steps through 13 iterations (15 iterations if the Initial Study and the final **Optimal** design scenario are included). As the optimization process proceeds, **Iteration** columns are added to tabulated results beneath the graphics screen while graphic images of the model are briefly displayed in the graphics area. Notice that part geometry associated with some iterations is undesirable or invalid based on the practical desire to have a complete fillet between mating parts. See circled area in Fig. 19.

Figure 19 – Undesirable results due to miss-match of sizes. (Iteration 2)

Results are reviewed below to gain further insight into the findings.

Overview of Results

We begin by making some general observations applicable to all results displayed on the final screen and in the Optimization Design table (located beneath the graphics area). First, notice that results are displayed in the **Results View** tab rather than the **Variable View** tab where this study was defined. Also, it is assumed that most monitors are not wide enough to display all 13 iterations simultaneously. Therefore, results only up to **Iteration 6** are shown in Fig. 20 (more are displayed on wide screen monitors). To see additional iterations, click-and-drag the horizontal scroll bar located beneath the table.

General Observations

1. To display results of a particular iteration, click the **Iteration** *name* located at the top of each column. Example: **Iteration 1, Iteration 2, ...** etc. The image shown in Fig. 20 is that of the **Optimal** solution. Its name is circled in Fig. 20. The **Optimal** solution column is highlighted light green.

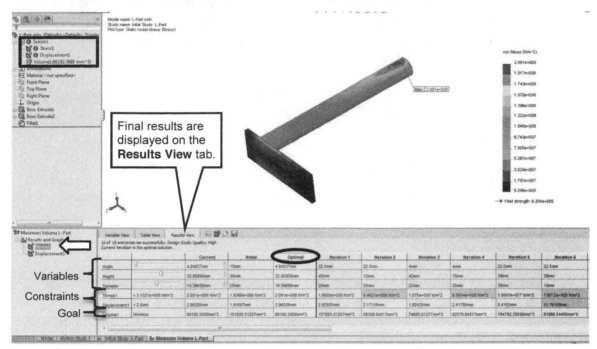

Figure 20 - Table summarizing results of the first six iterations of the optimization design process for the **L-Part**.

2. To the left of the **Optimal** column are listed results of the **Initial Study** and the **Current** column. As implied by its name, the **Current** column contains the same results as those in the currently selected column.

3. At the far left of the optimization table part dimensions (**Width, Height,** and **Diameter**) are displayed as sliders showing current sizes relative to the design **Range**. These sliders can be moved to update the model (not recommended until you become proficient using optimization studies). Also shown are the original **Constraints** (**Stress1** and **Displacement1**) and the optimization **Goal** (**Volume1**).

4. Design constraint plots for **Stress1** and **Displacement1** can be displayed in the graphics area by double-clicking the appropriate **Results and Graphs** folder. See arrow below and to the left of the graphics area. The **von Mises** stress plot shown in Fig. 20 corresponds to the **Optimal** solution. (Numbers may vary slightly.)

5. **Sensors,** shown boxed in the SolidWorks feature manager at the top left of Fig. 20, are updated to show the currently displayed **Volume1**. Note that **Stress1** and **Displacement1 Sensors** are indicated by an information ⓘ symbol only. See the optimization table for current values of these two **Variables**.

6. All columns highlighted in light red indicate cases where one or both of the design **Constraints** is violated. The darker red cells in these columns indicate the specific **Constraint(s)** violated. For example, in **Iteration 2** the **Stress1 Constraint** is violated (i.e., actual **Stress1** > ½*Yield Strength). The maximum stress is also exceeded in several other iterations. However, in **Iterations 4, 6, 8, 10,** and **12** both the **Stress1** and **Displacement1 Constraints** are violated because actual **Stress1** > ½*Yield Strength > (3.102e+008 N/m^2) and **Displacement1** > 2.50 mm. Scrolling to the right in the optimization table reveals **Iterations** that violate one or both **Constraints**.

7. Click the **Iteration** *name* at top of any of the red columns to display the model and corresponding **Stress1** or **Displacement1** plots.

8. **Iteration** columns highlighted in light gray satisfy all **Constraints**. However, those solutions do not satisfy the design **Goal** which results in *minimum volume* for the L-Part.

Local Trend Graphs

A series of Trend Graphs can be plotted at the conclusion of an Optimization Design Study. A trend graph displays either the **Goal** or a **Constraint** with respect to a design **Variable**. Alternatively, a trend graph can display variation of a **Constraint** relative to a selected design **Variable**. Examples of each are illustrated on the following pages. NOTE: **Local Trend Graphs** are not available when *discrete* variables and a **High Quality** study are selected.

Local Trend Graph of the Design Goal versus a Design Variable
Begin by examining a typical graph showing the relationship between a design **Variable**, in this case cylindrical rod diameter, and the design **Goal** (the "Objective") which is to minimize part volume. Proceed as follows.

1. To the left of the tabulated results, right-click **Results and Graphs** and from the pull-down menu, select **Define Local Trend Graph...** The **Local Trend Graph** property manager opens as shown in Fig. 21(a).

2. In the **Design variables (X-Axis)** dialogue box, select **Diameter** from the pull-down menu.

3. In the **Y-Axis** dialogue box, select ⊙ **Objective** then from the pull-down menu, select **Volume1**.

Notice that **Volume1** is the *only* choice available. This is because, in SolidWorks Simulation jargon, the design **Goal** (in this case minimum volume) is also named the "**Objective**" of the design optimization process. The **Local Trend at** dialogue box should show the **Optimal** solution as currently selected; if not, change it.

4. Click **[OK]** ✓ to close the property manager and the graph shown in Fig. 21(b) appears.

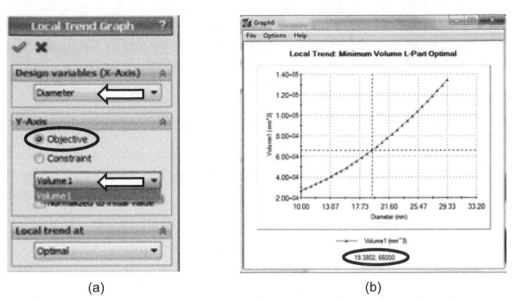

(a)   (b)

Figure 21 – Definition of a **Local Trend Graph** showing the relationship between cylinder diameter (a **Variable**) and part volume (the **Objective** or **Goal**) of this optimization study.

Observations

a. Figure 21(b) reveals the full **Range** of possible rod diameters [10mm ≤ **Range** ≤ 30mm (approx.)].   In Fig. 21(b), the cursor was moved into the graph and intersecting horizontal and vertical dashed lines automatically appear.

b. At the intersection point, *approximate* values of the *optimum* cylinder **Diameter** (19.38 mm, rounded value) and *minimum* part **Volume** (66000 mm^3, also a rounded value) occur. See circled values beneath the graph.

c. Similar graphs of **Height** vs **Volume** or **Width** vs **Volume** can be made.

d. Software default captions appear for the graph title and axis labels in Fig. 21(b). Titles can be altered as demonstrated in Chapter 1.

---

5. Click ☒ to close the current graph. Notice that **Graph1** is now listed beneath the **Results and Graphs** folder in the Simulation manager tree.

Local Trend Graph of a Constraint versus a Design Variable

Next examine a typical graph showing the relationship between a design **Variable** and a design **Constraint**. The design **Variables** remain the same as above (**Height, Width, and Diameter**). However, the **Constraints** applied to the current model include a maximum **Stress1** value and a maximum **Displacement1** value. Proceed as follows to examine one of these graphs.

1. Right-click **Results and Graphs** and from the pull-down menu, select **Define Local Trend Graph...** The **Local Trend Graph** property manager opens as shown in Fig. 22(a).

2. In the **Design variables (X-Axis)** dialogue box, select **Height** from the pull-down menu. Note that either of the remaining two variables (**Width**, or **Diameter**) also could be selected.

3. In the **Y-Axis** dialogue box, select ⊙ **Constraint** then from the pull-down menu, select **Displacement1**. It is also possible to select **Stress1** if it is of primary interest.

4. The **Local Trend at** dialogue box should show the **Optimal** solution as currently selected; if not, change it.

5. Click **[OK]** ✓ to close the property manager and the graph shown in Fig. 22(b) appears.

|(a)|(b)|

Figure 22 - Definition of a **Local Trend Graph** showing the relationship between **Height** of the rectangle (a **Variable**) and **Displacement1** (a **Constraint**) applied to the part. Values are plotted for all iterations necessary to find an optimum design.

The **Local Trend Graph** plots variation of **Displacement1** with respect to **Height** of the rectangular beam section. In general, the graph in Fig. 22 (b) reveals that as beam height increases, the maximum displacement decreases up to approximately **Height** = 37.97 mm. Above this value, displacement components, due to twisting of the model, may contribute to increasing the *resultant* displacement.

Observations

a. Intersecting dashed lines are located at the approximate intersection of the *maximum* **Displacement** (2.50 mm, rounded value) and the *corresponding* part **Height** value (23.7 mm, rounded value). (Values may vary.) Because the maximum displacement occurs at a height less than the **Optimal** height, it is evident that other design constraints limit optimization of this design.

b. All displacement values to the left of or above the dashed lines correspond to displacement magnitudes that exceed the **Constraint** which states **Displacement1** < 2.50 mm.

c. The **Local Trend Graph** of Fig. 22(b) plots the variation of **Displacement** with respect to **Height** of the rectangular member. **Local Trend Graphs** assume the other two design variables (**Width**, and **Diameter**) are set to their optimum values as shown in the **Optimal** design scenario column.

d. A custom title and axis labels are added to Fig. 22(b) using procedures outlined in Chapter 1.

e. Although not investigated here, if *discrete* rather than *continuous* variables are investigated, then either the **Variable View** tab or the **Table View** tab in the optimization study table can be used. Also, for *discrete* variables, a **Design History Graph** is used rather than the **Local Trend Graph** described here.

6. Click ⊠ to close the current graph. **Graph2** appears beneath the **Results and Graphs** folder.

Next, proceed to close the current file without saving results.

7. From the main menu, select **File > Close** followed by selecting **Don't Save** as shown in Fig. 23.

Figure 23 – Close the Study without saving results.

Closing Observations

The above Optimization Design Study introduces only some of the more salient and frequently used capabilities available within the design optimization module of SolidWorks Simulation Premium. This capability is not available in the Standard version of SolidWorks Simulation and is available to a more limited extent within the Simulation Professional version. Beyond this basic example, it is possible to optimize designs based on other parameters such as shape, safety factor, mass, weight, and others. The optimization search scheme within SolidWorks Simulation is based on the "design of experiments" approach to find an optimum solution using a minimum number of iterations.

When should the optimization process be applied? It is highly recommended to run a design optimization near the *beginning* of the design process. This approach allows the designer to benefit from software recommended changes to model geometry early in the design process when the influence of those changes can be factored into the design of related components and sub-components.

Also, the user should *not* consider completion of a single design optimization Study to be the "best" solution. For example, in the current example a value of 4.0 mm was arbitrarily specified for the lower range of **Width** for the rectangular beam cross-section. However, the **Optimal** solution converged to a value just slightly greater than 4.0 mm (4.04037 mm to be exact). This observation, combined with the fact that both the optimal **Stress** and optimal **Displacement** are lower than the maximums specified for these **Constraints**, leads one to believe that a more optimal design might be possible. Thus, further investigations are warranted. The interested reader should also access the available SolidWorks Simulation Design Optimization tutorials found under **Help > SolidWorks Simulation > Tutorials > Design Studies**.

CAUTION:
Use caution when specifying and/or accepting software suggested estimates for **Min:** and **Max:** values specified in the **Range** fields. Incorrect values, that is out-of-bound values or values that cause segments of the model to "self-intersect," may cause the design optimization process to fail. In these cases, the error message shown in Fig. 24 results. Therefore use caution when applying values to **Variables**, **Constraints**, and **Goals**.

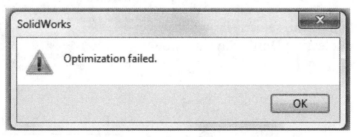

Figure 24 –Error received when "incorrect" estimates for **Range** values are used or if software suggested **Min:** and **Max:** values cause unrealistic events such as segments of a model "self-intersecting" with one another.

This concludes discussion for the current chapter.

EXERCISES

EXERCISE 1 – Design Optimization of a Milling Support

A milling support is being designed. It is to be bolted to the horizontal table of a CNC milling machine in the orientation pictured in Fig. E8-1. Bolts are inserted into "T" slots in the milling machine table (not shown) and pass through slots at the bottom left and right ends of the milling support base. The part is being designed to carry a maximum horizontal force F = 450 lb that acts as a *uniform pressure* over the area between the top end of the support and Split Line 1, which is also shown in Fig. E8-1. Material used for this part is **Cast Carbon Steel**. The part is manufactured as a casting to minimize final machining operations and thereby minimize production costs. As a consequence, the only machined surfaces are the bottom of the base, a 'finish cut' in the two bolt slots, and the surface to which the *uniform* pressure is applied. Also, because the support is in the early stages of design and because it is to be manufactured as a casting, it is desired to minimize the amount of material used in the part. However, to provide a minimum clamping area in the vicinity of force **F**, thickness of the vertical triangular portion of the model cannot be reduced below its original ¾ in thickness. Material reduction is to be accomplished without exceeding a maximum deflection (**URES** displacement) of 0.003 inch and without exceeding ¼ of the material Yield Strength. NOTE: Although this part is a casting, fillets and rounds are not shown on *all* external edges to simplify and, therefore, shorten optimization calculations within the software. Open the file **Milling Support** and perform a finite element analysis to optimize this design according to items requested below.

F

Split Line 1

Figure E8-1 – The **Milling Support** base showing force **F** applied to the area above Split Line 1.

- Material: **Cast Carbon Steel**, round-off yield strength to nearest 1000 psi.

- Mesh: System default **Curvature based mesh**.

- Fixtures: **Fixed (immovable)** restraints applied to all inner surfaces of Each bolt slot.

- External Load: Apply **uniform pressure** to the area above Split Line 1. Initial dimensions of this rectangle are: Height = 3 in, Thickness = ¾ in.

- Limitations: Maximum **von Mises** stress ≤ (¼)*Yield Strength. Maximum part deflection (**URES**) ≤ 0.003 in.

Determine the following:

Develop a finite element analysis that includes: material specification, fixtures, external load(s), mesh, and initial and optimized solutions. Do *not* defeature the model.

a. Create a plot showing all restraints and external loads applied to the model. This image is the finite element equivalent of a free-body diagram. Do not show stress or a mesh on this plot. Then, set-up and run an *Initial Study* to form the basis for an Optimization Design Study which is to follow. <u>IMPORTANT</u>: **SAVE** results of this *initial analysis* for possible re-use.

b. Based on the *Initial Study*, create a new design study to minimize the amount of material need to cast the upper (triangular shaped) portion of the milling support *and* its base. In the optimization design study, select **High quality (slower)** as the quality level to be used. Dimension changes are limited to those shown on the upper triangular segment *and* base of the model labeled in Fig. E8-2. Initial dimensions are:
    - Thickness of rectangular base = 0.75 in (this thickness cannot be reduced smaller than 0.30 inches due to minimum casting thickness limitations).
    - Vertical leg width = 1.00 in
    - Horizontal leg width = 1.25 in
    - Hypotenuse leg width = 1.00 in

NOTE: When defining variables the part initially appears with *all* dimensions shown. It is suggested that all dimensions, ***except*** those *shown in this figure,* be hidden (right-click the dimension and from the pull-down menu choose **Hide**). This approach simplifies choosing the correct dimensions.

Figure E8-2 – Dimensions that can be altered on the upper triangular section and base.

c. After completely filling in all boxes within the **Variables**, **Constraints**, and **Goals** sections on the **Variable View** tab, use techniques outlined in Appendix A to copy, paste and crop a readable image of the design table onto an 8 ½ x 11 sheet of paper. It may be necessary to click-and-drag the upper boundary of the table to reveal all values. Then run the optimization design study.

Potential Difficulties

1. If your design optimization terminates with the warning shown in Fig. E8-3, then review the **CAUTION** section found on pg. 8-24, immediately preceding this exercise. Then carefully check and edit values entered for **Min.:** and/or **Max.:** in the optimization table. Also check that **Range** is properly specified. Before doing so, however, read item (2) immediately below.

Figure E8-3 – Warning received if the optimization process fails. Such failures are typically due to bad data entered for **Variables**, **Constraints**, or **Goals**.

2. As of this writing (SolidWorks Simulation, Service Pack 1, 2013) simply editing values in the **Variables**, **Constraints**, or **Goals** tables and re-running the optimization solution may result in similar "**Optimization failed**" warnings. To avoid this possibility, it is best to close the file without saving results and then re-work it from the beginning. If the finite element model was **SAVED** as requested in step (a) above, then only the optimization design portion of the Study need be re-created.

---

d. Create a graph of each **Constraint** versus variation of the hypotenuse leg width. Move the cursor to place horizontal and vertical dashed lines at the intersection of each limiting **Constraint** value and the curve on the graph. Beneath each graph, write a brief statement indicating the significance of this point relative to the optimal solution for width of the hypotenuse leg. Modify the graph title and axis labels to best describe what is shown on each graph; include your name. Copy and paste each graph onto the upper and lower half of an 8 ½" x 11" sheet of paper.

e. Copy and paste all values shown on the **Results View** tab from the left side of that table up to the third or fourth iteration. Beneath this table show a calculation of the total annual weight savings of cast steel to be expected when comparing the initial part to the optimized design. For this calculation assume the density of steel = 0.282 lb/in^3 and that 2,500 parts are made per year.

f. Questions: (1)Which **Constraint** appears to be the "limiting factor" for this design optimization and why? (2) If **Min:** and **Max: Range** values could be changed, might a better solution be found? Give sound reasons for your answer by referring to values in the **Optimal** solution.

EXERCISE 2 – Design Optimization of Slotted Rectangular Block

The initial design of a slotted rectangular block, used to measure lateral (sideways) loads on an outdoor structure, is shown in Fig. E8-4. In its final state, not shown, strain gages are to be mounted on its left and right vertical legs to measure bending stress and correlate those stresses to loads on the structure. When in service, the part is fixed on its bottom surface and subject to a maximum horizontal force of 200 lb applied to its upper left edge as illustrated in Fig. E8-4 (a). To obtain larger strain magnitudes at the gage locations, if it is desired, reduce the width and thickness (depth into the page) of both vertical legs. The approach proposed is to minimize volume of the slotted block by reducing the width of the two vertical legs and thickness of the block. Common sense dictates that doing so will result in larger deflections with resulting higher strains measured by the strain gages. Practical limitations, however, restrict displacements to 0.05 inch or less and limit stress in the part to 32,000 psi or less. Open file: **Slotted Rectangular Block**.

(a)   (b)

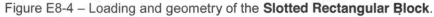

Figure E8-4 – Loading and geometry of the **Slotted Rectangular Block**.

- Material: **AISI 1020** steel

- Mesh: System default **Curvature based mesh**.

- Fixtures: **Fixed (immovable)** restraints applied to bottom surface.

- External Load: Apply a **200** lb horizontal force to the top left edge of the model.

- Limitations: Maximum **von Mises** stress ≤ 32000 psi.
  Maximum part deflection ≤ 0.05 in.

Determine the following:

Develop a finite element analysis that includes: material specification, fixtures, external load(s), mesh, and initial and optimized solutions.

a. Run an *Initial Study* for the original part to form the basis for an Optimization Design Study which is to follow. Create a plot showing the restraints and external loads applied to the model along with the initial von Mises stress distribution. IMPORTANT: **SAVE** the results of this *initial analysis* for possible re-use.

b. Based on the *Initial Study*, create a new Optimization Design Study that results in reduction of the width of the two vertical legs and thickness of the entire part. Dimension changes are limited to the dimensions labeled in Fig. E8-5. See step (c) for items to be done prior to running the optimization study. Initial dimensions are:

  - Left vertical leg initial width = 1.75 in
  - Right vertical leg initial width = 1.75 in
  - Thickness (depth into the page) = 2.00 in

NOTE: When defining variables the part initially appears with *all* dimensions shown. It is suggested that all dimensions, **except** *those shown in this figure,* be hidden (right-click the dimension and from the pull-down menu choose **Hide**). This approach simplifies choosing the proper dimensions.

Figure E8-5 – Dimensions that are to be reduced on the slotted rectangular block.

c. After completely filling in all boxes within the **Variables**, **Constraints**, and **Goals** sections on the **Variable View** tab, use techniques outlined in Appendix A to copy, paste, and crop a readable image of the design table onto an 8 ½ x 11 sheet of paper. It may be necessary to click-and-drag the upper boundary of the table to show all values in the table. Then, run the optimization design study. NOTE: *If* your design optimization terminates with the warning shown in Fig.

E8-3, then review the **CAUTION** section found on pg. 8-24. Also, follow guidelines outlined in the **Potential Difficulties** section of pg. 8-27 and carefully re-define **Min** and **Max:** values.

d. Upon completion of the optimization study, examine contents of the **Results View** tab. In particular, based on results displayed in the **Optimal** solution column, state whether or not a *more* optimal solution can be found. State specific reasons for your answer and include reference to values listed in the **Optimal** study column.

e. Create a graph of each **Constraint** versus the variation of leg width. On each graph, show horizontal and vertical dashed lines at the intersection of the limiting **Constraint** value and the curve on the graph. Modify the graph title and axis labels to best describe what is shown on each graph; include your name. Copy and paste each graph onto the upper and lower half of an 8 ½" x 11" sheet of paper. Beneath each graph, write a brief statement indicating the significance of the intersection point relative to the optimal solution for width of the rectangle legs.

APPENDIX A
ORGANIZING ASSIGNMENTS USING MS WORD®

This appendix is included to offer guidance in the use of Microsoft Word® for the preparation of deliverables associated with end of chapter exercises. It is assumed that users are familiar with Word® or some other word processor. However, a few procedures outlined below might be new even to seasoned Word® users. Although Chapter 5 demonstrates a semi-automated means to generate a **Report** using features embedded within the Simulation software, this section provides guidance for users desiring to output, into a neat report, *only* those items requested in end of chapter exercises. A fringe benefit of this approach is that, in addition to a professional looking assignment, the report (a) can be prepared simultaneously while working an exercise, and (b) can be printed on fewer pages, a real plus for students on a tight print quota.

The goal of this section is to show, through example, how to combine features of Word® with capabilities of SolidWorks Simulation to produce a concise and well organized report. Techniques described herein are the same procedures used to create and format text and images in this book. An example of the "final report" created below can be found beginning on page A-14. Be advised that *only the basics* of incorporating screen images into a document are described here.

Learning Objectives
Upon completion of this unit, users should be able to:

- *Copy and paste* images from SolidWorks Simulation into a word processor document. (It is presumed users already possess cut and paste capability).

- *Crop* and *Re-size* images extracted from SolidWorks Simulation.

- Apply *Text Wrapping* around images copied from SolidWorks Simulation into a Word® document.

- *Extract data* from **Probe Results** tables and include it in a document as an Excel® *spreadsheet* table.

- Append *Callouts* to images to label significant aspects of a model or results.

Problem Statement
The problem used in this example is based on the cam follower analysis performed in Chapter 1. As such, users should be familiar with technical aspects of the analysis thereby allowing us to focus attention solely upon how results of that problem might be presented in a report. Assume the following items are requested as part of the finite element analysis.

Deliverables:

a. Within a report, produce an image that documents **Fixtures** and **External Loads** applied to the model. Label applied force magnitudes on this image.

b. On the same page as part (a) create a plot of the most appropriate stress in the cam follower. See item (c) below for *where* on the model stresses are to be plotted.

c. Plot a graph of the most appropriate stress at one inch below the top end of the cam follower. On this graph include descriptive titles and axis labels.

d. On the same page as the graph in part (c), include an Excel table of stress values determined using the **Probe** tool for the graph of the previous step.

Software Version

Because of the growing adoption of Windows7® accompanied by lingering use of Windows Vista® and Windows XP®, and upgraded versions of Word® and Excel® that accompany newer versions of Windows®, instructions below are based on Microsoft Word® 2003-2007 and Word 2010® in Windows XP/Vista® and Windows 7® operating systems. Where significant differences exist between different versions of Word®, instructions are included for each. *Use only sections that apply to your software version.*

Setting Up the Necessary Editing Tools

WORD 2003-2007®   *(Word 2010® users skip to the section titled **Word 2010®**)*

Before demonstrating how to create an organized report, the necessary editing tools must be organized on the screen. Most of these tools are found in the **Drawing** toolbar. Assuming that this toolbar is *not* displayed in the Word® window proceed as follows to add it and modify its contents. NOTE: For many items demonstrated below there exist alternative ways to accomplish the same tasks. However, for the sake of brevity, only one method is demonstrated.

1. Right-click anywhere on the main menu and from the pull-down menu, select ☑ **Drawing**. This action adds the **Drawing** menu to the bottom of the screen (screen location may vary). The default **Drawing** menu is shown in Fig. 1.

Figure 1 – The default **Drawing** menu in MS Word 2003®.

2. If it is desired to relocate this menu, click-and-drag its "drag handle," circled in Fig. 1, to the desired location on the screen.

Next, several frequently used icons are added to the **Drawing** menu as follows.

3. Left click the **Toolbar Options** button, shown boxed in Fig. 1, and from the pop-up menu, first select **Add or Remove Buttons▼** followed by **Customize...** See Fig. 2.

Figure 2 – Menu selections to add buttons to the **Drawing** toolbar.

4. The **Customize** window opens in Fig. 3. Within this window, select the **Commands** tab circled in Fig. 3.

5. In the left column of the **Commands** tab, beneath **Categories**, select **Drawing**, shown at arrow in Fig. 3.

6. On the right side of this window, scroll through tools listed beneath **Commands** and click-and-drag the commands listed in Fig. 4 onto the **Drawing** toolbar and drop them there.

Figure 3 – Within the **Customize** window, buttons are selected to add to the **Drawing** toolbar.

Figure 4 – **Commands** copied onto the **Drawing** toolbar.

The **Drawing** toolbar now has sufficient tools to accomplish the tasks outlined in steps (a) though (d) of the **Problem Statement**. Thus, the process of creating a custom report begins below.

Word® 2003-2007 users should proceed to the section titled, **Creating a Custom Report (a demonstration)**

WORD 2010®

Before demonstrating how to create an organized report, the necessary editing tools must be placed on the screen. The necessary tools are placed on the **Quick Access Toolbar**. However, for those new to Word 2010®, some differences with prior versions are described first.

Word 2010® is organized differently than previous versions. Two menu bars are located at the top of the screen. The larger menu, now called the "**Ribbon**," contains many familiar commands. However, these commands are now organized beneath different *tabs* where similar items are grouped within a tab. A portion of the **Home** tab is illustrated in Fig. 5. Located just above the ribbon (default location) or below the ribbon, as shown in Fig. 5, is what is now called the "**Quick access toolbar**." This *customizable* toolbar is where the commands used to edit and create a report are placed. Various parts of the Word 2010® user interface are labeled in Fig. 5. NOTE: For many items demonstrated below there exist alternative ways to accomplish the same tasks. However, for the sake of brevity, only one method is shown.

Figure 5 – Upper portion of the Word 2010® user interface.

1. To move the **Quick Access Toolbar** beneath the ribbon, right-click the **Quick Access Toolbar** (in its default location above the ribbon) and from the pop-up menu shown in Fig. 6, select **#1, Show Quick Access Toolbar Below the Ribbon**.

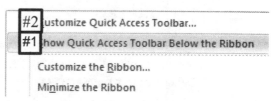

Figure 6 – Relocating and customizing the **Quick Access Toolbar** beneath the **Ribbon**.

Location of the **Quick Access Toolbar** is a user preference. However, the author finds it "closer to the action" and hence more convenient in the lower position. Next proceed to add the necessary icons to this toolbar. Although most icons are located beneath the various ribbon tabs, it is convenient to have the frequently used icons located where they are easily accessible. Proceed as follows.

2. Right-click the **Quick Access Toolbar** and from the pull-down menu, select **Customize Quick Access Toolbar...** shown at **#2** in Fig. 6. The **Word Options** window opens as shown in Fig. 7.

3. Beneath **Choose commands from:** located at the top of the left-hand column, select **Popular Commands** from the pull-down menu. See arrow in Fig. 7.

Figure 7 – Selecting commands to be added to the **Quick Access Toolbar**.

4. Scroll down the alphabetical listing of commands in the left-hand column and select **Shapes** highlighted in Fig. 7. Then click the **[Add >>]** button, circled in Fig. 7, to move this selection into the right-hand column labeled **Customize Quick Access Toolbar:**.

5. Return to **Choose commands from:** at top of the left-hand column and from the pull-down menu, select **Picture Tools │ Format Tab**.

Figure 8 – Commands selected for addition to the **Quick Access Toolbar**.

6. Scroll down the alphabetical listing to select the remaining commands, shown in Fig. 8, and **[Add >>]** each command to the right-hand column.

7. Commands in the right-hand column can be arranged in any order desired by selecting an item and then clicking the up ▲ or down ▼ arrows shown boxed in Fig. 7.

8. Click **[OK]** to close the **Word Options** window and the selected commands appear in the **Quick access Toolbar**.

Creating a Custom Report (a demonstration)

Incorporating Images into a Word Document

Begin by assuming that both SolidWorks Simulation *and* a Word document are open, side-by-side on the screen. Both these windows must be sized to fit on the monitor. *NOTE: It is also possible to switch from window to window by using the **Minimize** and **Restore** buttons at the top right of each window.* As larger monitors become more common, having two windows open simultaneously is less of a hassle. Dual monitors can also be used.

Because it can be tricky to place text onto a page *after* an image is placed on the page, it is a good practice to type your name, date, and exercise number at the top of a blank sheet in Word® before adding images.

There are three ways to incorporate images into a Word document. For all three methods, assume that the cam follower of Chapter 1 is displayed in the SolidWorks Simulation graphics area with **Fixtures** and **External Loads** applied to the model as shown in Fig. 9. The easiest method is described first. This method works for all versions of Word®, but only captures images in the graphics portion of the SolidWorks screen.

Figure 9 – Image to be pasted into a Word document. Note **Crop** marks around the image.

Before performing any of the steps below, choose a view of the model, plot, or graph that best displays the attributes you want to show.

METHOD 1 - Using SolidWorks Simulation "Screen Capture"

1. To add **Screen Capture** permanently to menus at the top of your SolidWorks screen, right-click anywhere on the menus and from the pull-down menu select **Screen Capture** . The screen capture toolbar, shown in Fig. 10 is added to the menus bar. To use this feature, simply click the camera [icon] icon to capture an image of the graphics area of the screen and place it on the clip-board.

Figure 10 – Using the **Screen Capture** capability built into SolidWorks.

2. Next, move the cursor to the desired location within a Word® document and select **Paste** from the Word® menu. A *full size* image, shown cropped and downsized in Fig. 9, is placed into the current document. Methods for cropping and resizing this image are described later.

The following sections describe alternate methods of placing SolidWorks Simulation images into Word® documents.

METHOD 2 – Using "Screenshot" in Word 2010

1. In the Word 2010® ribbon, select the **Insert** *tab*, and within the **Illustrations** sub-group, select the ▼ symbol adjacent to **Screenshot** [Screenshot]. Any currently *open* windows appear as thumbnail images as illustrated in Fig. 11. This feature does not display windows that are minimized to the taskbar.

Figure 11 shows that SolidWorks Simulation is the only other open window on the screen. If multiple windows are open, select the SolidWorks window containing the desired image.

Click the thumbnail of the image to be copied into Word®.

Figure 11 – Copying the contents of any open window into a Word document using the **Screenshot** capability of Word 2010.

2. Click the thumbnail image of the window to be copied and a full-size **Screenshot** of the image appears in the current Word® document as shown in Fig. 12.

Observe the difference between the image in Fig. 12 and the image in Fig. 9. Figure 9 shows only the model within the graphics area of the screen while Fig. 12 includes the *entire* SolidWorks screen image. Occasionally the entire screen image is desired in order to show some other details of the analysis. However, if only an image of the model is desired, then the **Screen Capture** capability within SolidWorks might be preferred. Both Figs. 9 and 12 require additional cropping and resizinig as described later in this example.

Figure 12 – Full-size image obtained using the **Screenshot** option within Word 2010®. No size alterations were applied to this image.

METHOD 3 – Using "[Ctrl] + [Print Screen]" Available in All Word Versions

1. By simultaneously pressing the **[Ctrl]** + **[Print Screen]** buttons on the keyboard, the *entire screen image* is copied to the clip-board. The image shown in Fig. 13 reveals that both the SolidWorks Simulation model *and* the currently open Word® document are copied. This approach can be used with all versions of Word®.

2. Next, move the cursor into the currently open Word document and select **Paste**. The entire image is placed into the open document.

Cropping handles

Figure 13 – The result of pressing the **[Ctrl] + [Print Screen]** buttons is to capture an image of the entire screen. If both SolidWorks and Word are open simultaneously, then images of both are pasted into the current document.

No matter what method is used to copy a screen image into a Word document that image typically *must* be further edited by either cropping or re-sizing the image, or both.

Editing Images Within a Word Document

This section outlines how images are cropped and/or resized using the editing commands that were added to either the **Drawing** or **Quick Access Toolbar**. Although reference is made only to the image in Fig. 13, the same editing process can be applied to images copied by any of the methods outlined above.

1. Within the Word document, begin by clicking the image to select it. When selected, "handles" (tiny circles) appear at each corner and tiny squares appear at the mid-side of the image. If desired, resize the image by clicking and dragging these handles.

2. Because the hypothetical 'assignment' requests only an image of the model and its **Fixtures** and **External Loads**, the image is next cropped by selecting the **Crop** tool. It should be found on either the **Drawing** or **Quick Access Toolbar**. Once selected, the **Crop** tool replaces the cursor and bold corners and short dashes appears at the mid-section on each edge of the selected image as shown in Figs. 9 and 13.

3. Using the **Crop** ⊹ tool, click and drag any of the "corners" or dark bars appearing on the image boundaries to crop the model to the approximate size shown by dashed lines in Fig. 13. Click anywhere outside the image to end cropping.

4. After cropping, the image may be too small. Therefore, click the image again to select it. The "handles" reappear. Click and drag any of these handles to re-size the image as desired. Because cropping occurs in finite steps, it is often helpful to enlarge the image, crop it again, and then return the image to its desired size.

NOTE: After cropping the image may *not* appear at its desired location. An image often jumps to a random location on the page. If the image is difficult to locate, typically look *above* the location where you clicked to paste it.

Part (a) of the problem statement also requests that magnitudes of the force components be labeled. Labeling can be done manually or as outlined below.

5. **Word 2003-2007:**
   On the **Drawing** toolbar, select the **AutoShapes** pop-up menu and from the list, select **Callouts**. Then select the **Callout** of your choice. For this example, the **Rectangular Callout** is used. See Fig. 14.

Figure 14 – Selecting a **Callout** to label the model.

Word 2010:

In the **Quick Access Toolbar**, select the **Shapes** 🔲 icon and from the pull-down menu select the **Callouts** of your choice; see **Callouts** at the bottom of the pull-down menu. A rectangular Callout is used in this example.

6. In Word, move the cursor near where the force component is to be labeled. The cursor symbol changes to a "+" sign. Click-and-drag the cursor to create a small text box. This box can be resized as needed by dragging its handles.

7. Click inside the **Callout** box and type a label for the X-component of force. Font style and font size can be changed by double clicking the callout boundary and selecting those items on the Word® menu (Word 2003-2007) or by right clicking the **Callout** boundary (Word 2010) for access to font style and size options. Drag the "pointer" on the **Callout** box to attach it to the appropriate force component as shown in Fig. 15.

8. An identical procedure is used to label the Y-force component. It is not repeated here.

To finalize this image, two additional steps are necessary. First, it is necessary to **Group** the image and its label. Grouping is necessary because the image and label are two different entities. As such, they *might* move independently and become separated during subsequent editing of the document. Any relative movement might separate the label from the force vector thereby rendering it meaningless. Proceed as follows to **Group** these items. Items can be un-grouped and positions changed at a later time if desired. However, un-grouping can get messy.

9. Simultaneously hold down the **[Shift]** key while clicking to select the **Callout** and then the image. Selection handles appear around each object as shown in Fig. 15. Then in the **Drawing** toolbar (Word 2003-2007) or the **Quick Access Toolbar** (Word 2010), select the **Group** icon.

A second step is required to finalize the image whenever typed text accompanies the image, such as Fig. 15 at right. Text can be placed in several different locations relative to the image. In this text, the most typical arrangement is either for text to appear adjacent to the image, like the text you are reading *and* the image in Fig. 15 at right. A second option is for text to appear above and below an image as illustrated in Fig. 13. Either selection is made by choosing the **Text Wrapping** icon and selecting either **Tight** or **Top and Bottom** from the pop-up menu. Click the **Text Wrapping** icon now to view these and other options for placing an image onto a page with text.

Figure 15 – Placing a label on an image and grouping the entities to effectively "lock" them together.

After applying **Text Wrapping** it is typically necessary to click the image and drag it to re-size it or to place it at its desired location on the page. Reminder, *if* various parts of an image are not **Grouped** together, then each part will need to be moved one-at-a-time and re-organized in the final position. Grouping eliminates this extra task.

Occasionally the **Bring to Front** or **Send to Back** icons must be used to show all important parts of an image. For example, if the **Callout** in Fig. 15 is hidden by the model image, we could either apply **Bring to Front** to the **Callout** or apply **Send to Back** to the model image. Either action results in properly stacked images so that the most visible item appears "in front."

A Word of Caution and Encouragement

Using the cut, paste, crop, callout, and group commands takes some getting used to. It easily frustrates individuals with a low tolerance for ambiguity. In other words, all kinds of unexpected things can happen. For example, after grouping items together, it is common for typed text to overlap the image. Don't panic, simply make a selection using the **Text Wrapping** tool and the text will nicely organize itself around (or) above and below the image. Using **Ungroup** ⬚ causes similar problems. Some of these frustrations have been remedied in Word 2010.

The procedures to cut and paste images from SolidWorks Simulation into a Word® document, to re-size those images, and to document them by the addition of labels is demonstrated above. The same procedure can be used to copy an image of the *most appropriate stress* [requested in part (b) of the problem statement] onto the same page as the image of Fig. 15. These two images are shown in Fig. 17 at the end of this example.

Incorporating an Excel Spreadsheet into a Word Document

Parts (c) and (d) of the problem statement request that a graph of the most appropriate stress (σ_y) be placed onto the same page with an Excel® spreadsheet that contains data used to produce the graph. Therefore, the last item to be demonstrated here is to capture data from the **Probe Results** table, to export it into an Excel® spreadsheet, and finally to insert the spreadsheet into a Word document. The procedure to accomplish this is outlined in the following section.

Capturing Probe Results Data and Exporting it to an Excel Spreadsheet

The following steps assume that the **Probe** tool is used to select nodes from left to right across the model at a location 1 inch below the top (fixed) end. It is also assumed that the **Probe Result** property manager is open and that stress values at each node location are stored in the **Results** table as shown in Fig. 16. One problem with the **Results** table is that, without resorting to scrolling through the data, its small size often prevents display of *all* values determined when using the **Probe** tool. This shortcoming is overcome by saving and displaying *all* the data in an Excel® spreadsheet. To capture this data into a spreadsheet, proceed as follows.

1. In the **Report Options** dialogue box, at the bottom of the **Probe Results** property manager, click the **Save** 💾 icon circled in Fig. 8. Immediately the **Save As** window opens and the **File name:** field contains the name assigned to the current Study. It is best to assign a descriptive name associated with this file such as:

"**Cam Follower Data.**" Then save this file to an easy to find location on the hard drive such as **C: \My Excel\Cam Follower Data.csv**" Also, at the bottom of this window note that the **Save as type:** field shows **Excel File (*.csv)**. Finally, click the **[Save]** button.

2. Also, click **[OK]** ✓ to close the **Probe Result** property manager.

3. Next, open the file in Excel® and copy the data by clicking and dragging over it to select it and then selecting, **Copy**. Carefully note the number of rows and columns of data.

4. Return to the Word® document and insert the Excel® file by clicking **Paste** and sizing the spreadsheet using its drag handles much like sizing an image.

Figure 16 – The **Probe Result** table populated with stress values sampled across the cam follower face.

5. Arrange the Excel® data table, Fig. 17, and the graph, Fig. 18, by clicking and dragging them to a desired location on the same page. See pg. A-15.

Exhibits of two pages of an "example report" are shown on the following pages.

EXAMPLE REPORT

Exercise 1, Chapter #1   NAME: ___YOUR NAME_____

Below are examples of figures requested in parts (a) and (b) of the example exercise used to demonstrate report preparation by copying and pasting multiple images from SolidWorks Simulation onto a single page in a Word document. Ordinarily this first paragraph would be used to describe technical data about the finite element models shown below.

Figure 17 - Figure (a) shows the cam follower and its associated **Fixtures** and applied **External Loads**. Figure (b) shows a plot of σ_y due to combined axial and bending stress in the cam follower.

A descriptive figure caption can be placed beneath the figures and answers to questions about the model can be typed in available space on the page adjacent to the images or above and below the image as shown on this page. The above figures were cut and pasted from SolidWorks Simulation. Then, labels were added and all items were grouped together using techniques demonstrated in this Appendix.

EXAMPLE REPORT (continued)

The spreadsheet at right contains all **Results** data found using the **Probe** tool.
In spreadsheet format, it is possible to compare stress magnitudes on both left and right sides of the cam follower with values calculated using classical stress equations. See below for notes appended to the Excel spreadsheet.

Maximum compressive stress on top left side of the cam follower.

Maximum tensile stress on top right side of the cam follower.

Node	Value (psi)	X (in)	Y (in)	Z (in)
95	-21507.3	-8.53E-16	4.4595	0.5
9801	-18674	0.071429	4.4257	0.5
534	-15833.1	0.14286	4.3919	0.5
7155	-13123.8	0.21429	4.3919	0.5
533	-10381.8	0.28571	4.3919	0.5
7161	-7640.5	0.35714	4.3919	0.5
532	-4850.7	0.42857	4.3919	0.5
7169	-2073.4	0.5	4.3919	0.5
531	724.4	0.57143	4.3919	0.5
7175	3496	0.64286	4.3919	0.5
530	6293.4	0.71429	4.3919	0.5
7179	9056.1	0.78571	4.3919	0.5
529	11832.4	0.85714	4.3919	0.5
8765	14736.3	0.92857	4.4257	0.5
27	17636.9	1	4.4595	0.5

Figure 18 – Data from the **Probe Result** table that was saved into an Excel® Spread-sheet and subsequently inserted into a Word® document.

This space can be used to discuss trends observed on the graph or values determined using the **Probe** tool.

Additionally, calculations of stress determined using classical stress equations can be included here and compared with finite element results.

All this can be accomplished in the neat and concise report format illustrated here.

Figure 19 – Graph of combined axial compressive stress and bending stress across the face of the cam follower at 1 below the top (fixed) end.

NOTES:

APPENDIX B

Alternate Method to Change Screen Background Color

This section describes an alternate method of changing the graphics area background color to white. The method outlined below occasionally works for computers that do not have the exact graphics board recommended for use with SolidWorks. Give it a try and if it works, so much the better. The procedure below assumes SolidWorks or SolidWorks Simulation is open.

1. Click the **Display Manager** icon shown circled at top of the SolidWorks feature manager tree Fig. 1.

2. Next, click the **View Scene, Lights, and Cameras** icon that appears near the top of the **Display Manager**, adjacent to the arrow in Fig. 1.

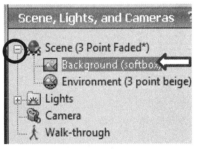

Figure 1 – Accessing the **View Scene, Lights, and Cameras** icon on the **Display Manager** tab.

3. Within the **Scene, Lights, and Cameras** display manager tree, click the "+" sign adjacent to **Scene (3 Point Faded***)**. This action reveals sub-menu choices shown in Fig. 2.

4. From this pull-down menu, double-click **Background (softbox)** to open the **Edit Scene** property manager partially shown in Fig. 3.

Figure 2 – Accessing the **Background (Gradient)** option.

5. Within the **Background** dialogue box, click ▼ to open the **Background Type** drop down menu, shown boxed in Fig. 3, and from the menu select **Gradient**.

6. Also, within the **Background** dialogue box the **Top gradient color:** field should appear white by default. If not, click the field to open the **Color** window shown to the right in Fig. 3.

7. In the **Color** window, select the color white, circled in Fig. 3, and press **[OK]**.

Figure 3 – Sequence of steps to change the background color to white.

8. Repeat steps 6 and 7 to change the color of the **Bottom gradient color:** field to white.

9. Next, within the **Background** dialogue box, check "✓" the ☑ **Keep background** box in oval on Fig. 3. This action *should* retain this setting during future SolidWorks Simulation sessions. *However, be prepared to repeat this simple procedure if the shaded background appears again.*

10. Finally, click **[OK]** ✓ (green check mark) to close the **Edit Scene** property manager and, if successful, the graphics area should now appear white. If not, the SolidWorks default display (gradient color) must be used.

11. Return to the **SolidWorks Feature Manager Design Tree** by clicking its icon located at top of the Feature manager tree, circled in Fig. 4.

Figure 4 – Select the SolidWorks Feature Manager Design tree icon to return to SolidWorks Simulation.

INDEX